Keeping Hold

What did it mean to possess something – or someone – in eighteenth-century Britain? What was the relationship between owning things and a person's character and reputation, and even their sense of self? And how did people experience the loss of a treasured belonging? *Keeping Hold* explores how Britons owned watches, bank notes and dogs in this period, and also people, and how these different 'things' shaped understandings of ownership. Kate Smith examines the meaning of possession by exploring how owners experienced and responded to its loss, particularly within urban spaces. She illuminates the complex systems of reclamation that emerged and the skills they demanded. Incorporating a systematic study of 'lost' and 'runaway' notices from London newspapers, Smith demonstrates how owners invested time, effort and money into reclaiming their possessions. Characterising the eighteenth century as a period of loss and losing, *Keeping Hold* uncovers how understandings of self-worth came to be bound up with possession, with destructive implications.

KATE SMITH is an associate professor in eighteenth-century history at the University of Birmingham. Her work explores how people related to the material world in the past. Her other books include *Material Goods, Moving Hands: Perceiving Production in England, 1700–1830* (2014) and *The East India Company at Home, 1757–1857* (co-edited with Margot Finn, 2018).

Keeping Hold

A Cultural and Social History of Possession in Eighteenth-Century Britain

Kate Smith
University of Birmingham

Shaftesbury Road, Cambridge CB2 8EA, United Kingdom

One Liberty Plaza, 20th Floor, New York, NY 10006, USA

477 Williamstown Road, Port Melbourne, VIC 3207, Australia

314–321, 3rd Floor, Plot 3, Splendor Forum, Jasola District Centre, New Delhi – 110025, India

103 Penang Road, #05-06/07, Visioncrest Commercial, Singapore 238467

Cambridge University Press is part of Cambridge University Press & Assessment, a department of the University of Cambridge.

We share the University's mission to contribute to society through the pursuit of education, learning and research at the highest international levels of excellence.

www.cambridge.org
Information on this title: www.cambridge.org/9781009617598

DOI: 10.1017/9781009617628

© Kate Smith 2026

This publication is in copyright. Subject to statutory exception and to the provisions of relevant collective licensing agreements, no reproduction of any part may take place without the written permission of Cambridge University Press & Assessment.

When citing this work, please include a reference to the DOI 10.1017/9781009617628

First published 2026

Cover image *A Young Girl and her Dog*, c.1780 (oil on canvas)/Joshua Reynolds/ Tokyo Fuji Art Museum / Bridgeman Images

A catalogue record for this publication is available from the British Library

A Cataloging-in-Publication data record for this book is available from the Library of Congress

ISBN 978-1-009-61759-8 Hardback
ISBN 978-1-009-61760-4 Paperback

Cambridge University Press & Assessment has no responsibility for the persistence or accuracy of URLs for external or third-party internet websites referred to in this publication and does not guarantee that any content on such websites is, or will remain, accurate or appropriate.

For EU product safety concerns, contact us at Calle de José Abascal, 56, 1°, 28003 Madrid, Spain, or email eugpsr@cambridge.org

For Will Millar

Contents

List of Figures	*page* viii
Acknowledgements	x
Introduction: Property, Possession and the Importance of Loss	1
Part I Challenging Property and Possession	27
1 Legal and Philosophical Understandings of Property and Possession	29
2 Cities of Loss	59
Part II Seeking Return	87
3 Systems of Reclamation	89
4 Who Lost and Who Looked	126
Part III Learning from Loss	149
5 Describing and Knowing Possessions	151
6 Valuing Possessions	179
7 Selfhood and the Importance of Keeping Hold	209
Conclusion: Legacies of Loss	232
Bibliography	243
Index	265

Figures

3.1 Warning carrier notice, 11 September 1729. Historic Warning Notices box O.J.V. page 93

3.2 Bar chart showing average number of 'lost', 'dropt' and 'misplac'd' notices which appeared in the December issues of the *Daily Courant* the *Daily Advertiser* and *The Times*. 97

3.3 Bar chart showing total number of 'lost', 'dropt' and 'misplac'd' notices which appeared in the December issues of the *Daily Courant*, the *Daily Advertiser* and *The Times*. 98

3.4 Chart showing percentage of different types of 'things' advertised in 'lost' notices which appeared in the December issues of the *Daily Courant* the *Daily Advertiser* and *The Times*. 100

3.5 Second page of *Daily Advertiser* (London), 18 December 1742. Mic. A. 5002-5058. 102

3.6 Bar chart showing average number of stolen notices that appeared in the December issues of the *Daily Courant* the *Daily Advertiser* and *The Times*. 104

3.7 Bar chart showing total number of stolen notices that appeared in the December issues of the *Daily Courant* the *Daily Advertiser* and *The Times*. 105

3.8 Bar chart showing total number of 'stopt' notices that appeared in the December issues of the *Daily Courant* the *Daily Advertiser* and *The Times*. 107

3.9 Bar chart showing total number of notices addressed to the owner, listing that an item had been 'found', 'left' or 'taken up' that appeared in the December issues of the *Daily Courant* the *Daily Advertiser* and *The Times*. 108

3.10 Bar chart showing total number of notices listing a person who had 'eloped', 'runaway', 'absconded' or 'deserted' (including escaped criminals or deserted soldiers, but not the pursuit of alleged criminals) that appeared in the December issues of the *Daily Courant* the *Daily Advertiser* and *The Times*. 109

3.11 Canonbury Grove by Islington Press, 1824. 303569.	116
5.1 William Henry Fox Talbot, 'Articles of China', 1843–44, Salted paper print. 2015.74.	152
8.1 'The Lost and Found Office', Handbill, 1777. 473402.	233

Acknowledgements

When reading books, it is often the acknowledgements page that I turn to first. Here is where the deception of the sole author ends, and the multiple contributors become clearer. Research, by nature, is a collaborative affair, and this book is no different. Its writing has accrued a range of debts that need acknowledgement.

The research and writing of this book were made possible by generous support from different institutions and organisations. Thanks to the Institute of Advanced Studies at the University of Birmingham for funding an interdisciplinary workshop at the start of this project and to the Past and Present Society for funding an international conference. I am grateful to the University of Birmingham for funding two periods of research leave that were essential to the development of the project. I am also indebted to the European University Institute in Florence for a visiting fellowship towards the end of the writing process, which gave me the space to bring the book together.

The process of identifying and locating the primary sources fundamental to this book was substantially aided by the expertise and generosity of archivists and curators. I particularly owe a debt of gratitude to Eleni Bide at the Goldsmiths' Company Archive; John Boneham at the British Library; Oliver House of the Bodleian Special Collections at the Bodleian Library; Julie-Anne Lambert of the John Johnson Collection of Printed Ephemera at the Bodleian Library and Catherine Pell at Leeds Castle.

This book has been researched and written while I was working in the Department of History at the University of Birmingham. Its development has been enriched by teaching undergraduate students, particularly those who took my special subject 'Stray Dogs: Confronting Loss in Eighteenth- and Nineteenth-Century Britain'. Our discussions of how eighteenth- and nineteenth-century Britons set about understanding and responding to loss distinctly shaped my work. I also received research assistance from three students who participated in the Student Research Scholarship Scheme funded by the University. A huge thank you goes to Anna Harrington, Emily Jones and Rik Sowden for hunting down references and helping me transcribe notices.

Acknowledgements xi

Alongside discussions with students, presenting my research at different institutions has been invaluable in allowing me to test my ideas and receive feedback from colleagues. Thanks to the following institutions for inviting me to speak and enriching the research process: Eighteenth-Century Seminar at the University of York; Material Witness Workshop at the University of Kent; Early Modern Seminar at the University of East Anglia; 1650–1800 Graduate Seminar at the University of Oxford; Animal History Group Seminar at King's College London; 'Gone Missing: Colonial Loss' seminar at the Renaissance Society of America Conference; Centre for Eighteenth-Century Studies at Queen's University Belfast; Material Culture in the Seventeenth and Eighteenth Centuries Seminar at the University of Edinburgh; Women's History Seminar at the Institute of Historical Research; Art History Department Seminar at UW-Madison; Long Eighteenth Century Seminar at the Institute of Historical Research and 'The History of Value' Conference at Princeton University.

At these different events and in other spaces, I have had conversations with colleagues that have significantly shaped the project. Such collegiality and generosity were important, helping me to rethink elements of the book anew. Thank you to Sarah Anne Carter, Joanna Cohen, Lynn Festa, Natasha Glaisyer, Jane Hamlett, Anna Harris, Hendrik Hartog, Helen Holmes, Aaron M. Hyman, Ben Jackson, Dana Leibsohn, Karen Lipsedge, Simon Newman, Sara Pennell, Sadiah Qureshi, Allie Stielau, Simon Werrett, Chloe Wigston Smith, Julie-Marie Strange, Ingrid Tague and Dror Wahrman. In thinking through loss and lost property, some of you offered stories, poems and songs that expanded my thinking. Thanks to Rebecca Earle, Elizabeth Eger and Malcolm Gaskill for these. Many of you have also simply offered support, encouragement and companionship along the way; thank you (as always) for making the process so enjoyable. Thank you to Clare Anderson, Maxine Berg, Helen Clifford, Sarah Easterby-Smith, Georgina Green, Harshan Kumarasingham, Sarah Longair, Margaret Makepeace, Jon Prown, Giorgio Riello, Molly Rogers, Holly Shaffer, Ellen Smith, Sally Tuckett and Phil Withington. Thanks too to my wonderful colleagues at Birmingham, particularly Henriette van der Blom, Chris Callow, Nathan Cardon, Tom Cutterham, Tara Hamling, Matt Houlbrook, Chris Moores, Mo Moulton, Kate Nichols, William Purkis, Hiroki Shin and Jonathan Willis. Thanks too to Marga Small – we miss you so much.

As I wrote and re-wrote chapters, colleagues kindly offered their time and expertise to read and comment on drafts. With the many draws on people's time, I am especially grateful for such generosity. Thanks to Margot Finn, Karen Harvey and John Styles for reading early iterations of what later became chapters. Special thanks to the expertise, time and effort supplied by Leonie Hannan and Bob Shoemaker in reading most of the chapters. Thanks too to

Carolyn Steedman for her invaluable expertise, advice and ideas when reading the entire manuscript – a big undertaking that was hugely appreciated. Finally, thanks to the two reviewers who provided such insightful comments on the manuscript and to the team at Cambridge University Press, including Liz Friend-Smith and Rosanna Barraclough, for your enthusiastic support.

Convention dictates that we end such acknowledgements with personal debts and thanks. Although last, it is often these thanks which are most heartfelt. Research is engrossing; it takes you away from friends and family for days, weeks and sometimes months at a time. Thanks to all the Smiths, but especially Mum and Dad and Uncle Pete and Bernard, for all your encouragement and support over the years. Thanks too to the Millars and Williamsons for your warmth and welcome. A special thanks goes to friends who have long borne my absence and presence with patience, cheer and laughter – Lucy, Nix, Al, Lauren, Kat, Doug, Nicole, Liz, Toria, Herj, Chris, Lydia, Miranda, Sian and Katie. I am more than lucky to have such friends in my life. Finally, my most significant and simple thank you must be left for my partner, Will. Thanks for always being there when I get lost.

Please note that parts of Chapters 3 and 5 have previously been published in an article titled 'Lost Things and the Making of Material Cultures in Eighteenth-Century London', which appeared in the *Journal of Social History* 55:4 in 2022.

Introduction
Property, Possession and the Importance of Loss

Writing to her sister Susanna (1755–1800) in March 1777, a year before the publication of her first novel, the writer Frances Burney (1752–1840) sought to entertain with tales of troublesome shoes. Burney had purchased, or rather 'rescued', a pair of shoes from a 'dark & dusty' warehouse and in possessing the shoes, Burney gave them purpose. Yet when walking, they proved fickle. They were 'false & worthless', more wedded to the mud than their owner. Burney complained of how they 'threaten me perpetually with desertion', as they were more attached 'to the mire' than to her feet and might have left at any time.[1] Burney would not have been surprised if 'some Day' they gave her 'the slip' for good. Here, in her letter, Burney constructed a philosophy of possession. She laid out the difficulty of achieving consistency and gaining compliance from the object itself. As such, Burney positioned possession as a relationship in need of ongoing enactment. Her writing up of a walk and the unsuitability of her shoes in dealing with the abundant mud introduces us to a broader problem within eighteenth-century society: the relationship of possession and what it was understood to be. As a writer who dwelt on questions of property in her work, and whose financial independence relied on her ability to lay claim to newly established copyrights, it is perhaps unsurprising that Burney looked to more whimsical questions of possession in her letters. Burney's joke, carefully constructed for her beloved Susanna, works because it is not the shoes that will up and leave, but rather the mud that will pull them away. Although anthropomorphised here, the shoes cannot (of course) act of their own volition, and thus the relationship of possession in this instance should be simple to sustain. In framing her story in this way, however, Burney touches upon a concern with which eighteenth-century Britons were familiar, namely what did it mean to possess? Examining this question is the purpose of this book.

What it might mean to be a proper possessor of things was pressing in the eighteenth century because greater numbers of people came to own more

---

[1] Frances Burney, *The Early Journals and Letters of Fanny Burney*, Vol. II (1774–1777), ed. Lars E. Troide (Oxford, 1988), 221.

things. We have long known that between 1675 and 1725, people owned more goods. Over this half century, a higher percentage of probate inventories came to include tables, cooking pots, saucepans, pewter dishes, pewter plates, earthenware, books, clocks, pictures, looking glasses, window curtains, knives and forks and china and utensils for hot drinks.[2] We also know that people worked harder and rearranged resources to privilege consumption and obtain these goods.[3] Since the 1990s, historians have largely approached the phenomenon of more people owning more goods as a question of consumption and material culture.[4] They have uncovered the systems and processes that created these goods and have asked why and how people consumed them and what these objects meant. As a result of this work, we better understand the global systems of racial capitalism that supplied new goods, such as sugar from the Caribbean.[5] At the same time we have learned that Britain's interventions in, and violent control of, global trade routes supplied South and East Asian goods, such as cotton textiles from the Indian subcontinent and porcelain wares from China.[6] Alongside knowledge of global connections, we have also gained a better understanding of how British manufacturers and makers produced innovative goods.[7] These new and novel products encouraged Britons into the marketplace and the sophisticated design of shops and print culture further consolidated the centrality of materialism and consumption within British society.[8] Once purchased, these possessions signified taste and

---

[2] Lorna Weatherill's analysis was based on a sample of 2,902 inventories. See Lorna Weatherill, 'The Meaning of Consumer Behaviour in Late Seventeenth- and Early Eighteenth-Century England', in John Brewer and Roy Porter (eds), *Consumption and the World of Goods* (London, 1993), 220. See also Lorna Weatherill, *Consumer Behaviour and Material Culture in Britain 1660–1760* (London, 1996).

[3] Jan de Vries, *The Industrious Revolution: Consumer Behavior and the Household Economy, 1650 to the Present* (Cambridge, 2012), 10; Hans-Joachim Voth, 'Work and the Sirens of Consumption in Eighteenth-Century London', in Marina Bianchi (ed.), *The Active Consumer: Novelty and Surprise in Consumer Culture* (London, 1998), 161–166.

[4] See, for example, Brewer and Porter, *Consumption and the World of Goods*.

[5] Sidney Mintz, *Sweetness and Power: The Place of Sugar in Modern History* (New York, NY, 1986); James Walvin, *Sugar: The World Corrupted, From Slavery to Obesity* (London, 2017); Maxine Berg and Pat Hudson, *Slavery, Capitalism and the Industrial Revolution* (Cambridge, 2023).

[6] On cotton see Giorgio Riello, *Cotton: The Fabric That Made the Modern World* (Cambridge, 2013); Sven Beckert, *Empire of Cotton: A New History of Global Capitalism* (London, 2014). On porcelain, see Maxine Berg, 'Cargoes: The Trade in Luxuries from Asia to Europe', in David Cannadine (ed.), *Empire, The Sea and Global History: Britain's Maritime World, c.1763–c.1840* (Hampshire, 2007), 60–82; Robert Finlay, *The Pilgrim Art: Cultures of Porcelain in World History* (Berkeley, CA and London, 2010).

[7] Maxine Berg, *Luxury and Pleasure in Eighteenth-Century Britain* (Oxford, 2005).

[8] Claire Walsh, 'Shop Design and the Display of Goods in Eighteenth-Century London', *Journal of Design History*, 8:3 (1995), 157–176; Nancy Cox, *The Complete Tradesman: A Study of Retailing, 1550–1820* (Aldershot, 2000); Helen Berry, 'Polite Consumption: Shopping in Eighteenth-Century England', *Transactions of the Royal Historical Society*, 12 (2002), 375–394; Maxine Berg and Helen Clifford, 'Selling Consumption in the Eighteenth

knowledge, constructing status, gender, belonging and exclusion.[9] More recently, we have learned that these were feeling things that bound and negotiated relationships.[10] They were also material things, which shaped how people and their bodies moved through the world.[11] Such scholarship has produced a deep understanding of how eighteenth-century society constructed, experienced and made meaningful their material world. Within such varied and fruitful enquiries, however, the question of ownership – the relationship of possession, rather than the possession itself – has been little explored. While this question has not been granted historiographical significance, this book finds that it was historically important. As more people came to possess more things, ownership increasingly shaped people's connection to themselves and others. The question of who could own, and who could own what, provided a means of deciphering legal personhood and impacted understandings of the self.[12] As such, possession uncovers and explains a wide range of 'social' relationships.[13] Given its importance, we must shift our attention from possessions to the relationship of possession to examine how eighteenth-century society and culture reckoned with it. *Keeping Hold* uncovers how understandings of self-worth came to be bound up with possessing things at the dawn of the modern age.

On Caring and Character

In the eighteenth century, land ownership was out of reach for most and was arguably becoming more so.[14] *Keeping Hold* turns away from real property, to

---

Century: Advertising and the Trade Card in Britain and France', *Cultural and Social History*, 4:2 (2007), 145–170; Jon Stobart, Andrew Hann and Victoria Morgan, *Spaces of Consumption: Leisure and Shopping in the English Town, c. 1680–1830* (London, 2007).

[9] John Styles and Amanda Vickery (eds), *Gender, Taste and Material Culture in Britain and North America 1700–1800* (London and New Haven, CT, 2006).

[10] Stephanie Downes, Sally Holloway and Sarah Randles (eds), *Feeling Things: Objects and Emotions Through History* (Oxford, 2018).

[11] Karen Harvey, 'Men of Parts: Masculine Embodiment and the Male Leg in Eighteenth-Century England', *Journal of British Studies*, 54:4 (2015), 797–821.

[12] Susan Staves, 'Chattel Property Rules and the Construction of Englishness, 1660–1800', *Law and History Review*, 12:1 (1994), 123; Lynn Festa, 'Personal Effects: Wigs and Possessive Individualism in the Long Eighteenth Century', *Eighteenth-Century Life*, 29:2 (2005), 48.

[13] I am using 'social' in its widest sense here to include human actors and non-human actants. See Bruno Latour, *Reassembling the Social: An Introduction to Actor-Network Theory* (Oxford, 2005), 71.

[14] On the changing role of landownership, see J. V. Beckett, 'The Pattern of Landownership in England and Wales, 1660–1880', *The Economic History Review*, 37:1 (1984), 21–22. Also see, J. M. Neeson, *Commoners: Common Rights, Enclosure and Social Change in England 1700–1820* (Cambridge, 1993); Carl Griffin, 'Becoming Private Property: Custom, Law, and the Geographies of "Ownership" in Eighteenth- and Nineteenth-Century England', *Environment and Planning A*, 42:3 (2010), 747–762; Briony McDonagh, *Elite Women and the Agricultural Landscape, 1700–1830* (Woodbridge, 2017). For the importance of moveable

instead examine everyday forms of property relations that were engaged in by many. Focusing on other forms of property relations, such as moveable property, is pertinent not only because more people came to own moveable property in the period, but also because the role of such property in people's lives and social relationships changed as urban spaces became more important.

To consider moveable goods, we might think back to all those cooking pots, dishes, plates, clocks and books recorded in probate inventories: we might look to the household. In doing so, we would be reminded of the importance placed on economy and more particularly of care and caring. In the early modern period, households needed to be well ordered and well managed to make the most of the resources they had.[15] A neat house reflected a good character, which remained crucial to social relations and obtaining credit.[16] Key to household order was the care of possessions. Manuals on domestic management suggest there were high expectations of what constituted care. Furniture needed to be 'washed clean' and 'rubbed daily' if it was 'to carry a gloss and look well'.[17] These standards were mirrored in diaries and day books, which reveal that pewter was regularly 'scowered', and 'old shifts, shirts and sheets' were frequently mended.[18] To clean, to care, or more particularly, to put 'a little fragrant wax' on a table with 'the woolen [sic] cloth that lends warmth to everything' was a key means of cherishing possessions.[19] Such care was given by mistresses and masters, but more usually their capacity to labour, to care, was exercised by servants. Trial reports show the fraught importance of such work: the never-ending demand for clean clouts sometimes became too much for the servants involved.[20] Care was also enacted by people with specialist skills. For instance, when ceramic objects were broken, they were taken to menders and dirty hats were sent off to be

property rather than land see, Alexandra Shepard, *Accounting for Oneself: Worth, Status, and the Social Order in Early Modern England* (Oxford, 2015), 1.

[15] Amanda Vickery, *Behind Closed Doors: At Home in Georgian England* (New Haven, CT and London, 2009), 296–299; Simon Werrett, *Thrifty Science: Making the Most of Materials in the History of Experiment* (Chicago, IL and London, 2019), 6.

[16] 'Neat' was an important term in eighteenth-century society and culture. It denoted styles that lacked ostentation and pretension but also indicated order: things being in place. See Amanda Vickery, *The Gentleman's Daughter: Women's Lives in Georgian England* (New Haven, CT and London, 1998), 147; Amanda Vickery, '"Neat and Not Too Showey": Words and Wallpaper in Regency England', in Styles and Vickery, *Gender, Taste and Material Culture*, 201–224.

[17] Anon., *Domestic Management, Or the Art of Conducting a Family; with Instructions to Servants in General* (London, 1800), 42.

[18] Vickery, *The Gentleman's Daughter*, 149 and 151. See also Vickery, *Behind Closed Doors*, 298–299.

[19] Gaston Bachelard, *The Poetics of Space: The Classic Look at How We Experience Intimate Places* (Boston, MA, 1994), 67–68.

[20] See the case of Ann Mead in Carolyn Steedman, *Labours Lost: Domestic Service and the Making of Modern England* (Cambridge, 2009), 228–254.

cleaned.[21] To care meant to clean and mend, but it was also about order and security. Mistresses and masters regularly inventoried the goods within their households to ensure everything was still where it should be. Valuable items such as silks and lace were locked away and securing the house each night was an important task.[22] To care was to keep things in good order.

Caring for possessions was important to achieving a good character, but it was also understood in moral and religious terms in eighteenth-century British culture. Yourself, your loved ones, your possessions and your estate were believed to have been given to you by the grace of God: they were on loan from God.[23] As such, these gifts should be valued and cared for. It was, of course, easier to be of good character if you could employ someone to exercise your labour (and do all that caring) on your behalf. In the later eighteenth century, children were taught the importance of looking after things from an early age. More particularly, they were reminded of the sheer labour involved in maintaining things and were also subtly alerted to the fact that someone might do it for them. In Dorothy Kilner's (1755–1836) *The Life and Perambulations of a Mouse* (1790), we see the child Miss Nancy behaving rudely to her Nurse. Nancy's mother Mrs Artless uses the incident as an opportunity to teach her about Nurse's value and the importance of taking care of things, including children and babies. She asks Nancy how capable she would be of enacting the skills and labour needed to take care: 'Could you buy, or dress your own victuals? Could you light your own fire? Could you clean your own house, or open and shut the doors and windows? Could you make your own cloaths [sic], or even put them on without some assistance, when made?'[24] The aptly named Mrs Artless hammers home Nancy's incapacities and reminds the reader of all that needs to be done for children. A large part of caring for children was looking after their things. Mrs Artless constructs caring as an adult act, requiring maturity and skill. In seemingly defending Nurse, Mrs Artless also underscored who it was that most often laboured away,

---

[21] Sara Pennell, '"For a Crack or Flaw Despis'd": Thinking about Ceramic Durability and the "Everyday" in Late Seventeenth- and Early Eighteenth-Century England,' in Tara Hamling and Catherine Richardson (eds), *Everyday Objects: Medieval and Early Modern Material Culture and Its Meaning* (Abingdon, 2010), 37; Sara Pennell, 'Invisible Mending: Ceramic Repair in Eighteenth-Century England', in Ariane Fennetaux, Amélie Junqua and Sophie Vasset (eds), *The Afterlife of Used Things: Recycling in the Long Eighteenth Century* (New York, NY, 2014), 107–121. For hats being sent to be cleaned see Bodleian Library, MS. Rawl. D. 1114, 'The Diary of an Anonymous Man', 16 March 1710.
[22] On locking up silk gowns, see *Domestic Management*, 54. On the importance of locking up the house, see Steedman, *Labours Lost*, 85; Vickery, *Behind Closed Doors*, 31.
[23] John Mason, *Self-Knowledge. A Treatise, Shewing the Nature and Benefit of the Important Science, and the Way to Attain It* [1745] (5th edn, London, 1755), 157.
[24] Dorothy Kilner, *The Life and Perambulations of a Mouse*, Vol. I (London, 1790), 27.

cleaning and making things. In this instance, it was certainly not Mrs Artless.[25]

As children grew older, they were encouraged to learn the importance of looking after their things themselves. In the it-narrative *Cato, or Interesting Adventures of a Dog of Sentiment* (1816), the dog Cato recounts an early experience in which a child in his household was inconsiderate of her gloves and hat. One day, the child Ellen is taken with the brightness of the morning and boldly removes her hat and gloves to dash outside. As soon as she has run away, the dog Cato and his sister Flora pick up her gloves and disperse them around the garden. A moment later, they get hold of her bonnet and in playfulness rip it apart. On seeing the destroyed bonnet and unable to find her gloves, Ellen realises the error of her ways: 'I am really so vexed and ashamed, I think I shall never be disobedient again; one feels so comfortable when acting properly.'[26] Ellen is clear about the lesson she has learned: to act properly, to be responsible and respectable, is to look after your things.

While caring continued to be important across the eighteenth century, the changing role of possessions in peoples' social lives prompted questions about what it was to care and why caring was important. In the early modern period, possessions acted as stores of wealth. In the 'culture of appraisal', household possessions were the basis upon which people calculated another's worth and offered credit.[27] In the eighteenth century, such calculations began to change. As historian Alexandra Shepard has shown, establishing trust relied on reputation and, in the eighteenth century, this was no longer dependent on 'a household's stock of assets' but rather on the 'selective representation of social and cultural capital'. In this period of increasing mobility and urbanisation, shopkeepers were no longer able to establish the value of a household's assets. Instead, they became 'more *heavily reliant* on judgements about reputation and character'.[28] And, as we know from Margot Finn's research on the continued relationship between character and credit, by the nineteenth century, 'the idea of character pervaded English society and culture'.[29] In urban environments, people secured the 'personal and social identities' crucial to character by utilising the 'partial and selective processes of display'.[30] Possessions accompanied people into urban spaces and reputations were built through their presence. The shifting ground upon which reputations and identities were forged – from household stock to the selective display of mobile things – did not diminish the importance of caring for things. Mobile items still needed

---

[25] On the difficulty of knowing who did the labour, see Kate Smith, 'In Her Hands: Materializing Distinction in Georgian Britain', *Cultural and Social History*, 11:4 (2014), 493.
[26] Anon., *Cato, or Interesting Adventures of a Dog of Sentiment* (London, 1816), 19.
[27] Shepard, *Accounting for Oneself*, 2.   [28] Ibid., 302.
[29] Margot C. Finn, *The Character of Credit: Personal Debt in English Culture, 1740–1914* (Cambridge, 2003), 20.
[30] Shepard, *Accounting for Oneself*, 311.

to be cleaned, maintained and mended. However, *Keeping Hold* argues that in the eighteenth century an increasingly critical part of caring for your things, of having a good character, was the ability to *maintain* possession over time. It became more important, this book will show, because in a world of increasingly mobile people and things, keeping hold proved difficult and required new forms of action. In the eighteenth century, as the basis for evaluating character switched from the household to 'selective representation', we begin to see how the relationship of possession came to exist as a 'thing' that itself required maintenance and care.

On Possessions

The question of what it meant to own was pressing in the eighteenth century, not only because more people came to own more things and the role of such things in the social life of Britons was substantially changing, but also because the question of *what* could be owned loomed large, particularly in terms of personal property. Historian Susan Staves asserts that after largely focusing on real property, the rapidly expanding commercial world of the eighteenth century prompted the law 'to develop (or, less sympathetically, to complicate) the law of chattels'.[31] In this period, new attention was paid to moveable goods and how the law should deal with them. In Book II of his *Commentaries*, Blackstone noted two categories of chattels. First, 'chattels real' were 'interests issuing out of, or annexed to, real estate'.[32] These things were immobile, but of an indeterminate duration and thus existed as chattels, rather than real property. The other category of chattels, and it is this form which this book largely focuses upon, was 'chattels personal' (sometimes referred to as 'chattels moveable').[33] These were distinctly mobile things: those 'which may be annexed to or attendant on the person of the owner, and carried about with him from one part of the world to another.'[34] Blackstone included a list to clearly articulate what such things might be. He named chattels personal as 'animals, household-stuff, money, jewels, corn, garments', but tellingly he also included 'every thing else that can properly be put in motion, and transferred

---

[31] Staves, 'Chattel Property Rules and the Construction of Englishness, 1660–1800', 124.
[32] William Blackstone, *Commentaries on the Laws of England: Book II Of the Rights of Things*, ed. Simon Stern (Oxford, 2016), 261.
[33] On 'chattels moveable' see Samuel Clapham, *A Collection of the Several Points of Sessions' Law, Vol. 1* (London, 1818), 204.
[34] Blackstone, *Commentaries on the Laws of England: Book II Of the Rights of Things*, 262. Blackstone's definition proved influential and was, in part, used by Samuel Clapham in his guide for magistrates. See Clapham, *A Collection of the Several Points of Sessions' Law, Vol. 1*, 204.

from place to place'.³⁵ That he included 'everything else' was reflective of an age in which there was a steady supply of new things which could be 'put in motion, and transferred from place to place'. The list was ever-changing and one of the reasons the law sought to increasingly focus on the law of chattels was due to the increasingly commercial nature of the British economy and society.³⁶ However, Blackstone's use of 'every thing else' also points towards the uncertainty of the category: its distinct fluidity in this period. Not only were the boundaries of ownership under development, so too were understandings of what should be subject to certain forms of possession.

Possibly due to a reliance on certain sources, such as inventories, or because of the dominance of material culture approaches, recent historical scholarship on personal possessions has largely focused on clothes and household goods.³⁷ However, as Blackstone reminds us, a much broader set of 'things' existed as property in the eighteenth century. We must remember that in this period, alongside clothes and household goods, it was possible for Britons to own money, animals and even people. Examining what people understood ownership to be – what the relationship of possession was and what it meant – requires that we reckon with a broader range of possessions. Doing so is important not only in answering the question central to this book, but also in challenging our current assumptions about what counted as possessions in the past.

In its analysis, *Keeping Hold* focuses on the relationships at stake in four different possessions: watches, financial instruments (a category that here includes money – coins and bank notes – but also instruments such as bills of exchange, and Exchequer bills), dogs and people (including enslaved people, but also servants, apprentices and spouses). As we will explore, this choice of 'things' is largely guided by the relevant primary sources. Dogs, financial instruments, people and watches appeared most regularly in the 'lost' notices of the age. However, focusing on these 'things' is also driven by the need to engage with an eighteenth-century worldview, which held the capacity to understand people as property. Watches, financial instruments and dogs would largely have been understood as chattels personal in the period. So too,

---

[35] Blackstone, *Commentaries on the Laws of England: Book II Of the Rights of Things*, 262.
[36] David Lieberman, 'Property, Commerce, and the Common Law: Attitudes to Legal Change in the Eighteenth Century', in John Brewer and Susan Staves (eds), *Early Modern Conceptions of Property* (London and New York, NY, 1995), 147.
[37] See for example Weatherill, *Consumer Behaviour and Material Culture in Britain 1660–1760*; Maxine Berg, 'Women's Consumption and the Industrial Classes of Eighteenth-Century England', *Journal of Social History*, 30:2 (1996), 415–434; Berg, *Luxury & Pleasure*; Styles and Vickery, *Gender, Taste and Material Culture in Britain and North America 1700–1800*; John Styles, *The Dress of the People: Everyday Fashion in Eighteenth-Century England* (New Haven, CT and London, 2007); Serena Dyer, *Material Lives: Women Makers and Consumer Culture in the Eighteenth Century* (London, 2021).

Introduction 9

as we will see in Chapter 1, could people in the form of enslavement. Beyond enslavement, people such as wives, servants, apprentices, the poor and children could also be considered possessions. Engaging with these different forms of property illuminates how they each shaped what the relationship of possession was understood to be and mean.

Studying dogs, financial instruments, people and watches forces us to reckon with eighteenth-century culture and the elisions it countenanced between objects, non-human animals and humans. In this period, the large-scale invasion, encroachment and exploitation of lands and peoples by European nations produced new questions about the category of the human.[38] The parameters governing what it meant to be human 'needed to be flexible enough to incorporate the world's variety within it'.[39] The construction of the category of the human took place across a range of sites, from epistemological questions about 'man' to taxonomical renderings within natural history, and from political questions of human rights to philosophical questions on human understanding, and then to literary conceptions of sensibility and sympathy.[40] Prior to the final quarter of the eighteenth century, the question of who and what counted as human loomed large. For example, in the early eighteenth century, rather than a question of political rights, discussions on the rights of mankind were more fundamental, referring 'to what distinguished humans from the divine on one end of the scale and from animals on the other'.[41] Writers, artists and philosophers were deeply uncertain as to 'what and who counted as human' and sought to produce means by which humanity could be elicited and produced.[42] Alongside interiority and sympathy, Lynn Festa has argued that literature produced the category of the human thematically, formally and performatively.[43] Festa argues that artwork and literature often did so with recourse to non-human animals and objects. As such, 'humanity arrived in a "field of conflict" flanked by animals, machines, and all manner of things'.[44] Writers and artists created innovations in non-human perspective, characterisation and voice, which constructed boundaries between animal, human and thing. Art and literature elicited the reactions needed to perform

---

[38] Daniel Carey, *Locke, Shaftesbury, and Hutcheson: Contesting Diversity in the Enlightenment and Beyond* (Cambridge, 2009), 4.
[39] Felicity A. Nussbaum, *The Limits of the Human: Fictions of Anomaly, Race, and Gender in the Long Eighteenth Century* (Cambridge, 2003), 2.
[40] Lynn Festa, *Fiction without Humanity: Person, Animal, Thing in Early Enlightenment Literature and Culture* (Philadelphia, PA, 2019), 5.
[41] Lynn Hunt, *Inventing Human Rights: A History* (New York, NY, 2007), 23.
[42] Festa, *Fiction without Humanity*, 1 and 8. See also Lynn Festa, *Sentimental Figures of Empire in Eighteenth-Century Britain and France* (Baltimore, MD, 2006), 3.
[43] Festa, *Fiction without Humanity*, 2.   [44] Ibid., 6.

humanity and created practices central to being human such as reading and reasoning.⁴⁵

In a similar vein, Jane Spencer has demonstrated the centrality of human–animal representation in political discussions of rights and personhood. Those advocating for the extension of human rights did so within a context where human–animal relations were undergoing changes. Animals came to be understood as 'fellow creatures', which needed to be cared for and sympathised with by humans.⁴⁶ At the same time, however, any claim to humanity was always dependent on a distinction between human animals and non-human animals.⁴⁷ Like Festa, Spencer underscores the need to understand the construction of humanity within literary and political forms that grappled with non-human things, and more particularly in this case, non-human animals. Of course, such forms were not only producing conceptions of humanity and the human, here we see that they also manifested understandings of non-human animals and objects, which were themselves undergoing processes of creation.⁴⁸

More broadly, we see that other spheres also reflected elisions between humans, non-human animals and objects in the eighteenth century, creating the possibility of regarding humans as 'things'. For example, the marketplace existed as an important space that produced these understandings. As Margot Finn has argued, when 'seizing men's bodies for their debts, the civil law substituted persons for things in market exchange, allowing the human body to serve as collateral for goods obtained not through productive labour and the cash nexus but rather through the operation of consumer credit.'⁴⁹ Similarly, Tawny Paul has underscored how the practices of debt repayment and punishment enacted the 'commodification of the debtor's body', because if someone failed to repay 'their body was taken to stand in for the debt, much like the object submitted to the pawnshop'.⁵⁰ Another means by which people came to be understood as 'things' was through pricing and monetary relations. Deborah Valenze has demonstrated that enlisting 'money as a vehicle for comprehending and regulating social relations' made it 'possible to conceive of certain categories of persons as private possessions over whom certain individuals

---

⁴⁵ Ibid., 254.
⁴⁶ As cited in Jane Spencer, *Writing about Animals in the Age of Revolution* (Oxford, 2020), 4.
⁴⁷ Spencer, *Writing about Animals*, 8.
⁴⁸ See for example, Laura Brown on the 'production' of animals in Laura Brown, *Homeless Dogs and Melancholy Apes: Humans and Other Animals in the Modern Literary Imagination* (Ithaca, NY, 2010). See particularly the work of Mark Blackwell and Liz Bellamy on the construction of the objects and animals and their relationship to humanity in Mark Blackwell (ed.), *The Secret Life of Things: Animals, Objects and It-Narratives in Eighteenth-Century England* (London, 2007).
⁴⁹ Finn, *The Character of Credit*, 10.
⁵⁰ Tawny Paul, *The Poverty of Disaster: Debt and Insecurity in Eighteenth-Century Britain* (Cambridge, 2019), 20.

Introduction

(usually property-owning men) claimed authority'. Valenze argues that enslaved people, women, children, servants and apprentices were 'subject to such status'.[51] Similarly, Christopher L. Brown has argued that we can see 'domestic analogues' with chattel slavery when we look to the restrained autonomy and mobility of day labourers, the poor, impressed soldiers and sailors, and of dependents such as wives, children and servants.[52] While such 'analogues' existed and will be further explored in this book, as Valenze acknowledges, enslavement was the 'most extreme form' of the 'tendency to enlist money as a vehicle for comprehending and regulating social relations'.[53] In the eighteenth century, enslavement not only took place within the Caribbean, Americas and South Asia. We know that enslavers brought enslaved people from these sites to Britain in the seventeenth and eighteenth centuries and that people were bought and sold on British soil at this time.[54] Although it was legally ambiguous as to whether people could own the body and person of another, or their capacity to labour, Britons were often invested in such ambiguity and the possibilities it opened up for conceiving of people as chattel property, as 'things', within Britain.[55] The construction of race, and the forms of dehumanisation and commodification that accompanied it, became increasingly central to understanding enslavement and its enactment in later eighteenth-century Britain.[56]

To examine what British culture and society understood the relationship of possession to be, it is crucial to connect with this eighteenth-century worldview in which humans, non-human animals and objects could all be considered property and possessions. In other words, *Keeping Hold* adds new knowledge by showing that to understand what it meant to own, including

---

[51] Deborah Valenze, *The Social Life of Money in the English Past* (Cambridge, 2006), 224–225.
[52] Christopher L. Brown, *Moral Capital: Foundations of British Abolitionism* (Chapel Hill, NC, 2006), 44. Brown describes 'domestic analogues' because he asserts that in 'the British Isles, there was nothing remotely like chattel slavery'. More recent work has shown that enslaved people were brought to Britain, were bought and sold in Britain and were regarded as property, although it remained legally ambiguous. See Chapter 1 and see Simon P. Newman, 'Freedom-Seeking Slaves in England and Scotland, 1700–1780', *English Historical Review*, 134:570 (2019), 1143 and 1148.
[53] Valenze, *The Social Life of Money*, 225.
[54] Newman, 'Freedom-Seeking Slaves', 1137 and 1148.
[55] On the 'contemporary investment in keeping it [the status of Black people in Britain] unclear', see Catherine Molineux, *Faces of Perfect Ebony: Encountering Atlantic Slavery in Imperial Britain* (Cambridge, MA and London, 2012), 11. On the distinctions drawn between enslavement and marriage see Katherine Paugh, 'The Curious Case of Mary Hylas: Wives, Slaves and the Limits of British Abolitionism', *Slavery & Abolition*, 35:4 (2014), 629–651.
[56] Newman, 'Freedom-Seeking Slaves', 1150; Catherine Hall, *Lucky Valley: Edward Long and the History of Racial Capitalism* (Cambridge, 2024), 25; D. Rabin, '"In a Country of Liberty?": Slavery, Villeinage and the Making of Whiteness in the Somerset Case (1772)', *History Workshop Journal*, 72 (2011), 5; Dana Y. Rabin, *Britain and Its Internal Others, 1750–1800: Under Rule of Law* (Manchester, 2017), 89.

what it meant to own people, we need to see how such meanings were highly interdependent in this period. However, although there are important reasons for considering humans, watches, financial instruments and dogs within my analysis, it is a problematic move. In fact, it is a devastating position to take. It is so because it risks perpetuating a logic that objectified and dehumanised people, seeing them as 'things', as possessions, as forms of display. Such a move risks perpetuating a historical violence and a legal fiction in which people were transformed into what they are not: things.[57] Yet, we must engage with the fact that people *were* subjected to the relationship of possession and the moral flatness this suggests at. Placing humans-as-property within the same analytical frame as other forms of property makes visible this eighteenth-century possibility and requires that we grapple with it more fully.

On Loss and Losing

Historians' ability to uncover what people understood the relationship of possession to be and mean has been limited by historical records that tend to name ownership rather than describe what people thought it to be. Again, if we return to probate inventories, or similarly to wills, we learn what people owned, but not how they understood such ownership (as opposed to loaning it, for instance). To probe the meanings and understandings at stake within such relationships, *Keeping Hold* breaks new ground by looking to loss. In the eighteenth century, historical actors defined loss and losing in different ways. Samuel Johnson (1709–1784) had much to say about loss and losing in his highly anticipated *A Dictionary of English Language* (1755). A loss was to forfeit something, to miss it, be deprived of it or to witness its destruction. To lose something was to 'have any thing gone so as that it cannot be found, or had again'. It was to 'be deprived of it' or 'To possess no longer'. To lose was 'contrary to keep'.[58] By 1773, William Kenrick (1725–1779) was more concise. His dictionary asserted that when something was lost, it was 'No longer possessed or perceptible'.[59] In looking to experiences of loss, the book looks to moments when things fell out of possession, when they were no longer readily available or when their location was entirely unknown, and examines what people thought, felt and did in such instances. *Keeping Hold* argues that Britons enunciated their understandings of property most clearly in such moments, particularly through what they *did* in the face of such absence. It considers their responses to the loss of their possessions (all those doings) as

---

[57] Holly Brewer, 'Creating a Common Law of Slavery for England and its New World Empire', *Law and History Review*, 39:3 (2021), 796.
[58] Samuel Johnson, *A Dictionary of the English Language, Vol. 2* (London, 1755), n.p.
[59] William Kenrick, *A New Dictionary of the English Language* (London, 1773), n.p.

articulations of what it meant to own. By focusing on what people did, we begin to learn what it was to possess.

Recent work in anthropology and sociology has shown the importance of loss and absence in our relations with possessions. Early on in such debates, sociologist Kevin Hetherington argued that consumption needed to be considered in broader terms. Rather than the point of purchase, he studied the range of social activities linked with consuming. He focused on the importance of disposal and understood it not as an end point but rather as a form of 'placing'.[60] Possessions could be placed in spaces to enact disposal, but they might also be removed from those spaces to be consumed further at a later point. We might consider here the glassware placed in a box to take to a charity shop before being swiftly taken out again one evening when extra guests unexpectedly arrive. Understanding disposal in this way allows it to be comprehended not as closure but rather as part of a larger array of performative activities important to consuming. Hetherington asserted that while in such positions of disposal, of absence, possessions continue to have impacts. He argued that the 'absent can have just as much of an effect upon relations as recognisable forms of presence can have'.[61] The letters boxed up in the attic, or the shoes given to a friend, still resonate. Although the possession is no longer seen, the 'translating effects' of the object are still present.[62]

More recently, anthropologists Mikkel Bille, Frida Hastrup and Tim Flohr Sørensen have built on Hetherington's insights but have moved beyond consumption. Bille, Hastrup and Sørensen have argued that 'absences are important social, political and cultural phenomena that impinge on people's lives'.[63] As with Hetherington, they see absent things as having important impacts upon the world and in need of study. For Bille, Hastrup and Sørensen, 'absence – even if absence is only perceived absence – may have just as much effect as material presence.'[64] In seeking to explore absent objects, they have advocated for the need to examine not only people's experience of absence, but more fully to also consider what people do in response to absence.[65] More recently still, building on work by sociologist Susie Scott who has studied 'nothing' as a social process and action, sociologist Helen Holmes has focused on the materiality of nothing.[66] Holmes has shown how 'material affinities',

---

[60] Kevin Hetherington, 'Secondhandedness: Consumption, Disposal, and Absent Presence', *Environment and Planning D: Society and Space*, 22 (2004), 159.
[61] Hetherington, 'Secondhandedness', 159. [62] Ibid., 166.
[63] Mikkel Bille, Frida Hastrup and Tim Flohr Sørensen, 'Introduction: An Anthropology of Absence', in Mikkel Bille, Frida Hastrup and Tim Flohr Sørensen (eds), *An Anthropology of Absence: Materialization of Transcendence and Loss* (New York, NY and London, 2010), 7.
[64] Bille, Hastrup and Sørensen, 'Introduction', 10. [65] Ibid., 11.
[66] Susie Scott, *The Social Life of Nothing: Silence, Invisibility and Emptiness in Tales of Lost Experience* (Abingdon, 2020), 3. See also Susan A. Crane, *Nothing Happened: A History* (Stanford, CA, 2020).

namely, how 'objects and materials conjure connections beyond kin and kin-like relations', can be important even within everyday objects and can continue when the object is absent.[67] Thus, Holmes underscores how the relations an object creates do not disappear if the object is lost, allowing that lost things continue to impact.[68] Such work prompts us to take seriously absent objects and the effects they have on people and their relationships. It also suggests at the possibilities studying loss offers for understanding property and possession. It is an obvious but important point that for loss to exist, for people to count the object as lost, the object must first have been possessed. As the songwriter Lucy Dacus eloquently puts it, 'Can't lose what you never had'.[69] If we follow Bille, Hastrup and Sørensen and explore what people did in response to absence, we can see their reactions as enunciations not only on loss, but also, more pertinently, on possession and ownership. It is when Burney experiences her shoes being pulled away by the mud that she writes to her sister about the nature of possession.

It is important that Frances Burney *wrote* about her experience of loss. The question of what experience was and how we, as historians, might seek to understand it in the past has been central to the enquiries of social historians. Edward Thompson's *The Making of the English Working Class* posited that workers' experiences were central to the emergence of the working class.[70] Within this position, Thompson understood experience broadly, as subjective responses to activities, events and exploitation. Reacting to Thompson's work in 1990, William H. Sewell, Jr. advocated for a narrower understanding of experience that followed more closely what was offered in *Webster's New International Dictionary*. Such a definition understood experience as concerned with 'actual living through an event or events' or 'actual enjoyment or suffering'. More recently, historians of emotions and the senses have argued for the need for a 'contextualised understanding of human experience'. In other words, that emotions, such as 'enjoyment' or 'suffering', open to historical actors, are historically and culturally dependent.[71] For Rob Boddice and Mark Smith, experience is 'the lived, meaningful reality of historical actors, whether as subjective or collective reality' and that any analysis must incorporate 'all the features of past perception in their own terms, be they sensory, emotional, cognitive, supernatural or whatever'.[72] Their definition of experience draws

---

[67] Helen Holmes, *The Materiality of Nothing: Exploring Our Everyday Relationships with Objects Absent and Present* (Abingdon, 2023), 4.
[68] Holmes, *The Materiality of Nothing*, 17–37; Helen Holmes and Ulrike Ehgartner, 'Lost Property and the Materiality of Absence', *Cultural Sociology*, 15:2 (2021), 253.
[69] Lucy Dacus, 'Night Shift', *The Historian* (2018).
[70] E. P. Thompson, *The Making of the English Working Class* [1963] (London, 2013), 8–9.
[71] Rob Boddice and Mark Smith, *Emotion, Sense, Experience* (Cambridge, 2020), 25.
[72] Boddice and Smith, *Emotion, Sense, Experience*, 17.

Introduction

upon a wider range of perceptions and sees them as historically and culturally contingent. Such insights have implications not only for how historical actors thought and felt about events but also how they were able to construct and construe such experiences. Invoking Clifford Geertz, Sewell himself underlined the importance of thinking through experience as something 'construed': as something consciously encountered and constructed.[73] Building on Sewell's intervention, Carolyn Steedman has asked 'But *how* construed?'. Steedman has advocated for the importance of recognising that historical actors use language to construe experience and that it is through such (historically bound) language that historians come to see experience. There is value then in applying stylistic analysis to more fully understand the linguistic possibilities open to historical actors in construing an experience in a particular moment.[74] *Keeping Hold* studies the understandings of possession and ownership by looking to experiences of loss. However, it accesses such experiences – the sensory, emotional and cognitive responses and interpretations of reality – not only through language, but also through response and action. It sees that thoughts and feelings about loss were not always articulated through language, but rather that they were also construed through responsive actions such as marking objects, printing notices and writing advertisements. *Keeping Hold* sees such interpretative acts as articulations of feelings about loss, and ultimately about ownership.

Revealing understandings of possession by looking to experiences of loss is particularly fruitful when studying eighteenth-century Britain because loss and losing were plentiful in this period. Historians have primarily written eighteenth-century Britain as a period of accumulation and expansion; however, loss and losing were significant preoccupations. They come into view if we see the eighteenth century as what I call an 'age of loss' shaped by wars, shipwrecks and fires. While concerned by their own losses, Britons were largely oblivious to the losses they forced on others through conquest, enslavement and coercion. Here is another example of the 'well-tended conditions of disregard' central to imperial projects.[75] Such disregard becomes more pointed when we consider that in their own experiences of loss, Britons acted. Rather than listen to sermons which reminded them that losses were a sign of God's

---

[73] William H. Sewell, Jr, 'How Classes are Made: Critical Reflections on E. P. Thompson's Theory of Working-Class Formation', in Harvey J. Kaye and Keith McClelland (eds), *E. P. Thompson: Critical Perspectives* (Oxford, 1990), 64.

[74] Carolyn Steedman, *An Everyday Life of the English Working Class: Work, Self and Sociability in the Early Nineteenth Century* (Cambridge, 2013), 26.

[75] The concept is Ann Laura Stoler's and has been invoked recently by Catherine Hall in her work on racial capitalism and disavowal. See Ann Laura Stoler, *Along the Archival Grain. Epistemic Anxieties and Colonial Common Sense* (Princeton, NJ, 2009), 256; Catherine Hall, *Lucky Valley: Edward Long and the History of Racial Capitalism* (Cambridge, 2024), xxix.

will and should be borne with patience, Britons were increasingly keen to mitigate the impacts of loss in this period.[76] The rapid expansion of fire, marine and life insurance industries in Britain over the century, for example, testifies to British society's attempts to allay the effects of loss.[77] Fire and life insurance grew exponentially, particularly in the late eighteenth and early nineteenth century. While there were just 567 current life assurance policies in 1772, by 1796 there were 5,000 and by 1845 there were 100,000.[78] Similarly, by 1775, 'over one third of domestic assets were insured' against fire.[79] Looking to the insurance industry also reminds us that losses had significant ramifications in people's everyday lives. For all the changes in buildings after the Great Fire, the eighteenth century still witnessed devastating fires, such as that in Cornhill in 1748.

The eighteenth century was also a period filled with much more mundane forms of loss. In her work on debt and insecurity, Tawny Paul has argued that 'individuals experienced the world of goods through the process of loss as much as through the pleasures of acquisition'.[80] Paul discusses how people lost objects through distraint or having to pawn or sell them to pay off debts. *Keeping Hold* sees that people also lost 'things' due to theft, forgetfulness or having them up and leave.[81] In novels, diaries and letters, people moaned about their lost things, or, as we saw with Burney, the possibility of losing them or of having them go. In September 1775, Elizabeth Shackleton (1726–1781) noted that her servant Nancy Nutter had thrown "her clothes out of the Red room window and run home". At the time, Shackleton was sanguine about the departure, remarking "Keep her there".[82] In a letter to his brother Thomas Robinson, 2nd Baron Grantham (1738–1786) dated

---

[76] Joseph Stennett, *The Works of the late Reverend and learned Mr. Joseph Stennett: in Five Volumes, Vol. 3* (London, 1731–1732), 264 and 279; John Tillotson, *The Works of the Most Reverend Dr. John Tillotson, the Late Lord Archbishop of Canterbury* (London, 1735), 80.

[77] Christopher Kingston, 'Marine Insurance in Britain and America', *Journal of Economic History*, 67:2 (2007), 379–409; A. B. Leonard, 'Underwriting British Trade to India and China, 1780–1835', *The Historical Journal*, 55:4 (2012), 983–1006; A. B. Leonard, 'Underwriting Marine Warfare: Insurance and Conflict in the Eighteenth Century', *International Journal of Maritime History*, 25:2 (2013), 173–185; Geoffrey Clark, *Betting on Lives: The Culture of Life Insurance in England, 1695–1775* (Manchester, 1999); Michael Lobban, 'Slavery, Insurance and the Law', *The Journal of Legal History*, 28:3 (2007), 319–328; Robin Pearson, *Insuring the Industrial Revolution: Fire Insurance in Great Britain, 1700–1850* (Aldershot, 2004).

[78] Liz McFall and Francis Dodsworth, 'Fabricating the Market: The Promotion of Life Assurance in the Long Nineteenth-Century', *Journal of Historical Sociology*, 22:1 (2009), 35.

[79] Pearson, *Insuring the Industrial Revolution*, 30.   [80] Paul, *The Poverty of Disaster*, 18.

[81] For more on distraint see Sara Pennell, 'Happiness in Things? Plebian Experiences of Chattel "Property" in the Long Eighteenth Century', in Michael J. Braddick and Joanna Innes (eds), *Suffering and Happiness in England 1550–1850: Narratives and Representations: A Collection to Honour Paul Slack* (Oxford, 2017), 208–226.

[82] As cited in Vickery, *The Gentleman's Daughter*, 144.

Introduction

2 December 1785, Frederick Robinson noted that he had 'had the misfortune to lose [his dog] Vicky'. He reported that 'she was missed on the other side of Barnet & has not been heard of since'.[83] In the late 1820s when Prince Hermann von Pückler-Muskau (1785–1871) conducted a tour of England, he recorded his experiences in lengthy epistles to his former wife Lucie (they had recently divorced by agreement in order that he could find a wealthy English wife whose fortune might help save his beloved Muskau Park).[84] In a letter dated 5 October 1826, von Pückler-Muskau discussed how he had 'left a purse with eighty sovereigns in a drawer' in his 'quayside sleeping quarters'. He proved lucky, however, as when a messenger went to recover the purse, he found it 'lying untouched in the very drawer' he had described.[85] People were constantly losing things or having them leave, yet such experiences have received little historical attention.

Losing Possession

To bring everyday occurrences of loss into view and use them to consider property and possession, this book looks to cities and focuses on *the* city: London. By the end of the century, it had become the first modern city to reach one million and a greater proportion of the population lived there. While in the early 1500s only 2 per cent of the population lived in the capital, by the late 1600s that proportion had risen to 10 per cent.[86] Rather than permanent migration, a growing proportion of the population lived in London for part of their life.[87] The capital operated a 'revolving door' system which saw ever-greater numbers moving in and out, bolstering the city and increasing the proportion of the national population that experienced it. People were drawn to the capital by its cultural and social resources but also by its economic strengths as a port city and manufacturing hub and the employment opportunities it allowed. London became increasingly understood as a city of wealth and commerce in this period of growth. It was also, however, a space in which people lost things.

Historians have shown us the centrality of theft in eighteenth-century London. While it is difficult to track the true levels of crime within the capital,

---

[83] Bedfordshire Record Office, Wrest Park Manuscripts, L30/14/333/331, Letter from Fritz [Frederick Robinson] to Thomas Robinson, 2nd Baron Grantham, 2 December 1785.
[84] Prince Hermann von Pückler-Muskau (Linda B. Parshall trans.), *Letters of a Dead Man* (Cambridge, 2016), xxix.
[85] von Pückler-Muskau, *Letters of a Dead Man*, 34.
[86] Leonard Schwarz, 'London 1700–1840', in Peter Clark, Martin J. Daunton and David Michael Palliser (eds), *Cambridge Urban History of Britain, Vol. 2: 1540–1840* (Cambridge, 2000), 644.
[87] Schwarz, 'London 1700–1840', 653.

concerns over crime regularly emerged, particularly during periods of demobilisation after war.[88] As we will further explore in Chapter 2, such concerns shaped understandings of urban life, as did the stories of loss included in guidebooks, poetry, newspapers and novels. In the late eighteenth century, the trope of the city as a threatening space emerged.[89] London was understood as a dangerous space not only due to the numbers of people in it, but also because of the distractions it held and the uncertainties they produced. The stories of the capital written and published in this period showed that things could be stolen, but also that they could be dropped and mislaid as city diversions distracted their owners. As London came to be increasingly understood as a site of hustle and bustle, it produced uncertainties over loss: the lost possession might have equally been stolen or fallen loose in the jostle of the crowd. Similarly, the economic and social opportunities presented by cities often provided the necessary inducements needed for servants and apprentices to leave or escape. *Keeping Hold* reveals how these experiences of loss in urban spaces and the uncertainties they presented prompted people to articulate their understandings of possession and ownership and challenged and reconfigured those very understandings.

Rather than looking to Providence, in an 'age of risk', the majority of eighteenth-century Britons came to understand that threats could be managed and prevented and took steps to ensure they were.[90] For example, in the second half of the eighteenth century, the government brought in a slew of legislation that sought to prevent house fires.[91] It was also a period that saw the development of technologies aimed at stopping the spread of fires.[92] Similarly, alongside caring for possessions through cleaning, maintenance order and repair, the eighteenth century increasingly witnessed forms of caring linked to prevention and the mitigation of risks. As Chapter 2 will show, eighteenth-century Londoners developed means of preventing the loss of possessions carried on their person as they travelled the streets of the capital. The when, where and with whom of any urban outing required consideration. Certain items of

---

[88] J. M. Beattie, *Policing and Punishment in London, 1660–1750: Urban Crime and the Limits of Terror* (Oxford, 2001), 45–46; J. M. Beattie, *The First English Detectives: The Bow Street Runners and the Policing of London, 1750–1840* (Oxford, 2014), 8–10. On the need for scepticism about concerns over crime see Robert Shoemaker, 'Worrying about Crime: Experience, Moral Panics and Public Opinion in London, 1660–1800', *Past & Present*, 234 (2017), 71–100.

[89] Raymond Williams, *Keywords: A Vocabulary of Culture and Society* (London, 2014), 53–54; Alison O'Byrne, 'The Art of Walking in London: Representing Urban Pedestrianism in the Early Nineteenth Century', *Romanticism*, 14:2 (2008), 97.

[90] Alexandra Walsham, *Providence in Early Modern England* (Oxford, 2003), 333–334; Emily C. Nacol, *An Age of Risk: Politics and Economy in Early Modern Britain* (Princeton, NJ and Oxford, 2016), 2.

[91] Pearson, *Insuring the Industrial Revolution*, 44.   [92] Ibid., 35.

Introduction 19

economic or emotional value might be left at home. When people did take possessions with them, they increasingly used technologies to keep them secure. Pockets hid possessions away and kept them close. Chains, collars and locks secured 'property', making it harder for 'thieves' to steal items. These practices broadened what it meant to take care of your things.

When such strategies failed to prevent loss and things went missing, people also cared by working to get their possessions back. Chapter 3 will show how Londoners created systems for finding and reclaiming their things. In the age before lost property offices, missing person reports, dog homes and a uniformed police force, it was the great regime of print culture which aided urban denizens in their quests to get things back. Following the lapsing of the Licensing Act in 1695, print culture expanded rapidly, particularly in the capital. While there were estimated to have been twelve London newspapers in 1712, by 1811 that figure had risen to fifty-two.[93] The increase in the number of newspapers was accompanied by an increase in the number of newspaper purchasers. It is estimated that newspaper circulation increased 'twenty-fold between 1695 and 1855'.[94] When we look to newspaper readership, as opposed to purchase, we see that the figures are higher still. Joseph Addison estimated that at least twenty people read each copy of his *Spectator*.[95] While we might be cautious of Addison's boast, it has been estimated that the proportion of newspaper readers in the capital was much higher than elsewhere. Newspapers were distributed to coffeehouses, inns and taverns, meaning that non-purchasers had multiple opportunities to read them. Historian Michael Harris has argued that these forms of distribution 'meant that a single copy of London newspapers was likely to reach a very large audience'.[96] Notices were an increasingly important part of newspaper culture over the eighteenth century. Advertisements provided substantial financial support to any newspaper venture.[97] Such sections frequently included notices for lost and stolen items. As Chapter 4 will demonstrate people up and down the social scale printed handbills and placed newspaper advertisements to draw attention to their lost and stolen things.

In using handbills and advertisements, 'losers' sought the return of their possession and to avoid the legal obligation to pursue prosecution. Although it was unclear, particularly in urban spaces, whether 'things' had been stolen, most handbills and advertisements used the language of 'lost'. Victims were obliged to report crimes and to use their own resources to detect and track the

---

[93] Hannah Barker, *Newspapers, Politics and English Society 1695–1855* (Harlow, 2000), 29.
[94] Barker, *Newspapers, Politics and English Society 1695–1855*, 31.
[95] Jeremy Black, *The English Press in the Eighteenth Century* (Abingdon, 2010), 72.
[96] Michael Harris, *London Newspapers in the Age of Walpole: A Study of the Origins of the Modern English Press* (London and Toronto, 1987), 47.
[97] Harris, *London Newspapers in the Age of Walpole*, 58.

criminal and follow prosecutorial proceedings.[98] Although the judicial system offered monetary rewards to encourage victims and thief-takers to pursue prosecution in the late seventeenth and eighteenth century, 'the vast majority of crimes were not prosecuted'.[99] Instead, victims often sought to bypass the prosecution of misdemeanours (which included property worth less than a shilling, vice, regulatory and poor law offences, as well as offences against the peace), by using informal settlements.[100] Although informal settlements were illegal, particularly in the case of felonies, victims often found means of contacting the thief and settling.[101] Newspaper notices provided one such way. The careful use of 'lost' rather than 'stolen' in the great majority of notices allowed victims to reach thieves and finders and seek reclamation of their possessions, while simultaneously signalling that they would not pursue prosecution. Importantly, in some cases, these notices – and the information they might prompt – could also act as the beginnings of an investigation that might lead to prosecution. However, the popularity of the lost notices system (and its persistent focus on the possession lost rather than any potential suspect) demonstrates that for many urban denizens, the return of possessions was much more important than pursuing prosecution and punishing threats to property. Illuminating these strategies contributes to our understanding of histories of crime by further revealing the prevalence of a form of informal settlement that sat alongside judicial processes.

Keeping Hold primarily utilises a specially compiled database of over 4,000 'lost' and 'runaway' newspaper notices, which were identified in and transcribed from the period's most important daily newspapers, the *Daily Courant* (1702–1735), *Daily Advertiser* (1731–1796), *Public Advertiser* (1752–1794) and *The Times* (1785–present).[102] It argues that it is here in these many notices that we see what people did in response to losing possessions and thus where we find articulations of what it meant to own. Rather than formed through keyword searches, this database was created by systematically working through issues of these newspapers and transcribing each notice they

---

[98] Beattie, *Policing and Punishment in London, 1660–1750*, 85.
[99] Mary Clayton and Robert Shoemaker, 'Blood Money and the Bloody Code: The Impact of Financial Rewards on Criminal Justice in Eighteenth-Century England', *Continuity and Change*, 37 (2022), 107.
[100] Robert B. Shoemaker, *Prosecution and Punishment: Petty Crime and the Law in London and Rural Middlesex, c. 1660–1725* (Cambridge, 1991), 311.
[101] Shoemaker, *Prosecution and Punishment*, 316.
[102] These newspapers were accessed via Gale's Seventeenth- and Eighteenth-Century Newspaper Collection, the British Library Microfilms A5002–5058 (in the case of the *Daily Advertiser*) and *The Times* Digital Archive.

Introduction

contained.[103] This method allowed the identification and inclusion of a wide range of lost, stolen, found and runaway notices, and the variations of language and terms at stake within them.[104] To see changes over time, *Keeping Hold* analysed a sample of 1,655 lost and runaway notices, which included those notices published in December issues of the *Daily Courant* (1702, 1710, 1720, 1730), the *Daily Advertiser* (1742, 1752, 1760, 1771, 1782, 1792) and *The Times* (1800, 1810, 1820, 1830). December was chosen as the month with the most consistent extant issues and thus the most consistent and comparable data. Prior to the later eighteenth century, it was within the London season and thus December also has the advantage of being a period of the year when the capital included the widest range of social groups.

Many different 'things' appeared in lost notices in the eighteenth century. Snuffboxes, anchors, keys, jewellery, coins, papers, banknotes, trunks, monkeys, parrots, dogs and clothes all feature. Similarly, a range of different people are listed as having 'absconded', 'left' or 'run away'. Spouses, apprentices, enslaved people, soldiers, servants and children all went. Historians and literary scholars have examined 'lost' notices in London newspapers before, but these studies focused on the late seventeenth and early eighteenth century.[105] Historians have also studied notices appearing in the provincial press, but here the focus was largely on stolen rather than lost notices, and their relationship to policing strategies and criminal investigation.[106] In contrast, this book offers the first systematic study of 'lost' notices appearing in the London press over the long eighteenth century. *Keeping Hold* focuses on

---

[103] Tim Hitchcock, 'Confronting the Digital: Or How Academic Writing Lost the Plot', *Cultural and Social History*, 10:1 (2013), 9–23. Thanks to research assistance from Anna Harrington, Emily Jones and Rik Sowden in supporting this labour-intensive process.

[104] I use the term 'runaway' notice to cover the different people (enslaved people, wives, apprentices, servants) included in these notices. When only dealing with notices for enslaved people, I use the term 'freedom seeker' to denote the different power relationship at stake.

[105] Tim Wales has studied the lost notices in the *London Gazette* (1696) and all the papers in the Burney Collection, 1698–1700, while literary scholars Jonathan Lamb and Sean Silver have studied a selection of notices published in London newspapers from 1717–1725 and 1714–1725, respectively. See Tim Wales, 'Thief-Takers and Their Clients in later Stuart London', in Paul Griffiths and Mark S.R. Jenner (eds), *Londinopolis: Essays in the Cultural and Social History of Early Modern London* (Manchester and New York, NY, 2000), 69; Jonathan Lamb, *The Things Things Say* (Princeton, NJ and Oxford, 2011), 43–46; Sean Silver, *The Mind Is a Collection: Case Studies in Eighteenth-Century Thought* (Philadelphia, PA, 2015), 255.

[106] John Styles has examined crime advertisements in Leeds and York newspapers in 1729, 1730 and 1784. Similarly, David Churchill has looked to this phenomenon in the provincial press of the nineteenth century, including newspapers in Manchester, Leeds and Liverpool in 1830, 1835, 1855, 1860, 1882 and 1895. See John Styles, 'Print and Policing: Crime Advertising in Eighteenth-Century Provincial England', in Douglas Hay and Francis Snyder (eds), *Policing and Prosecution in Britain, 1750–1850* (Oxford, 1989), 55–112; David Churchill, *Crime Control and Everyday Life in the Victorian City: The Police and the Public* (Oxford, 2018), 167–169.

notices for those items which appeared most regularly, including watches, financial instruments (coin, bank notes and bills) and dogs, but also people (including servants, apprentices, enslaved people and spouses). The analysis included in *Keeping Hold* innovates by placing notices for lost possessions and lost people in dialogue with each other. As noted previously, it does so in order to grapple more fully with an eighteenth-century worldview that often saw and purposefully enacted slippages between these different 'things'.

Notices for white servants, apprentices, spouses and soldiers have been recognised as useful sources, but have only been studied sporadically.[107] In contrast, advertisements for freedom seekers (enslaved people who escaped) have been studied more fully, particularly in Atlantic World newspapers of the eighteenth century.[108] These notices have provided a vital source for historians seeking to further understand the lives of enslaved people. However, we must approach notices for freedom seekers with caution. We too must apply care. Seeking to understand property and possession by studying notices written by enslavers about enslaved people begets the possibility of perpetuating historic acts which commodified and objectified people. We read the notices advertising enslaved people who have 'absconded' and read only descriptions constructed by their enslavers. As Marisa J. Fuentes, who has worked on women's experiences of enslavement in urban Barbados, reminds us, the 'fragmentary nature and format of runaway ads confine enslaved women in a depiction of violence and commodification from the perspective of the slave owner and other white authorities'.[109] Often these notices are the only historic records attached to a particular person. Their larger world, relationships, hopes, dreams and fears are lost to us. Instead, in our focus on newspaper advertisements

---

[107] See Gwenda Morgan and Peter Rushton, 'Visible Bodies: Power, Subordination and Identity in the Eighteenth-Century Atlantic World', *Journal of Social History*, 39:1 (2005), 39–64; Joseph Cozens, '"The Blackest Perjury": Desertion, Military Justice, and Popular Politics in England, 1803–1805', *Labour History Review*, 79:3 (2014), 255–280.

[108] Martha J. Cutter, '"As White as Most White Women": Racial Passing in Advertisements for Runaway Slaves and the Origins of a Multivalent Term', *American Studies*, 54:4 (2016), 73–97; Marisa J. Fuentes, *Dispossessed Lives: Enslaved Women, Violence, and the Archive* (Philadelphia, PA, 2016); Simon Middleton, 'Runaways, Rewards, and the Social History of Money', *Early American Studies: An Interdisciplinary Journal*, 15:3 (2017), 617–647; Simon P. Newman, 'Rethinking Runaways in the British Atlantic World: Britain, the Caribbean, West Africa and North America', *Slavery & Abolition*, 38:1 (2017), 49–71; Sharon Block, *Colonial Complexions: Race and Bodies in Eighteenth-Century America* (Philadelphia, PA, 2018); Newman, 'Freedom-Seeking Slaves in England and Scotland', 1136–1168; Simon P. Newman, *Freedom Seekers: Escaping from Slavery in Restoration London* (London, 2022); Jonathan Prude, 'To Look upon the "Lower Sort": Runaway Ads and the Appearance of Unfree Laborers in America, 1750–1800', *The Journal of American History*, 78:1 (1991), 124–159; David Waldstreicher, 'Reading the Runaways: Self-Fashioning, Print Culture, and Confidence in Slavery in the Eighteenth-Century Mid-Atlantic', *The William and Mary Quarterly*, 56:2 (1999), 243–272.

[109] Fuentes, *Dispossessed Lives*, 44.

written by enslavers, we give room and air to the perspectives of enslavers. Similarly, in compiling databases, in counting and extracting we take a risk. As Simon P. Newman asserts, 'Historians today who collate and analyse these advertisements engage in an act of remediation that risks continuing the datafication of enslaved people.'[110] To combat such ever-present concerns, the book seeks out other sources, baptism records, material sources and newspaper reports of organising to illuminate where possible the lives (in their fullest sense) of the freedom seekers it touches upon.[111] It also frequently considers the why and how of the limitations of such attempts. Such working is important in giving depth to the lives of historic actors, their concerns and interests but also to show how and where the record obscures such depth and why. We must better understand the historic nature of caring for things but also the potential violence of caring when the possession in question was human.

Understanding the notices is important not only because of their ubiquity but also because of the range of social groups who wrote and read them. Pursuing lost possessions through advertising incurred investments of time, effort and money and yet, as Chapter 4 shows, a range of urban denizens engaged in the practice. We find evidence of the nobility engaging with these systems but also servants. They wrote these notices, aware that larger swathes of the capital's population would read them and that they might prove successful in relocating their lost item. While these notices were written by a range of social groups, they were also read by a wide variety of people. However, there were certain groups and occupations that were more involved in the system than others. We find that Hackney coachmen were important, as were pawnbrokers, dog dealers and kidnappers. These were people particularly on the lookout in eighteenth-century London. Central within the advertisements placed for lost objects and animals and runaway people was the textual practice of description. As we will see in Chapter 5, to write a notice required remembering features that could make the item visible and recognisable to others. In analysing these features, we see another form of caring in action. An important marker of ownership was knowing your possession and being able to adequately describe it should it go missing. Clearly, eighteenth-century Londoners did not always trust their memory in such an important task. We see people making notes about their possessions and their relevant characteristics: a watchmaker's name here, the number on a banknote there or the clothing gifted to a servant or apprentice. People cared for their things by writing down details about them. Such knowledge could then be picked up and used if the

---

[110] Newman, *Freedom Seekers*, xxiv.
[111] For more on interpreting the broader lives and pleasures of those people who were enslaved see Tara A. Bynum, *Reading Pleasures: Everyday Black Lives in Early America* (Champaign, IL, 2023).

item became lost. To keep possession was not simply a physical act, rather it required that certain forms of knowledge be remembered and stored over time. To possess something was to know it.

Locating Value

Possession was distinctly tied to questions of value in the eighteenth century. Property rights largely existed to protect and organise things of value. As William Blackstone argued, 'Whatever...hath a *Value* is the Subject of Property'.[112] Yet, what value was, how it was produced and where it was located was open to interpretation. The financial and monetary instabilities of the eighteenth century meant people frequently worried as to the nature of value. Given value's importance to property but also its instability in this period, the final two chapters of this book seek to interrogate its place and position. Looking to the range of values at stake in possessions offers a means of understanding why people invested time, effort and money in securing the return of lost and stolen goods. Thinking through value also provides a way of interrogating the importance of the relationship of possession and the forms of value it accrued.

Historian Rebecca L. Sprang argues that 'Value is a product of humans' interactions with objects and with each other.'[113] Yet losing things, distinctly reorientates such interactions, disrupting and sometimes intensifying the values at stake. As Chapter 6 explores, the act of writing a notice which sought the return of a lost item itself indicated that the item was valuable to the loser. More particularly, lost and runaway notices often included monetary rewards, which acted as inducements to return or report the 'thing' concerned. Rewards provide us with a measure of value which can be read in relation to the description of the 'thing'. In writing a notice, describing the possession and deciding upon the amount of reward offered, losers conjured with questions of value. Such decisions, Chapter 6 argues, both reflected the values at stake in the possession concerned and often forced the construction of new values. The absence of the 'thing' and the threat of it not returning decidedly changed the loser's interaction with and relationship to that 'thing'. Loss asked pertinent questions as to what the possession was worth and why.

Finally, Chapter 7 considers the value at stake in the relationship of possession (rather than the possession itself). It asks what value owners could claim by maintaining possession over time. As stated earlier, part of the calculation

---

[112] As cited in Paul Langford, *Public Life and the Propertied Englishman 1689–1798* (Oxford, 1990), 3. Citation from the case of *Tonson v. Collins* (1762).

[113] Rebecca L. Sprang, *Stuff and Money in the Time of the French Revolution* (Cambridge, 2017), 14.

here was clearly that of achieving and sustaining a good character. To show yourself as careful rather than careless meant maintaining and retaining your possessions. Yet, the final chapter of the book suggests we can push this idea a little further by looking to a fictional example in which the author Frances Burney imagined the loss of property and possessions more fully. In this period, possessions, particularly worn on or about the person, were material manifestations of your self; they reflected and communicated who you were. Thus, to keep an ordered assemblage of things about your person, to have them neat and tidy and *there*, also signified the state of your*self*. Such a connection was important because this was also a period in which self-possession was increasingly valued. The eighteenth century was an age that appreciated order but also control and composure. As we will explore in Chapter 7, to have things ripped from you, to have them rifled through, to have them lost entirely or have your servant leave was suggestive of the state you your*self* were in. Rather than composure, the loss of possessions marked disorder. Sustaining relationships of possession showed that you were of good character and that you were in control of your*self*. It was not simply that possessions held value, rather the relationship of possession itself had value too.

Keeping Hold shows that across the eighteenth century, possession and ownership were understood not as self-evident states but rather as ongoing relationships that people negotiated and re-asserted over time. Understanding possession as an active relationship that required care emerged in this period because of the rise of moveable property and the variety of formations that threatened it. Urban spaces and the increasingly dense social formations they contained meant keeping hold of your things became no easy task. The constant threat of loss significantly shaped conceptions of possession. At the same time, the importance of maintaining possession, and all that showed and did, also grew. The desire to 'keep', as Samuel Johnson would have it, shaped how people comprehended who and what they were and how they related to wider society. As such, the relationship of possession grew into an important and changing entity in eighteenth-century British society and culture.

Part I

Challenging Property and Possession

1 Legal and Philosophical Understandings of Property and Possession

Francis Coventry's (1725–1759) novel *The History of Pompey the Little* (1751) tells the story of Pompey a lapdog who regularly finds himself lost and in the arms of yet another 'owner'. Early on in Pompey's life, he is content with Lady Tempest, an owner who showers him with affection. Nevertheless, while on a walk in St James's Park, he is distracted by a bird (as dogs are wont to be), runs off and is lost.[1] Over the following eight years, Pompey's life is one of perpetual change. We see him travelling across the country, being passed between different hands. Towards the end of the novel, Pompey, now with yet another 'owner', finds himself back in St James's Park. By chance, he is reunited with Lady Tempest, who proceeds to walk 'off with little Pompey under her Arm'.[2] The question of who owns Pompey looms large and in their attempts to have their claims recognised, both 'owners' turn to the law. At this point in *The History*, Coventry grapples with a contemporary issue: that it was difficult to know what it meant to own things in the eighteenth century and that people looked to a variety of sources for clarity. As we will go on to see in this chapter, alongside philosophical treatise, the law offered an important means by which to understand property and possession. However, the law on moveable property, and more particularly on chattels personal, was still very much in development and remained ambiguous in the eighteenth century. This chapter explores and illuminates these legal uncertainties. It reads them as important cultural and social spaces indicative of wider concerns about possession and its illusory stability. Ambiguity created space for other ways of conceiving of possession and property to emerge. These 'other ways' are what the later chapters of this book will explore.

After Pompey's swift removal from St James's Park, it is Pompey's new 'owner' who lands the first blow. She sends a brief epistle, which insists that if Pompey is not returned to her, she would 'immediately commence a

---

[1] Francis Coventry, *The History of Pompey the Little*, ed. Nicholas Hudson [1751] (Buffalo, NY, 2008), 74.
[2] Coventry, *The History of Pompey the Little*, 208.

Prosecution against you in Chancery' to 'recover him by Force of Law'.[3] In response, Lady Tempest goes to see her solicitor at Lincoln's Inn to better understand her legal position. She wants the law to offer clarity but is disappointed. In the hallowed spaces of Lincoln's Inn, she is told of the law's inadequacy in the matter of dogs.[4] Years before William Blackstone's *Commentaries on the Laws in England* (1765–1769), which did have things to say about dogs as property, it is perhaps unsurprising that Coventry's character Lady Tempest does not know, has not even the faintest idea, that in the matter of dogs, and particularly in the matter of lap dogs, the law will not be helpful.[5] As her solicitor explains 'there is something very peculiar in the Nature of Dogs'.[6] The problem, as he outlines it, is their fickleness: they 'follow any body that calls them, and that makes it so difficult to fix a Theft'. The solicitor hits upon a problem that the law continued to grapple within into the nineteenth century, namely how can something be property when it is so difficult to prove whether it has been stolen or simply wandered off of its own volition?[7] Coventry's knowing wink here is that, of course, Pompey did indeed wander off of his own volition when the bird attracted his attention. This question of volition became increasingly important as a means of distinguishing between different types of property in the eighteenth century. As difficult as the case might be, the solicitor agrees to examine it. The case gets no further, however, as soon after Pompey dies.

It is unclear within the novel whether either of the two women 'owners' is married and thus subject to the rules of coverture and in principle unable to own property.[8] We do know, however, that Coventry has both his female characters quickly call upon the law to assert their property claims. We can

---

[3] This is not a 'lawyers' letter' but rather one from the lady herself threatening to go to the law. On lawyers' letters, see Carolyn Steedman, *History and the Law: A Love Story* (Cambridge, 2020), 59–82.

[4] Lawyers were often called upon to clarify the position of animals under the law, as we see with the 'lawyer' in *Tom Jones*. See Henry Fielding, *Tom Jones: History of a Foundling* [1749] (London, 1966), 161.

[5] William Blackstone, *Commentaries on the Laws of England: Book II of the Rights of Things* ed. Simon Stern (Oxford, 2016), 262–66. William Blackstone, *Commentaries on the Laws of England: Book IV Of Public Wrongs* ed. Simon Stern (Oxford, 2016), 156.

[6] Coventry, *The History of Pompey the Little*, 210.

[7] This issue was discussed at length by witnesses who appeared before the Select Committee in 1844. See *Report from the Select Committee on Dog Stealing (Metropolis)* (London, 1844).

[8] For more on the extent and limits of coverture in the everyday lives of married women in the eighteenth century see Susan Staves, *Married Women's Separate Property in England, 1660–1833* (Cambridge, MA and London, 1990), 148; Krista J. Kesselring and Tim Stretton, 'Introduction: Coverture and Continuity' in Krista J. Kesselring and Tim Stretton (eds), *Married Women and the Law: Coverture in England and the Common Law World* (Montreal and Kingston, 2013), 8; Amy Louise Erickson, *Women and Property in Early Modern England* (London, 1993), 150–1; Margot Finn, 'Women, Consumption and Coverture in England, c.1760–1860', *The Historical Journal*, 39:3 (1996), 709.

understand why Coventry made this authorial move. While philosophical frameworks provided a means of conceptualising property, they did not teach what it meant to own and possess things and how people might navigate such meanings in the social worlds of their everyday lives. Constructing such meanings was an important and ongoing project in the eighteenth century and the law contributed to that project in important ways. In this period, there was ready recourse to the law. People up and down the social scale called upon it to assert their rights, and in some instances to simply ensure that someone, somewhere, heard their grievances.[9] Such ready recourse to the law is also suggestive of how people were uncertain of what it meant to own. Even though both women hurry to consult the law, the novel tells us that the law was ambiguous when it came to dogs. Lady Tempest's surprise and concern at this news perhaps reflects wider frustrations experienced by those looking to the law. That someone might go to a solicitor to hear about the law was credible. However, it was also understood that the law did not hold all the answers, particularly for certain kinds of 'thing' and particularly in the eighteenth century. As this chapter will go on to show, although philosophical and legal frameworks provided a means of understanding property and possession, they also contained significant ambiguities. This chapter seeks to dwell in and on these different forms of ambiguity. As eighteenth-century culture would have it, ambiguity was the 'fact or quality of being difficult to categorize or identify'.[10] Showing what legal ambiguities were and did is the central to this chapter.

Philosophy and the Law

Legal and philosophical thinking as to the nature of property and possession began with the same agreed principle: all on earth was God given. As Blackstone acknowledged, the 'earth therefore, and all things therein, are the general property of all mankind, exclusive of other beings, from the immediate gift of the creator'.[11] The seventeenth-century philosopher John Locke (1632–1704) worked from the same principle: that God gave the earth to humankind in common. The problem then arose as to how it was possible for humankind to possess and claim property in certain parts of that earth. In his 1689 work *Second Treatise of Government*, Locke instituted a

---

[9] Tim Hitchcock and Robert Shoemaker, *London Lives: Poverty, Crime and the Making of a Modern City, 1690–1800* (Cambridge, 2015), 4; Carolyn Steedman, *Labours Lost: Domestic Service and the Making of Modern England* (Cambridge, 2009), 183 and 189; Steedman, *History and the Law*, 61; Peter King, *Crime and Law in England, 1750–1840: Remaking Justice from the Margins* (London, 2006), x.
[10] First use of this meaning of the word was recorded in 1661. See *Oxford English Dictionary*, s.v. "ambiguity, n., sense 3", July 2023. https://doi.org/10.1093/OED/7475551561
[11] Blackstone, *Commentaries on the Laws of England: Book II Of the Rights of Things*, 2.

significant shift in philosophical conceptions of property, which proved important in eighteenth-century Britain. Diverting from his contemporaries, who argued for the importance of occupation or mutual consent in claiming property, Locke asserted that it was the exertion of labour that made possible rendering parts of the earth as property. 'Whatsoever…he removes out of the State that Nature have provided' by mixing 'his *Labour* with' it and thus joining it to 'something that is his own' he makes 'his *Property*'.[12] For Locke, the *picking up* of the acorn from 'under an Oak' or the *gathering* of apples from the 'Trees in the Wood' was important. In other words, it was labour that 'fixed' a person's property in these things.[13]

Locke also asserted that people should only own what they were able to enjoy. For things to remain unused and decay in the possession of someone with too much was against the law of nature.[14] However, such understandings were only relevant for perishable goods. Locke was keen to assert that if a person gave their 'Nuts for a piece of Metal', 'or exchange his Sheep for Shells, or Wooll [sic] for a sparkling Peble [sic] or a Diamond', then that person might 'keep those by him all his Life' and would not invade 'the Right of others'.[15] These things would not perish unused, and a person could continue to enjoy them all through their life. Moreover, 'he might heap up as much of these durable things as he pleased'. It was only the perishing of previously useful things, the inability to realise utility, that was problematic. What Locke laid out then was a different route to property, a different route to living together in the world within the grace of God. Rather than occupation or mutual consent, for Locke labour was paramount to the creation of property rights. Nevertheless, such conceptions did not provide a means of thinking through what it might mean to have the shell or the pebble and keep it by you all your 'Life'. He did not examine what the experience and meaning of ownership and possession might be.

In the early eighteenth century, philosophical and legal thinking over property was intertwined and law dictionaries often quoted Locke on this subject.[16] However, unlike philosophy, the law played an important and distinct role within eighteenth-century discussions of property. It did so largely due to its function as a means of understanding yourself and your relationship to society.[17] The law had to grapple more readily with experiences of ownership and how they impacted people's social relationships. The law was not abstract, and people used and encountered it in different spheres and through a range of

---

[12] John Locke, *Second Treatise of Government* and *A Letter Concerning Toleration* [1689] (Oxford, 2016), 15.
[13] Locke, *Second Treatise of Government*, 16.   [14] Ibid., 21.   [15] Ibid., 25.
[16] For the use of Locke in early eighteenth-century legal dictionaries see G. E. Aylmer, 'The Meaning and Definition of "Property" in Seventeenth-Century England', *Past & Present*, 86 (1980), 95.
[17] Steedman, *Labours Lost*, 30.

publications and genres, including novels.[18] Through examining discussions around legislation, the judgements passed on cases, and the reports, commentaries and fiction increasingly published about the law, we begin to see how it acted as a particular frame for understanding and experiencing property.

The law recognised two primary categories of property: immoveable and moveable. Immoveable property was real property, primarily land, and was understood to last the duration of time. In contrast, moveable property was largely chattels, goods which were mobile and of an indeterminate duration. In his hugely popular four-volume *Commentaries on the Laws of England*, published between 1765 and 1769, William Blackstone principally focused on common law and its administration.[19] In the introduction to *Book II Of the Rights of Things*, Blackstone outlined how he considered moveable property as the first form of property. He imagined nomadic peoples owning moveable property (tools and herds of animals), prior to settling, cultivating and making claims to particular lands.[20] Such distinctions between immoveable and moveable property contributed to the imagining of 'things' in eighteenth-century society as distinctly mobile items that were connected to, and thus moved with, people. Each of the 'things' under discussion in this chapter, and book – dogs, watches, financial instruments, and even sometimes people – came under the purview of chattel (moveable property) law in the eighteenth century.

In the early modern period, the law of chattels had remained relatively under-developed, but in the eighteenth century, it was subject to much change. In the long eighteenth century, the state and judicial system sought 'to develop (or, less sympathetically, to complicate) the law of chattels'.[21] Such developments, as we will see, created ambiguities in what it meant to own these mobile things. Blackstone's *Commentaries* proved important to administering common law on 'chattels personal', featuring as it did in later guides to administering these laws.[22] As such, it acted as an important marker in the process of defining ownership. In Book II titled *Of the Rights of Things*, he noted two categories of chattels. First, there were 'chattels real'. 'Chattels real' were 'interests issuing out of, or annexed to, real estate'.[23] These things were

---

[18] Steedman, *History and the Law*, 22.
[19] The *Commentaries* went through eight editions before Blackstone's death in 1780. See Katherine Paugh, 'The Curious Case of Mary Hylas: Wives, Slaves and the Limits of British Abolitionism', *Slavery & Abolition*, 35:4 (2014), 633.
[20] Blackstone, *Commentaries on the Laws of England: Book II Of the Rights of Things*, 3.
[21] Susan Staves, 'Chattel Property Rules and the Construction of Englishness, 1660–1800', *Law and History Review*, 12:1 (1994), 124.
[22] See for example Samuel Clapham, *A Collection of the Several Points of Sessions' Law vol. 1* (London, 1818), 204. This is perhaps in contrast to the lack of reference to Blackstone on coverture in 'guides to administering the poor laws and the laws of settlement'. See Steedman, *History and the Law*, 93.
[23] Blackstone, *Commentaries on the Laws of England: Book II Of the Rights of Things*, 261.

immobile but were of indeterminate duration and thus existed as chattels, rather than real property. The other category of chattels, and it is this form which this chapter and book largely focuses upon was 'chattels personal' (sometimes referred to as 'chattels moveable').[24] These were distinctly mobile things: those 'which may be annexed to or attendant on the person of the owner, and carried about with him from one part of the world to another.'[25] Blackstone listed out what might be included in this category. He named 'animals, household-stuff, money, jewels, corn, garments, and every thing else that can properly be put in motion, and transferred from place to place'.[26] By listing out specific types of things – all that corn and those jewels – Blackstone gestured towards the stability of the category of chattels personal. Yet his almost breathy inclusion of 'every thing else' turns the category into something open-ended. His inclusion of this term was perhaps reflective of the commercial age in which he lived. There was a steady supply of new things which could be 'put in motion, and transferred from place to place'. The list was ever-changing and one of the reasons property law changed rapidly over the eighteenth century was due to the increasingly commercial nature of the British economy and society.[27] It also points towards the uncertainty of the category, its distinct fluidity in this period. Not only were the parameters of ownership under development, so too were understandings of what should be subject to certain forms of ownership.

Blackstone's list of chattels personal does not include people, yet he did have comments to make on the possibility of people as 'things'. Relationships of possession related to servitude and subordination largely appeared in his *Book I Of the Rights of Persons*. Here Blackstone dealt with contracted relations of marriage, service and apprenticeship; however, he also commented on enslavement. In fact, his earliest mention of enslavement is arresting. He argued that 'a slave or a negro, the moment he lands in England, falls under the protection of the laws, and with regard to all natural rights becomes *eo instanti* [from that instant] a freeman'.[28] Blackstone also included a later

---

[24] On 'chattels moveable' see Clapham, *A Collection of the Several Points of Sessions' Law* vol. *1*, 204.
[25] Blackstone, *Commentaries on the Laws of England: Book II Of the Rights of Things*, 262. Blackstone's definition proved influential and was, in part, used by Samuel Clapham in his guide for magistrates. See Clapham, *A Collection of the Several Points of Sessions' Law*, vol. *1*, 204.
[26] Blackstone, *Commentaries on the Laws of England: Book II Of the Rights of Things*, 262.
[27] David Lieberman, 'Property, Commerce, and the Common Law: Attitudes to Legal Change in the Eighteenth Century', in John Brewer and Susan Staves (eds), *Early Modern Conceptions of Property* (London and New York, NY, 1995), 147.
[28] William Blackstone, *Commentaries on the Laws of England Book I Of the Rights of Persons* ed. Simon Stern (Oxford, 2016), 86. However, in the third edition of the *Commentaries*, Blackstone was more circumspect on the liberty of 'slaves' arriving in England. William M. Wiecek, 'Somerset: Lord Mansfield and the Legitimacy of Slavery in the Anglo-American World', *The University of Chicago Law Review*, 42:1 (1974), 99.

mention of enslavement in his *Book II Of the Rights of Things*. Here, he was more conservative as to the possibilities of freedom and argued that 'negroservants' continue 'in some degree the property of their masters who buy them' though that 'property consists rather in the perpetual *service*, than in the *body* or *person*, of the captive'.[29] While Blackstone could conceive of buying people, he argued that it was the person's capacity to exercise labour that was owned rather than the body of the person. As we will see later in this chapter, this question of whether enslaved people might be legally regarded as chattels or servants on British soil remained pressing and deeply impacted the lives of Black people living in Britain. Changes in the law of chattels through legislation and common law produced new understandings of what might be owned and by whom. However, the slow and contradictory nature of such change produced much ambiguity in this period.[30] It was often difficult to know what it meant to own and possess things in the eighteenth century and in certain cases such difficulty was purposeful.

The next section of this chapter lays out some of the answers and ambiguities produced by the law in eighteenth-century England to show how it offered, and sometimes entirely failed to offer, a means of understanding possession. It begins with the most difficult history: the possibility of owning people.[31] Following this, the chapter then goes onto to look at a very different kind of being: dogs. Finally, the last section of the chapter focuses upon more obvious forms of chattels personal: watches and money. By exploring the legal frameworks that shaped how people, dogs, watches and money could and could not be understood as property, we see the complexity at stake in possessing things in the eighteenth century. More particularly, this analysis highlights how the under-developed nature of chattel law in this period meant that the legal system often failed to offer clear direction as to what it might mean to 'possess'. The concept of possession was open and ambiguous in the eighteenth century, marking the need for other ways of understanding how 'things' might belong. As the book will go onto show in later chapters, it was loss, particularly in cities, that forced people to recognise this need. Loss and losing challenged Locke's simple assumption that once acquired, a person, or rather in Locke's telling a man, would keep his metal, shells, pebbles and diamonds 'by him all his Life'.

---

[29] Blackstone, *Commentaries on the Laws of England Book II Of the Rights of Things*, 272.
[30] Steedman, *History and the Law*, 1–2.
[31] For more on the difficulties and importance of encountering histories of enslavement, see Marisa J. Fuentes, *Dispossessed Lives: Enslaved Women, Violence, and the Archive* (Philadelphia, PA, 2016), 1–12.

People as Property

Over the long eighteenth century, Britons owned people. They were highly active in the slave trade and encouraged the continuation of slavery.[32] That British people forcefully enslaved people is often considered a phenomenon that took place 'over there' in sites such as the Caribbean, rather than 'here' in Britain. Yet recent research has shown that this was not the case: Britons enslaved people on British soil in the seventeenth and eighteenth centuries.[33] Prior to the *Somerset v. Stewart* case in England in 1772 and *Knight v. Wedderburn* in Scotland in 1778, the case law on slavery in Britain was particularly confused. As Catherine Molineux reminds us, however, we need to be mindful of the 'contemporary investment in keeping it [the status of Black people in Britain] unclear.'[34] We begin with owning people because here we see that legal ambiguities were not simply confusion but were sometimes actively courted in this period. Ambiguity could do cultural and social work, in this case, it allowed racialised hierarchies to flourish.

In the eighteenth century, Britons compelled enslaved people to travel from the Caribbean, Americas and South Asia to 'work' as servants in Britain.[35] Some of these individuals managed to move towards freedom and worked as indentured, apprenticed or hired servants and employees. Nevertheless, the presence of enslaved and previously enslaved people prompted questions as to their legal position within Britain. Over this period, cases often focused not only on whether slavery could exist in Britain but also, if it did exist, whether it meant that enslaved people were chattels or servants.[36] While we explore these nuances in the following paragraphs, it is important to remember that newspaper advertisements printed in England and Scotland in the first three-quarters of the eighteenth century show that 'white masters were in no doubt that the black men, women and children they brought to Britain were still slaves and property'.[37]

In England in 1696, Chief Justice Holt (1642–1710) concluded that previously enslaved people could not be defined as merchandise under English law.[38] As such, Holt's ruling challenged an important 1677 case *Butts v. Penny* overseen by Chief Justice Sir Richard Rainsford, which ruled that people could

---

[32] Katie Donington, *The Bonds of Family: Slavery, Commerce and Culture in the British Atlantic World* (Manchester, 2019); Maxine Berg and Pat Hudson, *Slavery, Capitalism and the Industrial Revolution* (Cambridge, 2023); Catherine Hall, *Lucky Valley: Edward Long and the History of Racial Capitalism* (Cambridge 2024).

[33] Simon P. Newman, 'Freedom-Seeking Slaves in England and Scotland, 1700–1780', *English Historical Review*, 134:570 (2019), 1137.

[34] Catherine Molineux, *Faces of Perfect Ebony: Encountering Atlantic Slavery in Imperial Britain* (Cambridge, MA and London, 2012), 11.

[35] Newman, 'Freedom-Seeking Slaves', 1137.

[36] Ruth Paley, 'After *Somerset*: Mansfield, Slavery and the Law in England, 1772–1830', in Norma Landau (ed), *Law, Crime, and English Society, 1660–1830* (Cambridge, 2002), 168.

[37] Newman, 'Freedom-Seeking Slaves', 1147. [38] Wiecek, 'Somerset', 90.

be considered 'goods' under English law.[39] Holt understood that while a master might not have a right to an enslaved person's 'person' as property and thus to pursue claims of trover (the recovery of damages for the wrongful taking of specific chattels), they did have a right to their service or labour as property. Holt's judgment worried planters and plantation owners who understood the impact of English law in colonial sites and felt the judgment undermined their claims to own, sell and purchase people there.[40] In response, in 1729 a group of merchants and planters approached the Attorney General Sir Philip Yorke (1690–1764) and Solicitor General Charles Talbot (1685–1737) for an opinion on the legality of enslavement in England. Yorke and Talbot gave their opinion that an enslaved person coming to England with or without their master remained enslaved (property in person unchanged) and that their master could legally compel them to return to a plantation.[41] Nevertheless, the *Galway v. Vadee* case of 1750 and the *Shanley v. Harvey* case of 1762 upheld Holt's earlier judgment that an enslaved person became free once in England. And as we saw earlier, William Blackstone similarly recognised this possibility in the first edition of his *Book I of the Rights of Persons*.[42]

While the abolition lobby had yet to emerge as a significant political force, individuals such as Granville Sharp (1735–1813) sought to utilise the law to bring about change.[43] In the 1770s, he was keen to find a case which would allow for a more definite ruling on Holt's earlier judgement. In 1772, *the* case presented itself. Charles Stewart had brought his domestic 'slave' James Somerset with him from Virginia to London in 1769. While in Virginia, Stewart's ownership of Somerset had not been in question, but this changed when in England. In February 1771, Somerset was baptised at St Andrew's in Holborn, a process which had long been understood to grant freedom to Black men and women in England.[44] Then in November 1771, Somerset ran away, a process also understood to denote freedom, or at least its pursuit, by enslaved people.[45] Tracked and captured, Somerset was forcibly held on the ship the

---

[39] Holly Brewer, 'Creating a Common Law of Slavery for England and its New World Empire', *Law and History Review*, 39:3 (2021), 794.
[40] For the relationship between English law and colonial law see Brewer, 'Creating a Common Law of Slavery for England and Its New World Empire', 766; Lee B. Wilson, *Bonds of Empire: The English Origins of Slave Law in South Carolina and British Plantation America, 1660–1783* (Cambridge, 2021), 2.
[41] Wiecek, 'Somerset', 93–94.
[42] Blackstone, *Commentaries on the Laws of England Book I Of the Rights of Persons*, 86.
[43] Christopher Brown, *Moral Capital: Foundations of British Abolitionism* (Chapel Hill, NC, 2006), 1.
[44] The principle that conversion to Christianity might denote freedom was established in *Butts v. Penny* (1677). See Brewer, 'Creating a Common Law of Slavery for England and Its New World Empire', 795.
[45] Douglas Lorimer argued that enslaved people running away was an important part of the wider 'resistance' project key to the abolition movement. See Douglas Lorimer, 'Black Slaves and English Liberty: A Re-Examination of Racial Slavery', *Immigrants & Minorities*, 3 (1984),

Ann and Mary with a view to being transported to a Jamaican plantation. With the support of Sharp, the case was brought before Lord Mansfield (1705–1793) who eventually ruled that there was no positive law or Act of Parliament existing in England to support the idea of slavery *here* and thus Somerset must be released.[46] The case was important in seeming to delineate enslavement as a colonial practice, enacted 'over there'.[47] As such, it highlighted the importance of race, building associations between liberty and whiteness.[48] The case persuaded many that it was no longer legal to enslave people on English soil.[49] The case of *Knight v. Wedderburn* (1778) brought about a similar shift in Scotland when the Lords of Session in Edinburgh upheld a ruling by a lower court that noted that an enslaved person entering the country became free.[50] Yet in both cases, the resolution was distinctly partial. Mansfield was clear about the limited parameters of his ruling. He had gone 'no further than that the master cannot by force compel him [the enslaved person] to go out of the kingdom' and that an enslaved person could prevent such removal by securing a writ of habeas corpus.[51] After Somerset, slavery continued to exist within England, just as it did in Scotland after 1778. Although newspaper notices advertising enslaved people for sale or seeking their recapture largely disappeared after about 1780, other evidence shows that the enslavement of people continued in Britain.[52]

The case of the servant Charlotte Howe in 1785 underlines how the position of previously enslaved people on British soil remained legally ambiguous after the Somerset and Knight cases. The case also reminds us of the importance of looking beyond enslaved men to consider the significance of the Somerset case for enslaved women.[53] Captain Tyringham Howe had purchased Charlotte in America when she was a young child and changed her name. He brought her to England in 1781 and she was forced to stay in Thames Ditton with his wife.[54]

121–150. For more on the different versions of freedom being pursued by running away see Simon P. Newman, 'Rethinking Runaways in the British Atlantic World: Britain, the Caribbean, West Africa and North America', *Slavery & Abolition*, 38:1 (2017), 49–71.

[46] Wiecek, 'Somerset', 106. [47] Paugh, 'The Curious Case of Mary Hylas', 636.

[48] D. Rabin, '"In a Country of Liberty?": Slavery, Villeinage and the Making of Whiteness in the Somerset Case (1772)', *History Workshop Journal*, 72 (2011), 5; Dana Y. Rabin, *Britain and Its Internal Others, 1750–1800: Under Rule of Law* (Manchester, 2017), 89.

[49] Thomas Clarkson was clearly persuaded that this was the case. See Thomas Clarkson, *An Essay on the Slavery and Commerce of the Human Species* (London, 1786), xiii–xiv.

[50] Newman, 'Freedom-Seeking Slaves', 1144.

[51] As cited in James Oldham, *English Common Law in the Age of Mansfield* (Chapel Hill, NC, 2004), 314. See also Wiecek, 'Somerset', 87.

[52] Particularly, Newman shows, the cases of Charles Bibbie and Peter Williams. See Newman, 'Freedom-Seeking Slaves', 1166–7.

[53] For more on the importance of thinking through gender within the Somerset case see Paugh, 'The Curious Case of Mary Hylas', 635.

[54] Steedman, *History and the Law*, 150.

We can only begin to imagine the traumas created by such seismic events in young Charlotte's life. We have no historic means by which to comprehend the desires of this young girl who abruptly found herself in Surrey but need to pause to consider them.[55] Charlotte had wishes, dreams and fears, and in resistance to the Howes' enslavement of her in Thames Ditton, she sought to enact them. Captain Howe died in 1783 and at this point Charlotte 'Howe' got herself baptised. Early in 1784, the widow Mrs Howe moved Charlotte to Chelsea in London and then in June, Charlotte walked out. Needing a means of subsistence, she applied to the parish officials of St Luke's, Chelsea, before going to Thames Ditton and applying there.[56] After further to-ing and fro-ing between the two parishes as to who might be liable, the parishes applied to the King's Bench for further guidance. Lord Mansfield was once again involved in the judgment, and he was clear: to claim relief under the Poor Law, claimants needed to prove their settlement. The 1662 Settlement Act (and its amendment in 1692) stipulated that people could gain settlement in a particular parish through birth, residence, apprenticeship, marriage, office-holding, purchase or paying rates. Another means was through earning it by serving for a full year. Mansfield ruled that as an enslaved person there had been no hiring and thus no settlement or poor relief. He stated, 'it cannot be contended that this was a voluntary hiring, and [it is] therefore not a service'.[57] As Carolyn Steedman has asserted, the problem (one of the many) for Charlotte Howe was that legal procedure required knowledge of 'what kind of legal entity stood there, in a court of law'. For Howe though, 'there was no legal category for her condition of existence', rather the status and consequences marked by the original enslavement remained pressing.[58] As the experiences of writer Mary Prince (c. 1788–1833) and Grace Jones also show us, such legal 'technicalities' continued to severely restrict the life choices and freedoms of Black women even in 1820s Britain.[59] They reveal how the law entirely failed to recognise or categorise the legal status of such individuals, binding their lives and opportunities.

Despite evidence of its continued existence, some considered that enslavement *in Britain* had ended in the 1770s.[60] Here we see the layers of ambiguity

---

[55] Although Saidiya Hartmann perhaps suggests a way. See Saidiya Hartman, 'Venus in Two Acts', *Small Axe: A Journal of Criticism*, 12:2 (2008), 1–14.
[56] Steedman, *History and the Law*, 152.
[57] As cited in ibid., 153. See also Oldham, *English Common Law in the Age of Mansfield*, 317.
[58] Steedman, *History and the Law*, 156.
[59] Ryan Hanley, *Beyond Slavery and Abolition: Black British Writing c. 1770–1830* (Cambridge, 2019), 84–85; Peter Fryer, *Staying Power: The History of Black People in Britain* (London, 1984), 130–132.
[60] The British Empire and the multiple legal systems it contained also created ambiguities across different geographies. See Lauren Benton, *Law and Colonial Cultures: Legal Regimes in World History, 1400–1900* (Cambridge, 2004), 3.

and confusion begin to emerge more fully. Abolitionist writings of the 1780s, which often highlighted the question of property in persons, are particularly telling on this count. Thomas Clarkson's (1760–1846) *An Essay on the Slavery and Commerce of the Human Species* (1786) was highly popular. We know it was read by Frances Hamilton, a widow farming at her small family estate in Taunton, who borrowed it (as others must have done) from the Taunton Book Society, as well as by William Wilberforce (1759–1833), who was soon to become a prominent abolitionist, possibly as a result of such reading.[61] In *An Essay*, Clarkson made a series of arguments about enslavement on the basis of a particular conception of property. Perhaps unsurprisingly for a man preparing to become a clergyman, his understanding was not overtly based on legal understandings, but rather seemed to draw upon Lockean conceptions of slavery, which saw people's bodies as given in trust from God, and thus that people did not have absolute power over their bodies and nor should anyone else.[62] Clarkson principally argued that to own and enslave another person was against the laws of nature and of God.[63] Clarkson further asserted that 'nature made every man's body and mind *his own*'.[64] That being so 'men' cannot 'be considered as lands, goods, or houses, among *possessions*', they must be understood as distinct.[65] Moreover, because 'all *property* should be inferior to its possessor', people cannot be conceived as property.[66] Clarkson went on to argue that people should not be enslaved as this would lead to them being unaccountable for their actions before God.[67] Similarly, to deny that the human species was distinct, and more particularly was distinct from other animals, or from seemingly inanimate things such as stones, was to go against Providence, 'which did not create a variety of natures without a purpose or design'.[68] As such, Clarkson spoke to a broader issue within late

---

[61] For more on Frances Hamilton's reading see Steedman, *Labours Lost*, 91–2. For more on William Wilberforce's reading see Hugh Brogan, 'Clarkson, Thomas (1760–1846), Slavery Abolitionist', *Oxford Dictionary of National Biography,* n.p. 23 Sep. 2004; Accessed 24 September 2021. www.oxforddnb.com/view/10.1093/ref:odnb/9780198614128.001.0001/odnb-9780198614128-e-5545.

[62] Locke, *Second Treatise of Government*, 14. For more on Clarkson preparing to become a clergyman see Brogan, 'Clarkson, Thomas', n.p. As discussed earlier in the chapter, Clarkson's view can also be understood as an echo of Blackstone's understanding. See Blackstone, *Commentaries on the Laws of England Book II Of the Rights of Things*, 272.

[63] See Locke, *Second Treatise of Government*, 15.

[64] Clarkson, *An Essay on the Slavery and Commerce of the Human Species*, 69. See also Locke, *Second Treatise of Government*, 15.

[65] Clarkson, *An Essay on the Slavery and Commerce of the Human Species*, 69 and 243.

[66] Ibid., 69.

[67] Ibid., 69 and 249. For an important discussion on the question of enslaved people being regarded as accountable for actions ordered by their 'master' see Fuentes, *Dispossessed Lives*, 100–123.

[68] Clarkson, *An Essay on the Slavery and Commerce of the Human Species*, 72.

eighteenth-century society concerning the impetus to understand certain 'things' as inhabiting different categories.

Writing in 1785 (and being published in 1786), Clarkson was clearly influenced by the earlier Somerset and Knight cases. For him, the cases meant that 'as soon as any person whatever set his foot in this country, he came under the protection of the British laws, and was consequently free'.[69] Clarkson understood enslavement was no longer possible on British soil, such ideas only operated 'out there' in the colonies and it was largely colonial slavery which abolitionists would seek to affect. Similarly, in his 1789 publication *The Substance of the Evidence of Sundry Persons on the Slave-Trade*, although Clarkson did include depositions from the case of Little Ephraim Robin John and Ancona Robin Robin John, two free Africans who were imprisoned onboard a Bristol ship bound for Virginia in 1773, there were no other references to enslaved people being brought to Britain or bound and taken to the colonies from Britain.[70] These were not the questions Clarkson was asking in the late 1780s: they were resolved in Clarkson's mind.[71]

However, as the case of Charlotte Howe demonstrates, such resolution was not met elsewhere and the continuing ambiguity sustained enslavement in Britain. It is important to remember that the law was largely administered by magistrates: it relied on *their* understanding of the law and *their* interpretation of it. Wider cultural understandings of legal rulings often played a part in such interpretations and as Clarkson's writings demonstrate, the Somerset case had captured the imagination of the country, shaping later cases. For instance, although the judgment in *Forbes v. Cochrane* (1824) was ambiguous, Ruth Paley has shown that it is clear that 'two of the three presiding judges believed that Somerset had indeed abolished slavery in England'.[72] While two of the three judges held this belief, it must be acknowledged that one did not. Clarity finally arrived nine years later, in 1833, when definitions were finally and categorically 'redrawn across the empire to exclude property in people'.[73] When slavery was abolished in Britain and many of its territories in 1833, no individual was recorded as receiving compensation for an enslaved person living in England.[74] However, it is important to remember that such distinct

---

[69] Ibid., xiii–xiv.
[70] Thomas Clarkson, *The Substance of the Evidence of Sundry Persons on the Slave-Trade, Collected in the Course of a Tour made in the Autumn of the Year 1788* (London, 1789), 4–11.
[71] For more on the questions Clarkson was asking see Clarkson, *The Substance of the Evidence of Sundry Persons on the Slave-Trade*, v.
[72] Paley, 'After *Somerset*', 181.
[73] Julian Hoppit, 'Compulsion, Compensation and Property Rights in Britain', *Past & Present*, 210 (2011), 120. Here Hoppit is referencing the work of Stanley L. Engerman, *Slavery, Emancipation and Freedom* (Baton Rouge, 2007), 43.
[74] Paley, 'After *Somerset*', 181.

and final redrawing did not take place throughout Britain's imperial territories.[75]

Across the long eighteenth century, it was possible for people within England to lay claim to owning other people. Cases tested the parameters of the law, but owning people as chattel property remained a legal possibility until 1833. The ambiguities set up by the cases that were brought in the eighteenth century, the knowing and unknowing set-in play by Mansfield's ruling, for instance, underlines how much uncertainty the law (and its administration) produced, and how it allowed a range of conceptualisations to emerge. Such ambiguity was not simply present in complex cases of enslaved people and their legal position; it was also visible in other categories of property, in wives for example, and their ability to possess.

Wives and Property

In strict legal terms, once married, women no longer enjoyed an independent legal existence. As Blackstone had it in his 1765–1769 *Commentaries*,

> the husband and wife are one person in law: that is, the very being or legal existence of the woman is suspended during the marriage, or at least is incorporated and consolidated into that of her husband: under whose wing, protection, and *cover*, she performs every thing; and is therefore called in our law-french a *feme-covert*...and her condition during her marriage is called her *coverture*.[76]

As Krista J. Kesselring and Tim Stretton have reminded us, it is important that we do not underestimate the power of such strictures: 'in ideological terms they counted for everything'.[77] Particularly in times of crisis, such as the breakdown of marriages, coverture's logic became an important reference point. Despite the significance of coverture in shaping worldviews, England's laws meant that never-married women and widows were in the unique position (in comparison to similar women in other European countries) of being able to own property.[78] Thus, around half of all women were able to be more economically active than their European counterparts.[79] At the same time, the practical need for married women to participate in the business of everyday life meant that the constraints of coverture were often ignored or

---

[75] For example, it is estimated that 'perhaps 8 to 9 million Indian slaves lived in bondage in territories under East India Company rule alone as late as the 1840s'. See Margot Finn, 'Slaves Out of Context: Domestic Slavery and the Anglo-Indian Family, c. 1780–1830', *Transactions of the Royal Historical Society*, 19 (2009), 184.
[76] Blackstone, *Commentaries on the Laws of England: Book I Of the Rights of Persons*, 284–285.
[77] Kesselring and Stretton, 'Introduction: Coverture and Continuity', 9.
[78] Amy Louise Erickson, 'Coverture and Capitalism', *History Workshop Journal*, 59 (2005), 2.
[79] Erickson, 'Coverture and Capitalism', 8.

reconceived. In such ways, coverture can be understood as a 'legal fiction', whose very flexibility allowed it to survive into the eighteenth century.[80] The use of the legal term 'coverture' seems to have declined in this period, however, marking the beginnings of a period of change which accelerated over the nineteenth century.[81] Here the ambiguities produced by the disparities between interpretation of the law and lived realities provided a space for married women to increasingly achieve independence and agency. Married women's lives and actions stretched at the ambiguities within the law, creating new spaces and new meanings of possession.

In the eighteenth century, multiple strategies existed to allow married women and men to live their lives around the law of coverture. Even if married women were theoretically not understood to exist as distinct legal entities, they could own separate property through the construction of specific clauses in marriage settlements. Such settlements were put in place for women up and down the social scale, ensuring that property owned before marriage would be safely protected during the marriage and would be wholly accessible afterwards.[82] The category of paraphernalia also opened the possibilities of owning separate property for married women. A wife's clothes and personal ornaments, known as 'paraphernalia', could be alienated by the husband during the marriage but could only be bequeathed by the wife.[83] Other forms of separate property also existed. Although practised in the early modern period, during the Restoration years and the early eighteenth century, it became increasingly popular to secure confirmation of 'pin money' within marriage settlements.[84] Pin money ensured that married women would be provided with a separate income to use as they saw fit. Over the eighteenth century, the increasingly common practice of including a provision for pin money within marriage settlements attracted controversy, particularly in terms of what married women might buy with such money. The purchase of houses or land, for example, was understood as problematic, but so was the acquisition of certain smaller items.[85]

'Necessaries' offered another means by which married women could claim independence as economic agents. Under common law, husbands had a responsibility to support their wives and supply them with the necessaries of life. If husbands failed to do so, women were able to contract debt on their

---

[80] Kesselring and Stretton, 'Introduction: Coverture and Continuity', 5. For more on 'legal fictions' as 'rhetorical devices deployed by lawyers in the courtroom to conceal disparities between the letter and the operation of the rule of law' see Margot Finn, *The Character of Credit: Personal Debt in English Culture, 1740–1914* (Cambridge, 2003), 13.
[81] Steedman, *History and the Law*, 109.
[82] Erickson, *Women & Property in Early Modern England*, 150.
[83] Staves, *Married Women's Separate Property in England*, 148. [84] Ibid., 132.
[85] Ibid., 149.

behalf to obtain the necessaries 'suitable to his rank'.[86] Creditors could then recover the debt from their customers' husbands. We might assume that the 'freedom' to purchase goods suitable to their husband's rank did not offer labouring and middling sort women a great deal of opportunity to make purchases beyond mundane household items, yet evidence suggests they were able to do just that.[87] At the same time, it provided privileged women with 'considerable discretion and room for manipulation in market negotiations and marital conflicts'.[88] When a marriage came unstuck, for example, and an informal separation was being sought, married women could seek to purchase a range of necessaries and acquire substantial debts, thus persuading their husbands to meet their demands.[89] As we will see in Chapter 2, such practices prompted husbands to issue notices publicly clearing themselves from the responsibility of debts accumulated by their wife. In cases where separated wives or other women accrued debt, it could be the shopkeeper who missed out. Using the law of agency, retailers assumed that wives had their husbands' consent to pledge credit if the couple were known to be cohabiting.[90] Otherwise the onus was on retailers to inquire as to the status of women and their ability to incur debt on behalf of their husbands. Keen for a sale, shopkeepers were naturally reluctant to make such inquiries and could end up liable for the debt themselves.[91]

While women could find ways to purchase items, they were also able to act on behalf of their husbands in courts. Married women regularly appeared as their husband's agents in small claim courts. Largely designed to deal with small debt litigation, involving married women in cases was crucial due to the understanding that they played a 'central role in contracting for household necessities'.[92] Married women could often speak directly to the moment when the original debt had been incurred. Similarly, when disputes were raised with magistrates as to servants' contracts, it was often married women that they dealt with as they had 'contracted with servants for their labour as if they had never heard of coverture'.[93] At the same time, the magistrates who heard such disputes did not record who had done the hiring. Such administrative oversights seem to suggest that magistrates only cared about *how* the hiring had been done and took for granted that married women could and did contract labour.

---

[86] Finn, 'Women, Consumption and Coverture in England', 709.
[87] Joanne Bailey, 'Favoured or Oppressed? Married Women, Property and "Coverture" in England, 1660–1800', *Continuity and Change*, 17:3 (2002), 358.
[88] Finn, 'Women, Consumption and Coverture in England', 710.   [89] Ibid., 711.
[90] Bailey, 'Favoured or Oppressed?', 355.   [91] Steedman, *History and the Law*, 104.
[92] Finn, 'Women, Consumption and Coverture in England', 714.
[93] Steedman, *History and the Law*, 88.

Although defined and understood as belonging to their husbands by the law, such understandings operated as fictions (albeit powerful fictions) in this period. Married women were active economic agents who held separate forms of property and issued and managed transactions in the marketplace. They could and did bequeath possessions and property to friends and family.[94] Wives regularly contracted labour to work within their households, and the creation of such contracts attracted little note. Living within such seeming contradictions, however, married women and the lives they led further underline the complexity of what it might actually mean to own and possess 'things' in eighteenth-century Britain. The law existed, but it was baggy and amorphous. Lived experiences proved the law was open to constant interpretation and reconfiguration.

Labouring Servants and Apprentices

While wives hiring servants was an unquestioned part of everyday life, the contracting of others to labour on your behalf raised broader questions about the relationship between labour and property. It prompted queries about ownership and possession both in terms of the energies outlaid by others and the products such exertions created. Masters may have owned their servants' labour; however, it must be remembered that they did not own their person. Or rather, that they did not in the case of white servants.

In the eighteenth century, the term 'servant' covered a wide range of workers.[95] Domestic servants made up a large proportion of this workforce, particularly in London, but have often been overlooked in analyses of labour and working conditions in the eighteenth century.[96] Domestic servants made up a distinct and significant population within British society and were a particularly important presence within London. Conservative estimates suggest that by the mid-eighteenth century, there may have been 52,000 domestic servants in London, while higher estimates put that figure at 90,000. It has also been suggested that 75–80 per cent of domestic servants in London were female.[97] Traditionally, servants have been obscured from the historical record because there was no recognisable 'product' emerging from their labours. The clouts would be washed, the floor scrubbed, and the table laid, but at the end of

---

[94] Maxine Berg, 'Women's Consumption and the Industrial Classes of Eighteenth-Century England', *Journal of Social History*, 30:2 (1996), 415–434.
[95] Douglas Hay and Paul Craven, 'Introduction', in Douglas Hay and Paul Craven (eds), *Masters, Servants, and Magistrates in Britain and the Empire, 1562–1955* (Chapel Hill, NC, 2004), 7.
[96] Steedman, *Labours Lost*, 33.
[97] For the 80 percent figure see Paula Humfrey (ed.), *The Experience of Domestic Service for Women in Early Modern London* (Farnham, 2011), 12. For the 75 percent figures see Steedman, *Labours Lost*, 13.

a domestic servant's working day there was not an item to pack up and sell and it would all need to be done again tomorrow. In trying to conceptualise what such labour was and who owned it, eighteenth-century Britons thoughts seem to have been shaped yet again by the work of John Locke. As mentioned earlier for Locke, 'Whatsoever...he removes out of the State that Nature have provided' by mixing 'his *Labour* with' it and thus joining it to 'something that is his own' he makes 'his *Property*'.[98] The labour, the doing, was key.[99] Locke was also clear that the 'turfs' cut by 'my servant' became 'my *Property*'.[100] In Locke's terms, the labour exerted by his servant to cut the turfs was *his* labour. By hiring the servant (and here Locke is referring to servant in the broadest sense), he had acquired their labour and 'bestowed on them' his 'own (unused) capacity to exercise' his 'own energies in labour'.[101] Rather than using their own labour, servants were hired to exercise their employer's labour on their behalf.[102]

In the 1760s, Blackstone continued to see the validity of such conceptions in his *Commentaries on the Laws of England*. He implied that 'the labour "really" belonged to the employer – was a capacity or attribute of him or her – and that the servant had been employed to perform, or act out, the potential labour of the he or she who had bought the servant's energies and time'.[103] In this conception, the servant became a non-person, a thing. Yet conceiving of a servant's labour, or rather the master' or mistresses' labour, in this way, as a social relationship, caused much consternation in eighteenth-century Britain. The concern was that the servant 'really' was the master or mistress, 'a detached body-part enacting the employer's atrophied – certainly unused – labour power'.[104] Such anxieties are visible to us through the many jokes that were told about servants in this period.[105]

Over the eighteenth century, and more particularly over the second half of the eighteenth century, a significant change took place in how people conceived of servants labouring away, chopping mounds of onions.[106] Carolyn Steedman has identified a shift from conceptualising labour as 'a social form (a form of relationship)' to it as 'a material thing, that could be owned, and perhaps *was* actually owned by the worker, as a form of property, and that was located in his or her body'.[107] Such a reconceptualisation can be understood as emerging from a series of processes and cultural productions including taxes, hiring contracts, settlement claims, abolitionist tracts and servant poetry.[108]

---

[98] Locke, *Second Treatise of Government*, 15.   [99] Ibid., 16.   [100] Ibid.
[101] Steedman, *Labours Lost*, 53.   [102] Ibid., 46.   [103] Ibid., 19.   [104] Ibid., 22.
[105] Carolyn Steedman, 'Servants and Their Relationship to the Unconscious', *Journal of British Studies*, 42 (2003), 349.
[106] On the importance of chopping onions, see Carolyn Steedman, 'Intimacy in Research: Accounting for It', *History of the Human Sciences*, 21:17 (2008), 27.
[107] Steedman, *Labours Lost*, 313.   [108] Ibid., 151, 110, 106–107, 114, 59 and 98.

By the late eighteenth century, rather than enacting the capacity of their master or mistress, servants were understood as enacting their own capacities, which they owned and contracted out. While changes took place for domestic servants in the nineteenth century, which eradicated the particularities of this period, servants emerged in this eighteenth-century moment as legal entities who engaged in contracted labour: as the beginnings of the modern labour force.[109]

Examining the ways in which different people – their bodies, their labour, their selves – were conceived through the frame of property over the long eighteenth century highlights three significant aspects of the law in the period. First, that the law could remain deeply ambiguous as to its standing on people as property. Such ambiguity could be purposeful, however, enacting important social and cultural work. For instance, ambiguities sustained the construction of racially-based hierarchies. Second, that while the law could be seemingly clear, the lived experiences that occurred under such laws could also challenge or perhaps more commonly obscure, such clarity. In the case of wives, we saw how the everyday experiences of married women's lives pulled legal understandings in different directions to create space for independence and agency. Finally, and unsurprisingly, we see that the law changed over the long eighteenth century. In the case of servants, contracts gave them greater power and control. Labour came to be understood as something, which could be possessed in itself and contracted out. Rather than linear though, such changes again shifted to a different position in the nineteenth century. In looking to people as a starting point for considering the legal parameters of property and possession in this period we are struck with the law's ambiguities. These uncertainties could do social and cultural work constricting and expanding people's freedoms. They also meant that conceptions of property and possession were not fixed or rigid but were continually challenged and changing: there was space for people to enact their own understandings of possession, and this proved crucial across the period.

Missing Canines

Historians have long known that dogs provide a particularly useful example with which to consider changing conceptions of property and the ways in which people responded to them.[110] Reflecting, as we have seen, broader

---

[109] Ibid., 356.
[110] Dogs are one of the featured categories in Susan Staves seminal article and have been considered by scholars, such as Ingrid Tague and Lynn Festa. See Staves, 'Chattel Property Rules', 125; Ingrid H. Tague, 'Eighteenth-Century English Debates on a Dog Tax', *The Historical Journal*, 51 (2008), 901–920; Lynn Festa, 'Person, Animal, Thing: The 1796 Dog Tax and the Right to Superfluous Things', *Eighteenth-Century Life*, 33:2 (2009), 1–44.

concerns around property, seventeenth- and early eighteenth-century British society asked *who* could 'own' which dogs, particularly in rural areas. In this period, the Game Laws (1671–1831) meant that dogs were of interest to the law because they were conceived as threats to, rather than as forms of, privilege and property. The central purpose of the Game Laws was to ensure that hunting game was exclusively enjoyed by the landed gentry.[111] The Laws only regarded hares, partridges, pheasants and moor fowl as game. They were not understood as belonging to the person on whose land they were found, but rather were the property of all qualified sportsmen: those men with landed wealth who had freeholds worth £100 a year or leaseholds worth £150 a year.[112] Any qualified sportsman could thus hunt game, no matter its location. Anyone hunting game who did not meet the property threshold would be regarded as a poacher. The Laws also meant that deer and rabbits came to be understood as property rather than game. The punishments for theft (of property) were harsher than those for poaching (game) and provided greater deterrents to taking these animals. Over the eighteenth century, hares, partridges, pheasants and moor fowl also started to be kept and cultivated on enclosed lands, but the law was slow to catch up and they were not regarded as property. Nevertheless, *poaching* was increasingly policed in the eighteenth century. It was so despite the fact most Englishmen did not consider it a crime to take that given to all by God in the Garden of Eden.[113]

The 1671 Game Act was important in policing hunting and thus the technologies of hunting and who could possess them. Certain property requirements had to be met in order that people could legally own hunting dogs. Pointers, setters, lurchers, hounds, greyhounds, beagles and spaniels all fell within the law's purview.[114] These provisions were enforced by local justices of the peace, who were regularly called upon to make judgements in such matters.[115] They were entitled to seize dogs illegally possessed by poor cottagers and give them to members of the local gentry who fulfilled the necessary property requirements.[116] While the confiscation of guns was relatively rare under the Acts, the confiscation of dogs was more common. Some landowners, such as William Cavendish, 5th Duke of Devonshire (1748–1811) in 1778, even sought to kill all dogs belonging to their tenants.[117]

In the later eighteenth century, the question shifted from who could own dogs to the question of owning itself and whether such a relationship would

---

[111] P. M. Munsche, *Gentlemen and Poachers: The English Games Laws, 1671–1831* (Cambridge, 1981), 8.
[112] Munsche, *Gentlemen and Poachers*, 9.   [113] Ibid., 6.
[114] Staves, 'Chattel Property Rules', 139; Munsche, *Gentlemen and Poachers*, 82.
[115] See Elizabeth Silverthorne (ed.), *Deposition of Richard Wyatt, JP, 1767–1776* (Guildford, 1978), 39, 50, 51 and 52.
[116] Staves, 'Chattel Property Rules', 140.   [117] Munsche, *Gentlemen and Poachers*, 82.

receive protection from the law. Such a shift reminds us how the relationship of possession was not self-evident and required consideration in this period. In questioning ownership, the issue shifted from what dogs did, to what dogs were. In the 1760s, Blackstone understood animals as 'things', as chattels which could be 'annexed to or attendant on the person of the owner'.[118] Blackstone made an important distinction between animals which were 'domitae' [tame] and those which were 'ferae naturae' [wild]. Important to such a distinction was the extent to which different animals 'can convey themselves from one part of the world to another'. Blackstone had much to say about this question of volition and its importance to conceptions of property. He noted that animals 'such as are of a nature tame and domestic (as horses, kine [cattle], sheep, poultry, and the like) a man may have as absolute a property as in any inanimate beings'. Blackstone argued that this was the case because such animals were 'perpetually in his occupation, and will not stray from his house or person, unless by accident or fraudulent enticement, in either of which cases the owner does not lose his property'.[119] He was wrong, of course, horses, sheep and cattle did wander off, or rather we know that eighteenth-century Britons were happy to explain their absence in such terms.[120] However, Blackstone argued that domestic animals, in our understanding farm animals, would *not* stray of their own volition and rejoin the common stock. Or rather, in terms that are reminiscent of those used about land, Blackstone conceived that horses, cows, sheep and poultry were constantly in 'his occupation' and therefore would not stray. Within such thinking around possession and volition, it was possible to maintain an absolute property right in domestic animals.

Surprisingly, Blackstone did not include dogs within the category of domesticated animals. Such an omission is surprising because working and hunting dogs were *trained* to be 'perpetually in his [the owner's] occupation' and were important to the processes of husbandry, such as guarding and herding animals.[121] In omitting dogs from this category, Blackstone suggested that dogs should be regarded as animals which 'can convey themselves from one part of the world to another'.[122] The reason for Blackstone's omission is

---

[118] Blackstone, *Commentaries on the Laws of England: Book II Of the Rights of Things*, 262.
[119] Ibid., 263.
[120] See for example 'Strayed on Thursday Night last, into the Yard of Mr. Wm. Brown, a bay Gelding', *Daily Advertiser* (London), 2 December 1771. Similarly, cattle thought to have strayed were impounded and advertised. See 'Pounded in Clapton Pound, in the Parish of Hackney, three Heifers, supposed to have strayed', *Daily Advertiser* (London), 18 December 1771.
[121] For more on training pointers for example, see William Augustus Osbaldiston, *The Universal Sportsman: or, Nobleman, Gentleman, and Farmer's Dictionary of Recreation and Amusement* (Dublin, 1795?), 542–548.
[122] Blackstone, *Commentaries on the Laws of England: Book II Of the Rights of Things*, 263.

suggested to us by the fictional solicitor in Francis Coventry's *The History of Pompey*. As you will remember, the solicitor noted that dogs were difficult to class as property because they 'follow any body that calls them'.[123] Dogs, and more particularly, dogs in urban spaces, were regarded as fickle things that could at any point simply run off when distracted by a passing bird. They were very much able to convey themselves.

Moreover, it seems Blackstone paid little attention to hunting, working and useful dogs, but rather focused on those 'only kept for pleasure, curiosity, or whim'.[124] In his *Book IV Of Public Wrongs*, Blackstone went still further and saw no distinctions at stake in the canine population. Instead, he stated that 'dogs of all sorts' did not serve for food and thus the law held them all 'to have no intrinsic value'.[125] Key within Blackstone's understandings of chattel property was the concept of 'intrinsic value'. Blackstone argued that if animals 'only kept for pleasure, curiosity, or whim' were taken, the taker could not be prosecuted for theft because the value of such animals was 'not intrinsic' but rather depended 'on the caprice of the owner'.[126] Alongside volition then, value was also important in conceiving of property, as we will explore further in Chapter 6. Value was not inherent to the dog but rather arose within the relationship between owner and dog. Nevertheless, Blackstone recognised that 'it is such an invasion of property as may amount to a civil injury, and be redressed by a civil action'.[127] He was beginning to see the possibility of dogs, not as threats to property but rather as property in their own right. Over the late eighteenth and early nineteenth century, the law increasingly came to recognise dogs as a form of property in need of the protection of the law.

Blackstone's *Commentaries*, written and published in the late 1760s, soon became outdated. The Dog Stealing Act of 1770 (10 Geo. III. C. 18) meant dog ownership enjoyed greater protection from the law in cases of theft. The Act noted that it had been brought in because 'the Practice of stealing Dogs hath of late Years greatly increased'.[128] The presence of dogs in urban spaces concentrated long-held practices of dog stealing, and greater loss prompted rethinking as to the nature of property and new provisions in law were designed to protect it. In the 1774 edition of *Commentaries,* William Blackstone noted how the

---

[123] This issue was discussed at length by witnesses who appeared before the Select Committee in 1844. See *Report from the Select Committee on Dog Stealing*.
[124] Blackstone, *Commentaries on the Laws of England: Book II Of the Rights of Things*, 266. Alongside hunting dogs, we need to also consider useful dogs such as watchdogs. See Tom Almeroth-Williams, 'The Watchdogs of Georgian London: Non-human Agency, Crime Prevention and Control of Urban Space', *The London Journal*, 43:3 (2018), 269; Thomas Almeroth-Williams, *City of Beasts: How Animals Shaped Georgian London* (Manchester, 2019), 188.
[125] Blackstone, *Commentaries on the Laws of England: Book IV Of Public Wrongs*, 156.
[126] Blackstone, *Commentaries on the Laws of England: Book II Of the Rights of Things*, 266.
[127] Ibid.   [128] 10 Geo. III. C. 18.

changes brought about by the Act meant 'very high pecuniary penalties, or a long imprisonment in their stead'. Blackstone remarked on the strangeness of the Act, that such penalties could be 'inflicted by two justices of the peace (with a very peculiar mode of appeal to the quarter sessions) on such as steal, or knowingly harbour a stolen dog, or have in their custody the skin of a dog that has been stolen'.[129] At this point, it was perhaps easier to conceive of a dog skin as property, than a dog. *The Annual Register* for 1770, which offered readers an overview of the 'history, politics, and literature' for that year, noted that the Act stipulated that any person found stealing dogs 'of any kind or sort whatsoever' from an owner or someone entrusted by the owner would face conviction. Similarly, it noted that anyone selling, buying, receiving, harbouring, detaining or keeping any dogs 'knowing the same to have been stolen' would also face the possibility of conviction. Such convictions could lead to fines ('not less than 20l' – twenty pounds) and would be committed 'to gaol' until the penalty and charges were paid. At the same time, the Act stipulated that Justices could 'grant warrants to search for dogs stolen or their skins' and anyone found in possession of such items would also be 'liable to like penalties'.[130] At this point, we see that legal attention had turned to question not what dogs did, but rather what they were.

Although the Dog Stealing Act of 1770 seemed to move dogs more firmly into the category of property, the status of dogs before the law continued to remain ambiguous. The question of dogs as property was raised again through attempts to tax dog owners. Calls for a dog tax began in the 1730s and evolved through frequent attempts at legislation (1755, 1761, 1776) before finally succeeding in 1796. Proponents of the tax often mooted it as a solution to problems of food shortage, the complex and outdated gaming laws, concerns over rabies and the need for greater government revenue. Significantly though, the 1796 tax demanded only a relatively limited tax on an owner's first dog but much on the second and much on sporting dogs. Such a distinction demonstrates that by the end of the eighteenth century, sporting dogs continued to be understood as belonging to particular social groups. In this moment, a broader conception of dogs was also present. Dogs came to be conceived of as pets that should be owned by a broader range of people. They were seen as a social good that created feelings and bonds.[131] At the same time, of course, in establishing the tax, legislators also

---

[129] William Blackstone, *Commentaries on the Laws of England Vol. 4* (London, 1774), 236.
[130] *The Annual Register*, 228.
[131] Tague, 'Eighteenth-Century English Debates on a Dog Tax', 917.

established that dogs were chattel, which could be owned, raising further questions and doubts about the status of dogs.[132]

Dog stealing continued to grow in the early nineteenth century, particularly within the capital, raising still further questions about the status of dogs and the protections they might receive. In 1837, the Metropolitan Police produced a report on dog stealing in London, which identified as many as 141 dog stealers, forty-five of whom they considered to live by the trade, forty-eight of whom used it to augment other occupations and forty-eight who were associates.[133] A Select Committee on Dog Stealing (Metropolis) was duly called in 1844 to investigate the continued problem. A key witness for the Select Committee was one of the Chief Commissioners of the Police of the Metropolis, Richard Mayne, Esq. One of the problems Mayne considered was that dogs were not covered by the 1827 Larceny (Advertisements) Act (7 & 8 Geo, IV. C. 29) because they did not come 'within the legal meaning of the word "property"'.[134] In making his case, Mayne quoted Blackstone that '"though a man may have a base property therein, and maintain a civil action for the loss of them, yet they are not of such estimation as that the crime of stealing them amounts to larceny"'.[135]

The issue raised by a fictional solicitor in a 1751 publication and then again by an entirely non-fictional William Blackstone in his 1765–69 publication continued to worry those who appeared as witnesses at the Select Committee hearings in 1844. They too saw that dogs were different to other animals, particularly farm animals: they could be enticed away and they could simply wander off, especially in urban spaces. For Mayne, there was something about dogs and the fact that they were allowed to wander the streets alone.[136] He noted that,

I hardly see how it can be got over in distinguishing between the cases of lost and stolen dogs. A dog is that sort of animal, allowed such liberty, and that runs about in that kind of way, that he may be enticed away in a manner that no other property can be. It is not

---

[132] Festa, 'Person, Animal, Thing', 3. For more on the ways in which the tax instituted the idea of dogs as commodities see Jodi L. Wyett, 'The Lap of Luxury: Lapdogs, Literature, and Social Meaning in the "Long" Eighteenth Century', *Lit: Literature Interpretation Theory*, 10:4 (1999), 277. The question of the relationship between property status and taxation had also been raised in regards to the enslavement of people. See Brewer, 'Creating a Common Law of Slavery for England and Its New World Empire', 798.

[133] Philip Howell, *At Home and Astray: The Domestic Dog in Victorian Britain* (Charlottesville, VA and London, 2015), 57.

[134] *Report from the Select Committee on Dog Stealing*, 2. Mayne's point is confirmed by the text of the Act; see also 7 & 8 Geo, IV. c. 29.

[135] *Report from the Select Committee on Dog Stealing*, 2.

[136] Chris Pearson, *Dogopolis: How Dogs and Humans Made Modern New York, London, and Paris* (Chicago, IL, 2021), 40.

possible for a horse or a sheep, or any such animal, to be enticed away like a dog. You do not find them straying about as dogs do.[137]

Given such 'liberty', being so easily duped and able leave of their own volition, it was difficult to know (or prove) whether dogs had been actively stolen. John Hardwick, Esq the Chief Magistrate of Marlborough Street, gave evidence to the Committee and noted the difficulties connected with dog stealing – namely, that unless someone was caught in the act of forcibly taking the dog, it was difficult to prove theft. He noted that 'very few cases' had been brought before him as a magistrate.[138] Similarly, the current state of the law meant that there had been cases where someone was indicted for stealing a collar, rather than the dog around whose neck it was.[139] It was more possible to conceive of the collar as property, than it was the dog, because the collar would not wander off of its own volition. Again and again, dogs come out as a particular kind of thing that lived in a particular way (especially in urban spaces). They were different to inanimate forms of property or even other types of animals such as sheep and pigs.

The Dog Stealing Act of 1845 (8 & 9 Vict. C. 47) sought to answer these issues by making dogs 'clearly identifiable as property'. The Act ensured that the 'full rigours of the law' could be brought to bear on offenders and that 'the hitherto untouchable receivers [were] now liable to punishment for misdemeanor'. Hence, 'what the Act accomplished was the decisive recognition that domestic dogs were *private property* and should be valued as such'.[140] Arriving at such recognition, however, had taken time. The law had struggled to conceive of what dogs were, the forms of liveliness they embodied and the way in which the law might protect people's relationships to them. The ambiguity of the thing's status led to an ambiguity in the law.

Placing the legal position of enslaved people, married women, servants and dogs side-by-side is a deeply awkward act. We feel its strangeness from our twenty-first century standpoint. Yet exploring these forms of property and possession together unearths larger themes and issues central to eighteenth-century worldviews. In each case, the law was ambiguous in the eighteenth century. Of course, in many ways, this is the nature of the law more broadly. It is a living thing which requires constant interpretation. It is not fixed.[141] Yet in the eighteenth century, such ambiguity did particular forms of work. In the case of enslaved people, the law's ambiguity as to their position and status made drawing upon it to uphold claims of freedom or settlement deeply challenging. With married women, the law of coverture appeared as a legal

---

[137] *Report from the Select Committee on Dog Stealing*, 3.   [138] Ibid., 11.   [139] Ibid., 13.
[140] Howell, *At Home and Astray*, 63.
[141] Hendrik Hartog, 'Pigs and Positivism', *Wisconsin Law Review*, 899 (1985), 13.

fiction which men and women worked around through the daily realities of their lives. Nevertheless, the ideological weight at stake within coverture could be and was called upon at times of crisis. It was an ever-important backstop. For servants, their ability to possess their own labour and lay claim to it grew over the period and they used the law to expand such claims. By contrast, in the case of dogs, the law struggled to form the means of protection sought by dog owners, creating a situation in which dog stealing could flourish. The law was slow to catch up. In seeing these ambiguities and the changes they encapsulated in this period, we see how amorphous concepts of property and possession could be. They played out across different relationships and assumed a range of shapes and meanings. To own something or someone was not a straightforward calculation in this period. As such, these ambiguities created spaces in which other forms of understanding about property and possession could emerge and be enacted. In the final section of the chapter, we now turn to some things which might be regarded as much more straightforward forms of property and look to why this was so.

'Dropt' Money and 'Lost' Watches

When discussing the question of dog stealing with the 1844 Select Committee, the editor of the sporting paper *Bell's Life* Vincent George Dowling made an important comparison. He stipulated that the uncertain status of dogs as property was most evident in moments of theft. In such moments, dogs were 'not protected as other property is; they have not been dealt with as a watch, or anything else which is stolen.'[142] Dowling was clear in his analogy: while dogs did not receive such protection, other things did. Unlike dogs, watches would not wander off, they would not be enticed away, but they were regularly stolen. Dowling looked to watches as exemplar possessions: things that everyone saw and understood unequivocally as property.

The Old Bailey Proceedings are littered with cases of watch theft.[143] Courts, and the law more broadly, knew how to deal with them. Nevertheless, even in the case of watches, their ownership and what that might mean produced ambiguities and anxieties in the eighteenth century. Published in 1788, *The Adventures of a Watch*, demonstrates how watches were readily exchangeable items, passing or taken from one owner to another. As with other it-narratives, the watch in question narrates its passage between different hands, including

---

[142] *Report from the Select Committee on Dog Stealing*, 47.
[143] Anne Helmreich, Tim Hitchcock and William J. Turkel, 'Rethinking Inventories in the Digital Age: The Case of the Old Bailey', *Journal of Art Historiography*, 11 (2014),14; Sara Horrell, Jane Humphries and Ken Sneath, 'Consumption Conundrums Unravelled', *Economic History Review*, 68:3 (2015), 847.

from a lord to a pawnbroker, and from there to a nabob and a watchmaker. The watch, this thing, does not act of its own volition. Rather it is transferred from hand to hand in dizzying forms of circulation. The watch, though, is unperturbed by the frequent movements it is seemingly destined to undertake. It asserts that, 'My life has hitherto been of that irregular hurried kind, that I had neither time nor inclination to form particular prepossessions for my possessors; so that a change of situation caused no violent emotion, though under misfortunes, I made myself perfectly easy.'[144] For the watch, possession exists as a temporary and uncertain relationship: it will not last. As the narrative follows the watch, rather than its possessors, we are unaware if they too are 'perfectly easy' about the seemingly temporary nature of possession. The presence of it-narratives, however, suggests that eighteenth-century culture was actively trying to better understand not only things but also the question of ownership and the difficulty of sustaining possession. Such questions were also complicated by the purchase of such things. The credit regimes which underpinned ownership in this period made the question of who might own what at any one time a source of anxiety, as the literature of the period further demonstrates.[145]

Bank notes and other financial instruments, such as bills of exchange, became increasingly important over the period as 'debts upon simple contract', which facilitated transactions and remittances across ever-greater distances.[146] However, the movement of these 'things', whose central purpose was exchange and transaction, raised similar forms of concern about ownership. Bank notes, essentially promissory notes that promised values borrowed by the government from the Bank of England, circulated increasingly widely and frequently.[147] As Christine Desan has noted, 'By the end of the century, £15 million Bank of England notes circulated.'[148] During the Bank Restriction period (1797–1821) when convertibility to coin was suspended, Bank of England notes became 'the nation's foremost currency'.[149] Within the Bank Restriction period, the 1812 Stanhope Act made it illegal to refuse Bank of

---

[144] Anon., *The Adventures of a Watch* (London, 1788), 85–86.
[145] See James Thompson, *Models of Value: Eighteenth-Century Political Economy and the Novel* (Durham, NC, 1996); Deidre Lynch, *The Economy of Character: Novels, Market Culture and the Business of Inner Meaning* (Chicago, IL, 1998).
[146] Blackstone, *Commentaries on the Laws of England: Book II Of the Rights of Things*, 315. Bills of exchange order someone in a distant location to pay a specified sum of local currency and became crucial to international trade. See Stephen Quinn, 'Money, Finance and Capital Markets', in Roderick Floud and Paul Johnson (eds), *The Cambridge Economic History of Modern Britain, Volume 1, 1700–1860* (Cambridge, 2004), 153.
[147] On definition of Bank of England notes see Christine Desan, *Making Money: Coin, Currency and the Coming of Capitalism* (Oxford, 2014), 295; Hiroki Shin, *The Age of Paper: The Bank Note, Communal Currency and British Society, 1790s–1830s* (Cambridge, 2024), 180.
[148] Desan, *Making Money*, 328.   [149] Shin, *The Age of Paper*, 3.

England notes, and by 1833 they had become legal tender.[150] Bank of England notes moved over greater geographical distances during this period and were used by a wider range of social groups.[151] The issue of bank notes, and the forms of ownership that could be claimed around them, were present during such changes. In 1758, Lord Mansfield heard the case of *Miller* v. *Race* and decreed that bank notes were forms of property with rights and responsibilities attached to them.[152] The extensive nature of bank note forgery in the 1810s prompted the Bank of England to compel individuals to take forged notes to the Bank if they found them. However, individuals such as Thomas Ranson and Robert Boyce challenged these demands by refusing to surrender forged notes.[153] These cases challenged the question of where ownership lay and sought to establish the primacy of the possessor (rather than the Bank of England) within ownership claims. While such cases sought to fix the nature of property with regard to bank notes, the rapid circulation of notes often loosened understandings of who possessed and who owned at any one time. The metaphors and other linguistic frameworks that surrounded money and made it culturally legible and stressed the crucial significance of their circulation. Money was understood as 'vital'.[154] It was the life 'blood' of the economy, allowing for ever-more rapid transactions.[155] In contrast to other 'it narratives', in Thomas Bridges' *The Adventures of a Bank-Note*, the note changes hands almost every page.[156] Like the watch, the bank note was passed along rather than acting of its own volition, but here it was passed along at a much faster rate. Such speed meant deciphering ownership on an everyday level could be difficult. The prolonged use of endorsements on bank notes perhaps provides further evidence as to the concerns surrounding the ownership of notes and the strategies individuals used to assert ownership. As James Thompson has argued, endorsement acted as an importance means of individualising paper money in the eighteenth century. With each intermediary bearer adding their name, it became possible to 'read the history of a bill or note in its endorsements'.[157] That 'transactions of paper currency were usually accompanied by an exchange of personal information' demonstrates both a desire to avoid forgery and improve security, but also the ways in which these objects were made unique and individual.[158]

Bills and bank notes, in particular, were peculiar forms of property. Unlike other forms, they declared their belonging (to a bank) and that they contained a

---

[150] Ibid., 190 and 266.   [151] Ibid., 93 and 103.
[152] Kevin Hart, *Samuel Johnson and the Culture of Property* (Cambridge, 1999), 135.
[153] Shin, *The Age of Paper*, 219.
[154] Valenze, *The Social Life of Money in the English Past*, 70.   [155] Ibid., 66.
[156] See Thomas Bridges, *The Adventures of a Bank-Note*, Vol. I (London, 1770).
[157] Thompson, *Models of Value*, 137.   [158] Shin, *The Age of Paper*, 135.

promise (to the bearer).[159] They were technologies that articulated their place in relationships of obligation and demand. At the same time, they were constantly changing. New varieties of bills and notes emerged to 'fill new needs and desires'. Similarly, coins might seem anonymous, but in the eighteenth century, they were 'clipped, bitten, counterfeited, chucked, and generally abused'.[160] As *The Adventures of a Ruppee* and *The Adventures of a Silver Penny* remind us, coins had tales to tell of their making.[161] Such making shows us that coins could become recognisable and unique, but it also underscores their physical mutability. Coins and paper money were constantly evolving. In the case of money and financial instruments then, it was not so much the law but the ever-changing nature of the thing itself that made understanding ownership and possession difficult.

Conclusion

The new philosophical frameworks of the late seventeenth century shifted understandings of the relationships at stake in property. In the eighteenth century, the development of chattel law, and particularly chattels personal, meant that different 'things' came to be increasingly understood as distinct forms of property. While the law produced the fiction that people could be 'things' which could be enslaved, owned, and understood as chattels, social practices meant that the 'ownership' of wives was largely a legal fiction. Over the eighteenth century, servants were increasingly recognised as legal persons who owned and contracted their labour. At the same time, outside of the realm of people, dogs experienced a different trajectory. Over the century, they came to be understood not only as pets, but also as things which people could possess and own: as property, as 'chattels personal'. Watches were much less troublesome; they were clearly 'chattels personal' throughout the period, whereas for financial instruments their position was not as transparent, and the law struggled to keep up with ever-changing commercial innovation.

Chattel law developed over the eighteenth century. It grappled with questions of what could and should be owned, who should be allowed to be owners and what it meant to be an owner, to possess such things. The process of development ensured that the legal frameworks important to conceptions of property and possession were in flux. They introduced ambiguities and uncertainties as much as understandings. Alongside acknowledging the ambiguities

---

[159] Many thanks to Carolyn Steedman for highlighting this particular form of strangeness in money.
[160] Valenze, *The Social Life of Money in the English Past*, 1.
[161] Helenus Scott, *The Adventures of a Ruppee* (London, 1782), 2; Anon., *The Adventures of a Silver Penny* (London, 1786), 15.

at stake in the law, particularly with chattel law, in the eighteenth century, it is also important to see the limited reach of the law in shaping understandings. Lord Mansfield was deeply sceptical as to contemporary understandings of property law. He observed in a typical ruling that 'generally speaking, no common person has the smallest idea of any difference between giving a person a horse and a quantity of land. Common sense alone would never teach a man the difference'.[162] These limitations meant that other means of knowing what 'possession' and property might be could grow and develop too. As such, it is important to look to other sites in which people encountered and conceived their broader understandings of property and possession. In the following chapters, *Keeping Hold* will do just that.

People learned about property and possession from novels like *The History of Pompey the Little*. Towards the novel's end, as the two women grapple over the ownership of Pompey, it is the law they turn to the law. They hoped the law would clarify the thorny question of ownership and would ultimately uphold their understanding of it regarding Pompey. In this instance, 'the law', or an interpretation of it, was delivered to Lady Tempest by a solicitor at Lincoln's Inn. But the moment is also important in that it underlines the centrality of loss in thinking through possession. Coventry utilises this moment of loss to have Lady Tempest think about the parameters of property and possession. More broadly, eighteenth- and early nineteenth-century literature consistently underlined the fragility of possession to its readers. Novels and 'it' narratives taught that such fragility was particularly marked in certain sites and spaces. Possessions came to be understood as vulnerable in urban spaces. In these sites, there was always another pair of hands ready to grasp the lapdog should it get distracted by a bird and wander away. It is to these spaces, to London, that we now turn to better understand why possession and property became such key issues in the eighteenth century. Chapter 2 will show how maintaining possession of your belongings became a particularly difficult thing to do in the rapidly expanding urban spaces of the eighteenth century. Cities were sites of loss and as such they challenged people's ability to maintain possession, to keep hold.

---

[162] As cited in Lieberman, 'Property, Commerce, and the Common Law', 153.

2 Cities of Loss

London has long been a city marked by imaginings. Residents and visitors have required some means of making sense of all the people, and all the places. In the eighteenth century, perhaps due to the centrality of the Thames and its tides, writers often grasped at images of waves. To walk down London's streets was to be confronted by 'tides of passengers', borne along the pavement by their collective energy.[1] By the 1770s, writers saw the capital's streets as chaotic spaces. No longer a single stream of pedestrians, here 'hurrying' and 'scrambling' abounded. Writers pitched the hustle and bustle of the city as contrasting with the 'country' where 'all things are generally calm and still'.[2] There were no waves in the 'country', no unstoppable rushes of people. While these descriptions of the social life of London can be likened to those for other European capitals, such as Paris, they diverged from the descriptive logics applied to other English cities.[3] Andrew Hooke's *Bristollia: or, Memoirs of the city of Bristol* and William Barrett's *The History and Antiquities of the City of Bristol* focused on the ancient history of the city and its built environment.[4] In a similar vein, John Wood's *Description of the Exchange* made a case for the importance of Bristol by focusing on its newly built Exchange.[5] Other guides had much more practical concerns. They placed cities like Bristol in their wider context, focusing on the costs of travelling to and from.[6] In contrast

---

[1] John Gay, 'Trivia; or the Art of Walking the Streets of London', in John Gay (ed.), *Court Poems* (London, 1716), 19.
[2] Anon., *The Countryman's Guide to London* (London, 1775), 94.
[3] Commentators on Paris were also overwhelmed 'by the din, the confusion of traffic, animals, cries, the crowds of people'. See David Garrioch, *The Making of Revolutionary Paris* (Berkeley, CA, 2004), 1.
[4] Andrew Hooke, *Bristollia: or, Memoirs of the City of Bristol* (London, 1748); William Barrett, *The History and Antiquities of the City of Bristol* (Bristol, 1789). For the importance of history in guidebooks, see Rosemary Sweet, *The Writing of Urban Histories in Eighteenth-Century England* (Oxford, 1997), 100–141.
[5] John Wood, *Description of the Exchange* (Bath, 1745).
[6] Anon., *The Tradesman's and Travellers Pocket Companion: OR, THE Bath and Bristol Guide: Calculated for the Use of Gentlemen and Ladies Who Visit Bath; Inhabitants of Bath and Bristol; and All Persons Who Have Occasion to Travel* (Bath, 1753); *The Bath and Bristol Guide: or, The Tradesman's and Traveller's Pocket Companion* (Bath, 1765).

to these descriptions focused on architecture and transport, writers primarily conceived of London as a 'seat of perpetual change, incessant noise, and constant hurry': as a deeply social space.[7]

People moved at pace in the capital. Vibrant fairs and markets contained throngs of ever-changing faces.[8] London had long been a busy port city, but its commercial activities intensified in the eighteenth century and hurrying came to define it. Significantly for this book, writers increasingly considered the intensity of the capital in terms of loss. They produced narratives in which the bustle of the city increased the possibility of possessions falling, or of them falling from a pocket without the owner even realising. They also created stories of servants running away into the dense anonymity of the city. Ever-broader forms of print culture reached a greater number of people, and poems, novels and guidebooks focused on London increasingly articulated fears. Stories about eighteenth-century London consistently featured tales of loss.[9] As we saw in Chapter 1, philosophical and legal texts were ambiguous as to the nature of property and possession in the eighteenth century, creating space for other meanings to emerge. In this chapter and those that follow, we seek out those other understandings by looking to loss. As discussed in the Introduction, examining moments in which Britons lost their possessions and what they did in response provides us with articulations of what it meant to possess. Here, practices, what urban denizens did, are read as enunciations on property. To begin this work, we must first seek out moments of loss. This chapter turns our attention to urban spaces and the city, London, because the imaginings that emerged to make sense of it were full of tales of losing.

London was hugely significant in the eighteenth century. While in the early 1500s only 2 per cent of the population lived in the capital, by the late 1600s, that proportion had risen to 10 per cent.[10] By 1800, London had become the first modern city with a population of one million.[11] People moved in and out of the capital, rather than permanently migrating there. Flows of migrants bolstered the city and increased the proportion of the national population that experienced capital life. At the same time, London's growing economic, social, political and cultural importance meant that the metropolis came to

---

[7] Sir John Fielding, Jr, and Richard King, *The New London Spy: Or a Modern Twenty-Four Hours Ramble through the Bills of Mortality* (London, 1771), 7.
[8] Benjamin Heller, 'The "Mene Peuple" and the Polite Spectator: The Individual in the Crowd at Eighteenth-Century London Fairs', *Past & Present*, 208 (2010), 143.
[9] As Vic Gattrell reminds us, however, other urban narratives also emerged which centred on pleasure, sex and laughter. See Vic Gattrell, *City of Laughter: Sex and Satire in Eighteenth-Century London* (London, 2006), 32.
[10] Schwarz, 'London 1700–1840', 644.
[11] James Vernon, *Distant Strangers: How Britain Became Modern* (Berkeley, CA, 2014), 24.

play an ever-more significant role in Britons' imaginations.¹² The question of property became more relevant in the long eighteenth century, not just because more people owned more things and the law was ambiguous as to what ownership meant but also because greater numbers of people came to live in London and the intensity of this city's social world asked questions about it. By making visible how growing urban spaces asked questions about possession through instances of loss, we further see how the eighteenth century has a particular story to tell.

This chapter examines how and why eighteenth-century London and the stories written about it raised present questions of property and possession. It shows how guides to London came to focus on experiences of loss and losing and that as such they asked about ownership, particularly in terms of possessions carried on the person, but also through 'runaway' people. The chapter places such concerns in conversation with how urban denizens increasingly came to protect and secure their possessions in urban sites: it looks to the care they put in. While it is difficult to prove whether possessions were at greater risk of theft in this period, by looking to the growth of security, we see that people conceived of such threats and sought to protect against them. In the methods people developed to prevent loss, we see our first set of articulations of what it meant to own.

London Stories

As London grew over the eighteenth century, so too did the print culture designed to aid people in navigating the multifaceted metropolis. As David Pike asserts, 'once it has become impossible to grasp a certain city in an instant, once a single person can no longer summon up its entirety in a single mental image ... we can say that it has become a modern city'. Modernity and urbanisation rely on scale. Londoners and visitors to the capital faced the impossibility of grasping the entirety of the city in the long eighteenth century. At this point of growth, Pike argues, 'new vantage points are needed from which to begin to understand it'.¹³ Various technologies sought to provide 'vantage points' in this period. Prospects, maps, itineraries, guidebooks, novels and poems all tackled the problem of finding the means to comprehend the capital. Among their many uses and purposes, guidebooks were particularly adept at offering different vantage points. As with other cities, some guides focused on encouraging visitors to 'see' the city and consume it in largely

---

[12] Pamela K. Gilbert, 'Introduction: Imagining Londons', in Pamela K. Gilbert (ed.), *Imagined Londons* (New York, NY, 2002), 1.

[13] David L. Pike, *Metropolis on the Styx: The Underworlds of Modern Urban Culture, 1800–2001* (Ithaca, NY, 2007), 36.

aesthetic terms. Guides, such as *The Stranger's Guide through London and Westminster* (1786), provided visitors with itineraries and information for touring the landmarks of the city. Under these modes of looking, the sites remained starkly unpopulated and instead focused the visitor's attention on the aesthetics and histories at stake. Such works underlined the importance of looking and the ability to see London as a built environment. In contrast, many other guides and writings sought to show the capital as a social space, made lively by the ever-increasing numbers of people within it. Nevertheless, these guides still had to consider which vantage points might allow visitors to understand London and know it in this way. When he was about to leave Britain in 1749, the Swedish traveller Samuel Schröder noted that new arrivals to London would do well to 'go to the top of St Paul's church-tower ... from where one at once can make a General Idea about London'.[14] Alongside gaining this perspective, Schröder also thought it was valuable for visitors to walk through London's streets and engage with the different sensory and social experiences they offered.[15] Almost one hundred years later, George Smeeton had his characters Peregrine and Mentor take a similar approach. Towards the end of his 1828 publication *Doings in London; or Day and Night Scenes of the Frauds, Follies, Manners, and Depravities of the Metropolis,* after much rambling along the streets and byways of London, the pair head up to see the view from St Paul's. '"Do you perceive the crowd beneath us?" said Peregrine: "they look, from hence, a swarm of Lilliputians."'[16] For most guidebooks, however, the different vantage points they offered through which to 'see' the city were not dependent on height, but rather on access. They took potential visitors into different parts of the city, to places inaccessible to those not in the know. In doing so, they wrote London as a social formation.

The 'ramble' through the city was a key strand within the guidebook genre of the eighteenth century and continued to develop over the nineteenth and twentieth centuries.[17] Edward Ward's (1667–1731) *The London Spy* set the

---

[14] As cited in Göran Rydén, 'Viewing and Walking: Swedish Visitors to Eighteenth-Century London', *Journal of Urban History*, 39:2 (2012), 255.

[15] Rydén, 'Viewing and Walking', 256.

[16] George Smeeton, *Doings in London; or Day and Night Scenes of the Frauds, Follies, Manners, and Depravities of the Metropolis* (London, 1828), 384.

[17] For other eighteenth-century iterations see Fielding Jr. and King, *The New London Spy*; *London Unmask'd*; B. Crosby, *A Modern Sabbath, Or, A Sunday Ramble, and Sabbath-Day Journey* (London, 1794); I. Roach, *A Fortnight's Ramble through London, Or, A Complete Display of all the Cheats and Frauds Practised in the Great Metropolis* (London, 1795); John Roach, *Roach's London Pocket Pilot, Or Stranger's Guide through the Metropolis* (London, 1796). For nineteenth- and twentieth-century iterations, see George Augustus Sala, *Twice Round the Clock, Or the Hours of the Day and Night in London* [1858] (New York, NY, 1971); Virginia Woolf, *Street Haunting: A London Adventure* [1927] (Nottingham, 2017). We might also understand Samuel Selvon's 1956 novel *The Lonely Londoners*, as part of, or a challenge to, this genre. See Samuel Selvon, *The Lonely Londoners* [1956] (London, 2006), 1–4.

terms for this form of London narrative. First published as a series of eighteen monthly instalments between November 1698 and May 1700, *The London Spy* was published as a complete book in 1703.[18] Differentiating itself from late seventeenth-century works which sought to write London as a city boldly re-emerging from the disaster of the 1666 Great Fire of London, Ward struck a new tone in his insistence on satire and the tentative position from which his narrator articulated his experience.[19] The central protagonist of the work, new from the countryside, meets an old schoolfellow, the 'Spy', and welcomes his guidance around the metropolis. Moving quickly from site to site, their insights are often based on brief interactions and limited knowledge, and thus their vantage points appear almost speculative. In the later eighteenth century and early nineteenth century, the rambling genre continued and became more confident and secure with publications such as Sir John Fielding Jr and Richard King's 1771 work *The New London Spy, or a Modern Twenty-Four Hours Ramble through the Bills of Mortality* and George Smeeton's early nineteenth-century *Doings in London*.

These guides produced important stories about London, the people who inhabited it and the practices that aided and restricted social relationships. From the second half of the century onwards, many of the stories contained in guidebooks hinged on the idea of deception. They wrote London as a space in which inhabitants needed to be constantly vigilant of themselves and their possessions to thwart the host of characters intent on taking things through trickery.[20] Perhaps unsurprisingly, these guides underlined the need for guidance. *The Countryman's Guide to London* could understand the contentment that might come from being 'ignorant of the various forms of fraud and deceit practised in this busy scene of things' but considered that trying to navigate 'this maze of perplexity, without caution ... may prove his bane'.[21] Similarly, Richard King thought his guide would illuminate 'villainous and illicit proceedings' and thus allow 'country readers to escape the traps laid for them'.[22] Smeeton wrote London as a space filled with people bent on 'numerous and almost incredible frauds, deceptions, schemes and villanies', making it the 'most dangerous city in the world for a stranger to enter, unless he has a friend to advise him'.[23] Worryingly, people were not what they seemed in London. Fraud and crime lurked around each corner.

---

[18] Peter M. Briggs, 'Satiric Strategy in Ned Ward's London Writings', *Eighteenth-Century Life*, 35:2 (2011), 81.
[19] Briggs, 'Satiric Strategy', 80.
[20] O'Byrne, 'The Art of Walking in London: Representing Urban Pedestrianism in the Early Nineteenth Century', 97.
[21] Anon., *The Countryman's Guide to London*, ii.
[22] Richard King, *New Cheats of London Exposed* (London, 1780), iv.
[23] Smeeton, *Doings in London*, 4.

The emergence of deception as a key strand within guidebooks from the mid eighteenth century onwards mirrored a wider growth in crime literature. We do not know whether crime rose across the eighteenth century, but it is clear that a wide readership consumed polemical works, journalistic accounts of crime waves, criminal biographies and other sources between the 1670s and 1770s.[24] In this period, popular understandings of crime as a social problem came to be distinctly shaped by what people read, rather than what they experienced, expanding fears.[25] Crime writings saw the construction of particular types of criminal; for example, the 1720s saw greater coverage of and concern around the 'street robber' as distinctly violent, threatening and urban.[26] At the same time, the growth in different types of published writing about crime also meant the development of a range of voices and conflicting views.[27] In contrast, by the later eighteenth century, London guidebooks consistently voiced concern that deceptions were focused upon the theft of personal property.[28] Theft had always been a part of London life. Personal property such as pewter pint pots, watches, jewellery, shoe buckles, ribbons and clothes was under threat not only in homes and businesses but also on the street.[29] What was different in the eighteenth century was that fears about crime came to be written and expressed through a variety of channels. More particularly, guidebooks came to write threats to property as an intrinsic aspect of urban life.

In Ward's *The London-Spy Compleat*, the 'Spy' and visitor find themselves amid the crowd at St Bartholomew's Fair. Thinking that a woman is struggling in the throng of people, the visitor seeks to protect her: 'I laid my hands upon my Friends [sic] Shoulders, and by keeping her between my Arms, defended her from the rude Squeezes and Jostles of the Careless Multitude'. In response to such 'honourable' actions, the woman put 'her Hand behind her and pick'd my Pocket of a good Handkerchief'; once she had gone, the visitor 'discover'd my Loss'. When telling the 'Spy' he is met with laughter, 'for my over-care of

---

[24] Robert B. Shoemaker, 'The Old Bailey Proceedings and the Representation of Crime and Criminal Justice in Eighteenth-Century London', *Journal of British Studies*, 47:3 (2008), 579; Lena Liapi, *Roguery in Print: Crime and Culture in Early Modern London* (Martlesham, 2019), 6.

[25] Robert Shoemaker, 'Print Culture and the Creation of Public Knowledge about Crime in 18th-Century London', in Paul Knepper, Jonathan Doak, and Joanna Shapland (eds.), *Urban Crime Prevention and Restorative Justice: Effects of Social Technologies* (Abingdon, 2009), 1; David Lemmings, 'Henry Fielding and English Crime and Justice Reportage, 1748–52: Narratives of Panic, Authority and Emotion', *Huntington Library Quarterly*, 80:1 (2017), 81–82.

[26] Robert Shoemaker, 'The Street Robber and Gentleman Highwayman: Changing Representations and Perceptions of Robbery in London, 1690–1800', *Cultural and Social History*, 3 (2006), 386.

[27] Robert Shoemaker, 'Worrying About Crime: Experience, Moral Panics and Public Opinion in London, 1660–1800', *Past & Present*, 234 (2017), 85.

[28] J. M. Beattie, *Policing and Punishment in London, 1660–1750: Urban Crime and the Limits of Terror* (Oxford, 2001), 45.

[29] Drew D. Gray, *Crime, Prosecution and Social Relations: The Summary Courts of the City of London in the Late Eighteenth Century* (London, 2009), 73.

my Lady, and carelessness of my Self'.[30] Such mirth is suggestive for multiple reasons. Pickpocketing had been a capital crime since 1565, but it was difficult to prove and only a small proportion of these crimes reached court. For pickpocketing to be recognised, the victim had to prove they were unaware of the crime taking place at the time of the theft (thus the discovery after the event).[31] Court records suggest that men were the mostly likely victims, and that over half of these crimes were committed by women.[32] Significantly, Ward has the protagonists consider the event through the language of care and carelessness.

The New London Spy outlined another rouse. A 'mock' fight breaks out before the visitor and guide and they find that the distraction provides the opportunity for others to steal: 'in a few minutes one lost his watch, another his hat, another his handkerchief; one woman was stripped of her cloak, another had her pocket cut from her side'. The incident taught the visitor '(always in London especially) to run from a crowd, instead of running into one'.[33] Richard King also warned of the dangers of pickpockets in crowds in his *New Cheats of London*, noting that the 'opera, play-houses, capital auctions, and public gardens swarm with them, and, of late years, they have introduced themselves into our very churches'.[34] King noted that, 'Some pickpockets are very dextrous in this way, by introducing their hands, without being perceived, into the very bottom of the breeches pocket, and taking out the money'. Women were not immune from such practices though, as King recorded pickpockets 'introducing their hands up ladies petticoats, taking hold of the pocket, and making an incision with a knife or scizzars [sic], and letting out the contents into their hands without discovery'. The concern was that things might go missing 'without discovery' and people might have 'never after received any account' of their 'lost purses, watches, rings, and pocketbooks'.[35] Similarly, *The Countryman's Guide to London* described how, using the distractions of a crowd, pickpockets would pick 'your property from you imperceptibly' using a 'kind of slight [sic]'.[36] Women were seen to be particularly vulnerable to such strategies because with the use of tie-pockets 'their watches and tweezers...are easily cut from their sides'.[37] Crowds offered the opportunity to pickpocket, nevertheless, court cases suggest that they were mainly spaces in which men operated and that more private

---

[30] Edward Ward, *The London-Spy Compleat* (London, 1703), 247.
[31] Deidre Palk, 'Private Crime in Public and Private Places: Pickpockets and Shoplifters in London, 1780–1823', in Tim Hitchcock and Heather Shore (eds), *The Streets of London: From the Great Fire to the Great Stink* (London, 2003), 137.
[32] Palk, 'Private Crime in Public and Private Places', 137 and 144.
[33] Fielding Jr and King, *The New London Spy*, 26.
[34] King, *New Cheats of London Exposed*, 61.   [35] Ibid., 63.
[36] *The Countryman's Guide to London*, 20.   [37] Ibid., 21.

domestic spaces and quiet streets were significant locations often utilised by women.[38]

What is perhaps more telling in these stories of crowds and pickpockets is their concern for the way in which possessions might go missing through sleights of hand. The ambiguities of loss demonstrated the ambiguities of possession. These same concerns were amplified through other forms of print culture in the later eighteenth century. It-narratives such as *The Adventures of a Watch* (1788) have watches telling stories of when a woman 'softly' conveyed the watch from its 'pendant situation, into her pocket; she then gently released a small note book, and his Lordship's purse from their hiding places' before 'carefully' depositing them alongside the watch in her pocket.[39] While these imagined objects might know what was happening to them, their owners were often blithely unaware. Pickpockets received much attention in London guides because they raised the concern of not knowing what happened until it was too late (although such ignorance would have been important in prosecuting the thief as a pickpocket). It also begins to show us the complex concerns about loss in an urban space full of 'hurryings', 'scramblings' and skilful sleights of hand.[40] It was felt that the intensity of London life made it possible to lose possessions without knowing whether they had been dropped or stolen. Cities produced this problem of uncertainty, and it in turn produced anxiety.

Concerns over losing items and not knowing how it had happened reflected a reality of city life, of course. The bustle of the metropolis, the jostling crowds and streets, meant that it *was* possible to simply drop your possessions, rather than have them stolen. In fact, multiple forms of print culture encouraged people to imagine this possibility. In the *Adventures of a Rupee* (1782), the coin is lost in St James's Park, where it 'might have remained amongst the grass for many years, had it not been for a Westminster lover, who had reclined himself on the verdant turf to enjoy the zephyrs of noon'.[41] Taking a tumble could also result in loss. In the 1770 it narrative *The Adventures of a Bank-Note*, the apothecary loses 'both his hat and wig' after tripping up, but the author reminds the reader that this is commonplace in the capital: 'that nobody wonders at [it] that knows London'.[42] In his 1786 publication *London Adviser and Guide*, the Reverend John Trussler (1735–1820) showed his understanding of the possibility of simply dropping things. He warned that if 'you should drop any thing of value in the street, whilst you are looking for it, you will have

---

[38] Palk, 'Private Crime in Public and Private Places', 141; Peter K Andersson, '"Bustling, Crowding, and Pushing": Pickpockets and the Nineteenth-Century Street Crowd', *Urban History*, 41:2 (2014), 296.

[39] Anon., *The Adventures of a Watch* (London, 1788), 30.

[40] *The Countryman's Guide to London*, 94.

[41] Helenus Scott, *The Adventures of a Ruppee. Wherein are Interspersed Various Anecdotes Asiatic and European* (Dublin, 1782), 208.

[42] Thomas Bridges, *The Adventures of a Bank-Note*. vol II (London, 1770), 8.

many ask you what you have lost, and offer to assist you in the search'. Again, he warned urban denizens to be careful of such ploys and to insist that the item was 'nothing of any consequence'. If you did not, Trussler warned, you would 'likely never find it, as they will probably find it for you and keep it.'[43] Prince Herman von Pückler-Muskau was of the same opinion. When travelling in Ireland, he was surprised when a gentleman returned his pocketbook to him. He noted how 'In England there would have been scarcely any chance of seeing my pocketbook again, even if a *gentleman* had found it, for he would just have let it lie there or...kept it.'[44] Like von Pückler-Muskau, Trussler knew how easy it was to drop something without realising or forget an item somewhere amid the distractions of the urban space. If this happened, it was doubtful that the item would be there when you returned. Trussler and von Pückler-Muskau envisaged everyone to be on the lookout, everyone a potential finder. The writer Samuel Johnson joked: even orange peel found in the street would be scraped, dried and then sold to distillers.[45] Everything had value, nothing would be left.

Finding and claiming things on the street was a legal possibility and could be used as a defence in cases of theft. William Blackstone, in his attempts to make common law into a recognisable system, underlined the possibilities inherent in finding. He noted that 'whatever movables are found upon the surface of the earth, or in the sea, and are unclaimed by any owner, are supposed to be abandoned by the last proprietor'. Such 'abandonment' meant that they were 'returned to into the common stock and mass of things: and therefore they belong, as in a state of nature, to the first occupant or fortunate finder'.[46] Yet, of course, cities were becoming spaces in which the line between abandonment, forgetting and simply dropping something unaware was rather hazy. For finders, there was no haziness. In 1778, just like the famous chimney sweep boy who came before her, the widow Ann Brown knew the important distinction of *finding* an item.[47] Robert Crosby was indicted for stealing a watch, which he had apparently got from Brown, when she appeared as a witness in the Old Bailey, she underscored her innocence by asserting that she had *found* the watch 'between eight and nine at night, near Panton Street on the pavement'.[48] When Crosby went to pawn it, however, the pawnbroker John Wood became suspicious and stopped it. Brown stated to the

---

[43] John Trussler, *London Adviser and Guide* (London, 1786), 147.
[44] Prince Hermann von Pückler-Muskau (Linda B. Parshall trans.), *Letters of a Dead Man* (Cambridge, 2016), 461.
[45] Jerry White, *London in the Eighteenth Century: A Great and Monstrous Thing* (London, 2012), 200.
[46] Blackstone, *Commentaries on the Laws of England: Book II Of the Rights of Things*, 272.
[47] The mention of the chimney sweep boy refers to the case well known to law students, that of Armory v. Delamirie, EWHC J94 (1722) 1 Strange 505. See John Strange, *A Collection of Select Cases Relating to Evidence. By a Late Barrister at Law* (London, 1754), 90.
[48] *Old Bailey Proceedings Online* (hereafter 'OBPO') (www.oldbaileyonline.org, version 8.0, 09 August 2019), April 1778, trial of Robert Crosby (t17780429-6).

court that the pawnbroker 'had no right to stop the watch I had found'. In doing so Ann Brown, who described herself as a widow who ran a lodging house in Little Britain, was confident of her understanding of the law: that items that are 'found upon the surface of the earth' and are 'unclaimed by any owner' are 'supposed to be abandoned' and thus belong 'to the first occupant or fortunate finder'.[49] Brown also told the court that she 'went and claimed it [from the pawnbroker], which I would not have done if I had stole it.' Women often defended themselves by stating in court that they had acquired the item not by theft but by having it delivered to them, loaned to them or through finding it somewhere.[50] The makeshift nature of economic lives, in which items were loaned between friends and kin, or temporarily pawned to free up money, made such given reasons highly plausible.[51] When asked when she found it, Brown was specific in her answer, increasing its plausibility: 'between eight and nine at night, near Panton Street on the pavement'. While the court seemingly believed Brown's explanation, Crosby was found guilty.[52]

In the long eighteenth century, London came to be written and imagined as a space where possessions were under threat. The trope of the dangerous city space became well established. Deceivers and tricksters apparently prowled every street, ready to use some ploy to relieve you of your possessions. The distractions of the city, the spectacles it contained, were also seen to prove problematic: while your attention was captured, pickpockets would swoop in and with a sleight of hand remove you of the things upon your person. The 'scramblings' of city life and the 'tides of passengers' upon the pavements produced still further issues. Your possessions might simply fall out of your pocket, and you might not be sure how it had happened. You might have simply dropped them in the throng of other bodies. City life was imagined to create deep uncertainties around loss. Understanding London in this way, meant that people were also warned of how they should act and be. They were increasingly warned of the need to take care of their possessions and be alert to such dangers. Here we begin to see possession being asserted as an active process, requiring effort and attention. In this period, part of caring for things was finding ways to keep hold.

---

[49] Blackstone, *Commentaries on the Laws in England: Book II Of the Rights of Things*, 272.
[50] Lynn MacKay, 'Why They Stole: Women in the Old Bailey, 1779–1789', *Journal of Social History*, 32 (1999), 626.
[51] Beverly Lemire, *The Business of Everyday Life: Gender, Practice and Social Politics in England, c.1600–1900* (Manchester, 2005), 17.
[52] OBPO (www.oldbaileyonline.org, version 8.0, 09 August 2019), April 1778, trial of Robert Crosby (t17780429-6).

The Runaway

Over the eighteenth century, London was increasingly written as an urban space characterised by deception, crime and loss not only because objects were taken or fell out of possession but also because enslaved people, servants and apprentices regularly went 'missing'.[53] The bustle of life meant that cities were places in which people could abscond or runaway unseen and unheard. Layering these different forms of loss on top each other might appear awkward and unconnected to us, after all, we know people and labour are very different 'possessions' to watches and bank notes. Nevertheless, we must move past our own understanding to re-engage with an eighteenth-century worldview that took a capacious view of possessions. Placing these different things in conversation underscores the different experiences of loss and explains why London stories regularly picked at this theme. By viewing them together, we also see the interdependent nature of understandings of property and possession, which drew on a multiplicity of relationships.

Stories of runaways or running away appeared in print in this period, particularly in the later eighteenth century. These stories echoed those about lost objects and contributed to understandings of the city as a space of loss and uncertainty. They were also part of a larger narrative about the capital as a social space difficult to grasp. These stories featured in works such as William Godwin's (1756–1836) *Caleb Williams* (1794) and *Onesimus; or, the Runaway Servant Converted* published by the Cheap Repository for Moral and Religious Tracts possibly in 1795. They highlighted the importance of urban spaces in providing anonymity. When the fictional character Caleb Williams is falsely accused of theft by his master and seeks to escape his persecution, he heads for London. Williams imagines that the city will provide 'an inexhaustible reservoir of concealment'.[54] Similarly, set in Ancient Rome (that earlier city of one million), in *Onesimus*, we see that after robbing his master and running away, Onesimus goes to Rome, where it would be easy for him 'to conceal himself'. The anonymous author sees a similarity in Onesimus's actions with those of the eighteenth century: 'just as it is easy for a man who has played the villain somewhere at a distance in this country, to lie hid in

---

[53] People living in eighteenth century Britain would not have called it that though. The concept of missing persons did not emerge until the nineteenth century. The *Oxford English Dictionary* has its first recorded use as 1850. See "missing, adj. and n.2". *OED Online*. September 2021. Oxford University Press. www.oed.com/view/Entry/119997?redirectedFrom=to+go+missing (accessed 2 November 2021). For more on the origins of missing persons, see Robert Douglas-Fairhurst, *The Turning Point: A Year That Changed Dickens and the World* (London, 2021), 95–97.

[54] William Godwin, *Caleb Williams* [1794] (Oxford, 2009), 246.

London now'.[55] These stories set up the runaway as seeking to escape their misdeeds, and as part of a broader story of deception and intent in which people's identities were easily blurred or rewritten in urban spaces.[56] But such dramatisations are unhelpful to us in trying to understand the sometimes mundane and often diverse reasons at stake within 'running'. London might have offered some anonymity, but more importantly it also offered economic opportunities, institutions designed to aid mobility and support groups that helped those seeking escape.

For white servants and apprentices, running away was a technical term, used to describe 'leaving a hiring before its term, or without notice'.[57] A useful definition of service as an eighteenth-century institution was 'a household worker hired on a year's term'.[58] In the first half of the eighteenth century, manuals designed to advise servants placed great importance on staying with a particular household. It was an argument that needed to be made, particularly in London. Published in 1725, *The Servants Calling with Some Advice to the Apprentice* consistently asserted the importance of humility and obedience on the part of servants. It noted, however, that the achievement of such qualities is 'of little Use to himself or others, if he is of a roving and unsettled Temper, moving from Place to Place'. Rather, it advised servants to 'settle' and incorporate themselves 'with the Family'.[59] Understanding the needs of a family and proving a good character took time. In her 1743 publication *Present for a Servant Maid*, Eliza Haywood (d. 1756) also asserted the advantages of remaining with a particular family over time. Haywood stressed the (very) long term advantages of commitment to one family. Women who entered service at a young age might by continuing in 'one Place eight or ten Years' be 'of a fit Age to marry' and might then gain the support of their mistress when seeking positions for their children further down the line.[60] The anonymous author of *The Footman's Looking-Glass* (1747) also prized stability. The publication noted that those employers who took a chance on an inexperienced servant should be rewarded by having that servant provide 'good and constant Services' rather than trying to 'get into a Place of some more Benefit'.[61] After this point, however, servant manuals desisted from

---

[55] Anon., *Onesimus; or, the Run-Away Servant Converted: A True Story* (London, 1795?), 3.
[56] Robert B. Shoemaker, *The London Mob: Violence and Disorder in Eighteenth-Century England* (London, 2007), 15.
[57] Carolyn Steedman, *Labours Lost: Domestic Service and the Making of Modern England* (Cambridge, 2009), 44.
[58] Paula Humfrey, 'Introduction' in Paula Humfrey (ed.), *The Experience of Domestic Service for Women in Early Modern London* (Farnham, 2011), 10.
[59] Anon., *The Servants Calling with Some Advice to the Apprentice* (London, 1725), 63.
[60] Eliza Haywood, *A Present for a Servant Maid* (1743), 49.
[61] Anon, *The Footman's Looking-Glass: or, Proposals to the Livery Servants of London and Westminster, &c. for Bettering Their Situations in Life, and Securing Their Credit in the World* (London, 1747), 6–7.

highlighting the importance of longevity. Instead, from this point on, manuals focused much more fully on the 'how' of servants' tasks. Cleaning, polishing, marketing, pickling and cooking took up space from the 1750s onwards.[62]

The shift in focus within servant manuals might be suggestive of employers, and metropolitan society more broadly, becoming used to the mobility of domestic servants. Historians have demonstrated that from the late seventeenth century onwards metropolitan servants, and particularly female servants, were likely to leave an employer before the end of the year they had been hired for.[63] On 5 April 1803, the London bookseller William Upcott (1779–1845) certainly bemoaned the loss of servants. He noted in his diary 'And yeh, many times, the house has been in the greatest confusion – Changing servants continually.'[64] As we saw in Chapter 1, completing a year-long contract as an unmarried servant or apprentice in a parish household was an important means of gaining settlement and thus future access to poor relief. Peter Earle has argued that female servants 'made an effort to spend over a year in at least one place so that they might have a parish settlement in London to fall back on in their time of need'.[65] Once settlement in a London parish was secured, however, servants tended to fulfil a series of 'relatively short stays'.[66] Paula Humfrey's work has been important in stressing the mobility of *female* domestic servants in London. As metropolitan hirings were not tied to the autumnal hiring fairs important in agricultural locations, and due to the constant influx of people to London, female servants could find new places throughout the year.[67] London households were constantly 'losing' servants.

Such demand had important implications for the experiences of domestic service. As with other parts of the country, in London it seems that domestic servants ran away when faced with violence.[68] The three most recorded

---

[62] For the shift in focus to the 'doing' of service, see Mary Johnson, *Madam Johnson's Present: Or, the Best Instructions for Young Women, in Useful and Universal Knowledge* [1755] (4th edn, London, 1766); Anne Barker, *The Complete Servant Maid: Or Young Woman's Best Companion* (London, 1770); Anon., *The Accomplished Lady's Delight in Cookery: Or, the Complete Servant's Maid's* [sic] *Guide* (Wolverhampton, 1780); *Domestic Management, or the Art of Conducting a Family*.

[63] D. A. Kent, 'Ubiquitous but Invisible: Female Domestic Servants in Mid-Eighteenth Century London', *History Workshop*, 28 (1989), 120; Tim Meldrum, *Domestic Service and Gender 1660–1750: Life and Work in the London Household* (Harlow, 2000), 23; Amy M. Froide, *Never Married: Singlewomen in Early Modern England* (New York, NY, 2005), 90; Humfrey, 'Introduction', 3. For more on how such mobility differed from the experiences of servants in the early seventeenth century, see Peter Earle, *A City Full of People: Men and Women of London, 1650–1750* (Methuen, MA, 1994), 274–276.

[64] British Library, BL Add MSS 32,558, Diary of William Upcott of London, January 1803–1807, 1809 and 1823, 18.

[65] Peter Earle, *The Making of the English Middle Class: Business, Society, and Family Life in London, 1660–1730* (Berkeley, CA, 1989), 129.

[66] Meldrum, *Domestic Service and Gender*, 25. [67] Humfrey, 'Introduction', 11, 14–15.

[68] For London see Meldrum, *Domestic Service and Gender*, 121. For elsewhere, including the Morda Valley in Shropshire, see Steedman, *Labours Lost*, 190–197.

reasons for departure were illness, violence and sexual assault.[69] While domestic servants actively utilised their right to seek out a Justice of Peace to hear their complaint as to treatment or wages, sometimes they simply left. From 1766, the law allowed a justice to send to the House of Correction any servant who had absented themselves before their term was up.[70] Despite this, London servants continued to leave. They were in high demand and alternative employment could always be found.[71] The metropolis provided other opportunities, making leaving before the end of their term of employment a viable and ever-ready possibility. Again, the social and economic formation that was the city made keeping hold a particularly difficult thing to do.

Similarly, London apprentices regularly went before finishing their term.[72] Although there were different power dimensions at play in these relationships, as many apprentices were men and came from the gentry or wealthy families, we again see that in the eighteenth century, apprentices would find a 'balanced audience among justices of the peace' and therefore possessed 'voice and agency'.[73] Over a third of London apprentices left after three or four years due to a fight, the need to return home to support a family, or because they had fallen in love or into crime.[74] The frequency of war in the eighteenth century also provided alternative work opportunities for apprentices who wanted to 'runaway'.[75] If both master and apprentice agreed to the dissolution of the apprenticeship, no outside approval was needed. In London, even if the dissolution was contested, there was ready institutional support to ease this process, making the early ending of apprenticeships relatively straightforward. In contrast to the nineteenth century when the full force of the law was deployed to prevent apprentices quitting, between 1500 and 1800, institutions favoured 'exit over enforcement'.[76]

The Lord Mayor's Court, situated in the Guildhall in the City of London, offered youths 'a simple, cheap, and effective' means to abandon their

---

[69] Meldrum, *Domestic Service and Gender 1660–1750*, 121.
[70] Steedman, *Labours Lost*, 193.   [71] Humfrey, 'Introduction', 15.
[72] Patrick Wallis, 'Labor, Law, and Training in Early Modern London: Apprenticeship and the City's Institutions', *Journal of British Studies*, 51 (2012), 793; Ilana Krausman Ben-Amos, 'Failure to Become Freemen: Urban Apprentices in Early Modern England', *Social History*, 16:2 (1991), 155.
[73] Wallis, 'Labor, Law, and Training in Early Modern London', 794. Only a tiny proportion of London apprentices were women, or rather the historical record tends to minimise their roles, see Laura Gowing, 'Girls on Forms: Apprenticing Young Women in Seventeenth-Century London', *Journal of British Studies*, 55 (2016), 447–473; Laura Gowing, *Ingenious Trade: Women and Work in Seventeenth-Century London* (Cambridge, 2021), 2.
[74] Patrick Wallis, 'Apprenticeship in England', in Maarten Prak and Patrick Wallis (eds), *Apprenticeship in Early Modern Europe* (Cambridge, 2019), 275–276.
[75] Joan Lane, *Apprenticeship in England, 1600–1914* (London, 1996), 176.
[76] Wallis, 'Apprenticeship in England', 275.

indentures and recover part of their premiums.[77] The office allowed the youth to enter a complaint against their master; the master would then be summoned. When masters answered such summons, they often accepted the runaway apprentice back, particularly after 'parental intervention or negotiating compensation for embezzlements'.[78] Having an apprentice quit could be costly for the master and absconding was a serious offence if fully pursued.[79] By ending early, the master would be unable to offset their investment in training through enjoying the services of a skilled yet inexpensive worker later in the apprenticeship.[80] However, in reality, masters rarely answered the summons from the Lord Mayor's Court. At that point, the youth could be released from their contract and could find a new master or depart entirely. That masters tended not to show up at the Court suggests that there was little advantage in doing so and that apprenticeships were largely understood as unenforceable. The ready dissolution of apprenticeships was key to its continuation in the eighteenth century.[81]

As with domestic service and apprenticeships, leaving also acted as an important means of ending marriages. While middling and elite men and women involved in failing marriages could sue for legal separation in diocesan ecclesiastical courts and the Court of Arches, others used lawyers to draw up private articles of separation.[82] For people lacking resources in eighteenth-century Britain, however, absconding remained the simplest way to leave a marriage.[83] Evidence suggests that desertion (particularly by men) happened more frequently in urban parishes than those in rural areas, possibly because urban spaces offered more opportunities for economic mobility and anonymity.[84] Notices placed in London newspapers more frequently advertised wives as having eloped, rather than husbands. Husbands placed notices usually not to encourage the return of their wife, but rather to announce their having left and

---

[77] Wallis, 'Labor, Law, and Training in Early Modern London', 793.   [78] Ibid., 802.
[79] Lane, *Apprenticeship in England, 1600–1914*, 175. For a brilliant imagining of the stakes that were at play for some eighteenth-century apprentices in running away see Jordy Rosenberg, *Confessions of the Fox* (London, 2018).
[80] Wallis, 'Labor, Law, and Training in Early Modern London', 792.
[81] See Ibid., 817; Tim Leunig, Chris Minns and Patrick Wallis, 'Networks in the Premodern Economy: The Market for London Apprenticeships, 1600–1749', *The Journal of Economic History*, 71: 2 (2011), 418.
[82] Margaret R. Hunt, 'Wives and Marital "Rights" in the Court of Exchequer in the Early Eighteenth Century', in Paul Griffiths and Mark S. R. Jenner, *Londinopolis: Essays in the Cultural and Social History of Early Modern London* (Manchester, 2000), 109.
[83] David A. Kent, '"Gone for a Soldier": Family Breakdown and the Demography of Desertion in a London Parish, 1750–1791', *Local Population Studies*, 45 (1990), 27. As E. P. Thompson's research demonstrated, wife sales also offered a customary apparatus for publicly dissolving marriages and enabling new unions to form. See E. P. Thompson, *Customs in Common* (London, 1993), 428.
[84] Kent, '"Gone for a Soldier"', 29.

that they, the husband, were no longer liable for any debts their wife incurred. Due to the assumption that cohabitation implied a husband's consent to his wife's pledging credit, it was important to publicly announce that a spouse had left.[85] The frequent use of the term 'eloped' suggested the woman having left with another man.[86] A woman forced from the home because they had committed adultery lost their right to pledge credit and notices also sought to establish this. However, if a wife left to escape her husband's cruelty, she was legally allowed to continue to use her husband's credit.[87] Similarly, as we saw in Chapter 1, when a marriage faltered and informal separation was being sought, married women might make purchases to acquire substantial debts, thus forcing their husbands to meet their demands. Placing a notice acted as an attempt to prevent against such negotiations and more broadly to ensure that debts were not accrued by warning shopkeepers against granting credit. Although notices occasionally encouraged wives to return, notices were rarely about 'running away', but instead sought to control the narrative, strengthen a husband's reputation and character and release them from economic obligations.[88]

Rather than the drama that the term 'run away' might imply in our contemporary world, in the eighteenth century, it was an everyday occurrence for servants, apprentices and spouses. Yet, with few corroborating sources, it is difficult to know whether some of the cases advertised in newspapers did involve exploitative situations where individuals very much pursued their freedom by 'running away'. In considering these instances, we must turn to a different story. In fact, we need turn to a publication which was not a story at all, but rather a history, or in the words of its author an 'Interesting Narrative'. Published in 1789, Olaudah Equiano's (d. 1797) *The Interesting Narrative of the Life of Olaudah Equiano* provides an important counter to tales of white mobility. Equiano describes how in the spring of 1774, having experienced 'the dishonesty of many people here [in London]', he decided to set out for Turkey and obtained the role of steward on Captain John Hughes's ship.[89] He also recommended 'a very clever black man, John Annis, as a cook'. However, although Annis had parted 'by consent' from his former "master" William Kirkpatrick, and had worked upon the ship for two months, Kirkpatrick continued to pursue him. He ultimately found Annis and kidnapped him while

---

[85] Joanne Bailey, 'Favoured or Oppressed? Married Women, Property and "Coverture" in England, 1660–1800', *Continuity and Change*, 17:3 (2002), 355–356.
[86] "Elope, v.". OED Online. December 2021. Oxford University Press. www.oed.com/view/Entry/60582?redirectedFrom=eloped (accessed 2 December 2021).
[87] Margot Finn, 'Women, Consumption and Coverture in England, c.1760–1860', *The Historical Journal*, 39:3 (1996), 709.
[88] Joanne Bailey, *Unquiet Lives: Marriage and Marriage Breakdown in England, 1660–1800* (Cambridge, 2003), 58–59.
[89] Olaudah Equiano, *The Interesting Narrative and Other Writings* [1789] (London, 2003), 179.

the ship was docked at 'Union-stairs' on the south side of the Thames in Wandsworth. Despite being two years after the Somerset ruling and despite Equiano gaining habeas corpus on his behalf, and the help of Granville Sharp (1735–1813) and an attorney, Annis was forcibly transported to St Kitts, where Equiano reports he was tortured and died.[90] Rather than providing anonymity or economic opportunity, Equiano's rendering of this series of traumatic events acts as a powerful reminder that many were actively pursued in London (a reality further explored in Chapter 4).

Equiano's telling of the John Annis case is also important, however, in showing that London could offer networks of support. Equiano's narrative is after all a story of his attempts to *help* Annis. We must bear witness to these forms of support and their importance. Here we see very different forms of care at stake. For freedom seekers, London could provide communities of sustenance. Historians long ago revealed the significant population of free and enslaved Black men and women in eighteenth-century London. Crucially, the capital was also home to Black men and women who organised support for enslaved people who sought escape.[91] Such organisation was well-known and became remarked upon for its effectiveness. In his 1768 work, *Extracts from such of the Penal Laws*, Sir John Fielding (1721–1780) noted that,

> there are already a great Number of black Men and Women who have made themselves so troublesome and dangerous to the Families who brought them over as to get themselves discharged; these enter into Societies, and make it their Business to corrupt and dissatisfy the Mind of every fresh black Servant that comes to England.[92]

We can read against Fielding's attempts to mark Black men and women as 'troublesome and dangerous' to instead see evidence of how Black men and women connected with and supported newcomers to London. We glimpse the Black men and women who resisted and organised to ensure their freedom and that of others. Fielding's remarks on corruption and influence provide hints of what we might re-interpret as support and love. Similarly, evidence exists of social gatherings in taverns to enjoy music and dancing. Peter Fryer lists how a 'public-house in Fleet Street' hosted 'fashionable routs or clubs' for 'the Blacks or Negro servants'.[93] London then was an important context for

---

[90] Equiano, *The Interesting Narrative and Other Writings*, 180.
[91] Peter Fryer, *Staying Power: The History of Black People in Britain* (London, 1984); Greta Holbrook Gerzina, *Black London: Life before Emancipation* (New Brunswick, 1995), 23–24; Susan Dwyer Amussen, *Caribbean Exchanges: Slavery and the Transformation of English Society, 1640–1700* (Chapel Hill, NC, 2007), 220.
[92] Sir John Fielding, *Extracts from Such of the Penal Laws, as Particularly Relate to the Peace and Good Order of This Metropolis* (London, 1768), 144. See also Lorimer, 'Black Slaves and English Liberty', 127; Gerzina, *Black London: Life before Emancipation*, 24; Steedman, *History and Law*, 151–152.
[93] As cited in Fryer, *Staying Power*, 71.

people's attempts at running away, not in terms of the anonymity it offered but rather for the support it might accommodate. Such care helped enslaved people to reclaim and celebrate their personhood, challenging the very conceptions of property and possession we saw in Chapter 1 and will interrogate again in Chapter 6.

Over the eighteenth century, London was increasingly written as an urban space characterised by deception, crime and loss not only because objects were taken or fell out of possession but also because enslaved people, servants, apprentices and spouses regularly left. As runaway notices tell us, and as we will see in greater detail in Chapter 6, up until the 1770s, enslaved people were often unambiguously regarded as forms of property. That enslaved people ran away in urban spaces, and could stay away by accessing communities of support, undermined people's confidence in the security of property rights. At the same time, as we learned in Chapter 1, over the eighteenth century, the capacity to work was reformulated from a thing which could be exercised, to a thing which could be possessed and owned. As such, this form of possession and its ubiquity in the eighteenth century existed as an important part of wider conceptions of what it meant to own 'things'. Possessions existed within a capacious category in the eighteenth century. By re-engaging with such diversity and layering these everyday forms of loss on top of each other, we see the precarity of possession in this period. Noting these perceptions of precarity is important in beginning to understand the nature of possession as a relationship that needed enactment each day. If we turn our attention to another form of possession – dogs – we come to witness yet another layer in the collage that sees London as a space which made visible the precarious nature of possession.

Wandering Off

As we saw in Chapter 1, the eighteenth century changed the questions it asked about dogs. While in the early decades the law was largely focused on the question of who could own dogs, in the later decades, it came to grapple with the question of whether dogs could be owned at all. Similarly, we also see a shift from questions about what dogs were for, to concerns about what dogs were. The issue with dogs was that they could run off of their own accord or simply follow someone else. Their ability to act of their own volition made it difficult to know if they had been stolen and thus difficult for the law to protect them as property. As with people, the ability of dogs to act of their own volition created an important question in understanding possession and property. Nevertheless, it was not simply dogs and their volition which was problematic, but also the spaces into which dogs increasingly entered. The changing nature of urban spaces, and of London in particular, amplified questions about dogs and ownership.

People did not take their dogs for walks in eighteenth-century London. Or rather, they did not walk their dogs in particular ways in particular spaces.[94] They did not usually use leads or leashes and they did not purposefully exercise their dogs in parks, for example.[95] Even pet dogs would simply be let out to roam at will or would accompany their owners as they went about different tasks. Ideally, they answered to their names and would return quickly when called. (As we will see in Chapter 6, in lost notices owners made much of their dog's name and its ability to answer to it.) As the 1770 Dog Stealing Act informs us, dog theft was on the rise in eighteenth-century London and became an ever-growing problem in the nineteenth century. Yet, despite these threats, in fictional accounts of dogs being lost in London, it is often the city itself which momentarily entices the dog away, distracting them from their owner and quickly subsuming them within the bustle. In the anonymously authored 1816 work *Cato, or Interesting Adventures of a Dog of Sentiment*, the dog in question is overwhelmed by London. The dog, as narrator, described how 'London appeared such a noisy bustling place…the surprising number of people in some of the streets so confused me'.[96] Cato's owner Henry (it is increasingly possible to call him an owner by 1816) advised him to 'always keep close' as 'dogs, and even children, were often stole [sic], as well as lost, in the streets of London'. Henry promised he would buy Cato a collar to ensure his safe return should the worst take place, but the collar was too slow in coming and soon afterwards Cato is lost.[97] On a trip with Henry down Oxford Road, Cato thinks he sees his sister down a side street and forgetting 'my master's caution, away I ran, and soon convinced myself of my mistake'. On returning to Oxford Road, he cannot see Henry; he is lost and must fend for himself. As with other works within the 'it narrative' genre, *Cato* acts as a moral tale for children and underscores the need for obedience, empathy, kindness and carefulness. It also underlines the difficulty of dogs, that they could simply wander off. Dogs were as much beholden to the distractions of the city as anyone else. Similarly, as we will explore in greater details in Chapters 4 and 6, tracking dog stealing was difficult because in the hustle and

---

[94] Such practices began to emerge more fully in Edwardian London. However, anecdotal evidence suggests letting dogs out to wander the streets continued to be practised into the late twentieth century. See Philip Howell, 'Between the Muzzle and the Leash: Dog-Walking, Discipline and the Modern City', in Peter Atkins (ed.), *Animal Cities: Beastly Urban Histories* (Farnham, 2012), 222.

[95] Dog collars perhaps provide some contrary evidence though. Some extant dog collars from the eighteenth century do include rings to attach a lead to. However, these are largely dated to the Victorian period and later. See examples in the Leeds Castle Dog Collar Collection.

[96] Anon., *Cato, or Interesting Adventures of a Dog of Sentiment* (London, 1816), 67.

[97] Anon., *Cato*, 67.

bustle of the city, it was often hard to know who they might have followed or who might have enticed them away. Without a lead and faced with lots of people, it was difficult to keep track of a dog. As with objects and people, the city amplified the problem of uncertainty, of what exactly had happened. It also made precarious the relationship of possession.

Preventing Loss

While historians have shown that some individuals living in London in the early eighteenth century were largely unaware of crime and its threats, city guides demonstrate that by the later eighteenth century the connection between urban living and criminal threats to property and person had become an established trope.[98] Eighteenth-century London guides warned that pickpockets were a 'rabble of cheats' who had been 'trained to the base art' from their youth.[99] At the same time, the capital was understood as a space in which possessions might be lost through forgetfulness or distraction. Cities also inspired stories about runaway servants and the new opportunities urban spaces provided in terms of anonymity, alternative economic opportunities and communities of help and support. The rapidly increasing density of urban environments prompted questions about property and possession.

The fears over loss expressed in city guidebooks also demonstrate an underlying issue around the seeming lack of attention urban denizens paid to their possessions. Guidebooks understood such inattentiveness in terms of 'care'. As we saw previously, Ned Ward's 'Spy' mocked his visitor for the 'carelessness' he showed to his possessions and his self.[100] As cities grew, guides encouraged people to be more careful of themselves and their things in urban sites. Here we see new forms of 'care' coming into existence, which focused on the importance of maintaining possession. Evidence from diaries and the new technologies that emerged confirm that Londoners were quick to take up these practices. They took up new technologies which kept possessions secure while out and about. We do not know if threats increased in the city, but the use of such technologies suggests people perceived them to be present. Similarly, the take up implies that people were keen to ensure that they did not lose things through theft, or forgetfulness, or through the 'thing' running away. It also marks how people increasingly understood possession as an active relationship. While such care might be read as vigilance and virtue in the case of objects and even dogs, when such 'care' was applied to people it might be read in other ways: as surveillance, control and violence.

---

[98] For more on lack of awareness see Shoemaker, 'Worrying about Crime', 81. For more on establishment of this trope see O'Byrne, 'The Art of Walking in London', 97.
[99] *The Countryman's Guide to London*, 20.   [100] Ward, *The London-Spy Compleat*, 247.

Although there were instances in which tie pockets themselves fell off and were stolen, tie pockets offered women an important means of ensuring that possessions remained hidden on their person.[101] Women's tie pockets, which were tied round waists, kept beneath clothing, and accessed through openings in petticoats and dresses, were particularly innovative in the eighteenth century. Some surviving pockets show that they might include extra interior compartments or other containers to order and protect the variety of objects inside.[102] They could contain a panoply of things: snuffboxes, toothpick cases, seals, combs, pocketbooks, purses, money and smelling bottles.[103] Some objects, however, infrequently appeared in women's tie pockets. Compared to men, fewer women possessed watches and records suggest those that did rarely kept them in their pockets.[104]

Men also developed means of keeping hold of their possessions on their person. Although pockets could sometimes fail to hold the panoply of possessions men increasingly took with them, they were as important to them as they were for women. However, men's pockets were quite different to the tie pockets used by women.[105] The centrality of pockets in men's lives is underscored by the pocketbook. These small envelope-style wallets, which were often made from leather and could be decorated with embroidery, were used to secure financial instruments such as bills and notes. As we will explore further in Chapter 5, extant pocketbooks in the collections of the Victoria and Albert Museum demonstrate how these items often bore the name of their owner and the date of their making.[106] Their materials and decoration bear testimony to their importance and the ways in which men identified with them. A pocketbook from 1774 contains a piece of paper noting the provenance of the object. The pocketbook was original a gift from 'Uncle Winchilsee' to his nephew Captain Charles Fielding. On Charles's death in 1783, the pocketbook was then bequeathed to Charles's daughter Augusta Sophie Fielding 'to keep

---

[101] Barbara Burman and Ariane Fennetaux, *The Pocket: A Hidden History of Women's Lives, 1660–1900* (New Haven, CT and London, 2019), 12.

[102] Burman and Fennetaux, *The Pocket*, 116 and 121.   [103] Ibid., 111.

[104] Ibid., 125; John Styles, *The Dress of the People: Everyday Fashion in Eighteenth-Century England* (New Haven, CT and London, 2007), 101; Moira Donald, 'The Greatest Necessity of Every Rank of Men: Gender, Clocks and Watches', in Moira Donald and Linda Hurcombe (eds), *Gender and Material Culture in Historical Perspective* (Basingstoke, 2000), 55. For early nineteenth-century evidence, see Lemire, *The Business of Everyday Life*, 37. Nevertheless, there are some 'lost' notices that explicitly note that the watch has been taken from a 'Gentlewoman's Side'. See 'Lost from a Gentlewoman's Side', *Daily Courant* (London), 19 December 1720.

[105] Barbara Burman, 'Pocketing the Difference: Gender and Pockets in Nineteenth-Century Britain', *Gender & History*, 14:3 (2002), 453–454.

[106] See for example Pocketbook, Inscription 'Iam.s McEvoy, Piccadilly, LONDON 1768', Embroidered Moroccan Leather, 1768, T.56-1940. Victoria and Albert Museum; Pocketbook, Inscription 'HENRY DAVIS/NP. 25 Wiegate[?] Street/LONDON' 'TETUAN/ 1996', Embroidered red Morocco leather, 1776, T.108-1953. Victoria and Albert Museum.

for his Sake'.[107] The note, recording the history of the object, bears witness to its value not only as a keeper of things but also as a thing in its own right, worthy of securing.[108] It is perhaps unsurprising then that Richard King advised men of the best ways to keep their pocketbooks safe. He suggested that pocketbooks were 'only secure in the inside pockets' of their coat and that their coat should be 'buttoned'.[109]

Rather than in their coats, men stored and concealed their watches in the fob pockets of their breeches, often with the chain, seals and key hanging down and on show.[110] Such practices were so commonplace in the eighteenth century that it was noteworthy when watches were stored elsewhere upon their person. In September 1790, Henry Hare Townsend (1765?–1827) appeared at the Old Bailey to testify as to the events that led to his watch, money, seals and key being stolen at the races at Enfield Marsh on 1 September that year. The court asked Townsend whether he had missed his watch from his fob pocket and Townsend replied that it was in his waistcoat pocket. The court followed up, wanting to know whether the watch and appendages were all in his waistcoat pocket, Townsend replied 'Yes, the chain and all was put in.' The court pushed further and wanted to know why it was there. Townsend admitted that the reason for the shift to his waistcoat pocket was 'a new pair of leather breeches', which he was afraid the seals would make dirty. The case of Townsend's lost watch is also illuminating in that it shows how people also sought to take care of their possessions through regular sensory interaction with them. When asked about when the watch went missing, Townsend explained that he had 'felt' his watch in his pocket when he got to the races and that it was 'a quarter of an hour' before he missed it.[111] Townsend's testimony suggests that he regularly reached for his watch, checking it was there and that the experience of losing was particularly noted as a sensory experience. Lessening visibility and keeping possessions close to the body and in regular sensory contact were important means of increasing security. Failure to implement such measures appeared foolish.

Men's pockets, and the security measures connected to them, changed over the eighteenth century. The 1780 publication, *New Cheats of London Exposed*, advised men that they should run their watch chains 'through a small loop

---

[107] Pocketbook, Inscription '1774. TUNISLE.5.AVRIL', Embroidered velvet, 1774, Tunisia, T.51-1927. Victoria and Albert Museum.
[108] The note lists the item as a lettercase rather than a pocketbook, both objects were used to carry financial instruments, papers and correspondence. For more on lettercases see Pauline Rushton, 'Two Men's Leather Letter Cases: Mercantile Pride and Hierarchies of Display', in Chloe Wigston Smith and Beth Fowkes Tobin (eds), *Small Things in the Eighteenth Century: The Political and Personal Value of the Miniature* (Cambridge, 2022), 172–186.
[109] King, *New Cheats of London Exposed*, 63.   [110] Styles, *The Dress of the People*, 103.
[111] OBPO (www.oldbaileyonline.org, version 8.0, 12 July 2019), September 1790, trial of George Barrington (t17900915-10).

contrived for the purpose of securing the watch in the fob, of which I have seen many'.[112] In the early nineteenth century, men continued to use chains and ties to secure their watch to their person. In Francis Edward Paget's 1844 work *Tales of the Village Children*, Frederick Sutton used a 'black silk watch-guard [a silk string], which, being passed about his neck, and through a button-hole of his waistcoat, appeared to be attached to a watch in the waistcoat pocket'.[113]

Diaries also reveal how urban denizens were aware of loss and losing and mitigated against such threats, particularly for objects worn on or near to the body, such as watches. In 1761, a clergyman recalled how when travelling to Paddington his companions felt that their 'Money & watches began to tremble in their places'.[114] On 12 December 1767, diarist Sylas Neville (1741–1840) noted how he had taken steps to protect his watch case. He had bought a new outer case for this watch to 'preserve the original one' that bore the arms of his uncle, 'if I should by any accident lose the watch'.[115] Similarly, on 2 October 1786, the diarist Sophie von la Roche (1730–1807) recounted how one of her friends took the further precaution of leaving his entire watch at home, a step he was glad of when he encountered a crowd one day. As von la Roche told it, a 'big fire' had broken out in one of the streets, which 'burned nine houses down'. One of her friends went off to look at the blaze but found himself 'surrounded and buffeted by a number of people'. He had not followed Trussler's advice to 'Never stop in a crowd in the streets: if you do, it is two to one but you either lose your watch or your pocket-handkerchief'.[116] Just as Trussler would have predicted, when von la Roche's friend 'got free he made the discovery that his purse, containing three guineas, had stayed behind with the mob'. He was disappointed with himself for taking the money with him in his pocket, 'as he had taken precautions to leave his gold watch at home'.[117] In traversing the streets of London, people understood that their watch case or watch was vulnerable and utilised a range of strategies to prevent such loss.

---

[112] King, *New Cheats of London Exposed*, 63.
[113] Francis Edward Paget, *Tales of the Village Children* (1844), 121. Silk watch-guards also appear in two other anonymous works: *Tales of Chivalry; or, Perils by Flood and Field* (1840) and *The Olio, Or, Museum of Entertainment* (1832). Silk watch-guards are also mentioned in three Old Bailey cases in 1824, 1830 and 1863. See *OBPO* (www.oldbaileyonline.org, version 8.0, 31 July 2019), July 1824, trial of William Ramsden Robinson (t18240715-141); *OBPO* (www.oldbaileyonline.org, version 8.0, 23 December 2019), January 1830, trial of William Adams William Mealing (t18300114-5); *OBPO* (www.oldbaileyonline.org, version 8.0, 23 December 2019), January 1863, trial of Thomas Paul (20) Joseph Fookes (17) (t18630105-202).
[114] British Library, BL Add MSS 27951, 'Diary of an Anonymous Clergyman August–October 1761 and August to September 1772', 70.
[115] Basil Cozens-Hardy (ed.), *The Diary of Sylas Neville 1767–1788* (London, 1950), 28.
[116] Trussler, *London Adviser and Guide*, 147.
[117] Sophie von la Roche, *Sophie in London 1786*, trans. Clare Williams (London, 1933), 264.

Alongside small items kept on or near your person such as watches and pocketbooks, preventing the loss of other 'possessions' – such as dogs – also prompted the creation of new forms of security. Leads and leashes did not become commonplace in London until the later nineteenth century.[118] In the eighteenth century, the main means of preventing the loss of your dog was through using a collar. Collars signalled to others that the dog had an 'owner' and was not a stray. As noted previously, the fictional character Henry optimistically assumed that putting a collar on Cato in London would ensure that if he went missing someone would bring him 'home'.[119] Collars acted as a form of technology that visibly marked ownership as the dog moved around the urban space. In fact, the inscriptions on collars referred to their ability to mark ownership. A brass collar dated to the eighteenth century included the inscription 'Stop me not but let me jog for i [sic] am S. Oliver's Dog, Bicknell'.[120] Another collar inscription quipped: 'I am Mr. Pratt's Dog, King St. Nr. Wokingham, Berks. "Whose Dog are You?"'.[121] That collars marked ownership was also understood by authorities in the capital. In responding to a panic over rabid dogs in 1760, London authorities mandated the killing of 'street dogs' and asked owners to publicise their ownership by ensuring their dog was wearing a collar.[122] Collars also provided some means of controlling dogs and preventing them from being lost in the first place: they were a form of security.

It is strange that amid all these concerns over loss and control people did not start using leads and leashes earlier. None of the notices in the sample note that the dog was wearing a lead or a leash, suggesting they were not 'attached' to someone at the point of loss. It was the collar, rather than the lead, that became important. Around a third of lost notices for dogs placed in eighteenth and early nineteenth century newspapers noted that the dog was wearing a collar, strap, ribbon or cord of some kind around their neck. Collars came in different shapes and sizes. They ranged from 'a Red Ribbon round her Neck' to 'a large Leather Collar, with an Iron Ring', and from 'a black Collar with three Brass Bells', to 'a Piece of Cord about her neck', 'a Strap Collar', 'a steel chain collar' and 'a Brass Collar lined with red Cloth'.[123] Extant collars in the Leeds Castle collection suggest that brass collars were particularly popular in this

---

[118] Howell, 'Between the Muzzle and the Leash', 234.   [119] *Cato*, 67.
[120] Leeds Castle, Dog Collar Collection, 'A small English Brass Dog Collar', 18th century, 56080.
[121] Leeds Castle, Dog Collar Collection, 'A large English Brass Collar', Late 18th century, 56086. This collar was not the last to include this quip. See Leeds Castle, Dog Collar Collection, 'An English Brass Dog Collar', Early 19th century, 56032.
[122] Ingrid Tague, *Animal Companions: Pets and Social Change in Eighteenth-Century Britain* (Philadelphia, PA, 2015), 40.
[123] See 'a Red Ribbon round her Neck', *Daily Courant* (London), 2 December 1720; 'a large Leather Collar, with an Iron Ring', *Daily Advertiser* (London), 1 December 1742; 'a black Collar with three Brass Bells', *Daily Advertiser* (London), 21 December 1742; 'a Piece of Cord about her neck', *Daily Advertiser* (London), 23 December 1752; 'a Brass Collar lined with red

period (or were more likely to be kept and collected than a ribbon or cord).[124] The popularity of brass collars might be due to the fact they could be inscribed. Of those lost notices which listed the dog as wearing some form of collar, 72 per cent also noted that the collar included an inscription with the owner's name and/or their address. These noted not the dog's name, but rather the owner's name and sometimes their residence. Extant collars from the period corroborate this practice of inscribing the owner's, rather than the dog's name.[125] When Sancho went missing in December 1752, we know he was wearing a collar. An advertisement placed in the *Daily Advertiser* on 5 December 1752 noted that he had on 'a Leather Collar with a Brass Plate, on which was the Owner's Name and Place of Abode'.[126] Many advertisements underlined the distinction between the dog's name and that of the owner's, which (unlike the dog's name) would be found on the collar. One noted that 'answers to the name of Rover, when lost he had a collar about his neck, having on it the name of Lord Byron', while another similarly remarked that 'answers to Cato; had a Strap round his Neck, with a Brass Plate, with a Gentleman's Name on it'.[127] Such a formulation was a common occurrence in eighteenth-century newspaper notices from the 1740s onwards. Although the law was ambiguous as to whether dogs were property, newspaper notices and extant collars suggest that British people were clear as to their status.

By looking across categories we see that people were also subjected to technologies of possession. Here we see further evidence of the violence British people enacted in enslaving people on British soil. We also see the potential violence of 'taking care'. Notices placed to seek the capture of freedom-seekers in Britain contain examples in which people are described as having escaped while wearing steel, iron, copper, and even silver, collars and chains.[128] Such practices are further evidenced by cases in the Old Bailey, which record how in 1716 an enslaved man named Richard was forced to wear a collar. We know of Richard because Anne Smith and Jane Evans were

---

Cloth', *Daily Advertiser* (London), 9 December 1752; 'a Strap Collar', *Daily Advertiser* (London), 5 December 1771; 'a steel chain collar, *The Times* (London), 23 December 1830.

[124] Within the collection, there are sixteen brass collars dated to the eighteenth century.

[125] See the twenty-one extant collars dated to eighteenth-century England in the collections of Leeds Castle, Kent.

[126] See 'Lost on Saturday Last Near Cheapside, a White Pointing Dog', *Daily Advertiser* (London), 5 December 1752.

[127] See 'Lost about Eight Days Ago, a Young Spaniel Dog', *Daily Advertiser* (London), 11 December 1742 and 'Lost from Great Russell Street, Bloomsbury, a Large, White Spanish Pointer', *Daily Advertiser* (London), 13 December 1782.

[128] Simon P. Newman, 'Freedom-Seeking Slaves in England and Scotland, 1700–1780', *English Historical Review*, 134:570 (2019), 1160. See also Catherine Molineux, *Faces of Perfect Ebony: Encountering Atlantic Slavery in Imperial Britain* (Cambridge and London, 2012), 11; Amussen, *Caribbean Exchanges*, 223.

accused of biting through the silver collar to steal it.[129] Using metal meant that collars and chains could be welded shut. These manacles were fitted by 'masters and mistresses' who actively sought to limit the actions of individuals they enslaved and ensure that they were marked as 'property' if they managed to get away. Similarly, in the British colony of Barbados, enslavers forced metal collars onto those they enslaved to show that they were 'allowed' to be in the capital Bridgetown, selling goods.[130] Anne Smith and Jane Evans understood this. When they met Richard, he told them he had been 'long on his Errand, and fear'd to go home'. Smith and Evans persuaded Richard that 'his Collar would betray him' and he allowed them to break it and remove it 'with their Teeth'. Implicit within this telling of what took place is the notion that Richard was scared to go home and was contemplating escape. By allowing Smith and Evans to remove the silver collar valued at 15 shillings, a mark of ownership was removed expanding the possibilities of his getting away. However, in stealing the collar Smith and Evans also took Richard's potential economic subsistence: he would not be able to pawn or sell the silver collar. Instead, the *Proceedings* tell us that Richard went home and 'told his Master of it'.[131] Through different layers of mediation (a report of Smith's telling of what Richard said) we hear the edges of Richard's experiences and fears, as well as what collars were understood to be and do to people.

Given that manacles were designed to restrict movement, the few 'runaway' notices that list people who had been forced into collars and chains are likely evidence of a much wider practice.[132] It is also important that, just as with collars attached to dogs, the manacles forced on enslaved people 'routinely named masters rather than the enslaved people wearing them'. The absence of the enslaved person's name (a name that was likely changed by the master or mistress) further marked their 'social death': no longer bearing a familial name (as we see with Richard), no longer a person, they instead were regarded as chattel property.[133] As Simon P. Newman argues, these manacles also marked how the servitude forced upon enslaved people was different to that experienced by white people. Chains and collars were used for convicts but 'were never imposed upon white apprentices and servants as emblems and instruments of ownership'.[134] Situating how people were forced to wear collars

---

[129] *OBPO* (www.oldbaileyonline.org, version 8.0, 15 December 2022), January 1716, trial of Anne Smith (t17160113-18).
[130] Marisa J. Fuentes, *Dispossessed Lives: Enslaved Women, Violence, and the Archive* (Philadelphia, PA, 2016), 28.
[131] *OBPO* (www.oldbaileyonline.org, version 8.0, 15 December 2022), January 1716, trial of Anne Smith (t17160113-18).
[132] Newman, 'Freedom-Seeking Slaves', 1161.
[133] Ibid., 1162. For the concept of social death see Orlando Patterson, *Slavery and Social Death: A Comparative Study* (Cambridge, MA, 1982).
[134] Newman, 'Freedom-Seeking Slaves', 1162.

bearing an enslaver's name alongside the practice of having dogs wear collars underlines the full violence at stake in this practice. In fact, contemporaries were aware of the barbarity of such equivalences. As the Rev. Dr Findlay noted in a letter to Granville Sharp on 14 August 1772, the points of similarity – in this case the name, the collar – were horrifically difficult to ignore. He was particularly affected by an advertisement in the *Gazetteer* on 1 June 1772, which advertised 'a Reward for taking an East Indian Black Boy of about 14 Years of Age "of the Name of Bob or Pompey" who is further distinguished in the Advertisement as "having a Brass Collar" round his Neck'. Findlay asserted that "the Black Indian Pompey was publickly [sic] treated with as little Ceremony as a Black Dog of the same Name would be".[135] Alongside restricting movement, causing pain and marking the person as 'property', forcing people to wear collars and chains, a practice also used on animals, was yet another means of dehumanising that person. Here we see the violence of taking 'care'.

Conclusion

As London grew over the long eighteenth century, it became increasingly incomprehensible. Alongside their own experiences of standing in the street and observing the multitudes flow by or taking time to look down from the height of St. Paul's, people also looked to texts as a technology that offered a vantage point. Given the increasing diversity of experiences in the metropolis, texts such as guides, proved particularly important in producing a collective notion of what the capital might be. One of the ways in which they wrote the city was through depictions of deception and the impacts this had on property rights. London guides focused on the precarity of possession in urban spaces and as such the capital came to be understood as series of spaces in which possessions were under threat from the deceptions and tricks of criminals, but also from the distractions that caused inattention. Possessions could be lost at any moment and the hustle and bustle of urban life made it difficult to always know how and why the loss had taken place. Cities created this uncertainty. At the same time, London offered resources important in allowing servants, apprentices, spouses and enslaved people to run away, elope and abscond. The dense social worlds of cities provided opportunities for anonymity if an individual needed to lose themselves quickly. London's expansion also meant there were ready economic opportunities if needed: another form of employment could always be found, and such options provided ready means of negotiation. As a distinctly peopled space, London also offered community

---

[135] York Minster Archive, Granville Sharp Letterbook 1768–1773, 'Copy of Letter from Rev. Dr. Findlay 14 August 1772', COLL 1896/1, 93. Emphasis appears in manuscript source.

and support for those whose running required careful navigation: others could be found to help you on your way out to freedom. Stories and experiences of loss contributed to a perception that possession was a precarious relationship in the eighteenth century.

In the face of all these opportunities for losing and running, many 'owners' developed technologies of security to prevent loss. People felt concern and acted to keep hold of their 'things'. People kept their best watches at home, they attached collars to their dogs and in acts of brutality they also forced them on the people they owned. The increasingly elaborate nature of such technologies underscores the importance placed on keeping hold and maintaining possession in this period. Possession became understood as an active process. While people developed new technologies and strategies to keep hold of their possessions, these were not always effectual. As the next chapter will examine, individuals developed broader systems which allowed for reclamation when things got lost, or when people left. What we begin to see in this chapter extends in the next, namely that maintaining possession was important and deliberate. It required effort, time and money in the eighteenth century.

Part II

Seeking Return

3   Systems of Reclamation

On July 10, 1745, Thomas Piggott, Esq appeared at the Old Bailey to offer his version of the events that had taken place on the night of 23 May 1745, when he 'lost' his watch and 40 guineas.[1] Piggott described how he had spent that Thursday evening with 'some West India merchants at the King's Arms Tavern, in Lombard street'. At the end of the night, as 'no coach could be got', he walked home. As he passed Somerset House, he noticed two men behind him and one in front. He carried on but then mistakenly turned into Buckingham Street. Realising his error, he turned around to find three men waiting for him. In court, Piggott described how one of the defendants had grabbed him by the throat and put a pistol 'or something like it' to his temples, while another had threatened him with a sword and the other held a hanger over his head. They then ripped his breeches to remove his watch, took the 'silver and brass' from his pocket and got hold of his purse with some '40 odd guineas'. The assault was reported in the *Penny London Post* (24–27 May 1745) and *St James's Evening Post* (23–25 May 1745).[2] Both these reports used a different name 'John Piggott', but both noted that he had been 'seiz'd...by the Throat". In response to the assault, Piggott said he had called out to the watchmen who advised him to go home, change his clothes and then pursue his attackers.[3] Piggott decided against this course of action and instead went to see his watchmaker.

On losing his watch, Piggott's impulse was to return to the person he had purchased it from. Piggott 'acquainted Mr Bowley [sic], the watchmaker in Lombard Street with the robbery' and the pair decided to advertise the watch with a 'ten guineas reward'. They were clearly keen to offer a substantial reward, reflective of the watch's value. (In the later court case, the watch was

---

[1] *Old Bailey Proceedings Online* (hereafter '*OBPO*') (www.oldbaileyonline.org, version 8.0, 5 August 2019), July 1745, trial of William Kelly Thomas St. Legar Patrick Cave Sarah Cave (t17450710-27).
[2] *Penny London Post or The Morning Advertiser* (London) 24–27 May 1745; *St. James's Evening Post* (London) 23–25 May 1745.
[3] *OBPO* (www.oldbaileyonline.org, version 8.0, 5 August 2019), July 1745, trial of William Kelly Thomas St. Legar Patrick Cave Sarah Cave (t17450710-27).

valued at £20.)⁴ On 25 May 1745, the advertisement duly appeared in one of London's chief daily newspapers the *Daily Advertiser*:

> LOST on Thursday Night last, at the Corner of Villers-Street in the Strand, a Silver repeating Watch made by Bowly, no Number, a gilt Cap over the Movement, the Case pierced in Relievo, a Blank Space at Bottom in a black Shagreen Case, with Silver Bessel and Edges, and a green Silk String with two Seals set in Silver. Whoever brings the said Watch to D. Bowly, in Lombard-Street, shall receive Ten Guineas Reward, and no Questions ask'd; or if already pawn'd or sold, your Money again with Thanks. Note, No greater Reward will be given.⁵

Although Piggott later testified in court that his watch had been stolen from him under threat of violence and the incident was reported as such in two newspapers, Mr Bowly had advised him 'not to advertise it as stole, but as lost' in order that he 'might possibly have it again'.⁶

As we explored in Chapter 2, losing possessions was a distinct problem in eighteenth-century urban spaces. Concerns over loss were exacerbated in cities because it was not always clear what had happened. In the bustle of urban life, possessions might have been stolen, dropped, misplaced or could have left of their own volition. However, such uncertainties also meant it was possible for a victim to advertise a watch as 'lost', despite two newspapers reporting its violent theft. As Chapter 2 showed, owners responded to the threats of loss by finding further ways to 'take care' of their things, to keep hold. The pocket and the collar gained new importance in eighteenth-century Britain. Despite these technologies, as Thomas Piggott experienced, items still went missing. Yet, even when lost or stolen, eighteenth-century urban denizens found ways to 'take care' of their possessions. They did so by pursuing reclamation. Securing the *return* of lost or stolen possessions emerged as a new and important part of taking care of your things in eighteenth-century society and culture.

People understood that the judicial system would be of little help in securing the return of lost possessions. In the eighteenth century, it largely sought to protect property by severely punishing threats against it. With a focus on deterrent rather than detection, it was ill-equipped to facilitate the regular reclamation of stolen property. In the absence of such help, as this chapter explores, Londoners developed complex systems to seek reclamation. An early system was created by the Goldsmiths' Company in the sixteenth century. It involved the printing of 'lost' notices, and their distribution by Goldsmiths' Company beadles (messengers, or as they were known, 'warning carriers') to those involved in the luxury trades. Alongside the Goldsmiths' notices, people

---

⁴ Ibid. ⁵ 'LOST on Thursday Night last', *Daily Advertiser* (London), 25 May 1745.
⁶ *OBPO* (www.oldbaileyonline.org, version 8.0, 5 August 2019), July 1745, trial of William Kelly Thomas St. Legar Patrick Cave Sarah Cave (t17450710-27).

had handbills printed, distributed and pasted around the urban environment, providing another lever to pull on in cases of loss. From the late seventeenth century, urban denizens also utilised the growing numbers of newspapers and advertised their lost possessions. In the early eighteenth century, the newspaper lost notices system became particularly popular because it was further bolstered by the involvement of thief-takers, who established highly organised, large-scale systems for mediating between 'losers' and 'finders'. As thief-takers increasingly diversified their activities in the second quarter of the eighteenth century and stopped organising 'finding' at scale, the newspaper notices system changed again. In the middle and later decades of the eighteenth century, the number of newspaper notices expanded rapidly. This method of reclamation both relied on and forged the growth of newspaper culture, in this period. Through exploring the growth and importance of lost notices published in newspapers, we see how inevitable it was that Thomas Piggott failed to follow the advice of the watchmen and instead went to his watchmaker and published a 'lost' notice in a daily newspaper. He did everything he could to 'have it again'.

Warning Carrier Notices

The Goldsmiths' Company established an early means of reclaiming lost wares and valuables through the 'warning carrier' system. Formed by royal charter in the fourteenth century, the Goldsmiths' Company was tasked with testing and marking gold and silver and enforcing standards within the trade. With connections throughout the luxury trades, as early as the mid sixteenth century, it developed a system to warn goldsmiths, jewellers, watchmakers, bankers, refiners, toymen, salesmen and pawnbrokers of the circulation of stolen property.[7]

While in the sixteenth century, the warning system seems to have been principally designed to protect the Court and ensure the security of royal plate, by the mid seventeenth century, a wider variety of individuals used it. In 1652, the writer John Evelyn (1620–1706) paid for 500 notices to be printed and dispersed by the Company.[8] In contrast to handbills, which 'losers' also utilised to announce and reclaim lost things, and which were largely printed and pasted on visible surfaces around the urban landscape, Goldsmiths' Company beadles *distributed* notices across the city. As Judy Jowett has

---

[7] Judy Jowett, 'The Warning Carriers: How Messengers of The Goldsmiths' Company Warned the Luxury Trades of Criminal Activities in Eighteenth-Century London', *Silver Studies*, 18 (2005), 12. Jowett's extended publication builds on earlier work by Tessa Murdoch, see Tessa Murdoch, 'Second Generation Huguenot Craftsmen in London: From the "Warning Carriers" Walks', *Proceedings of the Huguenot Society of Great Britain and Ireland*, XXVI (1994–1997), 241–256.
[8] Jowett, 'The Warning Carriers', 12.

shown, a notebook dated 1744, includes details of the 'Warning Carriers Walks'. It reveals how warning carriers, such as Mr Holtom, Mr Weatherland and Mr Bulstrode, had walking routes of around five miles, each of which included areas in and around the City such as Smithfield, Holborn, Charing Cross, Westminster, Mayfair, Shadwell and Wapping.[9] Along these routes, they would drop a notice with each member of the luxury trades who had applied to be included. The warning notices operated on a two-tier system, in which distribution could include only goldsmiths or all trades.[10] Nevertheless, much remains uncertain about the administration of the system. It is unclear why certain businesses were included in the walks and others not, and it is not known how businesses applied to participate.[11] However, the purpose of such notices is clear. They alerted those in and connected to the luxury trades not to receive and sell stolen property and told them where the item should be returned to if they encountered it. The centrality of the goldsmiths within this system was due to their role as early bankers, their links to coinage and attributing marks through assaying, and thus their long-held position in determining and upholding value and ownership.

Despite evidence existing of the warning carrier system at work as early as the mid sixteenth century, the conventions of the notices prior to the eighteenth century are unclear. The Goldsmiths' Company archive contains a collection of sixty-nine unique warning notices. These notices only intermittently cover the period from August 1726 (Number 11489) to July 1731 (Number 11955).[12] Nevertheless, the extant notices are important in showing the eighteenth-century workings of the system.

The notice in Figure 3.1 includes details of where and when the item was lost (in this case on Wednesday 10 September, between the Royal Exchange and Lloyd's Coffee House in Lombard Street), what was lost (an oval brilliant), to whom it could be returned (Mr Richard Gines – a goldsmith) and for what reward (two guineas). As with most of the other extant notices, that featured in Figure 3.1 lists the item as 'LOST' and hopes that whoever 'has taken it up, will bring it'. While some items were noted as 'Dropt', 'Left' 'Stolen', 'Supposed to be left' and 'Lost or Mislaid', the majority (48 per cent) were simply 'Lost'.[13] By listing them as 'lost', the notices and warning carrier system suggested the thing had simply gone missing in some unknown way and thus justified pursuing return rather than prosecution. The types of items listed in these notices reflect the types of businesses on the warning carrier

---

[9] Ibid., 14. [10] Ibid., 18. [11] Ibid., 16.
[12] The Goldsmiths' Company Library & Archive, 'Copies of Warning Notices from a Private Collection', R13846.
[13] Thirty-three of the sixty-nine notices listed the item as simply 'lost'.

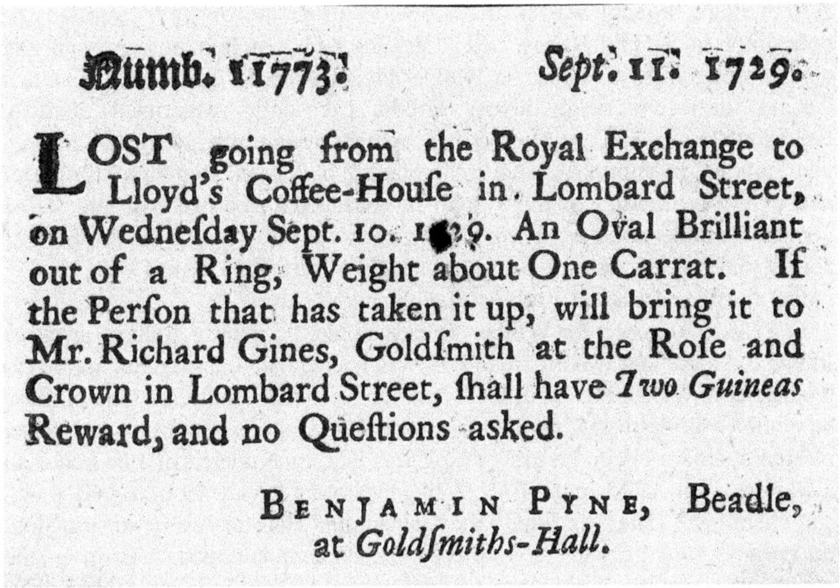

> **Numb. 17773.** **Sept. 11. 1729.**
>
> LOST going from the Royal Exchange to Lloyd's Coffee-Houſe in Lombard Street, on Wedneſday Sept. 10. 1729. An Oval Brilliant out of a Ring, Weight about One Carrat. If the Perſon that has taken it up, will bring it to Mr. Richard Gines, Goldſmith at the Roſe and Crown in Lombard Street, ſhall have *Two Guineas* Reward, and no Queſtions asked.
>
> BENJAMIN PYNE, Beadle, at *Goldſmiths-Hall.*

Figure 3.1 Warning carrier notice, 11 September 1729, Historic Warning Notices box O.J.V.
© The Goldsmiths' Company Archives, photography by Richard Valencia.

rounds. Rings, diamonds, snuffboxes, watches, plate and notes are all present, calling out to readers.

Although originally created in response to the loss of plate in the sixteenth century, the extant notices from the 1720s and 1730s and the 1744 notebook demonstrate that the system continued to operate in the eighteenth century. Cases heard at the Old Bailey, also attest to the goldsmiths lengthy involvement. In 1735, Patrick Gaffney was accused of stealing two tankards from Mr Shirley, the keeper of the Hoop Tavern, and James Barthelemi, a goldsmith located in Charing Cross, was alleged to have received the tankards as stolen goods. During the case, Mr Shirley noted how he had advertised the loss of the tankards by utilising the Goldsmiths' warning carrier system. A 'Messenger to the Goldsmiths' Company', John Holton (possibly the 'Mr. Holtom' named in the 1744 notebook), also gave evidence at the trial that he had left one of the warning notices with Barthelemi, thus making it difficult for the goldsmith to claim he had no knowledge of them having gone missing from their owner.[14] The case shows that the purpose of the 'warning' notices and the warning

[14] *OBPO* (www.oldbaileyonline.org, version 8.0, 5 August 2019), September 1735, trial of Patrick Gaffney James Barthelemi (t17350911-14).

system more broadly was to mark ownership of the object.[15] Similarly, a prosecutor in an Old Bailey case, Leonard Lee, reported how he had had clothes stolen from his house on Wednesday, 12 March 1755. We see here that despite these not being luxury goods, Lee duly 'advertised them at Goldsmith's [sic] hall' and found that 'by distributing bills', they had ensured that 'all the pawnbrokers and such places' had been alerted within 'four hours'.[16] The rapidity of the system in getting out news of lost and stolen goods was understood as an important part of its veracity and we see here its ability (or its need, in response to newspaper advertising) to deal with a wider range of lost possessions in the mid eighteenth century.

In 1766, the prosecutor William Bready noted that after a night of drinking 'rather too hard' and waking to find his watch and chain missing, he 'applied to the beadle of Goldsmiths [sic] Hall, and delivered out handbills'. One of those handbills was delivered to the goldsmith Mr Smith in Holborn and when offered a similar chain, he grew suspicious and remembered that he had 'had a warning from Goldsmiths [sic] Hall' 'and found it was about a gold watch and chain lost'. After sending to the Goldsmiths' Hall for further information, he became sure he had been offered the chain mentioned.[17] Even in the nineteenth century, newspaper notices included mentions of Goldsmiths' Hall. A notice placed in *The Times* on 29 August 1820 for a 'lost' pocket-book and some bills noted that 'Fifty pounds' would 'be paid to whoever will bring them to Goldsmiths [sic] hall, Foster lane'.[18] As we will see in Chapter 6, the reward offered here is unusually high, perhaps indicating that the bills were for large sums or that the pocket-book was particularly valuable. It also underscores how determined the owner was to get these things back.

In the early modern period and well beyond, the Goldsmiths' Company was recognised as playing an important role in communicating instances of loss and theft. However, the warning carrier system was not the only institutional response to 'lost' possessions. Just as the Goldsmiths' Company developed a system designed (initially at least) to deal with plate produced by its members and subsequently lost, so the Bank of England developed its own system for dealing with Bank of England notes that went missing from their owners. Bank of England notes held a promise to pay a denominated amount to the bearer of the note. As such, the Bank was required to pay that amount, even if the note

---

[15] Without the notice itself, we do not know if the item was listed as 'lost', therefore it is not possible to be more specific here, but it does reveal how the system in general was perceived to warn members of the luxury trades of stolen goods.
[16] *OBPO* (www.oldbaileyonline.org, version 8.0, 12 May 2020), April 1755, trial of Francis Pryer John West Edward Wright Winifred Farrel (t17550409-25).
[17] *OBPO* (www.oldbaileyonline.org, version 8.0, 12 May 2020), February 1766, trial of Susanna M'kenzie Edward Tricket (t17660219-20).
[18] 'Fifty Pounds Reward – Lost', *The Times* (London), 29 August 1820.

itself was lost.[19] Ensuring that the promise was met was an important means of building trust in the fledgling bank notes system. Over the eighteenth century, the Bank of England developed an increasingly sophisticated system for dealing with lost notes.

Founded in 1694, in its early years, the Bank of England vouched to reimburse lost notes if the loser provided 'good security'. By 1696, however, the Bank was clearly inundated and issued notices encouraging 'all persons concerned…to take greater care of their Bank notes'.[20] The Bank also stipulated that alongside 'good security', certain details needed to be supplied to it when seeking reimbursement for lost notes, such as the name and abode of the loser, and the sum, serial number and date of the note.[21] The Bank sought to sift out bogus claims by increasing the means of validating ownership. At this point, it also established the need for a delay between the initial claim and reimbursement, initially six months but soon after twelve months, to give time for the lost note to potentially turn up.[22] In 1697, it also offered to stop notes to prevent double payment. It did so by maintaining a list of paid notes under indemnity, which cashiers could check (particularly for notes over twelve months old). In the eighteenth century, the Bank introduced further requirements, such as a refundable deposit and then a non-refundable fee to encourage people to let the Bank know if someone returned the note.[23] From 1721 onwards, it also became more stringent in requiring an affidavit which proved ownership and details as to the means of loss.[24] Such details were recorded into Lost Books, which remain extant in the Bank of England archives.[25] As Hiroki Shin has noted, the Lost Books record bank notes as being lost through a range of situations, including being mislaid, stolen or simply slipping out of pockets. Notes could also be lost if they were paid to the wrong person or if an employee or spouse ran away with them. They might also be burnt, washed to pieces or eaten by vermin.[26] Going to the Bank of England and recording such information about a lost note meant that if anyone attempted to redeem the note for coin of the same value, it would be flagged. The system thus provided some security by creating a way in which the note, or simply its value, could be returned to the owner.

Alongside more specialised systems, broader practices covering a range of possessions also developed. As we will explore later in the chapter, handbills,

---

[19] Hiroki Shin, *The Age of Paper: The Bank Note, Communal Currency and British Society, 1790s–1830s* (Cambridge, 2024), 80.

[20] As cited in Wilfred M. Acres, *The Bank of England from Within, 1694–1900*, Vol. 2 (Oxford, 1931), 606. Many thanks to Hiroki Shin for this reference.

[21] Acres, *The Bank of England*, 606; Shin, *The Age of Paper*, 80.

[22] Acres, *The Bank of England*, 605–606.   [23] Ibid. 607.   [24] Ibid., 608.

[25] The extant Lost Books series begins on 13 August 1706 and ends on 31 October 1947. See Bank of England Archive, Cashier's Department: Record of Bank Note Issue: Lost Books, C101.

[26] Shin, *The Age of Paper*, 80.

pasted to surfaces around the city, or handed out with hopeful purpose, were important in the seventeenth century and remained so in the eighteenth and nineteenth. However, in this period, a new form of technology emerged, which proved increasingly important to the ever-present problem of lost possessions and people: the newspaper.

Newspaper Notices

The *London Gazette* (1666–1792) is often understood as the first English newspaper and as a 'governmental bulletin'. Its layout as a news*paper* was highly influential on future publications.[27] Its influence is perhaps explained by its success: circulation figures for the paper were impressive. Natasha Glaisyer has found that, if circulation is calculated as sales plus giveaways, across the period between 1695 and 1697, the *London Gazette's* circulation peaked at 19,062, dropped to 9,900 and averaged 13,846 per edition. Such figures meant that it outstripped any other newspaper or periodical. They even look impressive in comparison to the best-selling books of the period.[28] After the lapsing of the Licensing of the Press Act in 1695, newspaper culture expanded further, particularly in London. Alongside weekly and tri-weekly newspapers, the capital was the first to develop daily newspapers. London's first daily newspaper, the *Daily Courant*, which became a key player in lost notices, is estimated to have sold around 1,000 copies per day in the early eighteenth century.[29] With its 'tacit connections' to government, the *Daily Courant* had no direct competitors in the 1700s and 1710s.[30]

While in issue 62 (14–18 June 1666), the *London Gazette* sought to notify readers 'once for all, that we will not charge the Gazette with Advertisements, unless they be [a] matter of state', the paper clearly admitted defeat and slowly began to contain advertising, including notices for lost items and runaways.[31] Advertisements in the *Gazette* were expensive. They cost 10s per notice and by the mid-1690s, the paper carried an average of sixteen per issue for books, lotteries, auctions and lost and stolen items.[32] Following the *London Gazette*, over the eighteenth- and nineteenth-century London newspapers, especially

---

[27] Carolyn Nelson and Matthew Secombe, 'The Creation of the Periodical Press, 1620–1695', in John Barnard, D. F. McKenzie and Maureen Bell (eds), *The Cambridge History of the Book in Britain Volume 4: 1557–1695* (Cambridge, 2008), 545.
[28] Natasha Glaisyer, '"The Most Universal Intelligencers": The Circulation of the *London Gazette* in the 1690s', *Media History*, 23:2 (2017), 259.
[29] Hannah Barker, *Newspapers, Politics and English Society 1695-1855* (Harlow, 2000), 31; Michael Harris, 'London Newspapers', in Michael F. Suarez and Michael L. Turner (eds), *The Cambridge History of the Book in Britain* (Cambridge, 2010), 419.
[30] Harris, 'London Newspapers', 420.
[31] *London Gazette* (London), 14–18 June 1666. See also Jason McElligott, 'Advertising and Selling in Cromwellian Newsbooks' in Shanti Graheli (ed.), *Buying and Selling: The Business of Books in Early Modern Europe* (Leiden, 2019), 471.
[32] Glaisyer, '"The Most Universal Intelligencers"', 266.

Systems of Reclamation 97

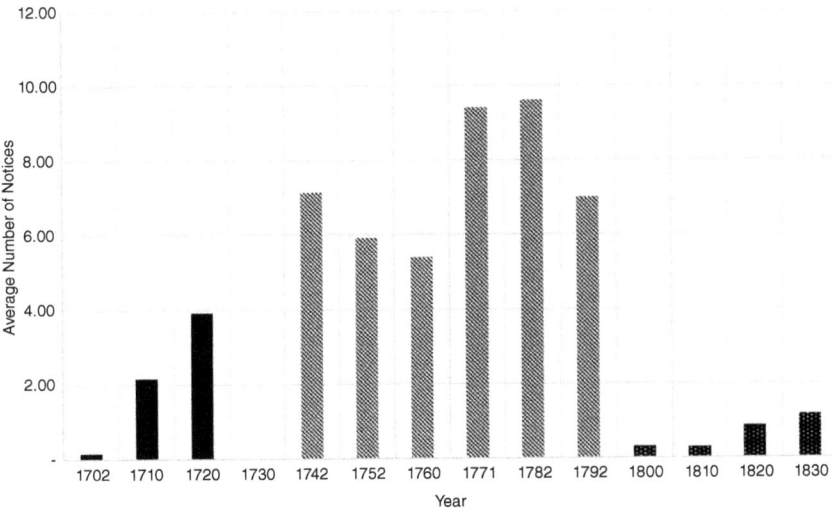

Figure 3.2 Bar chart showing average number of 'lost', 'dropt', and 'misplac'd' notices that appeared in the December issues of the *Daily Courant* (1702, 1710, 1720, 1730), the *Daily Advertiser* (1742, 1752, 1760, 1771, 1782, 1792) and *The Times* (1800, 1810, 1820, 1830). The different publications are represented through different patterns on the bars.[33]

daily newspapers such as the *Daily Courant*, *Daily Advertiser* and *The Times* regularly included 'lost' notices advertising snuff boxes, spaniels and lottery tickets as 'lost', 'misplaced', 'dropt' and 'found'. A survey of these three daily London newspapers at ten-yearly intervals over the period from 1700 to 1830 shows that lost notices became a regular and consistent feature (see Figures 3.2 and 3.3). Although London pioneered these forms of newspaper advertisement, the innovation soon took hold in other sites. Examples found in Leeds and Yorkshire newspapers in the eighteenth century demonstrate their wider prevalence.[34] Further afield, in its debut issue in 1704, the *Boston News-Letter* (1704–1726) offered reasonable rates for individuals wanting to print notices regarding sales, lets, runaway servants and lost and stolen goods.[35] Similarly,

---

[33] The analysis focuses on notices found in the December issues of the *Daily Courant* (1702–1735), *Daily Advertiser* (1731–1796), and *The Times* (1785–present), in the years 1702, 1710, 1720, 1730, 1742, 1752, 1760, 1771, 1782, 1792, 1800, 1810, 1820, 1830. To include the full range of forms that made up such notices, this sample was constructed by going through each issue rather than using key word searching. Sample includes notices published more than once.

[34] John Styles, 'Print and Policing: Crime Advertising in Eighteenth-Century Provincial England', in Douglas Hay and Francis Snyder (eds), *Policing and Prosecution in Britain, 1750–1850* (Oxford, 1989), 61.

[35] Simon Middleton, 'Runaways, Rewards, and the Social History of Money', *Early American Studies: An Interdisciplinary Journal*, 15:3 (2017), 633.

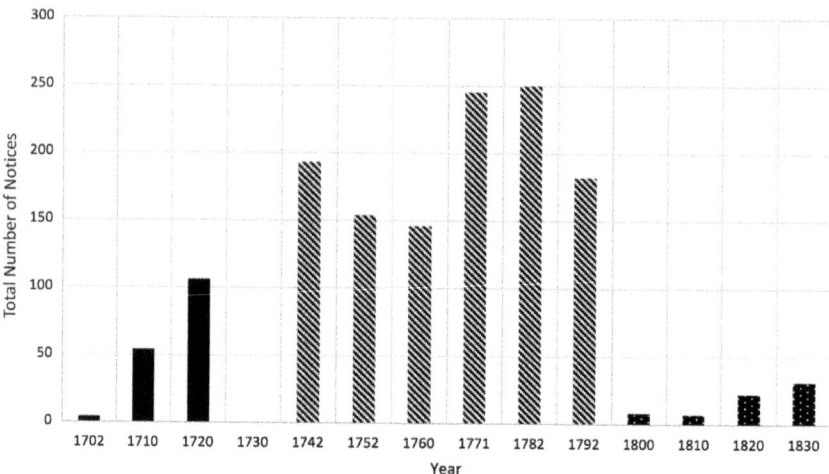

Figure 3.3 Bar chart showing total number of 'lost', 'dropt', and 'misplac'd' notices that appeared in the December issues of the *Daily Courant* (1702, 1710, 1720, 1730), the *Daily Advertiser* (1742, 1752, 1760, 1771, 1782, 1792) and *The Times* (1800, 1810, 1820, 1830). The different publications are represented through different patterns on the bars.[36]

The India Gazette; or, Calcutta Public Advertiser (1780–1790?) also featured lost and found notices. In British imperial cities of the eighteenth century, such as Boston, Calcutta and London, as in those in the British provinces, reclaiming 'lost' property was increasingly facilitated by the growth of the press.[37]

The first notice for a lost watch appeared in the 30 November–4 December 1671 issue of the *London Gazette*, and an advertisement from the 12–16 March 1674 issue is illustrative of how conventions slowly stabilised in the newspaper format.

Lost on Sunday the eighth of this instant March, about twelve a clock, between S. Pauls and S. Dunstans Church, a French Gold Watch enameld [sic] with Flowers, in a Case studded with Gold studs. Made by Solomon Chesnon at Blois, tyed [sic] with a Pink coloured Ribbon. Whoever shall bring the said Watch to Major Pinkneys Shop, at the three Squirrels over against the West end of S. Dunstans Church in Fleet street shall have forty shillings.[38]

---

[36] Sample includes notices published more than once.
[37] Historians have also looked at 'lost' notices in other countries, such as Sweden. See Karin Sennefelt, 'A Discerning Eye: Visual Culture and Social Distinction in Early Modern Stockholm', *Cultural and Social History*, 12:2 (2015), 175–195.
[38] 'Lost on Sunday the eighth of this instant March', *London Gazette* (London), 12–16 March 1674.

The notice lists where the item had been lost and when, what it was and who it could be returned to for what reward. Over the eighteenth and nineteenth centuries, lost notices appearing in publications, such as the *Daily Courant* (1702–1735), *Daily Advertiser* (1731–1796) and *The Times* (1785–present), largely followed this pattern. Significantly, these conventions also align with those found in the extant warning carrier notices of the 1720s and 1730s. Although it is not possible to trace which form influenced which, the warning carrier and newspaper notices demonstrate that multiple systems were at play to deal with lost or stolen property in the late-seventeenth and eighteenth centuries and that such systems were shaping and building on each other.

The emergence of daily newspapers as a key site for advertising was important. Perhaps most significantly, it allowed for the advertisement of a much broader range of lost 'things'. The notices included objects which had been advertised through the Goldsmiths' Company's warning carrier system, such as plate, watches, snuffboxes, jewellery and canes, but they also listed others. Lost notices in eighteenth-century daily newspapers included keys, spectacles, pictures, bag pipes, saddles, papers, anchors, trunks, wigs and bags. As London's material and commercial cultures expanded and an increasing number of people moved around urban streets, new systems of reclamation that operated beyond the luxury trades and encompassed a much broader range of objects were required and changes in print culture made them possible.

Newspapers also allowed the range of things advertised as lost to expand beyond the realm of objects. From the outset, the lost 'things' included in newspapers were diverse. In 1666, the *London Gazette* included a notice for George Howard, who was of 'a full stature, near six foot high, above 30 years old, fair Brown Hair, and a Perri-wig of that colour', and had run away.[39] In November of the same year 'a little Fallow-coloured Grey-Hound Bitch, her Ears crop'd round, belonging to the Lord General', was advertised as 'Lost'.[40] The following year a veritable menagerie appeared in the pages of the *London Gazette*. A 'Sore Ger-Falcon of his Majesties' was advertised as 'lost', as was 'a dark brown Gelding about 14 hand [sic] high, with a shorn Main [sic], and a fair star in his forehead'.[41] Alongside objects then, lost notices also featured animals such as horses, dogs, pigs and birds. At the same time, newspapers also increasingly included notices for servants, enslaved people, apprentices and soldiers who had 'eloped', 'absconded' and 'run away'. The move to

---

[39] 'An Advertisement. GEorge [sic] Howard of a full stature', *London Gazette* (London), 14–17 May 1666.
[40] 'LO*st* [sic] *upon Wednesday the Seventh of* November', *London Gazette* (London), 12 November 1666.
[41] See 'A Sore Ger-Falcon of His Majesties', *London Gazette* (London), 29 August–2 September 1667; '*Lost on Wednesday the 9th Instant*', *London Gazette* (London), 14–17 October 1667.

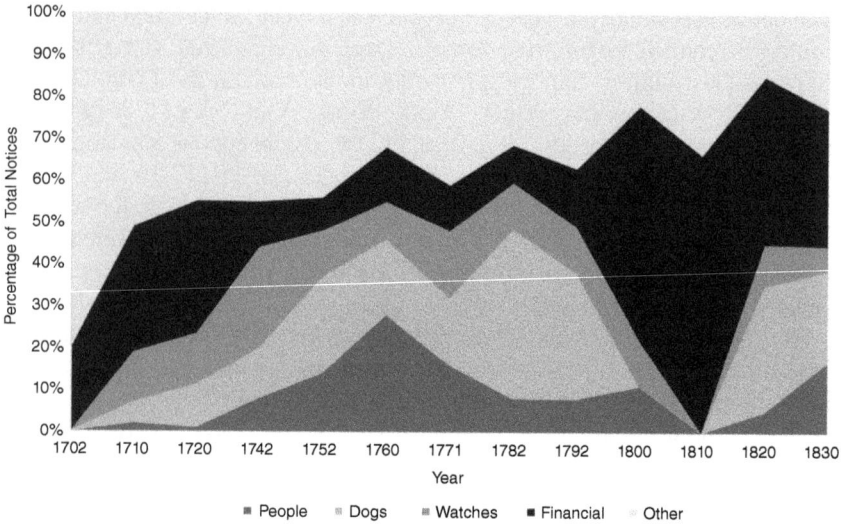

Figure 3.4 Chart showing percentage of different types of 'things' advertised in 'lost' notices which appeared in the December issues of the *Daily Courant* (1702, 1710, 1720), the *Daily Advertiser* (1742, 1752, 1760, 1771, 1782, 1792) and *The Times* (1800, 1810, 1820, 1830).[42]

newspapers marked an important shift in lost notices. They placed a wider diversity of 'things' in relationship to each other, marking them as possessions, or as subject to the relationship of possession.

An analysis of the notices published in a series of daily newspapers across the long eighteenth shows that the four primary 'things' featured in lost notices were dogs (22 per cent), money and financial instruments (14 per cent), people (13 per cent) and watches (13 per cent). The proportion of notices for different possessions changed over time (see Figure 3.4).[43] In the early eighteenth century, notices for watches and financial instruments appeared frequently. Across the century, dogs became an increasingly significant category of lost 'thing' but dipped in 1800 and 1810. By contrast, those notices for runaway people only filled a substantial proportion of the notices in the middle decades of the eighteenth century. While the extent to which these 'things' could be regarded as property was, as Chapter 1 has shown, ambiguous and

---

[42] Note that the data for 1730 has been removed from this chart as there were no notices in the *Daily Courant* that year. Sample excludes duplicate notices.

[43] The data is most robust for the samples taken from the *Daily Advertiser* (December issues in the years 1742, 1752, 1760, 1771, 1782, and 1792) when a much larger number of notices were published (see Figures 3.2 and 3.3).

ever-changing, their regular presence in the lost notices clearly marked them as items in need of reclamation: as possessions.

While the conventions for the text contained in these notices were important and will be explored in more depth in this chapter and Chapters 5 and 6, we must pause here to consider where they appeared on the printed page and what that position did. Skimming the first page of the 18 December 1742 issue of the *Daily Advertiser*, the reader would have been met with details of ships (or a lack of ships) at Deal in Kent, and mails arrived from Ireland and the news they contained. They might have read the notice announcing that Officers of the Sheriff of Middlesex were searching for an alleged thief Charles Williams or that 'on Monday next' the Theatre Royal was presenting 'a Comedy, call'd The Recruiting Officer'. They might then have turned the page. Scanning from left to right, they would have been quickly struck by the notices for lost things (see Figure 3.5). The notices were not an afterthought but rather they occupied a prime position on the second page. In following the structure offered by the columns, the reader would have seen first the notices for people who had 'runaway' or 'absconded', and then a mixture of lost notices for objects and animals. We know that people regularly read these notices. A 'servant Maid' described herself as reading them 'every Day' when necessary.[44] Some readers paid them the special attention of noting down what was included in them, as Sophie von la Roche did while in London in 1786.[45] These readers would not have been surprised by the order. They knew the format because this order was repeated across other newspapers before and after, including the *Daily Courant* (1702–1735), *Daily Advertiser* (1731–1796) and *The Times* (1785–present).

By placing these different lost 'things' next to each other on the printed page, newspapers suggested that they could and should be understood in relationship to each other. Printed handbills had placed notices for diverse lost and stolen items next to each other before. In sites, such as the Exchange, a notice for a servant wanting work and one for a lost 'Red-headed Monkey' could be pasted next to each other, creating a cacophony of voices and a range of relationships.[46] While the positioning of pasted handbills only suggested at relationships, however, in newspapers they were stabilised by the organisation of the advertisement section. Rather than a collage of pasted over notices, the

---

[44] The notice placed in the *Daily Advertiser* on 12 December 1760 read:

> A servant Maid found some Days past a Diamond Ring, between St James's and Charing Cross, and finding no Advertisement about it in the News-Papers (which she carefully reads every Day for that Purpose) she thinks it her Duty to advertise the Owner of it, that she will return it, on giving the just Tokens of it, and paying the Expence of this Advertisement. It is to be seen at Mr Stephen Vache's, Perfumer, next Door to Mr Lamb's in Pall Mall.

[45] Sophie von la Roche, *Sophie in London 1786* trans. Clare Williams (London, 1933), 100.
[46] As cited in Simon P. Newman, *Freedom Seekers: Escaping from Slavery in Restoration London* (London, 2022), 23.

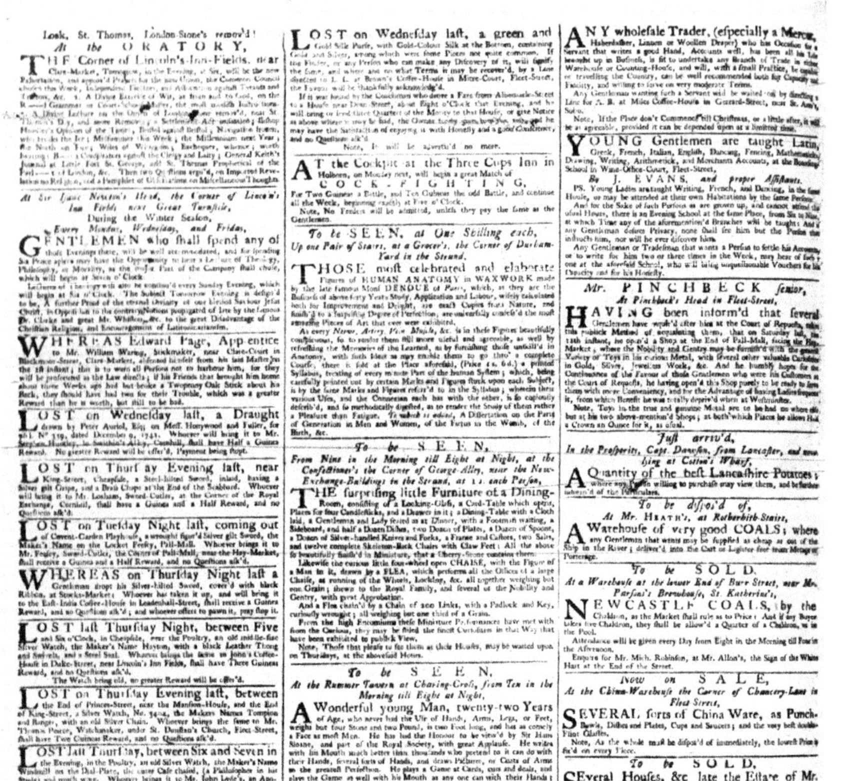

Look, St. Thomas, London-Stone's remov'd!
At the ORATORY,

LOST on Wednesday last, a green and

ANY wholesale Trader, (especially a Mercer,

YOUNG Gentlemen are taught Latin,

AT the Cockpit at the Three Cups Inn in Holborn

COCK-FIGHTING,

To be SEEN, at One Shilling each,

THOSE most celebrated and elaborate Figures of HUMAN ANATOMY in WAXWORK

GENTLEMEN who shall spend any of

WHEREAS Edward Page, Apprentice

LOST on Wednesday last, a Draught

LOST on Thursday Evening last, near

LOST on Tuesday Night last, coming out

WHEREAS on Thursday Night last a

LOST last Thursday Night, between Five

LOST on Thursday Evening last, between

LOST last Thursday, between Six and Seven in

LOST last Night, a Silver Watch, the

LOST Yesterday Se'nnight, (suppos'd) between

LOST on Thursday Evening last, from the

DROPT about Nine o'Clock Yesterday

LOST out of Albemarle-Street, a little black

STOPT Yesterday Se'nnight, at Mr. William

Mr. PINCHBECK senior,
At Pinchbeck's Head in Fleet-Street,

HAVING been inform'd that several

To be SEEN,

THE surprising little Furniture of a Dining-Room,

Just arriv'd,

A Quantity of the best Lancashire Potatoes;

To be dispos'd of,

A Warehouse of very good COALS;

To be SOLD,

NEWCASTLE COALS,

To be SEEN,

A Wonderful young Man, twenty-two Years of Age,

Now on SALE,

SEVERAL sorts of China Ware, as Punch-Bowls,

This is to give Notice,

THAT the Atherstone and Tamworth Waggon,

To be SOLD,

SEveral Houses, &c late the Estate of Mr.

To be SOLD,

THREE Leasehold Messuages, situate facing

On Monday next will set out from the King's Arms on Holborn-Bridge,

THE New Travelling Sedan, which runs

To be LETT,

THE Cross-Keys Inn in St. John's Street,

To be LETT,

A House and Shop, lately occupied by an Apothecary

ANY Gentleman, &c, that is desirous of

To be Lett, either entire or separate,

A House and Stables, with eight Coach-Houses,

Just imported,

A Parcel of Turky Carpets, some very large.

To be LETT,

A Very convenient House, two Rooms on a Floor,

Figure 3.5 Second page of *Daily Advertiser* (London), 18 December 1742, Mic. A. 5002-5058.
Image source: The British Library Collection.

layout of newspapers instituted an order over time. To advertise an apprentice absconding next to a lost bill of exchange contributed to the idea that these different things could both be understood as lost possessions. These newspaper notices all highlighted how things were gone, or rather that they were no longer accessible to someone with authority over them: their 'possessor'. As such, newspaper pages asserted again and again, in issue after issue, that each of these seemingly different 'things' existed in relationship *to* a possessor, and that therefore they were defined by or at least subject to this relationship. The positioning of newspaper notices did significant cultural and social work in perpetuating understandings that these different 'things' were all defined by the relationship of possession.

If we look more closely at the ordering of the notices within the section, we see that it suggests that there were differences in the relationships of possession. Remember that notices for people, both free and enslaved, who had absconded, eloped or runaway always came *before* a mixture of notices for lost objects and animals. The order of the notices implies that the relationships of possession governing connections between people were understood as distinct from those shaping associations with objects or animals. Such a distinction is noteworthy because, as we explored in the introduction to this book, the category of humanity and of the human was not inevitable or stable within eighteenth-century British culture: the distinction between humans, animals and objects was not set in place. However, while notices advertising servants, enslaved people, apprentices, soldiers and spouses who had 'eloped', 'absconded', 'deserted' or 'run' came before those advertising animals and objects as 'lost', their being placed together in the same section is telling. Here were people, animals and objects that could all be readily understood as 'things' in this period. Such conceptions were particularly stark for enslaved people who, as we will see in Chapter 6, were readily referred to as 'property' in these notices. Appearing in these pages, these notices further marked them as possessions. These notices did important cultural and social work in highlighting what possessions were and what and who was bound by the relationship of possession across the eighteenth century.

Lost Not Stolen

Lost notices featuring objects and animals were largely consistent in their form. They listed where the item had been lost and when, what it was and who it could be returned to for what reward. Throughout the long eighteenth century, notices listing possessions as 'lost' significantly outstripped those listing possessions as 'stolen'. If we look at Figure 3.2, we see that lost notices placed for objects and animals rose to an average of almost ten per issue in the second half of the eighteenth century. Similarly, Figure 3.3 shows that the

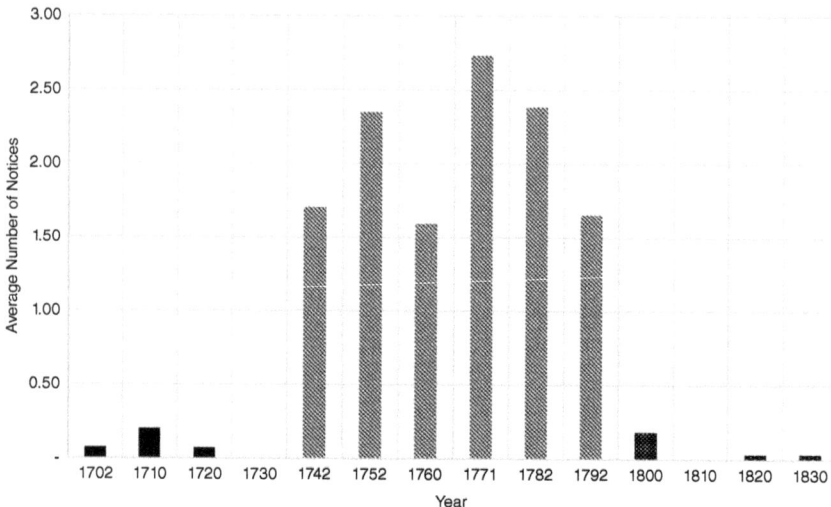

Figure 3.6 Bar chart showing average number of stolen notices that appeared in the December issues of the *Daily Courant* (1702, 1710, 1720, 1730), the *Daily Advertiser* (1742, 1752, 1760, 1771, 1782, 1792) and *The Times* (1800, 1810, 1820, 1830). The different publications are represented through different patterns on the bars.[47]

absolute number of lost notices peaked in 1782, with a total of 250 lost notices being published in the December issues of the *Daily Advertiser*. Significantly, with the publication of the *Daily Advertiser* from 1731 onwards we see a substantial and sustained rise in the number of lost notices included in newspapers. Such a shift stops when the *Daily Advertiser* ceases publication and our focus shifts to *The Times* in the final decade of the eighteenth century. If we compare figures for lost notices to those for stolen notices the differential becomes clear. The average number of stolen notices that were published in any issue within the sample was never above three (see Figure 3.6). Similarly, the stolen notices peaked in 1771 with a total of only seventy-one stolen notices being published in the December issues of the *Daily Advertiser* (see Figure 3.7). The use of the word 'lost' rather than 'stolen' was important. Lost notices were distinct from stolen notices: they did a particular job.

Over the long eighteenth century, victims of crime were legally obliged to pursue prosecution.[48] While the monetary rewards offered by the judicial

---

[47] Sample includes notices published more than once.
[48] J. M. Beattie, *Policing and Punishment in London, 1660-1750: Urban Crime and the Limits of Terror* (Oxford, 2001), 85.

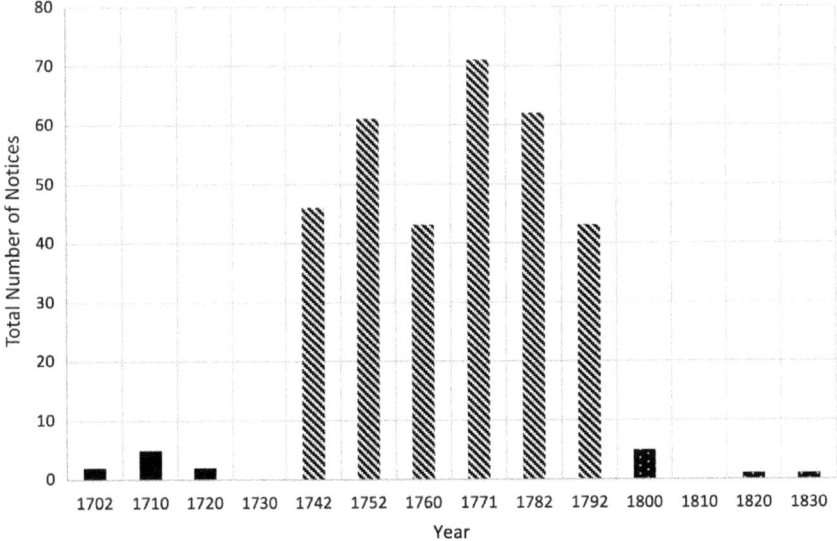

Figure 3.7 Bar chart showing total number of stolen notices that appeared in the December issues of the *Daily Courant* (1702, 1710, 1720, 1730), the *Daily Advertiser* (1742, 1752, 1760, 1771, 1782, 1792) and *The Times* (1800, 1810, 1820, 1830). The different publications are represented through different patterns on the bars.[49]

system in the late seventeenth and early eighteenth century worked to encourage victims to pursue prosecution, it remained the case that 'the vast majority of crimes were not prosecuted'.[50] Victims often by-passed the prosecution of misdemeanours (which included property worth less than a shilling, vice, regulatory and poor law offences, as well as offences against the peace), by using informal settlements.[51] When felonies took place (or were thought to have taken place), victims were legally required to report these crimes and pursue prosecution of the culprit. In these cases, informal settlements were illegal, but victims often found means of contacting the thief and settling.[52] Newspaper notices provided one such way. The careful use of 'lost' rather than

---

[49] Sample includes notices published more than once.
[50] Mary Clayton and Robert Shoemaker, 'Blood Money and the Bloody Code: The Impact of Financial Rewards on Criminal Justice in Eighteenth-Century England', *Continuity and Change*, 37 (2022), 107.
[51] Robert B. Shoemaker, *Prosecution and Punishment: Petty Crime and the Law in London and Rural Middlesex, c. 1660–1725* (Cambridge, 1991), 311.
[52] Shoemaker, *Prosecution and Punishment*, 316.

'stolen' in the great majority of notices allowed victims to reach thieves and finders and pursue reclamation of their possessions, while simultaneously signalling (potentially to the thief who had their possession) that they would not be pursuing prosecution. Here we see 'everyday' understandings of the law in action. Such understandings were significant not only in working with the law, as other historians have shown, but also in working around it.[53] Importantly, in some cases, these notices, and the information they might prompt, could also act as the beginnings of an investigation that might lead to prosecution, as in the case of Thomas Piggott. However, the popularity of the lost notices system (and its focus on the possession lost rather than any potential suspect) demonstrates that for many urban denizens, the return of possessions was more important than pursuing prosecution and punishing threats to property. In 1751, the principal magistrate for Westminster Henry Fielding (1707–1754) saw fit to berate victims for their misplaced priorities in this regard. He argued that 'such Advertisements are in themselves so very scandalous, and of such pernicious Consequence' because 'Men are not ashamed to own they prefer an old Watch or a Diamond Ring to the Good of Society'.[54] Even though the conditions of loss were always hazy, particularly, in urban spaces, people primarily used the term 'lost' to prioritise reclaiming their possessions, rather than meeting their prosecutorial obligations.

Alongside lost and stolen notices, others written by 'finders' rather than 'losers' also appeared in eighteenth-century newspapers. When objects understood as stolen were 'stopt' by a third party (often a pawnbroker), rather than received, the third party could alert the owner to the circumstance by advertising in the newspaper. However, the number of advertisements titled 'stopt' was low. A total of just fifty-eight were found across the sample (see Figure 3.8), a much lower figure than that for lost notices (objects and animals), which totalled 1,402 (including duplicate notices). While the number of these notices remained small, they show the range of possibilities open to finders. Similarly, there were instances in which people advertised to communicate that they had found what they understood to be someone else's possession or had one left with them. The finder addressed these notices to the owner in the hope they would come and collect the possession. These notices include instances where a horse had been left at a stable and the stable owner wished to free themselves from the expense of feeding and keeping the horse. In these instances, one outcome was for the stable owner to note that they would sell the horses to pay the charges incurred if the horse's owner

---

[53] For more on how those lower down the social scale understood and shaped the law see Tim Hitchcock and Robert Shoemaker, *London Lives: Poverty, Crime and the Making of a Modern City, 1690–1800* (Cambridge, 2015), 19; Carolyn Steedman, *Labours Lost: Domestic Service and the Making of Modern England* (Cambridge, 2009), 172–198.

[54] Henry Fielding, *An Enquiry into the Causes of the late Increase of Robbers, &c. with some Proposals for Remedying this Growing Evil* (2nd edn, London, 1751), 106.

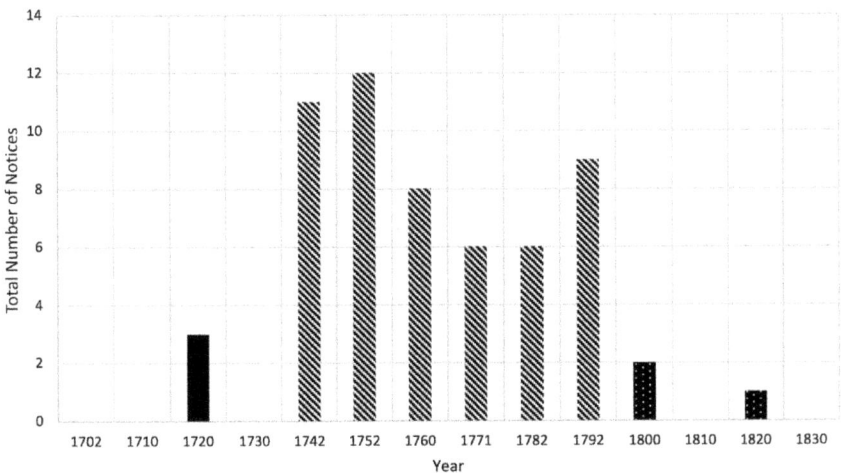

Figure 3.8 Bar chart showing total number of 'stopt' notices that appeared in the December issues of the *Daily Courant* (1702, 1710, 1720, 1730), the *Daily Advertiser* (1742, 1752, 1760, 1771, 1782, 1792) and *The Times* (1800, 1810, 1820, 1830). The different publications are represented through different patterns on the bars.[55]

did not return promptly. Again, the number of these notices is relatively small. In the sample, the number of 'found', 'left' or 'taken' notices totalled 268 (see Figure 3.9).

As we saw, lost, stolen, found and 'stopt' notices for objects and animals published in newspapers appeared directly after those publicising that servants and apprentices had absconded, spouses had eloped and soldiers had deserted. But advertisements for people never appeared with the same frequency as those for lost objects and animals (see Figure 3.10). For instance, while there was a total of 106 notices for lost objects and animals in the sample of *Daily Courant* issues (December 1702, 1710, 1720, 1730), just one appeared for a person. In the middle decades of the eighteenth century, the figures became more comparable. In the December issues of the *Daily Advertiser* in 1760, there were 146 lost notices for objects and animals and 71 for people. But such a comparison was short-lived. In the December issues of the *Daily Advertiser* in 1771 there were 245 lost notices for objects and animals and only 69 for people. The disparity in numbers is significant considering the attention that

---

[55] Sample includes notices published more than once.

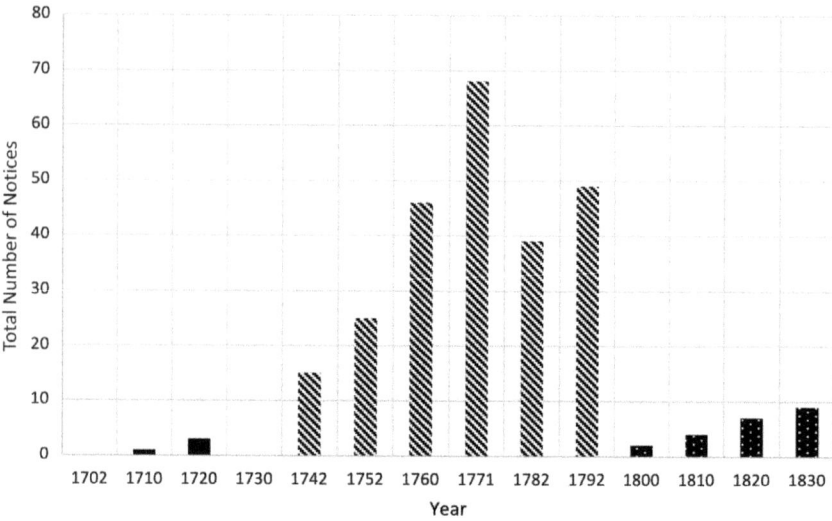

Figure 3.9 Bar chart showing total number of notices addressed to the owner, listing that an item had been 'found', 'left' or 'taken up' that appeared in the December issues of the *Daily Courant* (1702, 1710, 1720, 1730), the *Daily Advertiser* (1742, 1752, 1760, 1771, 1782, 1792) and *The Times* (1800, 1810, 1820, 1830). The different publications are represented through different patterns on the bars.[56]

has been paid to runaway notices and the lack of attention given to lost notices across the eighteenth century.[57] Placing these different forms in conversation with each other reconnects them to the context in which they operated.

---

[56] Sample includes notices published more than once.
[57] Simon P. Newman's work on the notices placed to capture freedom seekers in England has been crucial in highlighting the runaway notice and linking it the broader culture of runaway notices found across the Atlantic World in the seventeenth and eighteenth centuries. See Simon P. Newman, 'Freedom-Seeking Slaves in England and Scotland, 1700–1780', *English Historical Review*, 134:570 (2019), 1136–1168; Newman, *Freedom Seekers*. See also Gwenda Morgan and Peter Rushton, 'Visible Bodies: Power, Subordination and Identity in the Eighteenth-Century Atlantic World', *Journal of Social History*, 39:1 (2005), 39–64. Tim Wales has studied the lost notices in the *London Gazette* (1696) and all the papers in the Burney Collection, 1698–1700, while literary scholars Jonathan Lamb and Sean Silver have studied a selection of notices in published in London newspapers from 1717 to 1725 and 1714 to 1725, respectively. Historians and literary scholars have not focused on the later years of the eighteenth century. See Tim Wales, 'Thief-takers and their clients in later Stuart London', in Paul Griffiths and Mark S.R. Jenner (eds), *Londinopolis: Essays in the Cultural and Social History of Early Modern London* (Manchester and New York, NY, 2000), 69; Jonathan Lamb, *The Things Things Say* (Princeton, NJ and Oxford, 2011) 43–46; Sean Silver, *The Mind is a Collection: Case Studies in Eighteenth-Century Thought* (Philadelphia, PA, 2015), 255.

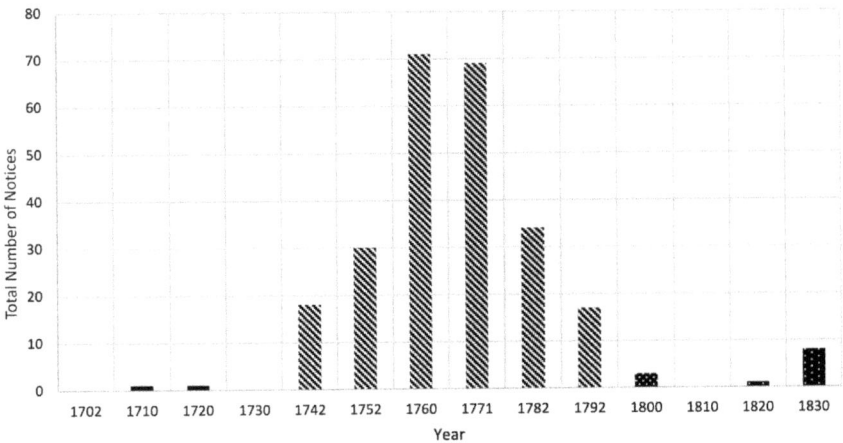

Figure 3.10 Bar chart showing total number of notices listing a person who had 'eloped', 'runaway', 'absconded' or 'deserted' (including escaped criminals or deserted soldiers, but not the pursuit of alleged criminals) that appeared in the December issues of the *Daily Courant* (1702, 1710, 1720, 1730), the *Daily Advertiser* (1742, 1752, 1760, 1771, 1782, 1792) and *The Times* (1800, 1810, 1820, 1830). The different publications are represented through different patterns on the bars.[58]

Ensuring Efficacy in the Early Eighteenth Century

Over the early eighteenth century, increasing numbers of people published 'lost' notices in newspapers. One means of explaining the growing popularity of publishing lost notices in the early eighteenth century is to see how thief-takers shored up the system in this period, making it particularly efficacious. From the early seventeenth century, thief-takers had worked on behalf of the judicial system and private individuals to pursue prosecutions. They also facilitated the return of stolen goods.[59] Victims of crime could hire a constable or any private citizen to discover a criminal and formulate charges, and it was thief-takers who often took on such detective work.[60] Thief-takers were increasingly encouraged to engage in such work by the rewards the judicial system offered, such as the £40 for the conviction of highwaymen from 1692

---

[58] Sample includes notices published more than once.
[59] J. M. Beattie, *The First English Detectives: The Bow Street Runners and the Policing of London, 1750–1840* (Oxford, 2014), 18.
[60] Beattie, *Policing and Punishment in London, 1660–1750*, 131 and 227.

onwards, coiners and clippers from 1696 and burglars from 1706.[61] Then from 1720, as property continued to come under threat, an extraordinary reward of £100 was offered on top of the usual £40 for the conviction of those committing robberies in the metropolis.[62] In the 1690s, pursuing the prosecution of coiners and clippers provided plentiful and relatively easy business for thief-takers, but as these sources of revenue began to dry up, they looked elsewhere. Side projects involving facilitating negotiations between the victims and thieves of stolen goods (rather than animals or people) began to grow for thief-takers in the 1690s and 1700s.[63] In facilitating such mediations, thief-takers focused on objects, such as watches and financial instruments, rather than animals or people. In the first three decades of the eighteenth century, watches and financial instruments were the most regularly advertised lost things (see Figure 3.4).

Thief-takers simultaneously worked within different systems. They could work for victims as middlemen and mediated contact with the thieves who had often stolen their supposed *lost* property, without ever referring to stealing or theft. It was not always possible to ensure that the thief or finder in question saw the notice and responded correctly, thief-takers made sure it took place, and in some cases, encouraged thieves to steal the item in the first place. Thief-takers made these connections in return for a reward from the victim, which was often then shared with the thief. At the same time, thief-takers continued to gain rewards by pursuing the prosecution of criminals on behalf of other victims and the judicial system. These different operations, in fact, complemented each other, as both relied on a thorough knowledge of criminal happenings.[64] As the eighteenth century began in earnest, the interlinked nature of these operations provided an opportunity for greater organisation and duplicity on the part of thief-takers.

Charles Hitchin (1675–1727) was one of the first thief-takers to devise a more organised network of connecting thieves with victims advertising their

---

[61] Ibid., 256. An inducement which continued until legislative change in 1818 ended the practice of giving £40 reward to those who obtained certain types of capital convictions. See Peter King, *Crime and Law in England, 1750–1840: Remaking Justice from the Margins* (Cambridge, 2009), 102. The Bank of England Inflation Calculator (www.bankofengland.co.uk/monetary-policy/inflation/inflation-calculator) states that £40 in 1692 is the equivalent of £7,102.03 today (as of October 2023).

[62] Beattie, *Policing and Punishment in London, 1660–1750*, 256. The £100 reward was withdrawn in 1745 and then reinstated in 1748 due to the increase in crime at the end of the War of Austrian Succession. All parliamentary rewards were finally abolished in 1818. Beattie, *The First English Detectives*, 8 and 209; King, *Crime and Law in England, 1750–1840*, 102. The Bank of England Inflation Calculator (www.bankofengland.co.uk/monetary-policy/inflation/inflation-calculator) states that £40 in 1720 is the equivalent of £6,828.85 today and that £100 in 1720 is the equivalent of £17,072.12 today (as of October 2023).

[63] Wales, 'Thief-Takers and Their Clients in Later Stuart London', 69; Beattie, *Policing and Punishment in London, 1660–1750*, 249.

[64] Beattie, *Policing and Punishment in London, 1660–1750*, 247–48.

'lost' things. Made Under City Marshall in 1712, Hitchin supposedly used Hatton's in Basinghall Street as his base for reading through the *Daily Courant* each morning to keep track of the lost advertisements.[65] However, the increasing number of complaints made against him slowed his business and he was suspended from his duties. Hitchin made the mistake of often handling the stolen goods himself, rather than requiring that the thieves or other intermediaries handled them.[66] Following the removal of Hitchin, his assistant Jonathan Wild (1683–1725) became the major thief-taker of London and was known as 'The Thief-taker General'.[67] As with Hitchin, Wild's primary work was ostensibly as a thief-taker who gained rewards for finding and convicting criminals. Such a position meant that he could operate legitimately as a trusted figure, whom the public would seek out if they lost a possession. However, he simultaneously worked with thieves, organising their activities to ensure maximum rewards. If the thieves slipped or proved troublesome, he could revert to his position as thief-taker and pursue their prosecution.

Thieves, victims and intermediaries willingly participated in Wild's system. For thieves, the system of mediation meant evading prosecution for their crimes (by classing them as 'lost') and yet receiving a monetary reward for committing thefts.[68] As receiving stolen goods became highly regulated from 1691 onwards, using a middleman and attributing the goods as lost became increasingly attractive to thieves, providing a level of ambiguity and protection.[69] In 1691, Parliament made the receivers of stolen goods accessories and thus made it possible to punish them as felons if the principal thief was convicted.[70] By 1702, such powers were strengthened further and it became possible to punish receivers as accessories to the felony, even if the principal thief escaped punishment by being offered the benefit of clergy or a pardon.[71] In 1706, a receiver could be convicted for a misdemeanour, even if the thief could not be taken.[72] By 1718, the nature of the punishments for receivers had also changed: receivers could be transported for fourteen years, if they were found guilty of being accessories to a felony.[73] Those accused of receiving

---

[65] Gerald Howson, *Thief-Taker General: The Rise and Fall of Jonathan Wild* (London, 1970), 51.
[66] Howson, *Thief-Taker General*, 67.   [67] Ibid., 55–56.
[68] Beattie, *Policing and Punishment in London, 1660–1750*, 249.
[69] Ibid., 39 and 250; Howson, *Thief-Taker General*, 36.
[70] Beattie, *Policing and Punishment in London, 1660–1750*, 250.
[71] The benefit of clergy was a means of sparing from the death penalty defendants found guilty of certain felonies. While earlier based on literacy, in the eighteenth century, it became more widely used. Hard labour or transportation were used as alternative punishments. Serious offences were non-clergyable.
[72] Beattie, *Policing and Punishment in London, 1660–1750*, 250.
[73] Heather Shore, 'Crime, Criminal Networks and the Survival Strategies of the Poor in Early Eighteenth-Century London', in Steven King and Alannah Tomkins (eds), *The Poor in England 1700–1850: An Economy of Makeshifts* (Manchester, 2003), 153.

often operated in the heart of communities, they were pawnbrokers, publicans and lodging-house keepers and were therefore often difficult to criminalise[74] Nevertheless, as legislative changes increasingly targeted receiving, receivers became wary, which reduced thieves' options for fencing goods and made lost notices ever more attractive.

Victims engaged with the lost notices system because they were reluctant to engage with the costly and time-intensive process of prosecution. Victims were also put off from pursuing prosecution because of the possible outcomes for the culprit. From 1699, shoplifting became a capital offence and in 1713 stealing from a house went the same way.[75] Such changes meant prosecution was a high-stakes pursuit and victims were reluctant to see the culprit hang if convicted. With such outcomes in play and with the difficulties victims faced in pursuing prosecution, victims sought to simply reclaim their property.[76] With the growth of daily newspapers, it became increasingly possible to do so, although it was not inexpensive.[77] It cost somewhere between 2s and 5s – a week's rent for a London artisan – to place a lost notice, and the conventions of the system required that victims also offer a reward.[78]

In his 1725 publication *The Life of Wild*, Daniel Defoe (1660–1731) noted how the practice of publishing 'lost' notices became common place in the 1710s and early 1720s.

> This practice of giving people notice of their goods after they were robbed becoming pretty public, and especially several people recovering their lost goods upon the easy condition of giving a gratuity to the discoverer, being known, it introduced another weak, foolish practice as a consequence, namely, that after this, when any person was robbed, they always published the particulars of their lost goods, with the promise of a reward to those who should discover them.[79]

Although, as this chapter has shown, the practice of publishing the particulars of lost items had a longer history, Defoe's writings show how the practice was thought to be further encouraged and enlarged by Wild, who essentially ensured that the 'system' worked more effectively (or, at least worked more effectively for him). On learning of a theft (or a theft's completion), Wild would go to a victim and suggest that they advertise the item or that he would

---

[74] Shore, 'Crime, Criminal Networks and the Survival Strategies of the Poor', 154.
[75] Beattie, *Policing and Punishment in London, 1660–1750*, 249.
[76] Even those notices that reference theft seem more concerned with getting the item back than pursuing prosecution. See 'Taken from a Gentleman by 3 Highway-Men', *Daily Courant* (London), 6 December 1710.
[77] Beattie, *Policing and Punishment in London, 1660–1750*, 250.
[78] Ingrid H. Tague, *Animal Companions: Pets and Social Change in Eighteenth-Century Britain* (Philadelphia, PA, 2015), 15; Joanne Bailey, *Unquiet Lives: Marriage and Marriage Breakdown in England, 1660–1800* (Cambridge, 2003), 57.
[79] Daniel Defoe, *The Life and Actions of Jonathan Wild*, in *Defoe on Sheppard and Wild*, ed. Richard Holmes (London, 2004), 86.

Systems of Reclamation

do it on their behalf.[80] As Wild became better known, the victims themselves would go to him and would then be encouraged to advertise.[81] The newspaper notices for 1720 show the prevalence of Jonathan Wild. He was listed as the person to whom a lost item could be returned in 15 per cent of the lost notices placed in the *Daily Courant* in 1720. In 1725, however, as the inducements grew, Wild overstretched himself and arranged too boldly for the return of stolen goods.[82] He was convicted and hung that year and his elaborate means of organising the 'lost' notices system ended.

The number of memoirs and essays published after Wild's death give some sense of his importance in early eighteenth-century British society, as does John Gay's (1685–1732) decision to feature him in his popular 1728 ballad opera *The Beggar's Opera*.[83] The extent and intricacy of Wild's exploits captured the imagination, particularly of early eighteenth-century Londoners, and continued to do so into the nineteenth century.[84] The memoirs and essays show that Londoners were aware of the systems at work, but were invested in remaining silent about the fallacy of 'lost', because it worked for them: we might assume that they got their things back.[85] In fact, some writers expressed concern that the system had worked too well. Bernard Mandeville (1670–1733) described how people had become so used to engaging with Wild's system of return, that the system actively encouraged criminals to steal more and possessors to be careless with their things. Mandeville felt that surety of return had created further loss:

I can't help thinking that if those Things were never to be heard of again, and the Loss irretrievable, many young Rakes, and other loose Reprobates, would be under great Apprehensions, and more upon their Guard, at least, when they had such a Charge about them, than the Generality of them now are...[86]

Mandeville expressed a more general feeling (explored further in Chapter 7) that maintaining possession of your things was socially and morally important:

---

[80] Howson, *Thief-Taker General*, 67.
[81] For the centrality of advertising, see also Capt. Alexander Smith, *Memoirs of the Life and Times of the Famous Jonathan Wild* (London, 1726), vi.
[82] Beattie, *Policing and Punishment in London, 1660–1750*, 381; Howson, *Thief-Taker General*, 227–236.
[83] Bernard Mandeville, *An Enquiry into the Causes of the Frequent Executions at Tyburn* [1725] (Los Angeles, CA, 1964); H. D., *The Life of Jonathan Wild, From His Birth to his Death* (Dublin, 1725); Anon., *The Life and Glorious Actions of the Most Heroic and Magnanimous Jonathan Wilde* (1725); Defoe, *The Life and Actions of Jonathan Wild*, 69–117; Smith, *Memoirs of the Life and Times of the Famous Jonathan Wild*; Henry Fielding, *Jonathan Wild* [1743] (Oxford, 2003).
[84] David L. Pike, *Metropolis on the Styx: The Underworlds of Modern Urban Culture, 1800–2001* (Ithaca, NY and London, 2007), 171–4. See also William Bishop, *Legal Protection of Dogs from the Increasing Evil of Dog-Stealers and Receivers* (London, 1844), 23.
[85] Silver, *The Mind is a Collection*, 256.
[86] Mandeville, *An Enquiry into the Causes of the Frequent Executions at Tyburn*, 5. The text also appears in the Preface to Smith, *Memoirs of the Life and Times of the Famous Jonathan Wild*, vii–viii.

it showed character. To be unaware and 'careless', to lose things regularly, was the behaviour not of a proper possessor but rather of 'Rakes' and 'Reprobates'. In the 1710s and early 1720s, the likes of Jonathan Wild shored up the possibilities of return. As such, according to Mandeville, people came to trust so thoroughly in the system that they became careless with their things. Mandeville underlined the importance of caring for your things, and ensuring they were not lost. He gave little credence to the time, effort and money (in other words, the care) expended on getting things back. But as the century moved on, such forms of care became increasingly important.

Expansion of the Newspaper System

While early eighteenth-century residents benefitted from the support of institutions such as the Goldsmiths' Company and figures such as Wild in reclaiming their lost things, from 1725 onwards the systems developed again. Thief-takers continued to operate in the capital over the course of the long eighteenth century, only ceasing in 1818 with the end of the £40 reward for certain capital convictions.[87] Over the century, thief-takers still returned stolen goods to their owners for a reward; however, none of them ran organised systems involving victims and thieves on the scale achieved by Wild.[88] Later thief-takers, such as Stephen McDaniel who himself was convicted and hung in 1754, operated on a large scale and like Wild was in essence involved in organising the committing of crime rather than its detection.[89] Yet in the mid to late eighteenth century, as Ruth Paley has shown, McDaniel and other thief-takers worked in a *variety* of ways to earn money. They ran debtor prisons and ale houses, were involved in credit networks, received stolen goods, set up crimes and caught criminals.[90] The diversity of operations undertaken by thief-takers underlines how returning stolen goods came to play a smaller role in their working lives.[91] As thief-takers involvement in the lost notices waned, the system did not wilt, but rather flourished in different ways.

From the second quarter of the eighteenth century, the growth, format and distribution of London newspapers, such as the *Daily Advertiser* (1731–1796), allowed the lost notices system to expand. In this period, lost notices

---

[87] King, *Crime and Law in England, 1750–1840*, 102.
[88] Beattie, *Policing and Punishment in London, 1660–1750*, 382.
[89] Ruth Paley, 'Thief-Takers in London in the Age of the McDaniel Gang, c.1745–1754', in Douglas Hay and Francis Snyder (eds), *Policing and Prosecution in Britain, 1750–1850* (Oxford, 1989), 323.
[90] Paley, 'Thief-takers in London in the Age of the McDaniel Gang, c.1745–1754', 306.
[91] Paley suggests that 'Arranging for the return of stolen goods may also have been a regular part of their business.' But underlines the difficulty of knowing how great a role it continued to play. Paley, 'Thief-takers in London in the Age of the McDaniel Gang, c.1745–1754', 311.

significantly contributed to the shape of newspaper culture (see Figures 3.2 and 3.3). By 1750, readers in the capital could choose between eighteen different papers (six weeklies, six tri-weeklies and six dailies), and by 1811 the total figure had reached fifty-two.[92] While choice grew, so did circulation: 'twenty-fold between 1695 and 1855'.[93] While the *London Daily Post* circulated almost 2,500 copies in 1746, the *Daily Advertiser* sold more.[94] In the mid eighteenth century, the *Daily Advertiser* and the *Gazetteer* started competing for the top circulation figures. However, it was not until 1775 that the *Gazetteer* managed to take top place, with a print run of 'about 5,000 copies per issue'.[95] Between the 1760s and 1790s, daily London newspapers then expanded further and began to increasingly serve national audiences. The newspaper that most successfully captured this enlarged market was *The Times* (1785–present), a newspaper which included lost notices amid its other advertisements. It was established in 1785 and by 1830 sold 'just over 10,000 per issue'.[96]

As historian Michael Harris has noted, advertisements bolstered the development of newspapers in the eighteenth century, providing crucial revenue streams which allowed for further growth.[97] Our analysis, the first to systematically assess advertisements for lost possessions, demonstrates that these notices were a significant presence. Between 1700 and 1830, the *Daily Courant*, *Daily Advertiser* and *The Times* were three of the biggest daily newspapers in London. As Figure 3.2 shows, lost notices were a consistent feature within these publications, but the high point of such advertisements was during the publication of the *Daily Advertiser*. Analysing the December issues of this publication, we see that issues included an average of 7.15 notices in 1742, a figure which dipped to 5.92 (1752) and 5.41 (1760), before rising to 9.42 (1771) and 9.62 (1782), before falling again to 7.00 (1792). Working with the same issues, we see that the *Daily Advertiser* also contained the largest number of runaway notices. With only 0.67 on average included in December issues in 1742, this figure rose to 1.19 (1752), 2.63 (1760) and 2.65 (1771), before dropping to 1.31 (1782) and 0.65 (1792). In *The Times*, the average number of notices included in each issue fell. In the December issues, the average number of lost notices was 0.3 (1800), 0.27 (1810), 0.85 (1820) and 1.15 (1830), while the average number of runaway notices was 0.11 (1800), 0 (1810), 0.04 (1820) and 0.30 (1830). The lower numbers of notices included in *The Times* might be explained by increases in advertising duty, which by the 1790s might be 2s or 3s on top of the cost of the advertisement at

---

[92] Barker, *Newspapers, Politics and English Society 1695–1855*, 29.   [93] Ibid., 31.
[94] Michael Harris, *London Newspapers in the Age of Walpole: A Study of the Origins of the Modern English Press* (London, 1987), 190.
[95] Harris, 'London Newspapers', 427.   [96] Ibid., 430.
[97] Harris, *London Newspapers in the Age of Walpole*, 58.

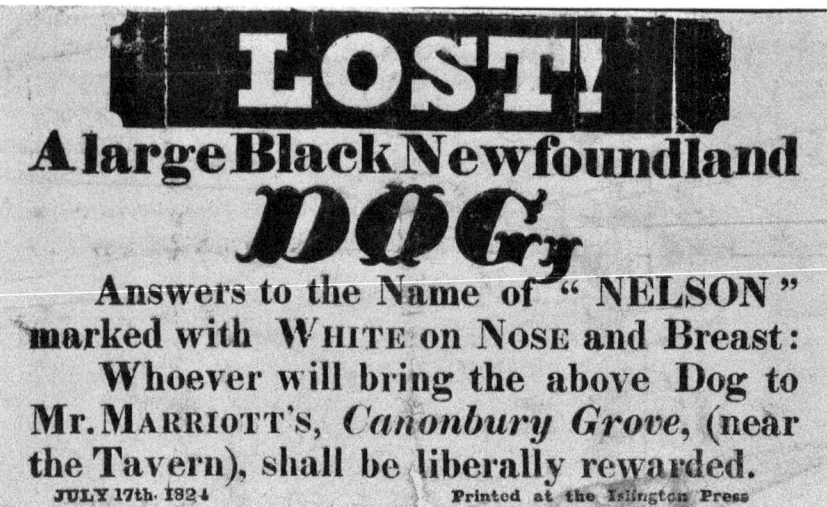

Figure 3.11 Canonbury Grove by Islington Press, 1824, 303569.
Image source: The London Archives (City of London Corporation).

around 5s.[98] It might also be explained by the expanding range of publications Londoners could advertise in. Although *The Times* was the most successful, by 1811 Londoners could choose between fifty-two newspapers.[99] Nevertheless, the number of lost notices included in London daily newspapers and most particularly the *Daily Advertiser* (1731–1796) reveals their importance to the commercial health of the industry. Newspapers needed Londoners to continue placing lost notices, as such they needed possessions to continue to go missing and losers to seek their reclamation through advertising. Here, we see a different kind of investment in loss, as well as reclamation. There existed what we might refer to as an 'economy of loss' in this period.[100]

Alongside placing notices in newspapers, individuals continued to print, paste and distribute privately printed handbills into the late eighteenth and early nineteenth century. Pieces of ephemera, handbills were designed for short time spans in the hope and belief that they would help locate the lost item. The typographic style of extant handbills (see Figure 3.11) shows that differing font sizes worked to alert and guide the reader as to what had happened, what was missing and what they might do should they come across the thing in question.[101] The text included on extant handbills shows that they

---

[98] Bailey, *Unquiet Lives*, 57.
[99] Barker, *Newspapers, Politics and English Society 1695–1855*, 29.
[100] Many thanks to Keith Wailoo for this observation.
[101] See also for example, Bodleian Library, Oxford, John Johnson Collection, Window Bill, 'Bank notes lost', 1797, Window Bills Box; Bodleian Library, Oxford, John Johnson Collection,

largely followed similar conventions to those found in lost newspaper advertisements. While they moved in quite different ways then, they shared important elements, perhaps explaining why victims saw them as linked strategies.

Evidence from court cases demonstrates that victims of theft, or those who had lost possessions, would often advertise in newspapers *and* print and distribute handbills. In November 1779, when Robert Davis's shop was allegedly burgled of coins and a bank note, he 'advertised the bank note by hand bills, and in the newspapers'.[102] Similarly, in June 1785, when the broker Mr. Sharpe realised that some precious stones in his care had gone missing, he 'advertised these pearls and diamonds, and circulated hand-bills in the usual form'. Albeit these methods 'produced no discovery', Sharpe clearly understood that this was the usual and expected response to such a discrepancy.[103] The coachman George Byers also understood the necessity of placing a newspaper advert and printing handbills. In August 1827, after generously assisting what he perceived to be a helpless woman, he discovered that 'she was then gone, and my watch also, with the chain, seals, and key – they were worth 7l. or 8l.'. In response he 'advertised it, and sent hand-bills round to the pawnbrokers', but rather than producing a discovery, it was a spontaneous trip to 'Mr. Joyce's, pawnbroker, or Euston-street, Euston-square' that located the 'watch and appendages, all complete, as I had lost it'.[104]

As with newspaper notices which were primarily placed in daily rather than weekly newspapers to ensure the rapid circulation of information, time was also seen as crucial in the printing and distribution of handbills. When advertising their services, printers stressed speed. In 1790, J. Rozea, a printer based on 'Wardour-street', claimed they could get 'Bills, relative to Goods, &c. Lost or Stolen, dispatched at Two Hours Notice'.[105] Whereas, in 1799, the Tottenham-based printer E. Brown noted that 'BILLS relative to lost property, [could be] printed in One Hour, by E BROWN, *Tottenham*'.[106] Such bills could then be quickly distributed around the city. In 1808 William Pyne

---

Window Bill, 'Gun. Lost this morning', 1784, Window Bills Box; Bodleian Library, Oxford, John Johnson Collection, Window Bill, 'Lost since Sunday evening', 1800?, Window Bills Box.

[102] *OBPO* (www.oldbaileyonline.org, version 8.0, 15 August 2019), December 1779, trial of John Hudson (t17791208-15).

[103] *OBPO* (www.oldbaileyonline.org, version 8.0, 4 May 2022), June 1785, trial of James Lockart (t17850629-61).

[104] *OBPO* (www.oldbaileyonline.org, version 8.0, 4 May 2022), September 1827, trial of Rosina Smith (t18270913-20).

[105] Bodleian Library, Oxford, John Johnson Collection, "J. Rozea, letter-press and copper-plate printer," c.1790, trade card, t161075.

[106] W. Daviss, 'Stolen or strayed, On Tuesday Morning last', Tottenham, 1799. Eighteenth Century Collections Online. Gale. University of Birmingham. 24 September 2020.

championed bill stickers, whose skills meant that 'within six hours, by the means of printed bills, the inhabitants of a great city can be advertised of a thousand things necessary to be publicly known'.[107] Rapidly announcing the loss of a possession was important in publicly marking ownership. If anything was 'found upon the surface of the earth, or in the sea, and are unclaimed by an owner', they were supposed to be 'abandoned by the last proprietor' and thus 'returned into the common stock'. If such abandoned possessions were found they were deemed to 'belong, as in a state of nature, to the first occupant or fortunate finder'.[108] Ownership was (and remains) deeply social. It relies on other people's recognition. When an item fell out of possession, ownership needed to be noted publicly within a strict temporal frame. Time became of the essence in trying to reclaim lost things in eighteenth-century London and daily newspapers, which were unique to the capital, allowed for the rapid movement of information.[109]

Over the middle decades of the century, without thief-takers' large-scale organisation of the lost advertisement system, its efficacy relied on the *daily* newspaper but also the substantial growth of newspaper buyers *and* readers. The number of newspaper readers was higher than those for newspaper buyers alone, particularly in the capital, which had high levels of literacy and ever-increasing numbers of sites and spaces in which to access newspapers.[110] Estimates suggest that while around 'one quarter of the capital's residents read a newspaper in 1750', a third did so 'in the 1780s'.[111] Over the long eighteenth century, reading newspapers became a central part of people's lives. As Natasha Glaisyer has shown by analysing correspondence for mentions of the *London Gazette*, for 'many correspondents, and not just those in government, the *Gazette* was a shared point of reference'.[112] Other sources show us how people understood newspaper culture as a phenomenon which collectively engaged people. Towards the end of Frances Burney's 1782 novel *Cecilia*, the irrepressible Mr Hobson, used daily readings of the *Daily Advertiser* as a mark of what it might mean to be a man of business, someone engaged in the world:

'Mr Hobson,' cried Mrs Belfield, very impatiently, 'you might as well let *me* speak, when the matter is all about my own daughter'.

---

[107] As cited in Robert Shoemaker, *The London Mob: Violence and Disorder in Eighteenth-Century England* (London, 2007), 247.
[108] William Blackstone, *Commentaries on the Laws in England: Book II Of the Rights of Things* ed. Simon Stern (Oxford, 2016), 272.
[109] Jeremy Black, *The English Press in the Eighteenth Century* (Abingdon, 2010), 1.
[110] Brian Cowan, 'Mr Spectator and the Coffeehouse Public Sphere', *Eighteenth-Century Studies*, 37:3 (2004), 347.
[111] Barker, *Newspapers, Politics and English Society 1695–1855*, 47.
[112] Glaisyer, '"The Most Universal Intelligencers"', 262.

'I ask pardon, ma'am,' said he, 'I did not mean to stop you; for as to not letting a lady speak, one might as well tell a man in business not to look at the Daily Advertiser; why its morally impossible!'[113]

Daily newspapers acted as a reference point in people's lives, a common ground upon which people relied to cultivate relationships and identities. Newspapers' ability to regularly engage such a high proportion of the capital's population meant they were well placed to facilitate a system which required the speedy circulation of information between losers and finders. With growing numbers of newspaper buyers and newspaper readers, lost notices came to be seen by an ever-growing section of the capital's population, increasing the efficacy of the system. In this period, as we will explore further in the next chapter, an ever-wider range of people were understood to be on the lookout for lost things.

The *Hue and Cry* of It All

Had Henry Fielding known that the number of lost notices published in newspapers expanded over the second half of the eighteenth century, he would have been deeply frustrated. In 1751, he bemoaned the popularity of lost notices and actively appealed to Londoners to desist from using them. He declared that he was keen to 'put an effectual Stop' to the lost notices system.[114] Like Defoe and Mandeville before him, Fielding felt it worked too well, encouraging theft and the receiving of stolen goods. In his *An Enquiry into the Causes of the Late Increases of Robbers,* he complained that 'if he [the thief] hath made a Booty of any Value, he is almost sure of seeing it advertised within a Day or two, directing him *to bring the Goods to a certain Place where he is to receive a Reward* (sometimes the full Value of the Booty) *and no Questions asked*'.[115] For Fielding, the lost notices provided thieves with a ready reward for their illegal efforts and a means of evading the judicial system. He contended that the problem of theft could be greatly reduced if people stopped placing lost notices offering rewards. In the second half of the eighteenth century, Fielding and his half-brother Sir John (1721–1780) sought to wean Londoners off lost notices and onto pursuing prosecution by developing crime prevention, enhancing policing, increasing crime reporting and supporting successful prosecutions.[116] Despite such changes, lost notices remained an important tactic into the nineteenth century.

---

[113] Frances Burney, *Cecilia* [1782] (Oxford, 2008), 877–78.
[114] Fielding, *An Enquiry into the Causes of the late Increase of Robbers*, 114.
[115] Ibid., 105–6.
[116] As such the period was not simply awaiting the establishment of the Metropolitan Police in 1829, but as rather marker by significant changes. See John Styles, 'Sir John Fielding and the

Certain developments in the later eighteenth century sought to prevent crime. A permanent foot patrol was created in 1783 and expanded in 1790. Such a shift was then further augmented in 1805 with the addition of a mounted patrol.[117] While prevention through policing was one aspect, changes were primarily focused on detection, apprehension and prosecution. Developments in these areas largely grew from the innovations imposed by Henry Fielding (until 1754) and then by his half-brother Sir John Fielding (who took over and remained until he died in 1780) when they each acted as principal magistrate in Westminster. These shifts centred on the Bow Street magistrate office, which became the most important office in the capital and remained so even after the 1792 Middlesex Justice Act. First, the Fieldings brought in changes that made it easier to report crimes. Access to magistrates was understood as key to crime reporting. In response, Sir John kept the Bow Street office open for long and regular hours. He also instituted a system of 'rotation offices', which meant that a magistrate would be available to the public at fixed times each week.[118] The 1792 Middlesex Justice Act built on these innovations, establishing seven police offices across the capital, each with stipendiary magistrates. Second, begun in 1749–1750 by Henry Fielding and then instituted more formally in 1754 by Sir John Fielding, a group of men were employed to detect and apprehend suspects. This group became known as the Bow Street runners.[119] They were available to act upon reports of crime and worked to detect and apprehend suspects. Their investigative capacity was crucial and became supported by other mechanisms, which allowed for the rapid flow of information. For example, the Bow Street runners benefitted from the systematic use of advertising. While this began with Henry in *The Public Advertiser*, Sir John expanded such advertising first through a section in *The London Packet or New Lloyds Evening Post* and then through his own newspaper *The Public Hue and Cry; or Sir John Fielding's Preventive Plan*.[120] Such advertising was largely focused on supporting the runners in detecting and apprehending suspects. It featured descriptions of escaped felons, people apprehended on suspicion of offences and descriptions of stolen

---

Problem of Criminal Investigation in Eighteenth-Century England', *Transactions of the Royal Historical Society*, 33 (1983), 127–149; King, *Crime, Justice and Discretion in England*; J. M. Beattie, *Crime and Courts in England, 1660–1800* (Oxford, 2002); J. M. Beattie, 'Sir John Fielding and Public Justice: The Bow Street Magistrates' Court, 1754–1780', *Law and History Review*, 25:1 (2007), 61–100; Beattie, *The First English Detectives*.

[117] Beattie, *The First English Detectives*, 49 and 172.
[118] Beattie, 'Sir John Fielding and Public Justice', 70; Beattie, *The First English Detectives*, 87.
[119] Beattie, 'Sir John Fielding and Public Justice', 69; Beattie, *The First English Detectives*, 17 and 24.
[120] Styles, 'Sir John Fielding and the Problem of Criminal Investigation', 136–7.

horses.[121] There were instances in which other things were included, such as a stolen silver pint Mug in 1774 and a lost watch in 1776, but they were rare.[122] The runners also cultivated their own information networks through building a knowledge of the city and relationships with informers.[123] In addition, they became adept at extricating evidence from crime scenes. These methods for apprehending suspects and building evidence were further supported by the development of pre-trial processes of re-examination where Sir John Fielding conducted secondary interviews with suspects to draw out further evidence and construct more robust prosecution cases.[124] In the second half of the eighteenth century and early nineteenth century, the judicial system became ever-more focused on encouraging prosecution and ensuring its success.

Although policing and prosecutorial efforts increased in the late eighteenth and early nineteenth century, lost notices remained popular. The conviction of cases, particularly those for simple larceny, remained difficult and faced 'evidentiary challenges at trial' into the early nineteenth century.[125] Although some Londoners' attempts to reclaim produced information that led them to pursue prosecution, their priority appears to have been the reclamation of their goods. Moreover, we see that people were comfortable in asserting (even in court) that this remained their primary aim. When the prosecutor George Wingfield, Esq gave testimony at the Old Bailey on 25 April 1770, he noted that he had been advised to advertise his stolen watch

---

[121] These categories were stipulated by John Fielding's 1772 General Preventive Plan and seem to have been adhered to in the publication. See the extant copies in the Bodleian Library collection N. 2287 b.7 which include information from the Public Office at Bow Street: *The London Packet and General Hue and Cry* (London), Monday 12 October to Wednesday 14 October 1772 (No. 46x [ripped]); Friday 30 October to Monday 2 November 1772 (No. 472); Friday 25 December to Monday 28 December 1772 (No. 496); Friday 12 February to Monday 15 February 1773 (No. 517); Friday 14 May to Monday 17 May 1773 (No. 556); Friday 25 June to Monday 28 June 1773 (No. 572); Friday 10 September to Monday 13 September 1773 (No. 607); Friday 24 September to Monday 27 September 1773 (No. 613).

[122] For the issue of *The Public Hue and Cry; or Sir John Fielding's General Preventive Plan* (London), featuring the stolen silver pint mug see Friday 25 March to Friday 8 April 1774 (No. 16). For the issue featuring the lost watch, see Friday 17 May to Friday 31 May 1776 (number illegible).

[123] Beattie, *The First English Detectives*, 67.

[124] Beattie, 'Sir John Fielding and Public Justice', 82–85; Beattie, *The First English Detectives*, 87.

[125] Bruce P. Smith, 'The Presumption of Guilt and the English Law of Theft, 1750–1850', *Law and History Review*, 23:1 (2005), 138. As Bruce Smith argues, this stood in contrast to cases of petty larceny (the theft of goods value at under 1s) and the misappropriation of goods such as wood, metals and textile materials, where summary proceedings were increasingly effective over the later eighteenth and early nineteenth century. See Smith, 'The Presumption of Guilt and the English Law of Theft', 133–71; Bruce Smith, 'The Emergence of Public Prosecution in London, 1790–1850', *Yale Journal of Law & the Humanities*, 18:1 (2006), 29–62.

and money as 'lost'.[126] Wingfield had been walking from Piccadilly to Green Park in the evening on 25 February, when a man had accosted him. Catching hold of his collar, he had asked for money and then also snatched his watch. He was keen to reclaim his watch despite it only being made of plain metal. In court, he stated that he had been advised by an unnamed person 'to advertise the watch as lost, as the best way to hear of it again'. In court, Wingfield was happy to assert that he prioritised the reclamation of his possession (or at least that he was advised to do so).

Wingfield had advertised 'that very evening; and the next day the watch was stopped' by a pawnbroker who became suspicious.[127] As noted earlier in the chapter, what we see here is that although the form of lost notices (when and where the item had been lost, what it was and who it could be returned to for what reward) underlined the return of the possession, lost notices could also act as part of investigative processes that secured prosecutions. Nevertheless, when 'lost' was used, it opened a particular possibility in the case concerned. Despite the suspicions of the pawnbroker, the defendant John Monro hoped that the use of the term 'lost' in the advertisement would provide him with some protection. At the Old Bailey, the court worked to discover whether the watch had been lost or actively stolen. This was before the 1808 change in the law, in this period victims were still required to prove that the pickpocketing theft had taken place without their knowledge.[128] As such, Wingfield was asked whether he had felt the watch being taken. He answered at first that 'I did not in my hurry miss it; but upon his running away, I put down my hand and missed it'. On further questioning, Wingfield was more specific: 'The man put his hand to my pocket, and I felt a snatch; a quick kind of a motion; but did not perceive my watch move from me at the time, till I felt'. In his defence, Monro noted that he had come upon the watch: 'I found this watch between Stable-yard gate and Spring-garden gate, going home'. He further stated that 'The watch being advertised as lost, proves that I found it.' He also produced the advertisement in the court but was dismissed by the Court officials who were recorded as noting that 'The prosecutor has told the reason he advertised it in that manner'.[129] The court accepted that using the term 'lost' in the advertisement was a fudge. It was a tactic primarily designed to secure the return of the possession rather than an accurate description of what had taken place. Monro was found guilty and sentenced to death.

---

[126] *OBPO* (www.oldbaileyonline.org, version 8.0, 9 August 2019), April 1770, trial of John Monro (t17700425-43).
[127] Ibid.   [128] Andersson, '"Bustling, Crowding, and Pushing"', 297.
[129] *OBPO* (www.oldbaileyonline.org, version 8.0, 9 August 2019), April 1770, trial of John Monro (t17700425-43).

Similarly, in the case of Robert Crosby, which was heard at the Old Bailey on 29 April 1778, the victim Margaret Wayte was happy to assert that her chief aim was reclaiming the item.[130] Under cross examination, Wayte, who had found that her watch was missing from her pocket while she 'went on to the Hay-market', noted that she had advertised her watch as lost. Like Wingfield before her, Wayte asserted that her reason for doing so was that 'I thought I might, by that means, get it sooner'. Victims were clear on this matter and were prepared to articulate it in court, even in the later decades of the eighteenth century.

In the early nineteenth century, people continued to believe that using the term 'lost' in advertisements was important as a means of securing the return of their possession and were keen to use it. In a trial at the Old Bailey on 6 December 1827, the solicitor Samuel Vines described how on 3 October 1827, he found that his purse and bank note had gone missing from behind a drawer in his secretaire.[131] In response, he recalled that he had decided to advertise them as 'Lost', even though his footman Robert Williams (the defendant in the case) was acting suspiciously. In the case, Vines was asked whether he had advertised it as 'lost' but supposed it had been stolen. Vines responded that he did not wish to answer the question and was 'afraid to do so'. When asked again, he responded 'I tell you honestly, I suspected the prisoner from the first, but if I had put "Lost or stolen" at the head of my advertisement, the note would not have been circulated, I think.'[132] Even though he was a solicitor and understood the responsibilities on him to prosecute, Vines also knew that advertising his purse and bank note as 'stolen' (or even 'Lost or stolen' rather than simply 'lost') would in all likelihood mean that he would not see them again.

Throughout the long eighteenth century, those who placed newspaper notices were aware that 'lost' was often a fallacy used to ensure that their item would be returned, the 'finder' would be protected, and prosecution would not be necessary. When cases of theft did go to court and victims had originally used a lost notice, they were more than prepared to say why they had done so. When they should have been focused on underscoring their commitment to prosecution, they constantly let slip that their priority was reclamation. In a period that witnessed substantial developments in the means of detecting, apprehending and successfully prosecuting defendants, Londoners did not always co-operate. The lost notices and their expansion in the second half of

---

[130] *OBPO* (www.oldbaileyonline.org, version 8.0, 9 August 2019), April 1778, trial of Robert Crosby (t17780429-6).

[131] *OBPO* (www.oldbaileyonline.org, version 8.0, 15 August 2019), December 1827, trial of Robert Williams (t18271206-5).

[132] *OBPO* (www.oldbaileyonline.org, version 8.0, 15 August 2019), December 1827, trial of Robert Williams (t18271206-5).

the century remind us that they had their own concerns and motivations, their own priorities. Attending to those concerns brings forth a more complex picture of the nature of crime, policing and prosecution in this period, making us see the importance of another 'p': possession.

Conclusion

We began this chapter with the case of Thomas Piggott, who had his watch and money stolen from him in Buckingham Street in 1745. We know of Piggott's case because it was heard and recorded at the Old Bailey, but Piggott's first response was not to pursue prosecution, but rather to try and get the watch (in particular) back. With the help of his watchmaker, Piggott advertised his watch as lost in the *Daily Advertiser* and in the end, it was his advertisement that proved effective. In court, Piggott was recorded as stating that 'I advertised it on Saturday the 25th of May. Mr Hall seeing the advertisement that morning, went to Mr. Bowley [sic], and told him that such a watch had been offered to him to be pawned to him for three guineas, and he refused to take it in.' Despite Mr Hall's conscience stopping him from receiving it, the lead he offered was enough. Piggott tracked the watch to 'Sarah Holland's in Stewart's Rents in Dirty Lane' and learned that it was kept in a chair there. When he got into the room, he 'went directly to the two armed chair, and found the watch in a white paper in the inside of the cushion among the hair'.[133] Piggott prioritised advertising his watch as lost, rather than chasing after his attackers and as such managed to reclaim his possession.

From the Goldsmiths' Company's system of printed notices, which their beadles walked round to members of the luxury trades, to the handbills people printed, distributed and posted upon walls around the city, urban dwellers had long accessed means of chasing after their lost things. In the later seventeenth century, newspapers proved an important additional means of facilitating reunions with errant possessions. They enlarged and expanded the possibilities of reclamation. The daily newspapers which were particular to London and began in the early eighteenth century further improved the efficacy of the system, by publicising notices to a wide range of people within a short time. The development of these different systems is indicative not only of the growing material and commercial cultures of eighteenth-century London, but also of the problems of loss produced by urban spaces in this period and the inability of the legal system to support the reclamation of property.

That people were prepared to develop these often-intricate systems and spend time and money on engaging with them to reclaim their possessions

---

[133] *OBPO* (www.oldbaileyonline.org, version 8.0, 05 August 2019), July 1745, trial of William Kelly Thomas St. Legar Patrick Cave Sarah Cave (t17450710-27).

shows us that people valued keeping hold of their possessions. To possess was not only to have but also keep hold. The diversity of things included in late seventeenth- and eighteenth-century advertisements also reminds us of how capacious the category of 'possessions' was. More than objects, animals, and even people, could be deemed possessions. Yet again we are reminded of the value of focusing on loss, rather than consumption and accumulation. Loss provides a very different lens by which to understand what the world of possessions was in this period. While we have been taught to think of eighteenth-century possessions in terms of clothes, mirrors, teacups, books and portraiture, focusing on lost items prompts a different list. Here we see watches but also the importance of the financial instruments such as bank notes, bills of exchange and Exchequer bills, we also come to see the importance of dogs and the centrality of people. These things were all understood as possessions in this period and contributed to people's consideration of what it might mean to own and possess. In exploring systems of reclamation as they operated in the capital, we see the relationship of possession as an active process, that took time and effort to maintain. We also see the diverse relationships of possession which were enacted in this period. The active process of possession took many forms and in the next chapter we will explore who engaged with such forms.

4 Who Lost and Who Looked

> A servant Maid found some Days past a Diamond Ring, between St James's and Charing Cross, and finding no Advertisement about it in the News-Papers (which she carefully reads every Day for that Purpose) she thinks it her Duty to advertise the Owner of it, that she will return it, on giving the just Tokens of it, and paying the Expence [sic] of this Advertisement. It is to be seen at Mr Stephen Vache's, Perfumer, next Door to Mr Lamb's in Pall Mall.
> – *Daily Advertiser* (London), 12 December 1760

On 12 December 1760, a notice appeared in the *Daily Advertiser*. It had been written and placed by someone who described themselves as a 'servant Maid' and who wanted to announce that they had found 'a Diamond Ring, between St James's and Charing Cross'. The notice insisted that the servant felt it was important to return the object to its owner and that she had pursued different strategies to achieve this aim. It contains a careful rendering of innocence and virtue. The notice claimed that the servant maid was well-versed in lost advertisements because she 'carefully' read them 'every Day'. The servant maid was not the only person to abide by such practices, the diaries of Sophie von la Roche tell us that she did so too. In fact, von la Roche went further and made notes of some of the notices she read including one 'about two missing men'.[1] Despite the servant maid's conscientiousness, on this occasion she found no advertisement for the diamond ring and thus finally decided to advertise herself, in fact she felt it was 'her Duty' to do so. Here we see how finding and placing a *found* notice could also be a question of character: the ability to care for things on behalf of others. Not only did the servant maid read and place advertisements she also knew not to part with the ring until she had received proof of ownership (and knew that a description of particulars, or 'the just Tokens', was the best proof). Finally, she announced that she would return it to the owner on them 'paying the Expence of this Advertisement'. The servant maid would not be out of pocket for her efforts,

---

[1] Sophie von la Roche, *Sophie in London 1786* trans. Clare Williams (London, 1933), 100.

rather the owner of the ring was expected to pay expenses (and we might assume a reward too).

The servant maid's brief notice illuminates how individuals found, as well as lost, possessions in the eighteenth century. Although they did not appear in anything like the numbers of lost notices, people regularly placed found notices in newspapers, particularly between the 1740s and 1790s.[2] The notice and the finding it announced, is important in introducing us to the readers of lost notices. The servant found the ring, a highly valuable item, and knew that if they wanted to return it rather than sell it, they needed to look to the advertisements in newspapers. When their careful 'every Day' reading failed to spot the required advertisement, the servant maid decided that they would advertise instead. Following the lead highlighted by this notice, this chapter looks to the writers and readers of lost notices. In examining who lost and who looked, we find that people from a range of different social groups, from the gentry to servants, placed and regularly read the lost notices published in newspapers. More than this, we find that people were largely expected to understand the system. Lost notices and the workings that upheld them were not peripheral, rather they were an intrinsic part of British, and more particularly London, culture in the long eighteenth century. Such an assertion is further supported by the chapter's exploration of who 'losers' thought they were addressing with their short notices. It finds that those who responded to lost notices ranged far beyond thief-takers. As the century drew on, 'losers' assumed they were writing to coffeehouse men, Hackney carriage drivers, pawnbrokers and dog sellers and dealers, as well as kidnappers. At the same time, the growth of newspaper culture explored in the previous chapter meant that they also believed in the possibility that everyone was on the lookout for lost things in London. Anyone might read their notices and return the item, including a 'servant Maid'.

Underlining the ubiquity of these practices broadens our understanding of the range of people who invested in the relationship of possession and keeping hold. It also changes our grasp of urban life. The lost notices system assumed the *possibility* of people seeing things in the city. While many of the notices were anonymous, their writing hints at an urban society bristling with proximity, connections and knowledge, rather than anonymity.[3] Strangers were not always to be feared and worried about.[4] The lost notices assumed something that we have already witnessed at work in the London guides: that to be a

---

[2] While there were 1402 'lost' notices in the sample analysed, there were only 268 for items 'found', 'left' or 'taken up'.

[3] For more on the importance of proximity as a social relationship see Lauren Berlant, 'The Commons: Infrastructures for Troubling Times', *Environment and Planning D: Society and Space*, 34:3 (2016), 393–419.

[4] James Vernon, *Distant Strangers: How Britain Became Modern* (Berkeley, CA, 2014), 37.

Londoner was to be on the lookout and in the know. We are reminded that although cities were often spaces in which people, animals and objects could escape, get lost and go missing, they were also places for seeing, recognising and finding in the eighteenth century.

Who Placed Notices?

Despite their sustained popularity, knowing who placed lost and runaway advertisements is difficult because notices rarely named or described owners or 'losers'.[5] The case of Marcus Polak, indicted for stealing a Gold Ring and heard in the Old Bailey on 29 June 1743, suggests that newspapers were reticent to include advertisements that named losers (or suspected thieves).[6] It also seems that those who placed notices largely wanted the lost item to be returned to a named intermediary rather than themselves.[7] Losers worked to retain their anonymity in order to protect their reputations. They did not want to be known as people who were careless with their things. As Bernard Mandeville saw it, to show such a lack of care was to be a 'rake' or 'reprobate': someone without character.[8] Despite the difficulties of identification, trying to understand who wrote and placed the notices is important in deciphering whose property was at stake in such moments of loss and who had the resources and inclination to seek its return. We must seek out the fragmentary clues to find who was writing these notices.

The clues that might lead us to understand who placed notices are different in notices for lost objects and animals than those for people who have runaway. For instance, while notices for lost objects and animals tended to omit any details about the loser, those for 'runaways' were more likely to identify the name, gender and occupation of the loser. In only 12 per cent of

---

[5] Examples of the 'victim' being named are very rare but did appear occasionally. For example, the following appeared in the *Daily Advertiser* on 26 September 1752: 'Lost from Mrs. De Paiba's, in Bury-Street, a Silver Table-Spoon, with a Cypher M R P. Whoever brings it to the Rainbow Coffee-House in Cornhill, shall have Five Shillings Reward.' Mrs De Paiba was the wife of Moses de Paiba (possibly the M R P of the cypher), an active member of the Jewish community in the City. In his will he left the house on Bury Street to his eldest son Abraham but noted that his wife should have residence of the house for the rest of her life. See, The National Archives, 'Moses de Paiba, St Katherine Cree Church', 22 March 1749, PROB 11/768/406.

[6] *Old Bailey Proceedings Online* (hereafter '*OBPO*') (www.oldbaileyonline.org, version 8.0, 21 December 2022), June 1743, trial of Marcus Polak (t17430629-50).

[7] For example, a notice placed in the *Daily Advertiser* (London) on 9 December 1760, does list the 'loser', and we see here that the finder is directed to return the item to someone else. 'Lost on Saturday the 6th of November last, a Pocket Book, and a Licence, belonging to William Kennedy, between the lower End of Cheapside and Westminster Infirmary. Whoever brings them to Mr Young's, at the Sign of the Crown in Petty France, Westminster, shall have Five Shillings Reward. They are of no Use to any but the Owner.'

[8] Bernard Mandeville, *An Enquiry into the Causes of the Frequent Executions at Tyburn* [1725] (Los Angeles, CA, 1964), 5.

the notices for lost objects or animals the gender of the loser is noted (or can be extrapolated from the information included, such as listing that a 'gentleman' has lost his dog). In these cases, 78 per cent are male.[9] Although only a small sample, the centrality of men as writers of these notices is corroborated by the gendered nature of the 'things' most regularly featured: dogs, financial instruments and watches.[10] Similarly, evidence from court cases heard in the Old Bailey sees men regularly advertising lost things.[11] Many of the notices for 'runaways', 49 per cent in total, listed the gender of the loser (or the gender can be extrapolated from the information included). The majority of those that listed the gender of the loser in 'runaway' notices, listed it as male – 93 per cent. Women certainly engaged with the lost notices system; however, men may have engaged with it more regularly. Given the nature of the 'things' concerned in the notices, the gender balance of newspaper culture and relationships to property, the tentative suggestion that men engaged more regularly with the system is perhaps unsurprising.

Unpicking the status or occupation of those who placed advertisements is also fraught. Of the sample of 1,169 notices for lost objects and animals (excluding duplicate notices), only 9 per cent included some clue as to the occupation or status of the owner.[12] Admittedly, the clues are often somewhat obscure. Some notices clearly list that a 'Gentleman' lost something. In others, clues to status can be uncovered, for example in the inclusion of 'Esq' when a name was listed on a dog's collar.[13] Of those that included some clue, the majority relate to the somewhat opaque category of 'gentleman' or

---

[9] There are instances of married women, or at least 'Mrs' being listed as the named owner on some of the dog collars transcribed within the lost notices. See for example, the inclusion of "Mrs Floyer Brent Pelham, Herts" in 'Lost on Wednesday the 24th instant, a liver and white colour'd Bitch', *Daily Advertiser* (London), 27 December 1760 and the inclusion of "Mrs Williams, Queen Street, Westminster" in 'Lost the 27th ult. in St. Martin's Lane, or thereabouts, a small black Bitch', *Daily Advertiser* (London), 4 December 1771. Unmarried women also appear, see the inclusion of "Miss Collier" in 'Lost a black German Dog', *Daily Advertiser* (London), 16 December 1782.

[10] For the proportions of different types of things listed in the lost notices, see Figure 3.4 in Chapter 3.

[11] See *OBPO*, (www.oldbaileyonline.org, version 8.0, 05 August 2019), July 1745, trial of William Kelly Thomas St. Legar Patrick Cave Sarah Cave (t17450710-27); *OBPO* (www.oldbaileyonline.org, version 8.0, 09 August 2019), April 1770, trial of John Monro (t17700425-43); *OBPO* (www.oldbaileyonline.org, version 8.0, 15 August 2019), December 1827, trial of Robert Williams (t18271206-5).

[12] Sample includes 'lost' notices which appeared in the December issues of the *Daily Courant* (1702, 1710, 1720, 1730), the *Daily Advertiser* (1742, 1752, 1760, 1771, 1782, 1792) and *The Times* (1800, 1810, 1820, 1830). Notices published more than once have been excluded within this calculation.

[13] The exception here is names recorded as inscribed on watches as they might be heirlooms, featuring the name of a previous owner.

'gentlewoman'.[14] Again, we need to be tentative in our assumptions of what such clues suggest. In contrast, a much greater proportion of the 'runaway' notices (especially those for apprentices) included a clear indication of the status of the loser. The loser's occupation was listed in 37 per cent of 'runaway' notices.[15] Stickmakers, tin plate workers, watermen, shoemakers, corkcutters and cutlers are all listed. The regular inclusion of the occupation can perhaps be explained by the importance of that information in locating the missing apprentice or servant: by signalling the type of work they were engaged in and thus where they might apply for work. In the case of notices for 'eloped' spouses, a broader social group might be at play, particularly as annulments and judicial separations were expensive and thus absconding was the simplest way to escape or end a marriage for most of the population.[16] While runaway notices (especially those for apprentices) were largely placed by male artisans and shopkeepers, we must be more tentative about the findings from the lost notices for objects and animals. Although male members of the gentry seem to be the most regular placers of lost notices for objects and animals where there is some clue as to the loser, we must remember that the evidence for who was placing these notices is very scarce (only 9 per cent). Nevertheless, the advertisements allow us to see the presence of the gentry and those in artisanal occupations. They also, as we saw in the notice that began this chapter, very occasionally allow us to glimpse engagement by those lower down the social scale.

That servants read and checked lost notices in newspapers and placed notices is clear from the advertisement at the start of the chapter. As we saw in Chapter 1, 'servant' existed as an expansive term in eighteenth-century society and although the majority were poor, servants came from a wide variety of social backgrounds. The Statute of Artificers had listed three categories of servant, including 'servants in husbandry (yearly hires); artificers and workmen (hired for varying periods); and day laborers'.[17] Domestic servants often fell between these definitions but were largely understood to be those hired for a year to work within households. Servants were important in freeing up household members to contribute to London's society and economy, but domestic servants were also important as readers and writers. Evidence exists of servants purchasing a range of practical and literary texts in

---

[14] Ninety-seven of the 109 notices that noted the status or occupation of the loser of the object or animal listed the loser as a 'gentleman' or 'gentlewoman'.

[15] Sixty-two of the 168 notices for runaways list the occupation of the 'master', or that person seeking the runaway.

[16] David A. Kent, '"Gone for a Soldier": Family Breakdown and the Demography of Desertion in a London Parish, 175091', *Local Population Studies*, 45 (1990), 27.

[17] Paula Humfrey, 'Introduction', in Paula Humfrey (ed.), *The Experience of Domestic Service for Women in Early Modern London* (Farnham, 2011), 10.

this period.[18] We also know that servants wrote and published poetry, and that servant poetry became fashionable in the second half of the eighteenth century.[19] Alongside these forms of literary engagement, extant newspaper notices tell us that male and female servants were engaged in newspaper cultures. They read newspapers, checked for notices and wrote and placed them.

Other newspaper notices reveal that servants advertised because they themselves had lost possessions. On 24 December 1742, a 'Gentleman's Servant' placed a notice for a lost 'plain Silver Watch', which was 'his own Property'.[20] That the servant felt the need to voice the distinction of 'his own' suggests that a servant placing such notices for themselves (rather than for their master) was rare. Nevertheless, the servant was able to describe the relevant features of the lost watch, such as the maker's name and its number. As we will see in Chapter 5, being able to do so was indicative of knowledge of the intricacies of the lost notices system and eighteenth-century material cultures more broadly. Similarly, on 3 December 1771, another 'Gentleman's Servant' placed a notice for their lost watch in the *Daily Advertiser*.[21] On this occasion, the servant found themselves without work ('out of Place') and thus also used the notice to advertise their willingness 'to serve a single Gentleman' and noted that they had 'a good Character'.[22] Rather than serving a single purpose, lost notices could be put to work in multiple ways.

Such keen engagement by servants also appears foreseeable when we recognise their engagement with and utilisation of official and unofficial systems. Plebian Londoners were accustomed to working with and around the criminal justice and poor relief systems in this period. In the eighteenth century, magistrates and courts gave credence to servants or apprentices. Apprentices, for example, used the law to protect themselves and their position. As we saw in Chapter 2, London apprentices were enabled to act through their demonstrations to Justices of the Peace, but also through application to

---

[18] Jan Fergus, 'Provincial Servants' Reading in the Late Eighteenth Century' in James Raven, Helen Small and Naomi Tadmor (eds), *The Practice and Representation of Reading in England* (Cambridge, 1996), 202–203.

[19] Carolyn Steedman, *Labours Lost: Domestic Service and the Making of Modern England* (Cambridge, 2009), 282. See also Cynthia Dereli, 'In Search of a Poet: The Life and Work of Elizabeth Hands', *Women's Writing*, 8 (2001), 169–182; William J. Christmas, *The Lab'ring Muse: Work, Writing and the Social Order in English Plebian Poetry, 1730–1830* (Newark, DE, 2001); Donna Landry, *The Muses of Resistance: Labouring Class Women's Poetry in Britain, 1739–1796* (Cambridge, 1990).

[20] 'Lost on Wednesday Night last, by a Gentleman's Servant', *Daily Advertiser* (London), 24 December 1742.

[21] 'Lost Yesterday Morning, in Cheapside, a Silver Watch', *Daily Advertiser* (London), 3 December 1771.

[22] The use of 'character' is specific to servants and refers to the reference from previous employers guaranteeing that they were of good character. See Bruce Robbins, *The Servant's Hand: English Fiction from Below* (Durham, NC and London, 1993), 34–38.

the Lord Mayor's Court in the outer chamber of the Guildhall. The court had both common law and equitable jurisdiction and 'at least one in ten apprentices who left their original master used the court'.[23] Similarly, as we saw in Chapter 1, the question of settlement was crucial to servants, who could, following the 1662 Settlement Act, gain settlement by serving for a year. Female domestic servants regularly forced legal questions about settlement and in doing so rendered settlement as something to *have*, 'as a form of possession'.[24] Servants and apprentices regularly used legal and judicial systems to protect themselves and their possessions. It is perhaps unsurprising then that they were also apt to utilise the means offered by the lost notices to further protect their property rights.

Other evidence goes further and suggests that there was an expectation within British culture that servants would be well-versed in the lost notices system. A case heard at the Old Bailey on 14 January 1789 saw members of court incredulous that the prosecutor Charles Cope was inattentive (or perhaps incompetent) in his use of the system. It is difficult to definitively place the occupational status of Cope. He worked for and lived in the household of Charles Minier, a seedman who was based at The Orange Tree on the Strand.[25] Cope referred to Minier (or Minees as it was spelt in the *Old Bailey Proceedings* and Charles Mariner as it was spelt in the session papers) as his master and so likely worked for Minier as his servant.[26] As such, he falls within the broader definition for 'servants' in use in this period. Cope was in court seeking to prosecute Aquila Cole for stealing his silver watch. Cope gave testimony that on the night of 6 January, as he returned 'not quite sober' to his master's house in the Strand, he was accosted by Cole and assumed he had stolen his watch. However, the watch was not found on Cole when he was taken by the night watch. Rather it was found the next morning by a servant maid, in an area 'about four feet down' where there was 'snow and dirt'. In eighteenth-century London, it seems, servant maids were good at finding things.

As the watch had not been found on Cole and was no longer in the possession of Cope, both parties advertised for the lost watch in the *Daily Advertiser* on 8 January 1789.[27] One party sought to reclaim the watch, and the

---

[23] Patrick Wallis, 'Labor, Law, and Training in Early Modern London: Apprenticeship and the City's Institutions', *Journal of British Studies*, 51 (2012), 797.

[24] Steedman, *Labours Lost*, 106.

[25] Ray Desmond, *Dictionary of British & Irish Botanists and Horticulturists* (London, 1994), 2140.

[26] London Metropolitan Archives, 'Old Bailey Sessions: Sessions Papers – Justices' Working Documents', 12 January 1789, 28–29, LMOBPS450370028–29. www.londonlives.org/browse.jsp?div=LMOBPS45037PS45037002.

[27] See '*Publick Office, Bow Street*, January 7, 1789. WHEREAS a Person is now in Custody', *Daily Advertiser* (London), 8 January 1789; 'LOST on Tuesday Night last between Twelve and One', *Daily Advertiser* (London), 8 January 1789.

other to prove their innocence. The two notices appeared almost next to each other in the bottom righthand corner of the second page of the paper. Nevertheless, when questioned by Mr. Silvester in court, Cope testified that he 'did not see' the other advertisement, he 'did not look at the advertisement'.[28] Mr. Silvester appeared incredulous that Cope was so unaware. 'Do not you know', he asked, 'that that advertisement stood next to your own, in the same paper?' Such inattentiveness to the advertisements on the part of Cope, joined with his drunkenness on the night, the character witnesses for Cole (who had 'been a butcher' and thus belonged to a powerful group in late eighteenth-century London), and the lack of the watch on Cole's person, meant that Cole was found not guilty.[29] Significantly, that Cope had not followed the lost notices into publication was seemingly detrimental to his credibility in court, possibly because he was expected to have known better. The case of Charles Cope thus demonstrates that there was a general expectation that a range of people would be able to utilise the lost notices system and that they would be diligent in doing so: to do so was to be of good character, to be a proper possessor. It also hints at another aspect of urban life: that urban denizens were understood to be on the lookout for lost things and therefore that no one was surprised when they found them 'about four feet down' in the 'snow and dirt'.

On the Lookout

Runaway notices were often directed at the runaway themselves in the hope they would spot it and return. Here, particularly in the case of some servants and apprentices, we see more evidence that those lower down the social scale engaged with the notices. In fact, they were expected to be so adept at using the lost notices system they could even be relied upon to spot notices advertising themselves. When the 15-year-old Thomas Tise ran away from his master, the cutler Thomas Cartwright, on a Monday in November 1752, the notice placed in the *Daily Advertiser* asserted that if he would return he would be 'kindly receiv'd'.[30] That it was expected that (often young, male) apprentices and servants would see these notices is revealing of the penetration of newspaper-reading cultures and the notices system among different social groups, particularly given the varied nature of apprentices social backgrounds.[31]

---

[28] *OBPO* (www.oldbaileyonline.org, version 8.0, 15 August 2019), January 1789, trial of Aquila Cole (t17890114-21).
[29] For more on the importance and power of butchers as a trade, see Ian Maclachlan, 'A Bloody Offal Nuisance: The Persistence of Private Slaughter-Houses in Nineteenth-Century London', *Urban History*, 34:2 (2007), 230.
[30] 'RAN away from his Master on Monday last', *Daily Advertiser* (London), 1 December 1752.
[31] Patrick Wallis, 'Apprenticeship in England', in Maarten Prak and Patrick Wallis (eds), *Apprenticeship in Early Modern Europe* (Cambridge, 2019), 264–5.

Other notices were directed at those who might have information and requested it be supplied directly to the 'loser' concerned, acknowledging a reliance on a wider range of lookouts. As we will explore in greater detail in Chapter 6, just over a fifth of runaway notices did not seek information to foster a return. Rather these notices (particularly those for servants and apprentices) sought to act as a warning to others not to 'harbour', 'employ', 'entertain' or offer credit to the individual concerned. As we saw in Chapter 3, advertisements for lost objects and animals held a particular narrative logic. They noted when and where the item had been lost, what it was and who it could be returned to for what reward. These notices told a story of the loss of the item and how reclamation would take place. The story had been written, and the narrative structure contained an air of inevitability. In contrast, advertisements listing people who had eloped and absconded did not contain the same narrative clarity. There was not the same assurance of how the story would end, of how the return would take place. Rather these notices more often acted as public statements delineating the parameters of possession to others.

The notices written about freedom seekers who had sought escape, however, left little doubt as to how the story would end. These advertisements requested that others 'bring' the individual concerned. As such, the ends sought in these notices highlight how certain Britons regarded enslaved people as 'things', which could be transferred from place to place by others. However, if we dig deeper, we see that while such terms might appear innocuous, they had specific meanings within eighteenth-century culture and suggest at the active presence of kidnappers within Britain. As such, they demonstrate the paradox in play whereby enslaved people were both understood as 'things' to be moved and people with the potential to escape anything but forceful capture.

In the late 1760s, Granville Sharp began to focus more fully on agitating for the freedom of enslaved men and women in England.[32] His extant correspondence from this period shows that he wrote to enslavers who pursued freedom seekers by placing advertisements. In May 1768, he wrote to Alderman William Beckford (1709–1770), a major absentee slaveowner in Jamaica, regarding a 'Copy of an Advertisement' that Beckford had recently placed in the *Daily Advertiser*.[33] Sharp copied the advertisement into his letter to Beckford, underlining and starring elements he considered to be particularly important.

Ran away from his Master, a Negro Boy, under 5 feet high, about 16 Years Old, named Charles, he is very ill made, being remarkably bow Legged, hollow Backed, and Pot-Bellied; he had on when he went away a Coarse dark brown Linen Frock, a Thickset

---

[32] For more on Granville Sharp and his relationship to abolitionism see Christopher Brown, *Moral Capital: Foundations of British Abolitionism* (Chapel Hill, NC, 2006), 93–100.

[33] Perry Gauci, *William Beckford: First Prime Minister of the London Empire* (New Haven, CT, 2013), 3.

Waistcoat, very dirty Leather Breeches, and on his Head an Old Velvet Jockey Cap. Whoever <u>will bring him</u>,* or give any Tidings of him to Mr Beckford, in Pall Mall, may depend upon being very handsomely rewarded.[34]

The notice includes a litany of neglect. It notes how 'Charles' is 'bow Legged, hollow Backed, and Pot-Bellied'. Ill-treated and malnourished, the description of Charles' body and the clothes he escaped in – his 'very dirty Leather Breeches' – speak to the lack of care he has received. Despite Beckford owning several plantations and enslaving numerous people in Jamaica, Sharp wanted to underscore to Beckford that 'holding slaves in this Island [Britain]' was likely to be 'productive of very bad Consequences' and that it was 'a growing Evil'. In writing the letter, he urged Beckford to consider 'the subject more seriously than you have hitherto done' and included a pamphlet – 'Remark concerning the Tenure of Negroe Slaves in England' (an offering that Beckford returned to Sharp three days later with a sixteen-word acknowledgement).[35] More particularly, Sharp added a note in relation to the underlining and star ('<u>will bring him</u>,*') he had included when copying Beckford's advertisement into his letter. He reminded Beckford that 'It is absolutely actionable for any indifferent Person to touch him [Charles], and has been proved so in the Courts of Justice.' Sharp was clear as to what 'will bring him' meant. For Sharp, it was about laying hands on Charles and capturing him by physical force. Perhaps referring to the case of Jonathan Strong in 1767, Sharp asserted that forced capture was illegal, an argument not wholly plausible until Lord Mansfield's Somerset ruling in 1772.[36] Nevertheless, in this short note at the end of his letter, Sharp provides us with a key to understanding the countless other inclusions of 'will bring him' (or 'whoever apprehends him, and brings him' or 'will give Notice of him, so that he may be taken, or will bring him') in freedom seeker notices appearing in English newspapers in this period.[37] By examining such phrases we see that in the case of freedom seeker notices, the encouragement of kidnapping litters these publications.

As we learned earlier, in contrast to those for runaways, notices for lost objects and animals did not name the loser as the point of contact for the return of lost or stolen possessions, but instead usually listed an intermediary. These intermediaries might be understood as the vanguard of a new population of

---

[34] York Minster Archives, Letterbook of Granville Sharp 1768–1773, COLL 1896/1, 3.
[35] Gloucestershire Archives, Gloucester, 'BECKFORD, Mr: Acknowledgement', 1768, D3549/13/1/B16.
[36] For more on the case of Jonathan Strong see Brown, *Moral Capital*, 93.
[37] 'Eloped on Wednesday last in the Evening', *Daily Advertiser* (London), 8 December 1760; 'Ran away about ten Days ago, a Negro Boy', *Daily Advertiser* (London), 16 December 1760; 'A Black Boy. Ran away from his Master', *Daily Advertiser* (London), 20 December 1771; 'Lost, or supposed to lose his Way on Wednesday last', *Daily Advertiser* (London), 21 December 1782.

people on the lookout. While a name and location might be listed for intermediaries, the occupation or business interest of that individual was not always included. Nevertheless, some types of business appeared regularly within the lost notices. The legacies and continued vibrancy of the warning carrier notice system perhaps meant that goldsmiths (2 per cent) appeared as intermediaries in lost property notices, as did watchmakers (3 per cent). Taverns also appeared with some regularity (5 per cent). In the eighteenth century, these were important spaces of fellowship, offering a social space for food, rest and care in urban sites.[38] However, it was coffeehouses that appeared most regularly as sites for intermediaries. They were listed in 10 per cent of lost notices.

The regularity with which coffeehouses were listed as containing people to whom items could be returned might be explained by the fact that they were spaces deeply embedded in the newspaper culture. Coffeehouses prided themselves on holding the growing range of newspaper publications. In the early eighteenth century, 'the Coffee-Men of London and Westminster' considered 'their Houses as the Staples of News, and Themselves as the fittest Persons in the World to furnish the Town with that Commodity'.[39] Alongside drinking weak coffee often made with river water, they were understood as sites in which people could studiously read the latest news, or rather indulge their passion for news, information and gossip.[40] Coffeehouses performed a range of functions, including holding auctions, acting as meeting houses for committees, serving as informal 'labour' markets for enslaved people and servants, offering courses in public education and scientific lectures, and serving as lost property offices for the return of lost and stolen items.[41] Coffeehouse men understood themselves as central to the lost notices system: 'The *Coffee-Men* are the Persons who do the Business of the *Advertisers*'. As they saw it, they not only held newspapers in their coffeehouses but rather actively circulated newspapers and thus all the advertisements they contained, passing 'them from Hand to Hand' and making 'them known to the whole Town'.[42]

Coffeehouse customers also recognised coffee-men as central to the lost notices system and would ask them for advice. On 26 October 1752, the Old

---

[38] Mark Hailwood, *Alehouses and Good Fellowship in Early Modern England* (Martlesham, 2014), 4.
[39] Anon, *The Case of the Coffee-Men of London and Westminster* (London, 1728), 4.
[40] For more on the nature of coffee in the eighteenth century, see Brian Cowan, *The Social Life of Coffee: The Emergence of the British Coffeehouse* (London and New Haven, CT, 2005), 80. For more on the idea of coffeehouses as sites of information exchange and gossip, see Brian Cowan, 'Mr Spectator and the Coffeehouse Public Sphere', *Eighteenth-Century Studies*, 37:3 (2004), 349; Christopher Kingston, 'Marine Insurance in Britain and America', *Journal of Economic History*, 67:2 (2007), 385.
[41] Richard Coulton, '"The Darling of the Temple-Coffee-House Club": Science, Sociability and Satire in Early Eighteenth-Century London', *Journal for Eighteenth-Century Studies*, 35:1 (2012), 46; Markman Ellis, *The Coffee House: A Cultural History* (London, 2004), 170–174.
[42] *The Case of the Coffee-Men of London and Westminster*, 17.

Bailey heard the case of Alexander Bourk who had been indicted for allegedly committing a highway robbery, which involved the theft of money and a gold watch. In court, Bourk argued that he had been given the watch by a highway robber, rather than being the robber himself. He noted how he had been to a coffeehouse to see if the watch had been advertised in the *Daily Advertiser* and to advertise it himself if necessary. The coffeehouse keeper Patrick Guy gave witness testimony in the case and noted that Bourk had asked him whether the watch had been advertised and advised him to look through the papers to check.[43] Similarly, on 6 December 1769, the Old Bailey heard the case of Lazrous Jacob who had been indicted for allegedly stealing 80 silver watches, several metal watches and 16 silver cases for watches from William Turner. As soon as Turner had found out about the thefts he visited Mr Howard, a coffeehouse keeper, and 'told him if he found any such things offered with which names and numbers, he should be obliged to him if he would let me know'.[44] Coffeehouse men supported and expanded the lost notices system by holding a range of newspapers but also by acting as points of advice on advertising and as lookouts for lost and stolen items.

Some notices for lost objects and animals were proactive not only in listing an intermediary site where it could be returned but also who might have seen it. Notices particularly focused on drawing the attention of Hackney coachmen, pawnbrokers and dog sellers and dealers. Hackney coaches were understood as spaces in which things easily fell from a passenger's pocket and quickly became subsumed within the body of the coach. In Dorothy Kilner's *The Adventures of a Hackney Coach* the coach itself is aware of papers fluttering from passengers' pockets. One day, the coach 'discovered' a paper containing a suicide note 'dropped' from a passenger's 'pocket in the confusion'; on another day, it 'discovered' a poem, which a 'gentleman from the London Coffee House' had 'dropped on my seat'.[45] While here the coach itself was aware of its changing contents, other eighteenth-century imaginings of city life, such as those in the 1755 publication *Low-Life: Or One Half of the World Knows Not How the Other Half Live,* saw Hackney coachmen as finders, on the lookout. These men were envisioned 'searching the Seats and Boots of their Coaches, in hopes of finding Things of Value, accidentally left there in the Hurry of the Night.'[46] There was value in checking the seats and being on the lookout for lost things.

---

[43] *OBPO* (www.oldbaileyonline.org, version 8.0, 12 July 2019), October 1752, trial of Alexander Bourk (t17521026-30).

[44] *OBPO* (www.oldbaileyonline.org, version 8.0, 09 August 2019), December 1769, trial of Lazrous Jacob (t17691206-43).

[45] Dorothy Kilner, *The Adventures of a Hackney Coach* (3rd edn, London, 1781), 63 and 127.

[46] *Low-Life: OR One Half of the World, Knows Not How the Other HALF Live* (London, 1755), 16.

Hackney coaches and coachmen were an important part of urban life. The statutory maximum for Hackney coach licenses was 800 in 1715, rose to 1,000 in 1771, and rose again to 1,200 in 1831.[47] Despite repeated attempts to regulate them, Hackney coachmen had bad reputations particularly when it came to where they waited for hire, their use of the streets and their role in the movement of stolen goods around the city.[48] In his diary entry from 1764, Gervase Leveland, the son of a woollen draper, recounted a conversation he had had with 'a drole genius' in a coach on the road towards London from Twickenham Green to Turnham Green. Leveland described how the gentleman had struck up a conversation regarding 'the impertinence of Hackney Coachmen'. Leveland recounted how 'every one told a story to prove the truth of this assertion'.[49] A particular issue concerning Hackney coachmen was the prices they charged. The regulation of prices placed emphasis on distance travelled. Elaborate guides to using Hackney coaches and the fares to be expected for multiple different routes were an important recourse for those navigating the city streets by coach.[50] The diminutive size of such guides suggests that people carried them with them, using them to negotiate the correct price.[51]

Despite their reputations, Hackney coachmen were often listed in lost notices, in the hope they would find lost possessions and return them.[52] Advertising in the *Daily Courant* on 28 April 1720, a gentleman noted that he had been 'taken up on Tuesday the 26th Instant past 6 in the Afternoon, in Cheapside and set down in Greek Street, Soho' and had 'left a Parcel of Linnen in the Coach'. The notice stated that 'The Coachman is desired to bring it to Mrs Allen's in Greek Street, Soho, who will gratify him to Content'.[53] Some notices were more direct and aggressive in their wording. Advertising in the *Daily Advertiser* on the 28 September 1742, one notice stated that 'The Coachman and Number are known, and if he does not deliver it, he will be

---

[47] Mark Jenner, 'Circulation and Disorder: London Streets and Hackney Coaches, c.1640–c.1740', in Tim Hitchcock and Heather Shore (eds), *The Streets of London: From the Great Fire to the Great Stink* (London, 2003), 41. For 1831 figure, see *London Hackney Carriage Act 1831* [1831 c.22 (Regnal. 1_and_2_Will_4), 122.

[48] Jerry White, *London in the 18th Century: A Great and Monstrous Thing* (London, 2012), 224.

[49] British Library, 'Diary of Gervase Leveland', July 1764–October 1765, BL Add MSS 19211, 34.

[50] See for example, John Playford, *Vade Mecum, or The Necessary Companion* (London, 1680); Anon., *The London Companion, or an account of the fares of Hackney Coachmen, Chairmen and Watermen* (London, 1773); *Hodson's Hackney Carriage Pocket Companion for 1839* (London, 1839).

[51] Anon., *Hodson's Hackney Carriage Pocket Companion* is smaller than an iPhone.

[52] Such requests were particularly common in the 1710 (10) and 1720 (25) samples. By the nineteenth century, they had become less common: 1800 (1), 1810 (3), 1820 (3), 1830 (3).

[53] 'A Gentleman who was taken up on Tuesday the 26th Instant', *Daily Courant* (London), 28 April 1720.

dealt with in another Way'.[54] Another noted that 'The Coachman's Face and the Number are well known' and if the coachmen did not comply, 'proper Methods' would be taken to 'find him out'.[55] The increased regulation of Hackney coachmen over the eighteenth century perhaps allowed passengers to be more strident. The Commissioners of Hackney Coaches and Chairs, based at Somerset House, issued coachmen with numbered licenses, which had to be displayed on painted tin plates hung on the coach.[56] These numbers allowed customers to hold coachmen accountable and more directly seek out lost things. In 1786, John Trussler advised travellers to 'always take the number' of the Hackney Coach before getting in 'as, if you leave any thing therein, you may then, by summoning the coachman or chairman, to the Hackney-coach-office, probably recover it'. He also stressed the need that 'every one should look round the coach or chair before they quit it.'[57] Clearly it was not only children who were advised how to take care of their things, guides like Trussler's dispensed important counsel to adults.

In the 1780s, some notices began to address themselves exclusively to coachmen. On 30 November 1782, a notice in the *Daily Advertiser* began with, 'To Hackney Coachmen. By Neglect of a Servant two Great Coats were left in the Coach, that on Tuesday last carried a Lady from Mile-End Turnpike to No. 66, in Bishopsgate-Street, near Artillery-Lane.'[58] The practice continued into the nineteenth century, with examples found in samples from *The Times* in 1810, 1820 and 1830.[59] Similarly, in the late eighteenth century, other passengers wrote notices which contained detailed directions as to what exactly the coachmen should do. One notice writer who had lost 'the inside Setting of [a] Ring' noted that they were aware of the number of the coach 'either 436 or 146'. The notice recommended that the coachman 'search

---

[54] 'Left last Night in a Hackney Coach, a Silver Watch', *Daily Advertiser* (London), 28 September 1742.

[55] 'Lost out of a Gentleman's Pocket, in a Hackney Coach', *Daily Advertiser* (London), 26 December 1752.

[56] For the increasing importance of the visibility of license numbers see Anon., *The Right of the City of London, and Their Proceedings, Touching the Regulations of Hackney-Coaches* (London, 1692/3); *The London Companion, Or an Account of the Fares of Hackney Coachmen, Chairmen and Watermen* (London, 1773), iv; *Hodson's Hackney Carriage Pocket Companion for 1839* (London, 1839), vii.

[57] John Trussler, *London Adviser and Guide* (London, 1786), 148.

[58] 'To Hackney Coachmen. By Neglect of a Servant', *Daily Advertiser* (London), 30 November 1782.

[59] See 'TO HACKNEY COACHMEN – LOST, on Friday last', *The Times* (London), 13 July 1810; 'TO HACKNEY COACHMEN and Others – Left in a Chariot', *The Times* (London), 18 February 1820; 'FOUR GUINEAS REWARD – To HACKNEY COACHMEN and Others.', *The Times* (London), 10 October 1820; 'TO HACKNEY COACHMEN and others – LEFT, last night, in a HACKNEY COACH', *The Times* (London), 1 February 1830; 'TO HACKNEY COACHMEN and others – LEFT, in a Hackney Coach', *The Times* (London), 29 April 1830.

between the outside and inside Pannels [sic] of the Right Hand Door of those Coaches, as by drawing up and letting down the Glass it may have fallen in there, as well as amongst the Straw at the Bottom'.[60] These notices were clear about who they wished to reach and increasingly tried to address those individuals as directly as possible.

Despite regular changes to the legislation regulating Hackney coaches across the eighteenth century, it was only in 1815 that the law insisted that Hackney coach drivers had to hand in items left in their coaches.[61] The 1815 legislation demanded that drivers take left property to the Hackney Coach Office; otherwise they would face a fine of up to twenty pounds. The owner could then claim the item but would need to pay expenses incurred and 'a reasonable Sum to the Driver'. If no one claimed the item within a year, it would be sold and the balance left after expenses had been paid, would go to the driver.[62] From this point, the law required that Hackney coachmen be active finders, or rather, the law called on them to support owners in taking care of their goods. Such change was further consolidated by the 1831 London Hackney Carriage Act.[63] Hackney coach drivers were responsible for carrying any property left in their carriages to the Head Office for Stamps in the City of Westminster within four days. Not doing so incurred a twenty-pound fine. It was hoped that lost property could then be 'returned to the Person who shall prove, to the Satisfaction of the said Commissioners, that the same belonged to him'. If no one claimed the item within a year, it would be 'delivered to the Driver who brought and deposited the same', and if they did not claim it, it would be sold.[64] Although there was an expectation throughout the eighteenth century that Hackney coachmen were on the lookout for lost things, by 1815 they were required to do so by law. Their finding and handing in also relied on the identification of an institutional intermediary – the Hackney Coach Office – that would take in the item and adjudicate the process going forwards. Here we see the beginnings of the *modern* lost property system in action, a shift we will discuss further in the book's conclusion.

Trials at the Old Bailey reveal that pawnbrokers were also on the lookout for 'lost' things and were increasingly expected to be so over the eighteenth century. On 18 October 1749, when Constantine Gahagen realised that he

---

[60] 'To Hackney Coachmen. Dropt the inside Setting of a Ring', *Daily Advertiser* (London), 14 December 1792.
[61] Across the long eighteenth hackney coaches were subject to changes in legislation in 1694, 1710, 1711, 1713, 1716, 1743, 1757, 1759, 1763, 1767, 1770, 1771, 1172, 1784, 1786, 1792, 1800, 1802, 1804, 1808, 1815, 1817 and 1831.
[62] 55 George III c. 159. See *The Statutes of the United Kingdom of Great Britain and Ireland 55 George III 1815* (1815), 843–848.
[63] House of Commons Transport Committee, *Seventh Report of Session 2010–2012 – Taxis and Private Hire Vehicles: The Road to Reform* (London, 2011), Ev 66.
[64] *London Hackney Carriage Act 1831* [1831 c.22 (Regnal. 1_and_2_Will_4), 137.

had lost his watch on London Bridge, he went to his watchmaker 'and had it advertised'. On 'the 2d day of advertising it', he 'heard of it'.[65] The person who had spotted the watch and become suspicious was Thomas Brown, a pawnbroker. Pawnbrokers became one of the most important audiences for lost notices in this period because they were often offered stolen goods. Due to their frequent dealings with criminality, a series of newspaper articles and legislative changes show that many Britons (particularly those within the elite) held a low opinion of pawnbrokers in the eighteenth century.[66] A recurring concern was that pawnbrokers too readily acted as receivers of stolen goods. Henry Fielding certainly voiced this concern in his 1751 publication *Enquiry into the Causes of the Late Increase of Robbers*.[67] In response to these concerns, in the middle decades of the eighteenth century, pawnbrokers sought to ensure that they became known as individuals who were alert to the possibilities of stolen and lost items and actively stopped suspicious goods. As Samuel Johnson recorded in his satirical summary of parliamentary proceedings, 'Proceedings and Debates in the Senate of Lilliput', published in the *Gentleman's Magazine* in September 1745, some members of parliament involved in the 1745 debate on pawnbroking, defended the trade by asserting that they were an important force in stopping stolen goods.[68] As the 'Proceedings' noted, some members of parliament argued that 'greater numbers of pawnbrokers appear at the Old Bailey upon account of goods and felons which they have stopt, than upon account of stolen goods which they have received'.[69] In fact, the parliamentary debate was noted as arguing that the 'very nature of their business' makes them 'more watchful in this particular than any other set of men.'[70] It was also noted in the debate that more than simply watching for stolen goods, pawnbrokers were also inclined to advertise items that they considered suspicious.[71]

In court cases, pawnbrokers regularly sought to present themselves as watchful individuals, suspicious of stolen goods. The case indicting Lawrence Savage for the theft of a silver watch from Constantine Gahagen

---

[65] *OBPO* (www.oldbaileyonline.org, version 8.0, 05 August 2019), January 1750, trial of Lawrence Savage (t17500117-49).
[66] Alannah Tomkins, 'Pawnbroking and the Survival Strategies of the Urban Poor in 1770s York', in Steven King and Alannah Tomkins (eds), *The Poor in England 1700–1850: An Economy of Makeshifts* (Manchester, 2003), 167.
[67] J. M. Beattie, *The First English Detectives: The Bow Street Runners and the Policing of London, 1750–1840* (Oxford, 2014), 17.
[68] Samuel Johnson regularly published his 'Proceedings and Debates in the Senate of Lilliput', in the *Gentleman's Magazine*, as a means of evading the legal constraints imposed on publishing parliamentary debates.
[69] *The Gentleman's Magazine*, 15 (1745), 452. Also cited in Warren Swain and Karen Fairweather, 'The Legal Regulation of Pawnbroking in England, a Brief History', in James Devenney and Mel Kenny (eds), *Consumer Credit, Debt and Investment in Europe* (Cambridge, 2012), 148.
[70] *The Gentleman's Magazine*, 15 (1745), 452. [71] Ibid., 453.

was heard at the Old Bailey on 17 January 1750.[72] The court heard how the pawnbroker Thomas Brown had been approached by a woman wanting to pawn a watch for 30 shillings. A woman approaching a pawnbroker and wanting to pawn an item for a relatively small amount was a regular occurrence in eighteenth-century Britain. The short-term loans provided by pawnbrokers constituted an important part of household finances and 'women were disproportionately responsible for the management of small-scale credit for activities based in the household'.[73] Francis Shipley owned a retail business based in Whitechapel that brokered pawns and loans and sold groceries and chandler's wares. When Francis died in 1749, his probate records show that women owned 'nearly 60 per cent' of the outstanding pawns.[74] Rather than the *woman* who brought the watch to pawn then, in the court case, Brown stated that it was the freshly cut string that made him suspicious (the technology designed to prevent loss had clearly been tampered with). Here Brown cast himself as the epitome of the 'watchful' pawnbroker on the lookout. Before giving the watch back, Brown 'took the name and number of it upon a card'. As Chapter 5 will go on to show, the name and number of watches were understood to be the most salient features, crucial in the identification of lost watches and proving ownership. Similarly, evidence from extant eighteenth-century pawnbroker records demonstrates that pawnbrokers often recorded the watch's number when recording the pledge of a watch.[75] When Brown then saw a watch with the same maker's name and 'number forgot' advertised on 20 October, he 'thought [it] proper to let the man know, that such a thing was offered to me, which I did'.[76] In doing so, and discussing it publicly within the court case, Brown made an important and timely claim to his own credibility and integrity. He presented himself as a pawnbroker who was vigilant about what took place within his shop and who was attentive to information advertised within newspapers.

In the mid eighteenth century, as questions were repeatedly raised about pawnbroker practices, London pawnbrokers became more vocal in defending their trade and outlining the precautions they took against the possibility of (inadvertently) receiving stolen goods. Over the year 1753, London pawnbrokers regularly placed the following notice in the *Public Advertiser*. '*THE principal Pawnbrokers within the Bills of Mortality have agreed to take in this Daily Paper; and if any lost or stolen Goods shall be advertised in it, they will, to their utmost, endeavour to secure the Property for the Owner, and bring the*

---

[72] *OBPO* (www.oldbaileyonline.org, version 8.0, 5 August 2019), January 1750, trial of Lawrence Savage (t17500117-49).
[73] Beverly Lemire, *The Business of Everyday Life: Gender, Practice and Social Politics in England, c.1600–1900* (Manchester, 2005), 17.
[74] Lemire, *The Business of Everyday Life*, 34.
[75] Tomkins, 'Pawnbroking and the Survival Strategies of the Urban Poor', 182.
[76] *OBPO* (www.oldbaileyonline.org, version 8.0, 5 August 2019), January 1750, trial of Lawrence Savage (t17500117-49).

Offender to Justice.⁷⁷ In regularly placing this notice, they hoped people would believe that they could be trusted to stop goods, return them to their owner and help bring the offender to justice. That they looked to the lost notices system in this instance underlines its centrality within eighteenth-century culture. Yet when we compare the number of notices for lost and stolen goods (objects and animals) appearing in the *Public Advertiser* and the *Daily Advertiser* in December 1752, just before the pawnbrokers' announcement began to appear, their pledge appears somewhat empty. In this month, the *Public Advertiser* contained only twenty-four notices for stolen goods, ten for stopped items, three for found items and one notice in which the status of the item was unclear. In contrast, in the same month, the *Daily Advertiser* listed 154 lost notices, sixty-one stolen notices, twelve stopped notices and twenty-five found notices. Even though they made their task easier by singling out a publication which contained so few notices, the pawnbrokers were understood to continually fail. In 1765, Sir John Fielding, who had become principal magistrate for Westminster following his brother's death in 1754, complained that pawnbrokers paid little attention to advertisements and the information they contained.⁷⁸ Nevertheless, some pawnbrokers clearly came to take seriously the possibilities of systematically engaging with the advertisements for lost or stolen goods.

Evidence from cases heard and recorded in the Old Bailey shows that pawnbrokers were keen to publicise that they kept records of advertised items. On 6 September 1769, Samuel Bailey was indicted at the Old Bailey for breaking and entering the pawnbroker Samuel Slater's house. Bailey then gave the watch he had allegedly stolen to Philip Backwell in order that he would pawn it at the shop of Mr. Curtois. At the shop, Curtois's suspicions were raised and he described how he 'looked in a book, in which we enter every watch that is advertised, with name and number, and not finding such advertised, I lent him 27 s. upon it.'⁷⁹ Similarly, on 10 February 1775, when the pawnbroker Richard Pharez suspected that a potential customer was offering him a stolen watch he referred to his 'book, by which I found this watch had been advertised'.⁸⁰ It is perhaps not surprising that certain pawnbrokers were

---

⁷⁷ See the notice in the header of the *Public Advertiser* (London), 5 January 1753. It was then repeatedly included in the *Public Advertiser* across the year, for example 10 January 1753 and 11 August 1753. See also Black, *The English Press in the Eighteenth Century*, 60.

⁷⁸ See the *Public Advertiser* (London), 1 January 1765. Quoted in Tomkins, 'Pawnbroking and the Survival Strategies of the Urban Poor', 171. Also cited in Beverley Lemire, 'The Theft of Clothes and Popular Consumerism in Early Modern England', *Journal of Social History*, 24 (1990), 259.

⁷⁹ *OBPO* (www.oldbaileyonline.org, version 8.0, 9 August 2019), September 1769, trial of Samuel Bailey (t17690906-39).

⁸⁰ *OBPO* (www.oldbaileyonline.org, version 8.0, 9 August 2019), September 1775, trial of Henry Jordan (t17750913-36).

keen to give testimony that publicised how they raised suspicions, stopped stolen items and advertised suspicious goods where necessary. In noting how they kept records of all the watches advertised, Curtois and Pharez demonstrated how they went above and beyond what was expected of them. An Act of 1757 required that pawnbrokers keep records of goods pledged and money lent, as well as the date of the transaction and the name and address of the customer.[81] If people pledged goods on behalf of someone else, the Act required that pawnbrokers also noted the owner's name. If they paid a small fee, customers could demand a duplicate of the register details. By 1784, a new act demanded that pawnbrokers give the customer a duplicate of the registered details.[82] Yet, there was no legislation requiring that pawnbrokers were obliged to make records of objects advertised as lost or stolen. In noting how they systematically recorded such advertisements, Curtois and Pharez showed the robust strategies they had in place to ensure vigilance. In 1785, the first attempts were made to define the trade and require all pawnbrokers be licensed. Despite claims of going above and beyond from individuals such as Curtois and Pharez, pawnbrokers remained difficult businesses to regulate. Nine further acts of a similar nature were instituted between 1784 and 1800. In 1800, the legislation was consolidated in the Pawnbroker's Act.[83]

As with goldsmiths, jewellers, watchmakers, bankers, refiners, toymen and salesmen, pawnbrokers had long been an important part of the lost notices system: they were one of the key businesses whom the warning carrier notices also served. In the eighteenth century, they continued to be important and increasingly positioned themselves as businesses actively on the lookout for lost and stolen goods. Doing so was important for their reputation and position within eighteenth-century society. Being on the lookout was part of the urban ecology and proved crucial to certain individuals and businesses.

Hackney coachmen and pawnbrokers were increasingly expected to be attentive to lost objects, but over the eighteenth-century dogs became the most regularly appearing 'thing' within the lost notices system. Fictional stories of dogs becoming lost on London streets suggest that an array of people would be inclined to simply pick up dogs that appeared ownerless. As we witnessed in Chapter 1, in Francis Coventry's 1751 publication *The History of Pompey the Little*, Pompey is picked up every time he is more than a moment absent from

---

[81] Tomkins, 'Pawnbroking and the Survival Strategies of the Urban Poor', 172. The Act also stipulated that pawnbrokers became the owners of any goods (for which a loan of up to 10 pounds was given) not reclaimed after two years. The Act also gave peace officers the right to search pawnbroker premises which they suspect of receiving stolen goods. See Melanie Tebbutt, *Making Ends Meet: Pawnbroking and Working-Class Credit* (London, 1983), 73.

[82] Tebbutt, *Making Ends Meet*, 75. But such regulation continued to be difficult to police, see Swain and Fairweather, 'The Legal Regulation of Pawnbroking in England', 151.

[83] Tebbutt, *Making Ends Meet*, 75.

his previous 'owner'.[84] Similarly, in the 1803 publication *The Biography of a Spaniel*, the narrative can move forward largely because individuals are so willing to buy but also simply take up lost dogs.[85] As we saw in Chapter 2, this pattern is also evident in *Cato, or Interesting Adventures of a Dog of Sentiment* (1816), Cato finds himself lost after running off from his owner Henry on Oxford Road.[86] Although lost, he is quickly 'found' and taken up by a young boy who tries to sell him and even considers killing him to be able to sell his skin. Luckily, Cato is then rescued by another boy named Frank, who ultimately gives him away.[87] These it-narratives, so concerned with circulation, saw dogs running off of their own volition but also included the idea that people would take up seemingly ownerless dogs, particularly in urban spaces. Importantly, the dogs featured in these tales would have been understood as lost rather than strayed because of their appearance and breeding.[88] To be a lap dog was always to be owned. With such dogs, the concern was that once out of sight, the dog would quickly be taken up by any number of people. In writing lost notices then, losers potentially wrote out to multitudes of urban denizens.

There is also some evidence that losers were aware that they were writing to those who had wilfully and intentionally stolen their dogs. The question of dog stealing became particularly relevant in the second half the eighteenth century and remained so until the late nineteenth century.[89] The 1770 Act for preventing the Stealing of Dogs noted that 'the Practice of stealing Dogs hath of late Years greatly increased'.[90] In response to the increased threat, the Act acknowledged dogs as property which should be protected under the law. The change brought about by the act impacted lost notices for dogs, which began to list that if the dog were 'found in the Possession of any Person', rather than returned following the publication of the notice, that person would be 'prosecuted accordingly'. Despite such threats and the greater weight of the law, in his 1781 publication *A View of Society and Manners in High and Low Life*, George Parker noted that making enquiries and advertising remained important. He advised that, if a dog were lost, the owner should look for a 'dog seller' near to the place the dog went missing. Parker reckoned that 'it is very probable' that the seller would provide information 'for a smaller reward that

---

[84] Francis Coventry, *The History of Pompey the Little: Or The Life and Adventures of a Lap-Dog* ed. Nicholas Hudson [1751] (Buffalo, NY, 2008).
[85] Anon., *The Biography of a Spaniel* (London, 1803).
[86] Anon., *Cato, or Interesting Adventures of a Dog of Sentiment* (London, 1816), 68.
[87] Anon., *Cato*, 72–97.
[88] Philip Howell, *At Home and Astray: The Domestic Dog in Victorian Britain* (Charlottesville, VA and London, 2015), 95.
[89] Jane Hamlett and Julie-Marie Strange, *Pet Revolution: Animals and the Making of Modern British Life* (London, 2023), 61.
[90] 10 Geo. III. C.18

what you would have proposed, besides saving you the trouble and expence [sic] of an advertisement'.[91]

Decades later in 1844, the evidence heard by the Select Committee on Dog Stealing (Metropolis) illuminates a long-established system within the city, by which dogs understood to have owners would be stolen not to sell them on, but rather to gain a reward by returning them. In giving evidence to the committee, the Chief Commissioner of Police, Richard Mayne, asserted that the system was sustained by the fact that owners were prepared to pay rewards to reclaim the dog.[92] Inspector Shackell of the Metropolitan Police gave evidence that he was aware of people operating in the city who would facilitate the return of a dog.[93] George Hoabdell, a dog dealer in the city, noted that he himself had facilitated the return of dogs on behalf of others. He told the Select Committee that 'I have had applications made to me to get dogs back, and in some cases I have done it, and in some cases I could not do it.'[94] Hoabdell also mentioned that dog stealers took dogs to dog dealers in order that they might act as go-betweens in the return of dogs.[95] Such dog dealers and other go-betweens could become infamous. One individual remained nameless but was instead referred to as 'the Jonathan Wild of the fraternity'.[96] Vincent George Dowling editor of the sporting paper *Bell's Life* (a sporting paper) gave evidence that when his own spaniel went missing and after he had ascertained it was not in the hands of dog stealers, he 'advertised, and recovered' his dog. He 'found that it had not been stolen, but that it had strayed away, and had been picked up by an individual who, upon payment of the reward, restored it'.[97] In these cases, owners' first port of call was often dog dealers within the city, and more particularly in Leadenhall and Club Row, who were understood to be able to provide information concerning who held the dog and the reward sought for them.[98] Given the established nature of the system outlined by witnesses before the Select Committee, it is likely that lost notices for dogs placed in the later part of the eighteenth century and early nineteenth century were written mindful of these dealers (and sellers). Here again we see the emergence of a particular group of people who were on the lookout and in the know when it came to lost and stolen goods. But we also see the likelihood of a larger audience at stake within the notices system. There was always the possibility

---

[91] George Parker, *A View of Society and Manners in High and Low Life* vol. 2 (London, 1781), 81–82.
[92] *Report from the Select Committee on Dog Stealing (Metropolis); Together with the Minutes of Evidence Taken before Them* (London, 1844), 5.
[93] *Report from the Select Committee on Dog Stealing*, 17.   [94] Ibid., 22.   [95] Ibid., 25.
[96] William Bishop, *Legal Protection of Dogs from the Increasing Evil of Dog-Stealers and Receivers* (London, 1844), 23.
[97] *Report from the Select Committee on Dog Stealing*, 45.
[98] Ibid., 22; Hamlett and Strange, *Pet Revolution*, 58.

that the dog had simply 'strayed away', been 'picked up by an individual' and that (like the 'servant Maid' we met at the start of the chapter) they would be ready to return it when they saw the advertisement and the reward.

Conclusion

In the eighteenth century, alongside kidnappers, dog sellers and dealers, pawnbrokers and Hackney coachmen, Londoners expected that an even wider range of people would be on the look-out for 'lost things'. When Charles Cope, who we met earlier, placed his notice in the *Daily Advertiser* on Thursday 8 January 1789, the 'whoever' he listed as hopefully being on the lookout and finding turned out to be a maid-servant named Mary Wilson who lived close by at Mr Bond's No. 39, Strand.[99] Although it has been suggested that London was becoming increasingly anonymous in this period, we should not ignore the cultures of observation and connection that also grew. As we saw in Chapter 2, although London was known for its 'inexhaustible reservoir of concealment', stories of people running away to the capital to hide, usually ended with the person being found.[100] Similarly, in that chapter we saw that guidebooks for London published in the long eighteenth century increasingly underlined that to be urban, to be a *Londoner*, was to be on the lookout and in the know. You might not know who had placed the lost notice, but as a Londoner, you were likely to have seen it and might perhaps even act if you did come across that silver watch, spaniel or eloped wife. The lost notices system was able to grow through the expansion of newspaper culture, but also because there was an expectation of response. We might understand such actions, such practices, then as producing a deep sense of the social nature of urban life: that people were understood to be on the lookout for lost things and in doing so were implicitly looking out for (or less optimistically, watching) each other.

---

[99] *OBPO* (www.oldbaileyonline.org, version 8.0, 15 August 2019), January 1789, trial of Aquila Cole (t17890114-21).

[100] William Godwin, *Caleb Williams* [1794] (Oxford, 2009), 246.

Part III

Learning from Loss

5   Describing and Knowing Possessions

Between 1835 and 1837, Louis-Jacques-Mandé Daguerre (1787–1851) worked in France seeking the means to permanently preserve the images created by the camera obscura. In the same period, William Henry Fox Talbot (1800–1877) was focused on similar objectives in England. By 1839, both had succeeded. Daguerre had created fragile daguerreotypes and Talbot had produced paper-based calotypes. It was not until the late 1840s, however, that both processes achieved reliable results. Throughout the 1840s, Talbot dedicated himself to testing and developing the possibilities of calotypes. In this period, Talbot was also keen to communicate the potential offered by his new technology. To this end, he published *The Pencil of Nature* between 1844 and 1846. The volume was one of the first commercially published books to include photographic illustrations (see Figure 5.1). The photographs included in each copy needed to be reproduced and inserted alongside the pre-printed text. Producing such reproductions was one of the calotype's marvels. Talbot described how 'The number of copies which can be taken from a single original photographic picture, appears to be almost unlimited.'[1]

Alongside capturing images of people and architecture, and producing facsimiles of images and texts, Talbot foresaw one of photography's potential uses as recording objects. Within the book, he included 'Articles of China' (see Figure 5.1), an image of multiple ceramic objects lined up on shelves. The photographs are two-dimensional: they capture the objects from the 'front' and render them static entities. The images supposedly offered clarity, a definitive record of the objects in question. Nevertheless, it is important to remember that the level of clarity was different in different copies of the book. Due to the photographic inserts needing to be copied for each book and the unreliability of the process at this stage, some of the reproductions were clearer than others. The extent of the detail captured in a particular copy was open to question.

In his introduction to *The Pencil of Nature*, Talbot noted that although the term 'photography' had become well known, he thought that some people

---

[1] Henry Fox Talbot, *The Pencil of Nature: The History of Photography* (London, 1844–46), 44.

Figure 5.1 William Henry Fox Talbot, 'Articles of China', 1843–1844, Salted paper print. 2015.74.
Image source: The Mary and Leigh Block Endowment Fund, The Art Institute of Chicago.

might still be 'unacquainted with the art' and that 'a few words...of general explanation' might be required.[2] Alongside his explanations of photography, Talbot also used the book to situate photography's potential functions in relation to the existing technologies. The text that accompanies 'Articles of China' notes that one benefit of such images is that they can depict 'on paper' 'the whole cabinet of a Virtuoso and collector of old China...in little more time than it would take him to make a written inventory describing it in the usual way'.[3] Talbot was clear that the process was as convenient as the 'usual' technologies for recording objects, such as written descriptions.

Writing in the 1840s, it is significant that Talbot saw photographic images like 'Articles of China' as being particularly useful forms of evidence. He considered that if a thief stole such treasures, photographic records could be used as 'mute testimony' in court to prove that they had belonged to

---

[2] See 'Introductory Remarks', Fox Talbot, *The Pencil of Nature*, 5.
[3] Fox Talbot, *The Pencil of Nature*, 18.

another. Here the camera could describe (although this was and is limited: a camera can never capture its 'own passage into the hands of a stranger').[4] In understanding how photographic representations might operate as evidence of ownership, Talbot drew upon a long-established practice. In the eighteenth century, people used *written* descriptions to make claims to ownership and to facilitate the return of lost possessions. Producing details, particularly relevant details, demonstrated knowledge of an item and thus acted as testimony of possession. Prior to the technological innovations pioneered by Talbot, it was written description that acted as not-so-mute proof of ownership.

Rather than focused on the intricacies of the lost notices *system* as the previous chapters have been, this chapter, and the one that follows, looks more closely at the texts included in the notices themselves. This chapter examines the new 'textual praxis' such notices drew upon: description.[5] Here again, we see lost and runaway notices as a particularly eighteenth-century story. In this instance, it is because they drew upon a textual praxis that was increasingly profuse at this time and would later be challenged by new technologies, such as photography. As we explored in Chapter 4, the lost and runaway notices system sought to reach out to Hackney carriage drivers, dog sellers and dealers, kidnappers and pawnbrokers, but also to the wider readership who daily engaged with London's newspaper culture. In these short notices, writers sought to lay before newspaper readers the circumstances of loss, the thing lost and where it could be returned to for what reward. Writers tried to set out what the lost thing was in terms that would prove their ownership and make it visible and recognisable amid the increasingly complex social life of urban spaces.[6] To achieve this difficult and pressing aim, writers embraced description.

Description was not new in the eighteenth century. It had a long and complex history.[7] As Brian Ogilvie reminds us, description was central to studies of nature and natural history. In the period between 1530 and 1630, as naturalists had sought to describe nature and catalogue 'its marvellous and mundane products', they had considered description in detail. While observation might be understood as attending to the natural world to perceive it more fully, description offered an important means of capturing the findings

---

[4] When Patti Smith forgets her camera on a bench on Rockaway Beach, she is unsettled by its inability to record its own loss. Patti Smith, *M Train* (London and New York, NY, 2016), 146.
[5] The idea of description as a 'textual praxis' comes from Philippe Hamon and Patricia Baudoin, 'Rhetorical Status of the Descriptive', *Yale French Studies*, 61 (1981), 6. As cited in Cynthia Wall, *The Prose of Things: Transformations of Description in the Eighteenth Century* (Chicago, IL, 2006). 20.
[6] I use 'social' in the broadest sense here, to include human and non-human things. Bruno Latour, *Reassembling the Social: An Introduction to Actor-Network-Theory* (Oxford, 2005), 71.
[7] Patrick Singy, 'Huber's Eyes: The Art of Scientific Observation Before the Emergence of Positivism', *Representations*, 95 (2006), 55.

facilitated by such attention. Ogilvie argues that we should see the 'process and result' of description as 'the central concern of Renaissance natural history'.[8] Unlike their predecessors or successors, Renaissance naturalists examined and developed descriptive practices. Other areas of enquiry also came to consider description in greater detail. Joanna Stalnaker has shown the importance of description within both science and literature. However, Stalnaker observes that in the eighteenth century, description became a 'site of growing tensions', that resolved 'themselves in our modern distinction between literature and science'.[9] To this end, Cynthia Wall has laid out how description emerged as an important *literary* textual praxis in the eighteenth century. Again, description as a textual practice was not new: textual praxes in seventeenth-century Britain had shown the importance of detail, setting the groundwork for further literary changes in the following century.[10] Wall has plotted the shifting nature of description as it operated in the novel and other prose genres of the period. In later eighteenth-century novels, characters began to enter described spaces, filled with significant and meaningful objects, rather than (in the Defoe tradition) suddenly picking up an object that lay previously unseen and unreferenced.[11] Description became crucial to literary forms in the eighteenth century, and object descriptions were particularly important. At the same time, object descriptions were utilised in a range of texts such as inventories, wills and lost notices, and thus to eighteenth-century material cultures more broadly.[12] With an ever-more complex range of objects in circulation, description emerged as a tool for 'making things visible'.[13] This chapter builds on Wall's work to show how lost notices were an important space in which a range of people engaged with and wrote descriptions, and in turn developed this textual praxis in new ways.

John Bender and Michael Marrinan assert that descriptions 'are based upon a finite and selective body of features' and 'employ different media to transmit the salient characteristics of those objects'.[14] Modes of description are

---

[8] Brian W. Ogilvie, *The Science of Describing: Natural History in Renaissance Europe* (Chicago, IL, 2006), 6.

[9] Joanna Stalnaker, *The Unfinished Enlightenment: Description in the Age of the Encyclopedia* (Ithaca, NY, 2010), 6.

[10] Wall, *The Prose of Things*, 43.   [11] Ibid., 112.

[12] Amanda Vickery, '"Neat and Not Too Showey": Words and Wallpaper in Regency England', in John Styles and Amanda Vickery (eds), *Gender, Taste, and Material Culture in Britain and North America 1700–1800* (New Haven, CT and London, 2006), 205; Amanda Vickery, 'His and Hers: Gender, Consumption and Household Accounting in Eighteenth-Century England', *Past & Present* Supp. 1 (2006), 35; Amanda Vickery, *The Gentleman's Daughter: Women's Lives in Georgian England* (New Haven, CT and London, 1998), 147 and 151; Maxine Berg, 'Women's Consumption and the Industrial Classes of Eighteenth-Century England', *Journal of Social History*, 30:2 (1996), 418.

[13] Wall, *The Prose of Things*, 14.

[14] John Bender and Michael Marrinan, 'Introduction', in John Bender and Michael Marrinan (eds), *Regimes of Description: In the Archive of the Eighteenth Century* (Stanford, CA, 2005), 4.

historically and culturally contingent, shaped by changing perspectives, context and media. Lost notices published in newspapers offered a particular form of media, which required certain kinds of description. Losers needed their descriptions to make a particular 'thing' visible and recognisable to others but had to do so within a relatively short space due to costs. What becomes clear in the notices is that a 'finite and selective body of features' emerged to ease the task of description and recognition. As the first half of this chapter will show, focusing on *relevant* and *distinguishable* features became particularly significant. For instance, the bank note or watch number became important. No such abstraction existed for dogs, however, and when describing these beings, we see more recourse to idiosyncrasies. Surprisingly, the use of such details was not common when describing people. Instead, the descriptions constructed in these instances relied on features such as name, age, stature, hair and clothes. An important and overlooked consequence of the different logics of description was their ability to signal differences between 'things'. As we have seen, lost notices were a space in which the seemingly blurry lines between humans, non-human animals and objects were tested and stretched in this period. They also demonstrate how different languages of possession existed and that owners held and understood different relationships of possession.[15]

Given that people might need to produce descriptions of their 'things' to prove ownership at some point, it is important to ask how eighteenth-century owners developed the necessary knowledge and this is what the second half of this chapter will go on to do. In cases of loss, as opposed to wills or inventories, writing descriptions relied upon the ability to recall and remember such knowledge. How then did people develop and *remember* all they needed to know? Seeing an apprentice or servant day in and day out would perhaps consolidate the ability to remember their stature, hair and the colour of their breeches. Similarly, the increasing proximity of dogs as members of the households also provided a way of knowing that belied memory. At the same time, watches were items that would have been on their person and used regularly. That people would have known things that existed in close relationship to them may perhaps seem obvious. Yet, in exploring how people were able to write descriptions of absent things, we see that they did not always feel confident in relying on their memories, but rather that they often used records or the skills and knowledge of others. In producing the photographs of rows of china then, Talbot drew upon an established practice of keeping records of possessions. Although the photograph would fade over time, it would have provided a record. Prior to photographs, people used day books, diaries and inventories to record salient features. The existence of such technologies

[15] Thanks to Karen Lipsedge for encouraging me to think about the different languages of possession.

156   Learning from Loss

shows people's awareness of the likelihood of loss and the need to pro-actively prepare for it. People worked to ensure that the means of reclamation were open to them, should their possession go missing. That such technologies were different for different things again underscores the varied relationships of possession in this period and how people enacted and distinguished those relationships through specific practices.

The Logics of Description

The descriptions for lost possessions focused on certain relevant details, and the choice of details was shaped by different practices and institutions, as the case of bank notes shows. On a Wednesday in November 1760, two bank notes went missing. They were lost 'either in Lombard Street, or between there and the Custom House'.[16] It was difficult to be definite about where the loss had taken place. At the Bank of England, Thomas Jones, clerk to Mr Samuel Lloyd, a merchant based in Devonshire Square, who was the owner of the notes, recalled how his colleague Mr Case (who was underage and thus unable to give notice to the Bank himself) had placed the notes in a Memorandum Book while in the shop of the banker Mr Martin based in Lombard Street, but on looking again to the Book 'he could not find the same' nor say 'what became thereof'.[17] Like promissory notes, bank notes were paper issues that did not bear interest. The Bank of England had tried to encourage the use of interest-bearing bank bills in the late seventeenth century, but it was bank notes that proved more sustainable, acting as forms of cash. By 1709 bank notes had begun to outnumber bills, but only in 1758 were bank notes recognised by the judiciary as money and it was not until 1833 that Parliament declared bank notes legal tender.[18] On 26 November 1760, trying to ensure the return of the two bank notes, Thomas Jones went to the Bank of England.[19] Here he used the lost notes system outlined in Chapter 3 to ensure that the notes were not erroneously cashed by the Bank. On 1 December 1760, Samuel Lloyd, the owner of the notes, also placed a notice in the newspaper to mark proof of ownership, alert other banks to the loss and potential theft and seek return. The description of the notes that appeared in the advertisement was concise. It remarked that there were 'two Bank Notes, viz. No. B 40, to William Best

---

[16] 'Lost last Wednesday, either in Lombard Street, or between there and the Custom House', *Daily Advertiser* (London), 1 December 1760. The notes were advertised again in the *Daily Advertiser* on 2 December 1760 and 11 December 1760. The reward offered increased in each notice.
[17] Bank of England Archive, Cashier's Department Record of Bank Note Issue: Lost Book, 19 February 1759–11 February 1764, C101/10, f.109.
[18] Christine Desan, *Making Money: Coin, Currency and the Coming of Capitalism* (Oxford, 2014), 327-28 and 311.
[19] Bank of England Archive, Cashier's Department Record of Bank Note Issue: Lost Book, 19 February 1759–11 February 1764, C101/10, f.109.

or Bearer, 100l. Dated April 29, 1760; 409, to Tim Smith or Bearer, 30l. dated Sept. 3 1760'.[20] The descriptive details given in the lost notice mirror those expected from losers when they recorded their loss at the Bank of England. Hiroki Shin has shown that the Bank usually noted the name and abode of the claimant, the serial number, the dates and amount on note and, finally, the situation in which it was lost.[21] The Bank clearly influenced what the relevant details were understood to be in cases of loss, and unique identifiers such as serial numbers, amounts and dates supported the finding process. Significantly, given their importance in making bank notes unique objects and showing ownership, details of endorsements were not required.[22] In this case, the process of identifying the notes was successful. The records in the Bank of England Lost Books tell us that the notes turned up again in the summer of 1761 and on 8 October 1761, Thomas Jones returned to the Bank to revoke the notice he had placed with them.

Another bank note was advertised as having gone missing on a Tuesday afternoon in December 1792, this time it was presumed that it had been lost between 'Newman Street' in Soho and 'Kinglands' (presumably Kinglands Road in the east of the city).[23] On 5 December, a 'Mr Loder' went to the Bank of England to give notice of the note going missing. Loader, who appeared in the newspaper advertisement as 'Mr Loader', identified himself to the Bank as 'Clerk of the works' and told of how a servant of Mr Bent (presumably the owner of the works and someone who also appears in the newspaper advertisement) had lost the note 'a few days ago'.[24] Loader told the Bank that the note was of the value of £30, was issued on 23 November 1792 and was numbered 8997. This seemingly brief description was repeated when the note was advertised in the *Daily Advertiser* the next day. The advertisement included the description 'for 30 l, No. 8997'.[25] In the eighteenth century then, the means of describing a bank note, the features crucial to ownership and reclamation were clearly delineated, with the amount and number being all that might be supplied in some cases. It is worth noting though that such limited descriptions might not be enough to ensure return. Twelve months later, the

---

[20] 'Lost last Wednesday, either in Lombard Street, or between there and the Custom House', *Daily Advertiser* (London), 1 December 1760.
[21] Hiroki Shin, *The Age of Paper: The Bank Note, Communal Currency and British Society, 1790s–1830s* (Cambridge, 2024), 80.
[22] On the importance of endorsements in creating bank notes as unique objects and showing ownership see James Thompson, *Models of Value: Eighteenth-Century Political Economy and the Novel* (Durham, NC, 1996), 137; Shin, *The Age of Paper*, 135.
[23] 'Bank Note. Lost on Tuesday Afternoon', *Daily Advertiser* (London), 6 December 1792.
[24] Bank of England Archive, Cashier's Department Record of Bank Note Issue: Lost Book, 23 December 1791–28 November 1793, C101/19, f.157.
[25] 'Bank Note. Lost on Tuesday Afternoon', *Daily Advertiser* (London), 6 December 1792.

note had not appeared, and the Bank refunded it after Mr Loader provided two guarantors.[26]

Another financial instrument that appeared regularly in lost notices was bills of exchange. Bills were an instruction by one person (the drawer) for the payment of money to another person (drawee). The money or amount at stake was then actually paid by a third party (usually a bank). The drawee would endorse the bill by signing it to indicate their acceptance of the obligation. Bills of exchange were usually payable at a particular point in the future and the person receiving the money had to demand it from the drawer on the day the bill became due. When a bill went missing in 1742, the owner placed a notice in the *Daily Advertiser*. Like the bank notes, the bill was noted as the 'Payment being stopt' and thus 'of no Service to any but the Owner'. The description included in the notice recorded how the bill was 'dated Norwich, November 26, 1742, for 24l, 1s drawn by John Cooper, on Henry Lawton, payable to Nicholas Kendle, the last of December'.[27] In including these details, the description largely recorded all the written and printed information contained on the bill. Bills usually included the amount concerned (in numerical and word form) ('24l'), the date at which the bill was drawn ('November 26, 1742'), the date it was due ('the last of December'), the person to whom it was to be paid ('Nicholas Kendle'), the signature of the person from whose firm the bill was drawn ('by John Cooper, on Henry Lawton') and a space for the acceptor's signature.[28] Similarly, when two bills were lost in November 1830, the notice placed in *The Times* recorded these same pieces of information. It noted 'one for £15 12s, drawn by J. W. Lyon on and accepted by B. and W. Blogg, due the 4th of March; and another for £22 15s drawn by J. W. Lyon on and accepted by William Rood, due 25th of February next'.[29] For bills, the amount, drawee, date and accepter were the salient points of information to record in the description.

In the eighteenth century, each different type of thing was described through a particular set of relevant details. In seeking to describe financial instruments such as bank notes and bills of exchange, losers recalled amounts, numbers and dates, but they very rarely mentioned the material nature of the item concerned. Helped in their endeavour by Jonathan Wild, when two Bank notes were 'Lost or dropt at the South Sea House' in 1720, the person advertising

---

[26] Bank of England Archive, Cashier's Department Record of Bank Note Issue: Lost Book, 23 December 1791–28 November 1793, C101/19, f.157.
[27] 'Lost Yesterday, between the Hours of Twelve and Two', *Daily Advertiser* (London), 24 December 1742.
[28] Mary Poovey, *Genres of the Credit Economy: Mediating Value in Eighteenth- and Nineteenth-Century Britain* (Chicago, IL and London, 2008), 37.
[29] 'BILLS LOST, on Friday, the 26th of November last:', *The Times* (London), 11 December 1830.

their absence noted that they were 'very much worn and torn in the Middle'.[30] Yet including such a sense of texture (and in this case, fragility) was uncommon. When reading lost notices for notes and bills, we are rarely given any clue that the lost thing is a piece of paper. Even in the case of coin, descriptions tended to list the amount and material, 'Four Guineas in Gold, and about Eighteenth Shillings in Silver', but no other features.[31]

Bank notes and coins are strange possessions, of course. Although the miser's dream might be to hoard wealth, making possession permanent, for most the ownership of bank notes and coins is only ever temporary. Despite such time limitations, the lack of material details notices provided in the case of coins is surprising as other evidence suggests people did recognise their material features. In the late 1820s when Prince Hermann von Pückler-Muskau conducted a tour of England, he proved forgetful. He left behind 'a purse with eighty sovereigns' in his 'quayside sleeping quarters'.[32] Later his pocketbook fell out of his breast pocket, and he was grateful to (and deeply surprised by) a young man who returned it.[33] Later still in his trip, while he was in Chepstow, he realised that he was missing his 'purse and notebook', which he always carried on him. Thinking that to pursue these things was a lost cause, he decided to pay his bill and leave. On getting his change, 'because of the slight nick above the eye of His Majesty George IV', he thought he 'recognized one of my own sovereigns among those I received'.[34] His response suggests at how he closely looked at the coins that crossed his path in everyday dealings. That he was able to recognise 'his' sovereign from such a minor detail is also suggestive of the detailed material understanding people had of money. In a world replete with counterfeits, it is perhaps unsurprising that people looked closely at the coins that passed their way.[35]

Despite Pückler's close eye for detail when it came to his lost coins, the descriptions for financial instruments included in lost notices rarely mentioned these material intricacies. Instead, the descriptions of notes, bills and coin largely rendered financial instruments as pure abstraction: not things or material forms, but rather just function. The dematerialisation of money within this form of representation is perhaps explained by money becoming increasingly

---

[30] 'Lost or dropt at the South Sea House, on Monday the 21st of November', *Daily Advertiser* (London), 21 December 1720.
[31] 'Lost Yesterday, between Two and Three o'clock in the Afternoon', *Daily Advertiser* (London), 12 December 1752.
[32] Prince Hermann von Pückler-Muskau (Linda B. Parshall trans.), *Letters of a Dead Man* (Cambridge, 2016), 34.
[33] von Pückler-Muskau, *Letters of a Dead Man*, 461.   [34] Ibid., 623.
[35] Katherine Smoak, 'The Weight of Necessity: Counterfeit Coins in the British Atlantic World, circa 1760–1800', *The William and Mary Quarterly*, 74:3 (2017), 467–502; Katherine Smoak, 'Circulating Counterfeits: Making Money and its Meanings in the Eighteenth-Century British Atlantic World' (Unpublished PhD Thesis, John Hopkins University, 2018), 84–117.

160   Learning from Loss

dematerialised in the eighteenth century.[36] In reading these 'descriptions', we are reminded of Christine Desan's argument regarding the reinvention of money in early modern England. Money came to be understood as a mode of payment that was 'more interesting for what it *does* than for what it *is*'. Yet Desan goes on to argue that, such a formulation is not 'natural' or inevitable, rather she states that the abstraction of money 'is part of the revolution's vanishing act'.[37] Here in the pages of eighteenth-century daily newspapers, in the descriptions people produced of their lost bills, banks notes and coins, we see how they contributed to this larger project of seeing money for what it did rather than what it was. Even when money and financial instruments went missing their 'thinginess' did not re-emerge within people's consciousness, rather what was retained were the details that allowed financial instruments to work, to transfer value and circulate wealth.[38] Such forms did not just reflect the increasing abstraction taking place, rather they also *produced* abstraction.

That financial instruments were objects, were pieces of paper or metal you could pick up and hand on, is only apparent because notices listed their containers. We know that when a set of promissory notes and receipts and two legal briefs went missing in 1720, they were in 'a yellow Letter Case'.[39] Similarly, 'a Note of Hand for Ten Pounds, and upwards, with some more Memorandums', were 'wrapt up in a Piece of Seal's Skin' when they were lost by a 'poor Man' in 1752.[40] In 1771, 'three Guineas and a Half, and some Silver' had been in a 'long green Silk Purse, containing a small Ivory Box' when they went.[41] The materiality of letter cases and purses was not in doubt and some types of carrying devices appeared regularly in lost notices. Pocketbooks in red leather were particularly popular. In 1771 'A red Leather Pocket Book with Silver Clasps, opens both Sides' went missing with three Lottery tickets inside and in 1830 another 'RED LEATHER POCKET BOOK' was lost with 'sundry papers and a Bank Post Bill for £55'.[42] Even here though, as the material nature of these carriers becomes present through the descriptions, the lack of detail is telling. Pocketbooks were often ornate items, decorated with embroidery and embossing and in some cases hand-painted

---

[36] Deborah Valenze, *The Social Life of Money in the English Past* (Cambridge, 2006), 22.
[37] Desan, *Making Money*, 1.
[38] For more on 'thinginess' see Kate Smith, 'Amidst Things: New Histories of Commodities, Capital and Consumption', *The Historical Journal*, 61:3 (2018), 856.
[39] 'Lost on Saturday the 20th of November last', *Daily Advertiser* (London), 8 December 1720.
[40] 'Lost last Tuesday, a Note of Hand for Ten Pounds', *Daily Advertiser* (London), 1 December 1752.
[41] 'If any Person has found a long green Silk Purse', *Daily Advertiser* (London), 18 December 1771.
[42] 'Left in a Hackney Coach on Tuesday the 26th ult.', *Daily Advertiser* (London), 2 December 1771; 'LOST, between the Bank of England and the St Katharine Docks', *The Times* (London), 15 December 1830.

silks.[43] They were also often objects that bore the name of their owner, yet these details were not mentioned in lost notices.[44] 'Losers' desire for anonymity perhaps explains such omissions, but the lack of detail here also belies the seeming immateriality of things connected to finance and their increased abstraction in this period. However, financial instruments were not the only things increasingly viewed through the prism of abstraction.

In 1745, when a certain Thomas Piggott Esq. wrote a notice for the *Daily Advertiser,* with the assistance of his watchmaker Mr Bowly, he described his lost watch in detail. We learn that he had lost 'a Silver repeating Watch made by Bowly, no Number, a gilt Cap over the Movement, the Case pierced in Relievo, a Blank Space at Bottom in a black Shagreen Case, with Silver Bessel and Edges, and a green Silk String with two Seals set in Silver'. As such, Piggott provides us with a largely representative advertisement: it lists many of the key features apparent in other lost notices for watches placed in London newspapers over the long eighteenth century, including the type of watch, the material it was made from, its maker, its lack of a number, its casing and the other objects (two seals) that were attached to it.

Noting the material the watch was made from did little to distinguish it from others, yet writers were keen to list this feature. They did so in 87 per cent of notices. The watches that went missing were mainly made of gold or silver. In fact, 52 per cent were listed as silver and 29 per cent as gold. From the 1740s onwards, other materials also came to be listed for watches, such as metal gilt, silver gilt and pinchbeck (alloy of copper and zinc), but these instances were occasional: gold and silver dominated watchmaking. While listing the material make-up of the watch might offer some sort of distinction to those involved in the reclaiming process, listing the maker's name and the number of the watch must have proved more helpful in making a particular watch discernible to others. Maker's names often appeared on the dial plate, or the back of the watch, sometimes accompanied by the city of making and the serial number identifying a particular watch.[45] Lost notices frequently included the maker's name: 77 per cent of the notices sampled. They included some of the most prestigious makers of the period, such as John Ellicott (1706–1772),

---

[43] See, for example, Victoria and Albert Museum, T.10801953, Pocketbook, Red Morocco Leather embroidered with Gilt Thread in Satin Stitch, Tétouan, Morocco, 1776; Victoria and Albert Museum, T.56-1940, Pocketbook, Embroidered Moroccan Leather, 1768; Victoria and Albert Museum, T.51-1927, Pocketbook, Embroidered Velvet, Tunisia, 1774. For pocket-book in silk with hand-painted watercolour decoration see T.143-1961, Pocketbook, Cream Silk, Lined with Pink Silk and Edged with Silver-Gilt Woven Lace, France, 1750s.

[44] Pauline Rushton, 'Two Men's Leather Letter Cases: Mercantile Pride and Hierarchies of Display', in Chloe Wigston Smith and Beth Fowkes Tobin (eds), *Small Things in the Eighteenth Century: The Political and Personal Value of the Miniature* (Cambridge, 2022), 180.

[45] Edward Town and Angela McShane (eds), *Marking Time: Objects, People, and Their Lives, 1500–1800* (New Haven, CT and London, 2020), 347.

Thomas Tompion (1639–1713) and Daniel Quare (c.1648–1724), as well as lesser-known makers such as John Ward, Thomas Hally and Charles Clay. Due to the high levels of subcontracting within the watch- and clock-making trade, the maker's name referred either to the finisher, or simply to the person who had requested the making and finishing of the piece and had their name attached before selling.[46] Rather than simply a form of 'branding', in looking at responses to loss, we see how the maker's name played other roles in material cultures. Including the maker's name in notices meant that writers could offer a clear identification mark that required textual literacy. We also begin to see how making cultures marked objects and that such material practices in turn shaped descriptions.

Making practices produced other marks that became crucial to descriptions. It was common for people to include watch numbers in their lost notices; 43 per cent of notices for watches did so. Watchmakers gave watches numbers to allow them to be tracked through finishing and future repairing processes.[47] The convention of including the watch's number in lost notices became quickly entrenched. By the time Thomas Piggott came to write and place his notice on 25 May 1745, he noted that the watch he had lost had 'no Number'.[48] Other individuals also sought to clarify their watch's number in notices. On placing a notice for 'a large old-fashion Silver Watch' in the *Daily Advertiser* on 21 December 1742, the writer noted that 'the Number not certain'.[49] Despite such uncertainty, they were prepared to hazard a guess, 'believ'd to be 4560'. Others placing notices mentioned that they had forgotten the number entirely.[50] In forgetting the number, losers rarely offered more detail as recompense. Nevertheless, that they felt compelled to include their forgetting underlines the importance of numbers in identifying specific watches (and proving ownership) from the middle decades of the eighteenth-century onwards. The importance of knowing the watch maker's name and the watch's number in instances of loss became still more important from 1754 onwards. At Bow Street, John Fielding began to require his clerks to keep an account of the numbers of any watches reported stolen. In the case of Bow

---

[46] Robert Campbell, *The London Tradesman* (London, 1747), 250.
[47] See, for example, Guildhall Library, London, Thwaites and Reed Collection, "Watch Repair Book", 1825–1842, MS09194.
[48] 'Lost on Thursday Night last', *Daily Advertiser* (London), 25 May 1745.
[49] 'Lost on Friday the 10th instant', *Daily Advertiser* (London), 21 December 1742.
[50] Keyword searching the Burney Collection, shows the earliest example of someone noting that they had forgot the number in a notice is in the *Daily Courant* on 15 May 1716. See 'Lost or mislaid, a small flat Silver Watch', *Daily Courant* (London), 15 May 1716. More examples of inclusion can be found in *Daily Courant* (London), 26 August 1720; 18 February 1723; 14 January 1724; 21 April 1724; 11 January 1725; *Daily Post* (London), 11 November 1729; 30 April 1730. After this point, 'number forgot' became more regularly used, see for example 'Lost on Sunday Night last, in Goodman's Fields', *Daily Advertiser* (London), 8 December 1742. For more on the problems of keyword searching digital databases, see Tim Hitchcock, 'Confronting the Digital: Or How Academic History Writing Lost the Plot', *Cultural and Social History* 10:1 (2013), 9–23.

Street, such information could prove helpful in trials at the Old Bailey. The clerks could produce evidence of the watch number from the 'watch book'.[51] It might even be argued that the lost notices and the descriptive practices they established encouraged Bow Street to establish these practices of recording.

The increasing importance of numbers constructed an abstract version of the watch, removed from its material properties. Unlike court practices, which often demanded victims list an object's damage or marks (particularly in the case humble objects such as a cake of beeswax, a plank of wood or mutton pies) to prove ownership, lost notices, particularly for personal objects such as watches, rarely noted such material details.[52] Only 7 per cent of 'lost' notices for watches listed damage or marks.[53] The centrality of cultures of repair in eighteenth-century Britain and the importance of watches might have meant that these items were largely free of damage. But it is also noteworthy that the advertisements rarely included descriptions of the watch or watchcase's decoration. Some notices mentioned that the watch or watchcase was 'plain', 'chased' or 'enamelled', but few included details of decoration or design. Rather, when describing watches in notices, writers were highly consistent. They focused on four features: the size of the watch, the material it was made from, who made it, and its serial number. Examining notices systematically across the long eighteenth century shows that writers understood these to be the salient characteristics. Noting these features seemingly made watches recognisable to people, and thus reclamation possible. As abstract as these features might be, they are distinct from those used in the case of notes and coins and underscore the different languages of possession that existed.

In contrast to descriptions for objects such as watches, those detailing animals, and more specifically dogs, were quite different again. They were

---

[51] J. M. Beattie, *The First English Detectives: The Bow Street Runners and the Policing of London, 1750–1840* (Oxford, 2014), 29–30.

[52] For more on the court case practice of listing damage and marks (and the difficulties victims faced in doing so), see Cynthia Herrup, 'New Shoes and Mutton Pies: Investigative Responses to Theft in Seventeenth-Century East Sussex', *The Historical Journal*, 27:4 (1984), 826–7; Bruce P. Smith, 'The Presumption of Guilt and the English Law of Theft, 1750–1850', *Law and History Review*, 23:1 (2005), 139–40; Sara Pennell, '"A Cake of Beeswax, Which I Knew to be Mine": Materiality and Identification Amongst the Mundane in Eighteenth-Century England," first given: Things Matter CRASSH seminar, 28 January 2015.

[53] Twelve of the 173 notices for watches listed forms of damage, such as 'a little Hole in the inward case', *Daily Courant* (London), 1 December 1720; 'Glass was broke when lost', *Daily Advertiser* (London), 28 December 1752; 'a little Piece on one side loose', *Daily Advertiser* (London), 30 December 1752; 'the Chrystal was crack'd in two Places', *Daily Advertiser* (London), 12 December 1760; 'broken China seal', *Daily Advertiser* (London), 2 December 1771; 'Half of the Gilding is worn off the case', *Daily Advertiser* (London), 3 December 1771; 'the Glass crack'd', *Daily Advertiser* (London), 31 December 1771; 'the Enamel Plate cracked', *Daily Advertiser* (London), 6 December 1782; 'small Piece of Enamel broke off the Back', *Daily Advertiser* (London), 10 December 1792; 'Lost some Time in June last', *Daily Advertiser* (London), 18 December 1792; 'the Watch is in very bad Condition', *Daily Advertiser* (London), 25 December 1792); 'Cases much bruised', *Daily Advertiser* (London), 29 December 1792.

distinct in that they frequently dealt in idiosyncrasies. The descriptions of dogs often noted the kind, 86 per cent of notices, in fact. Of those notices, the most frequently appearing kind was spaniels (34 per cent), and then pointers (19 per cent), terriers (9 per cent), Newfoundlands (7 per cent) and greyhounds (7 per cent). It is perhaps surprising that these notices so frequently specified the kind of dog concerned, or rather that people considered that listing the kind of dog was a meaningful detail. The Kennel Club of Great Britain was not founded until 1873 and it was only then that an official body sought to regulate canine breeding (and thus can we begin to talk about 'breeds' with more confidence).[54] Nevertheless, in the early modern period, dog varieties were increasingly included in classificatory systems: there had long existed a taxonomy of dogs. Clifford Hubbard cites that Fleming's *Of Englishe Dogges* (1576) lists only three 'kindes' of 'dogges',[55] whereas, Ralph Beilby included thirty different 'kinds' of dogs in his 1790 *General History of Quadrupeds*.[56] That notices often noted the kind of dog demonstrates that they expected readers to be able to name and differentiate such varieties. Pointer, terrier and greyhound were meaningful terms that allowed recognition.

A large proportion of the notices for dogs listed the dog's name (67 per cent). While there were a few Lions, Princes, Rovers and Sanchos, there were plenty of names that only appeared once including, Airolo, Basto, Cartouche, Darby, Fox, Gyp, Hazor, Julie, Lubin, Molineux, Nettle, Pincher, Rap, Skion, Trodo, Venus and Yacoty. During the eighteenth century, dogs continued to be kept for hunting and to act as watch dogs, but they were also increasingly understood as pets and, as Ralph Beilby's *A General History of Quadrupeds* tells us, as beings with characters.[57] The range of different names given to dogs is reflective of the increasingly individualised understanding of dogs which arose from these new forms of dog ownership. Such individualisation was also at work in cultural productions such as dog portraiture, which became increasingly popular from the seventeenth century onwards, and produced dogs as distinctly visual entities.[58] At the same time, notices often included the name

---

[54] Markman Ellis, 'Suffering Things: Lapdogs, Slaves, and Counter-Sensibility', in Mark Blackwell (ed.), *The Secret Life of Things: Animals, Objects and It-Narratives in Eighteenth-Century England* (Lewisburg, PA, 2007), 98; Michael Worboys, Julie-Marie Strange and Neil Pemberton, *The Invention of the Modern Dog: Breed and Blood in Victorian Britain* (Baltimore, MD, 2018), 117.

[55] Jodi L. Wyett, 'The Lap of Luxury: Lapdogs, Literature, and Social Meaning in the "Long" Eighteenth Century', *Lit: Literature Interpretation Theory*, 10:4 (1999), 296.

[56] See 'Advertisement' in Ralph Beilby, *A General History of Quadrupeds* (2nd edn, London, 1791), n.p.

[57] Beilby, *A General History of Quadrupeds*, 331.

[58] See Xavier Bray, *Faithful and Fearless: Portraits of Dogs* (Lewes, 2021), 6; William Secord, *Dog Painting 1840–1940: A Social History of the Dog in Art* (London, 1992), 44. That dog portraiture made dogs visible as individual entities can particularly be seen in the work of George Stubbs. See Secord, *Dog Painting 1840–1940*, 110.

because, the notice stated, the dog answered to it. In an age before leads and leashes, owners trained dogs to answer to their names, and needed to do so, especially in urban spaces. Giving someone the name of the dog provided a means of making the dog recognisable.[59]

The notices uniformly described the colour of lost dogs and some included further details as to the size and shape of the canine. These were important details for people trying to recognise dogs in comparison to all the others in the city. Some notices used their descriptions of the physical makeup of the dog to list unique, distinguishing features. On 17 February 1752, an advertisement listed a lost 'young Dog Puppy' that was 'remarkable for his Ugliness'. The notice described how the puppy had 'His Ears cropt, tho' not even, his Tail just cut, with White at the End, and he is very rough'. Nevertheless, the advertisement drolly stated that the puppy answered 'to the Name of Beauty'.[60] In December 1752, another lost dog was listed as having 'his hind Legs weak and a little crooked'.[61] Similarly, in 1760, a pointer's coat was listed as having 'some little Appearance of Mange' and in 1771 another pointer was noted as having 'lost some of his fore Teeth'.[62] The descriptions utilised such points to distinguish their dog amongst others. When writing their notice in 1782, the owner must have known that their dog was unusual in having 'his Jaw...broke in the Middle, so that one Side may be moved without the other'.[63] These idiosyncratic details were included to mark the unique nature of the dog, prove ownership and make the dog recognisable amid all the other dogs making their way in London. They also marked dogs as particular kinds of 'things'. The descriptions underscore them as beings which aged and got sick: as deeply mortal. However, in the context of lost notices, such details did other work too. As we will see in Chapter 6, in an age of dog stealing, they sought to lessen the value of the dog to try to ensure that the reward needed for its return was not exorbitant.

Alongside physical details, or perhaps 'defects', owners also often described their dog's behaviours and training in lost notices. Far from obedient dogs, the descriptions included in the pages of newspapers prompt us to see rebellious canines who were good for nothing. A notice for a lost 'not a true bred' pointer

---

[59] It is important to note, however, that the dog's name was rarely included on its collar. As discussed in Chapter 2, the inscriptions on collars noted the owner's name, not the dog's.
[60] 'Lost, a young Dog Puppy, remarkable for his Ugliness', *Daily Advertiser* (London), 17 February 1752.
[61] 'Lost out of a House in Hart Street, near Bloomsbury Square', *Daily Advertiser* (London), 8 December 1752.
[62] 'Lost the 17th instant, near Hyde Park Corner', *Daily Advertiser* (London), 20 December 1760; 'Lost on Monday the 25th of November last, a Pointer Dog', *Daily Advertiser* (London), 5 December 1771.
[63] 'Lost last Sunday from Bloomsbury Square, a large brown Dog', *Daily Advertiser* (London), 19 December 1782.

noted that he 'has not been broke or used…never will be good for Thing as such'.[64] Similarly, a greyhound was listed as 'not broke to any Thing', a spaniel as having 'never been hunted' and a pointer as 'useless, having never been taught'.[65] We will never know, of course, whether the pointer was useless and if so, what this might have meant. The inclusion of this comment in the notices should not be taken as evidence that the pointer was poorly behaved. After all, we might ask, how might knowing that a dog has never been hunting help to identify them on London's streets? What such details do reveal, once again, is that dogs were understood as quite particular, lively kinds of 'things'. Such details are also revealing of eighteenth-century conceptions of value. As we will explore in the next chapter, in including these remarks, owners actively sought to devalue their dogs to lessen the chances of extortion. We also see that despite being supposedly 'useless', dogs were sought. A well-trained dog was clearly valuable, but so too (for quite different reasons) was a badly trained one. Lost notices for dogs trod a fine rhetorical line and as such were deeply meaningful.

In contrast to such pontifications about the training levels of dogs, notices included in London newspapers for 'eloped' wives contained no description beyond the wife's name. As we saw in Chapter 1, this was primarily because these notices were designed to free the husband from the obligations of credit rather than to seek return. The descriptions for other people were also brief. Those for free and enslaved servants, and apprentices, who had 'runaway' or 'absconded', and soldiers who had deserted, contained surprisingly few details about skills, training, character, behaviour or even speech. Such omissions are remarkable given that people were contracted (or forced in) to these roles to undertake specific tasks. The absence of these details is also surprising given the regular inclusion of remarks on skills and abilities, bodily movements and gestures in notices for freedom seekers advertised in other parts of the Atlantic World.[66] We do know that Avis Phillips, a 'young Girl' that 'went away from her Father', was described as having 'an impediment in her Speech'.[67]

---

[64] 'Stra'd [sic] on Saturday Morning last, a yellow and white Pointing Puppy', *Daily Advertiser* (London), 5 December 1771.

[65] 'A Dog. Lost on Sunday last, about Noon', *Daily Advertiser* (London), 4 December 1782; 'Lost on Sunday Night, about Six o'Clock', *Daily Advertiser* (London), 31 December 1782; 'Lost from Great Russell Street, Bloomsbury, a large, white Spanish Pointer', *Daily Advertiser* (London), 13 December 1782.

[66] See David Waldstreicher, 'Reading the Runaways: Self-Fashioning, Print Culture, and Confidence in Slavery in the Eighteenth-Century Mid-Atlantic', *The William and Mary Quarterly*, 56:2 (1999), 255; Gwenda Morgan and Peter Rushton, 'Visible Bodies: Power, Subordination and Identity in the Eighteenth-Century Atlantic World', *Journal of Social History*, 39:1 (2005), 46; Martha J. Cutter, '"As White as Most White Women": Racial Passing in Advertisements for Runaway Slaves and the Origins of a Multivalent Term', *American Studies*, 54:4 (2016), 93; Simon Middleton, 'Runaways, Rewards, and the Social History of Money', *Early American Studies: An Interdisciplinary Journal*, 15:3 (2017), 641.

[67] 'Avis Phillips, a young Girl in the thirteenth Year', *Daily Advertiser* (London), 9 December 1760.

Similarly, it was noted that John Thorp, an apprentice who had 'eloped' from his master Robert Thompson, 'speaks thick'.[68] So too, was the 'Postillion Boy' James Black noted for his voice. An advert placed in the *Daily Advertiser* in 1752 asserted that 'by his Accent may be known to be born in Scotland'.[69] However, even the inclusion of details regarding a runaway's voice were relatively few. The lack of details on voice, or behaviours and skills, suggests at the centrality of visual features in these notices. There was little likelihood of apprentices and servants being captured and ransomed by others. Rather 'masters' and 'mistresses' believed that it was the runaway themselves that might institute their return, if it was sought or that such notices would warn others against 'harbouring', 'employing' or 'entertaining' the person concerned. These descriptions worked to make the runaway recognisable to themselves and to prompt others to give information: to see the apprentice and pass that on.

The notices focused on including details that would be visually recognisable, such as age, stature, hair and clothes. In 1720, Charles Adams was described as 'a Boy of about Fifteen, with a full round Face, and black Hair, born in Wales'.[70] Similarly, in 1742, James Fewtrell was described as being 'twenty-one Years of Age, of a fresh Complexion, and a middle Stature'.[71] Likewise, Thomas Tise was noted as being 'a Lad about fifteen Years of Age, wears his own Hair, and had on a Duffil Coat' in 1752.[72] In the first half of the eighteenth century, the descriptions included for runaways were particularly limited. However, from these scant details, and those such as the name of the person and their master or mistress, the runaway would be able to recognise themselves and anyone they approached for work might be able to recognise them too. By contrast, in the later eighteenth century, the descriptions included for people, or rather for their clothes, became more detailed, often including the particularities of type, materials and patterns. In 1760, Richard Wellstead was described as having 'on when he went away a blue Coat and Waistcoat, a Pair of Claret-coloured Breeches, blue Stockings, and a brown Cut Wig'. It also noted that he 'took with him his Buckskin Breeches, white Coat, Stockings, and Shirts, and Leather Apron'.[73] Similarly, when George Thomas Wright ran away in 1792, he was described as having 'on a

---

[68] 'Whereas John Thorp, Apprentice to Robert Thompson', *Daily Advertiser* (London), 11 December 1760.
[69] 'RAN away from a Gentleman's Service in Dover-Street', *Daily Advertiser* (London), 9 December 1752.
[70] 'Whereas Charles Adams, a Boy of about Fifteen', *Daily Advertiser* (London), 27 December 1720.
[71] 'Whereas James Fewtrell, went away from his Master', *Daily Advertiser* (London), 11 December 1742.
[72] 'RAN away from his Master on Monday last', *Daily Advertiser* (London), 1 December 1752.
[73] 'Whereas Richard Wellstead absented himself on the 28th instant', *Daily Advertiser* (London), 30 December 1760.

dark-brown Coat, Velveret Orange-coloured Waistcoat, spotted black dark-brown Kerseymere Breeches, light-blue Stockings, placed Buckles in his Shoes, plaid Silk Handkerchief round his Neck, and a round Hat bound'.[74] Finally, when 'two lads' 'left their home', they were described as wearing 'an olive frock coat and trousers, black waistcoat, and checked silk handkerchief' and 'a brown jacket, waistcoat, and trousers with a blue cap'.[75] The inclusion of more elaborate details of a runaway's clothes in these notices is telling of the levels of material literacy at work in eighteenth-century culture.[76] It also further highlights the lack of detail included as to the character, skills and behaviour of the person concerned.

What might we make of all these details (or lack of them), all these numbers, names and brown jackets? As we explored in Chapter 3, runaway and lost notices sat side-by-side in eighteenth-century newspapers. The order was always the same: in the advertisements section there would be runaway notices, followed by a mixture of those for animals and objects. Such proximity was meaningful; it constructed a sense of equivalency between these different things. The order mirrored an eighteenth-century conception of the world, in which people and things could be conceived as interchangeable. It also underscored how these different things could all be understood to exist in relationship to a possessor.[77] In this chapter, as we think through the descriptions contained in these notices and how they were written, it is important to pause here to think through the work done by the descriptions. We need to consider whether the logics at stake in the descriptions for people, dogs, watches and banknotes worked in similar ways, and if so, what that similarity did in the world.

As the previous paragraphs have explored, when we look closely at the descriptions included for different kinds of thing, we see distinct logics at stake. The descriptions people wrote for watches and bank notes increasingly drew on abstract, immaterial features to mark out their possession and prove their ownership. By contrast, notices for dogs laboured upon the idiosyncratic qualities of the hound in question, producing them often as mangy or ill or poorly trained, but as individuals, nonetheless. Descriptions of people did not work like this. While it was common to note a runaway's stature, hair or complexion, their skills or character traits were rarely mentioned. They were

---

[74] 'Supposed to be enticed from his Master's Service', *Daily Advertiser* (London), 5 December 1792.
[75] 'LEFT their HOME, in Newgate-street, on Sunday afternoon', *The Times* (London), 1 December 1830.
[76] Serena Dyer and Chloe Wigston-Smith, 'Introduction', in Serena Dyer and Chloe Wigston-Smith (eds), *Material Literacy in Eighteenth-Century Britain* (London, 2020), 1; Serena Dyer, *Material Lives: Women Makers and Consumer Culture in the 18th Century* (London, 2021), 9.
[77] Valenze, *The Social Life of Money in the English Past*, 224; Lynn Festa, *Fiction Without Humanity: Person, Animal, Thing in Early Enlightenment Literature and Culture* (Philadelphia, PA, 2019), 1.

made visible, but were rarely seen or understood as people. The diverse logics at work in these descriptions suggest that distinct languages of possession existed for different things. In other words, writing the descriptions so important to proving ownership and possession required different kinds of information. To write a description of a watch was a different task to writing a description of your dog, or for that matter your servant. In fact, those salient features provided for watches, financial instruments and even dogs could be used to prove ownership, in a way that those for servants and apprentices could not. By focusing on the descriptions used in these different lost notices, we see that people used different languages of possession and held different relationships of possession to watches, financial instruments, dogs and servants. As we will go on to explore in the next chapter, when we see these descriptions and logics at work in concert with other aspects of the lost notices, such as the rewards, an even more complex picture begins to emerge.

How to Know, Remember and Write

As we saw in Chapter 2, part of being a proper possessor, to be of good character, was the ability to take care of your things and keep them secure. People not only worked to ensure their items were regularly cleaned and repaired, they also sought to mark ownership and protect property by using pockets, chains and collars. Such 'care' meant that owners could maintain possession over time. Chapter 3 demonstrated that despite such strategies things still went missing, therefore another important facet of being a proper owner was to seek the reclamation of possessions when they were lost. Using the lost notices system prompted the need to describe possessions and thus demanded that owners knew their things. How then did these writers arrive at such knowledge? How was such knowledge shaped by differences in use, making practices and relationships? And how did owners retain and remember such knowledge?

Let us begin to consider this by focusing on financial instruments, the bills of exchange, bank notes, coins and Exchequer Bills that allowed monetary transactions to take place. As we have explored earlier in this book, these things were defined by their ability to circulate. They kept moving and so were likely to only be in anyone's grasp for a short space of time. More than this, in the eighteenth century, these things were rarely regarded as things at all. As we saw from the descriptions, paper forms such as bank notes and bills of exchange were rarely regarded as material presences. Rather they were valued more for what they could do than what they were. Given such seeming material absence, we might not be surprised that people rarely described the paper they were written on, but we might consider how it was they were able to know the numbers and names that appeared upon them.

In 1696, the Bank of England issued a notice encouraging 'all persons concerned...to take greater care of their Bank notes, and to keep a more exact Accompt of the Sumes [sic], Numbers and Dates thereof and to whom payable'.[78] More specifically, in 1786, John Trussler advised city dwellers and visitors to 'Never carry any bank-notes or bills about you, without first entering, in some book at home, the number and date, and particulars of such notes, that in case you lose them, or your pocket is picked of your book, you stand some chance of recovering them, or stop the payment.'[79] While bank note users remained limited in the eighteenth century, they significantly expanded during the Bank Restriction Period (1797–1821) when the Bank of England inputted £27 million of small denomination notes into circulation.[80] Despite such an expansion, handling paper money in this period was not universal and required care and skill to avoid forgeries and stolen notes.[81] Hiroki Shin has argued that 'the care note users took in their handling of notes' is 'striking'.[82] Such 'care' is apparent through the Bank of England's Lost Books in which claimants were required to provide details of the note's serial number, date and value.[83] Court cases also provide evidence of the strategies peopled developed for knowing *their* coins, notes and bills. Joseph Hodson was indicted for stealing a promissory note worth £500 at the Old Bailey on 18 May 1738. The victim Mr Pye recounted how he had taken precautions to keep his pocketbook safe: he 'thrust it down (square) into' his 'Breeches Pocket'. Nevertheless, in the bustle of 'the Crowd', the pocketbook went missing. Mr Pye 'felt for it', but recalled that 'there I found, that one of the Buttons of my Pocket was cut, or twisted off; the other unbutton'd, and the Pocket Book was gone'. When giving his testimony, he recalled his certainty about the note because of the records he had kept. In this case, Mr Pye's records appear informal. He knew the number (229) and date (2 June) of the note because of the 'Memorandum' he had taken.[84] Such details proved useful not only in the court case but also in allowing him to 'stop' the note (and others in his pocketbook) at the Bank of England.[85] Similarly, on 8 December 1779, John Hudson was indicted for 'stealing 3 guineas, a half-guinea, and 16 s. 6 d. in monies numbered, the property of Robert Davis; and a bank note for 10

---

[78] As cited in Wilfred M. Acres, *The Bank of England from Within, 1694–1900* vol. 2 (Oxford, 1931), 606.
[79] John Trussler, *London Adviser and Guide* (London, 1786), 147.
[80] Shin, *The Age of Paper*, 10 and 68.
[81] Margot Finn, *The Character of Credit: Personal Debt in English Culture, 1740–1914* (Cambridge, 2003), 80.
[82] Shin, *The Age of Paper*, 131.   [83] Ibid., 132 and 80.
[84] *Old Bailey Proceedings Online* (hereafter '*OBPO*') (www.oldbaileyonline.org, version 8.0, 23 April 2020), May 1738, trial of Joseph Hodson (t17380518-10).
[85] The Bank of England Archive, Cashier's Department Record of Bank Notes Issue: Lost Book, 8 February 1736–6 December 1744, C101/7, f. 25.

l. the money secured by the said note being due and unsatisfied to the said Robert Davis, the proprietor thereof' and his case was heard in the Old Bailey. Edward Lloyd managed the grocery business for Davis, and it was from here that Hudson allegedly stole the monies. Lloyd knew how much had been stolen because he had checked the till at nine and had taken no monies since then. He also knew exactly which ten-pound bank note was missing. He told the court, 'It was No. H 233, dated the 28th of May, 1779, payable to Thomas Hughes'. When cross examined, Edward Lloyd was asked how he came to have a 'perfect recollection of the note' and replied that he had 'had it down, I put it down that day; I had received it that day of a Mrs. Lawrence'. His wife Mary recalled how he had written the details of the note in his 'sort of memorandum book', which he usually did when they received notes at the shop. Edward, on the other hand, used the term 'account book'.[86] He wanted to persuade the court that he knew the details with confidence because it was what was written down and recorded. These cases are revealing of how both individuals and businesses kept such details to prove ownership.

In contrast to the circulation of financial instruments, people often retained watches over substantial periods of time, in some cases over generations. As we learned in Chapter 2, they were items worn upon the person, snugly located in the fob pockets of breeches. They would have been regarded daily, if not moment by moment when time was pressing, and every minute counted. Eighteenth-century watches bear witness to such use. Their patterns of wear provide evidence of regular handling.[87] They were important objects that demonstrated status and guided the rhythms of each day. Given their centrality within the everyday lives of their owners, we might assume that their daily handling produced a 'somatic memory' of certain features of the watch.[88] We certainly know that it was often regular habits of reaching for a watch that first alerted a victim to its loss.[89] However, we need to be wary of assuming that familiarity produced knowledge. In his *Philosophical Investigations*, Ludwig Wittgenstein explored questions of familiarity and recognition. He pondered his own desk – the one he saw and worked at each day. If someone asked him whether on entering his room, he recognised his desk, he felt he would answer '"Certainly!"'. However, on further consideration, he delineated that he doubted whether 'any recognizing had occurred'. He noted

---

[86] *OBPO* (www.oldbaileyonline.org, version 8.0, 15 August 2019), December 1779, trial of John Hudson (t17791208-15).

[87] See, for example, the signs of wear on the back of the outer case of the gold pair-cased cylinder watch with quarter repeat, made by George Graham in London in 1727, which is now in the collections of the British Museum, 1912, 1107.1.

[88] Susan Stewart, 'Prologue: From the Museum of Touch', in Marcus Kwint, Christopher Breward and Jeremy Aynsley (eds), *Material Memories: Design and Evocation* (Oxford, 1999), 19.

[89] See case of Henry Hare Townsend discussed in Chapter 2, *OBPO* (www.oldbaileyonline.org, version 8.0, 12 July 2019), September 1790, trial of George Barrington (t17900915-10).

that 'recognizing' is often misconstrued. People do not compare. They do not enter a room with a picture in their mind's eye of the object and then compare that picture with what is there before them. Rather, Wittgenstein suggested that people only consider whether the object 'coincides' with the picture in their mind.[90] Wittgenstein reminds us then that our daily interactions with everyday items might not elicit moments of recognition. We might not really see or reckon with our things at all and thus we might not be able to describe something just because we have looked at and used it every day.

The descriptions of lost watches found in notices rarely included details of wear, damage or decoration. The features highlighted by daily handling then – its look, its damage, its feel – appear largely unimportant to this genre of writing. Instead, over the eighteenth century, lost notices included features – the number, the maker's name – which produced essentially abstract and 'objective' versions of watches. As we have seen, such details were regarded as important not only in lost notices, but also from the 1750s by the judicial system. Given their significance, rather than relying on memory, individuals often recorded these salient characteristics. Watch numbers and makers' numbers were written down in diaries and stored away for future use. In his *London Adviser and Guide*, ever keen to advise people on how to take care of their things, John Trussler suggested people 'enter, in some book at home, the number, maker's name, &c. and description of your watch, and whatever else of value you carry about you, that you may know how to describe it, if lost.'[91] Londoners clearly followed such advice. When writing the first volume of his diary in the late 1780s, the coal merchant Elijah Goff decided to include a note to himself on the inside of his diary's cover: 'No. of my watch 7613 made by Ellicott.'[92] As his diary shows, Goff was a regular at 'the Change' [the Royal Exchange in the City], a place that was often listed in 'lost' notices as a site of loss. As such, Goff would have been aware of the possibility of having his watch go missing. In his memorandum to himself, Goff was careful to note that the number referred to 'my watch', demonstrating a keen sense of ownership. Significantly, Goff did not note the size of the watch, its material, decoration or damage, but rather the name of the maker ('Ellicott') and the number ('7613'). He noted those details which were crucial to the process of reclaiming the watch through the 'lost' notice system in eighteenth-century newspapers.

Goff was not alone in understanding that the maker's name and number of the watch were the 'salient characteristics' to record. At an Old Bailey trial in

---

[90] Many thanks to Lynn Festa for suggesting this source. See Ludwig Wittgenstein, *Philosophical Investigations*, trans. G. E. M. Anscombe, P. M. S. Hacker and Joachim Schulte (4th edn, Oxford, 2009), 165.
[91] Trussler, *London Adviser and Guide*, 147.
[92] Tower Hamlets Local History Library, London, Diary of Elijah Goff (Coal Merchants, St George in the East), 1788–1796, P/GOF/1.

1782, when Alexander Colderhead was asked how long he had owned his watch he remarked, 'Between eight and nine months, I am a journeyman baker, I know the man that made it, his name is Wilson, the number is 1,267.' When asked if he had known that information before he lost it, he answered, 'I always look at the number of my watch when I have it first, and commonly set it down; I have lost watches before now, and that makes me careful when I buy a watch to set down the number.'[93] Recording details of personal possessions acted as insurance against loss. They provided a ready means of remembering the salient features of their possession, allowing for processes of reclamation and proof of ownership. People paid attention to certain features that the 'lost' system (and then the judicial system) made significant, and rather than relying on their memory, they decided to put pen to paper. Making such records suggests that Londoners were aware of the workings of the 'lost' notices system and that the system (and their desire to maintain possession of their things through possibly using the system in the future) prompted the generation and recording of personalised systems of remembrance to help them in that task.

It was not owners alone who held knowledge of their possessions. People maintained and repaired possessions in eighteenth-century Britain.[94] However, such caring – all that cleaning and repairing – was often performed by other people. Servants, as much as mistresses, cleaned and repaired linens.[95] Men, particularly older men, sent their breeches out to be repaired.[96] Customers kept in contact with their watchmaker as the piece was produced and then remained reliant on makers to clean, maintain and repair the watches under their ownership. In 1756, Samuel Harper took his watch to the watchmaker Christopher Potter to have it cleaned.[97] In 1845, Annie Lambert recorded in her diary how on 24 February she had gone to the city and 'took my Watch to Wests to have a new face put in & the Case new lined'.[98] That watchmakers were called upon to enact such care also meant they held knowledge of these watches. It is unsurprising then, that their knowledge and their records proved

---

[93] *OBPO* (www.oldbaileyonline.org, version 8.0, 15 August 2019), December 1782, trial of William Seton (t17821204-42).
[94] Ariane Fennetaux, Amélie Junqua and Sophie Vasset, 'Introduction: The Many Lives of Recycling', in Ariane Fennetaux, Amélie Junqua and Sophie Vasset (eds), *The Afterlife of Used Things: Recycling in the Long Eighteenth Century* (New York, NY, 2014), 1; Susan Strasser, *Waste and Want: A Social History of Trash* (New York, NY, 1999), 22.
[95] Vickery, *The Gentleman's Daughter*, 149–51. For more on whether gentlewomen were actively involved, see Kate Smith, 'In Her Hands: Materializing Distinction in Georgian Britain', *Cultural and Social History*, 11:4 (2014), 493.
[96] Karen Harvey, 'Men of Parts: Masculine Embodiment and the Male Leg in Eighteenth-Century England', *Journal of British Studies*, 54 (2015), 803–4.
[97] *OBPO* (www.oldbaileyonline.org, version 8.0, 25 September 2020), February 1757, trial of John Howland (t17570223-18).
[98] Cadbury Research Library, University of Birmingham, Journal of Annie Lambert, 1845–1846, MS241.

important resources when watches went missing. The case of Thomas Piggott noted at the start of Chapter 3 suggests that people readily called upon the expertise of watchmakers when things went missing.[99] Other cases in the Old Bailey also show that people regularly engaged their watchmaker in the reclamation process. When a pawnbroker advertised a missing watch case in November 1729, Edward Yates 'went with the Watch-maker to see it, and he said it was mine'.[100] In recalling what he did after finding his watch missing, Constantine Gahagen recounted to the Old Bailey on 17 January 1750 that he 'went to the Maker, and had it advertised'.[101] Similarly, when James Weeden had his watch stolen from him on Saturday 27 May 1769, on the Monday he went to the 'watchmaker that made my watch' and had him draw 'up the advertisement'.[102] When a coach-master Samuel Heaven lost his watch at the Angel Inn on or around 3 August 1791 and thought he saw it at John Fielding's Bow Street offices, he 'could not swear to it without sending to my watchmaker, and he sent me the number to refresh my memory; I recollect the maker's name, Philip Page, London, No. 23626.'[103] While some individuals, such as Elijah Goff, were well-versed in the details of their possessions because of the records *they* kept, others relied on the material expertise (and records) of sellers and makers. Such insights reveal how even after purchase, makers remained important repositories of knowledge. They also prompt us to resituate individual and household practices of knowing within broader networks to show how material knowledge was held collectively and called upon at different moments. Household knowledge (in the form of a servant's memory or an inventory) and collective knowledge (in the form of watchmaker's memory, or their account books) were particularly important when navigating moments of loss. It also reminds us how being a proper possessor and holding a good character, so often relied on the labour and knowledge of others.

While the features people focused upon to describe watches were relatively narrow, when describing dogs, the writers of lost notices took a much more capacious view. In these notices, writers included seemingly minute details. We learn that a 'small black Bitch' was 'a little grey about the Nose' and that

---

[99] For more on the relationships between artisans and their customers, see Anita McConnell, 'From Craft Workshop to Big Business: The London Scientific Instrument Trade's Response to Increasing Demand, 1750–1820', *London Journal*, 19:1 (1994), 50.

[100] *OBPO* (www.oldbaileyonline.org, version 8.0, 31 July 2019), December 1729, trial of Mary Cox (t17291203-28).

[101] *OBPO* (www.oldbaileyonline.org, version 8.0, 5 August 2019), January 1750, trial of Lawrence Savage (t17500117-49).

[102] *OBPO* (www.oldbaileyonline.org, version 8.0, 9 August 2019), June 1769, trial of Robert Merry Richard Belcher Samuel Cornwall (t17690628-46).

[103] *OBPO* (www.oldbaileyonline.org, version 8.0, 15 August 2019), September 1791, trial of Richard Gardner (t17910914-35).

'a middle-sized Pug Bitch' had 'one Ear longer than the other'.[104] From the notices, we also know that a white Greyhound Bitch was lost in 1792 and that her owner remembered that she had 'a yellowish Dun Patch on the Left Side of her Face'.[105] In the age before photography, when painted dog portraits were an established, but expensive, luxury, dog owners were still able to recall the precise details of their dog. Of course, we do not know if such recollections are in fact precise; we have no dog to compare them against. What is perhaps more significant is that writers attempted at such detail, precise or not. Rather than drawing upon records, that owners were able to provide such detail is suggestive of the changing relationship to dogs in this period. As Ingrid Tague has argued, the term 'pet' only came into use in the eighteenth century. It marked a shift in which some domesticated animals might be kept purely for pleasure or companionship.[106] The changing nature of homes as places containing specialised and separate spaces meant it was possible to countenance keeping dogs in the house, particularly in cities where space was at a premium.[107] In the Victorian period, such ideas expanded further and increasingly the pet's place was seen to be in the home.[108] Yet as discussed earlier, we should not equate proximity with knowledge. What is also important to note is that there is evidence that owners engaged with their dogs in ways that allowed them to 'see' them: that they were taking care. For instance, when considering how best to ensure the health of dog, *The Sportman's Dictionary* suggested that *owners* should 'rub' their dogs 'with chalk, and brush or comb him once or twice a week'. Doing so ensured the dog would 'thrive much better' as 'the chalk will clear his skin from all greasiness, and he will be the less liable to be mangy'.[109] While the *Dictionary* does not provide evidence of whether anyone did indeed get down on their knees and rub chalk all over their dog once or twice a week, the lack of detail given as to how grooming should take place is suggestive of how regular grooming was an accepted and normalised practice (although all those mangy dogs appearing in advertisements also gives pause for thought).

The possibilities of proximity and interaction are perhaps equally important as a means of explaining how masters and mistresses were able to construct descriptions of what servants (free and enslaved) and apprentices, and their

---

[104] 'Lost on Thursday last out of Gray's Inn Passage, a small black Bitch', *Daily Advertiser* (London), 18 December 1752; 'Lost last Monday Evening, a middle-sized Pug Bitch', *Daily Advertiser* (London), 24 December 1760.
[105] 'Lost on Thursday Evening last, a white Greyhound Bitch', *Daily Advertiser* (London), 3 December 1792.
[106] Ingrid H. Tague, *Animal Companions: Pets and Social Change in Eighteenth-Century Britain* (Philadelphia, PA, 2015), 3.
[107] Tague, *Animal Companions*, 19.
[108] Philip Howell, *At Home and Astray: The Domestic Dog in Victorian Britain* (Charlottesville, VA and London, 2015), 37.
[109] Anon., *The Sportsman's Dictionary; or, the Gentleman's Companion* (London, 1800), 119.

clothes, looked like. In the early modern period, the multi-functional nature of household spaces meant that people lived closely together. Although the eighteenth century ushered in a period where houses contained specialised spaces and concepts of privacy, households continued to live in relative proximity to each other. Servants and apprentices would often be expected to sleep in the same bed as their master or mistress, in trundle beds below or at the end of their master's or mistresses' bed, or with the children.[110] On 9 March 1772, the Lancashire gentlewoman Elizabeth Shackleton noted in her diary that her servant 'Nanny Nutter lay with me for the first time'.[111] Even as servants began to sleep in beds unconnected to those of their masters and mistresses, they continued to sleep in rooms which were multi-purpose and to which the rest of the household had ready access.[112] While such proximity could be a regular occurrence, their position in the household also meant that their bodies were placed under scrutiny. Servants' bodies would be watched by mistresses for signs of pregnancy and such surveillance could take the form of touching to inspect the body.[113] Mistresses and masters remained on guard for any potential challenges to their household's reputation.

Mistresses and masters lived in proximity to their servants. They paid close attention to changes in the shape of their bodies and what others said about them. They also watched them work, sometimes worked alongside them and commented on the outcomes of such labour.[114] Masters and mistresses were aware that they may well need to write a 'character' of their employee at some point and thus also had other reasons to observe them.[115] Such close contact and surveillance would of course have provided ready opportunity for employers to know what their servants and apprentices looked like. At the same time, some of the clothes worn by servants and apprentices would have been given to them as gifts by their employer or enslaver, meaning that they would also have knowledge of the garments they ran off in and any extra clothes they managed to take with them. We know employers were aware of their servants' garments. Elizabeth Shackleton wrote of her servant 'Nanny Nutter put on her new stays and strip'd Callimanco gown & went home'.[116] While Shackleton's notes on Nutter are perhaps exceptional in their detail, they provide a glimpse

---

[110] Laura Gowing, *Common Bodies: Women, Touch and Power in Seventeenth-Century England* (New Haven, CT, 2003), 60.
[111] As cited in Vickery, *The Gentleman's Daughter*, 144.
[112] Amanda Flather, 'Gender, Space, and Place: The Experience of Service in the Early Modern Household, c.1580–1720', *Home Cultures*, 8:2 (2011), 180–81.
[113] Gowing, *Common Bodies*, 65.
[114] Vickery, *The Gentleman's Daughter*, 141–142; Carolyn Steedman, *Labours Lost: Domestic Service and the Making of Modern England* (Cambridge, 2009), 86.
[115] A 'character' was essentially a character reference written by a previous employer that the servant would need to produce if they wanted to be employed elsewhere. See Bruce Robbins, *The Servant's Hand: English Fiction from Below* (Durham, NC and London, 1993), 109.
[116] As cited in Vickery, *The Gentleman's Daughter*, 144.

of how possible it was for employers to know what a servant would be wearing as she left the house on a particular day. Without abundant wardrobes and with mistresses keeping regular inventories of their household possessions, employers were likely to know what their servant or apprentice left with. As such, they were able to draw up the relatively sparse descriptions that runaway notices required – age, stature, hair and clothes.

As with the logic that shaped descriptions, so the formation and remembering of knowledge that such descriptions relied upon happened differently for different types of 'things'. People took note and recorded the numbers of their bills and notes in 'Memorandum' and account books. The watch owner or its maker noted the watch's number, safely securing a crucial piece of information for future use in a lost notice. A note recording the stays or breeches gifted to a servant might become useful in the moment of their absconding. And all those hours rubbing chalk into the coat of a mangy dog might suddenly become important when you needed to recall where exactly that 'yellowish Dun patch' was. In thinking through the knowledge required to write a description of a possession and how such knowing might have been acquired we are struck with an eighteenth-century reality, that it was not necessarily the owner who laboured away caring for their possessions, often it was someone else: a servant, a mender, a watchmaker. As we saw in the introduction to this book, in Mrs Artless' lecture to her daughter about the importance and difficulty of taking care of possessions, it becomes abundantly clear that it is actually Nurse who labours to enact such care.[117] That knowledge was held collectively meant that others could be called upon when something went missing, and a description had to be written. To be a good possessor was to take care of your things and know them, but there was no expectation that owners themselves should enact such labour. So often it was others who exercised this labour on their behalf, and so often it was other devices (the memorandum, the diary, the account book, the inventory) that 'remembered' the necessary knowledge.

Conclusion

The expansion of photography that took place in the 1840s provided other ways of recording objects and proving ownership. As William Henry Fox Talbot conceived of it, photography would come to provide the 'mute testimony' so crucial to property claims. Prior to this decade, owners had to find other ways of pinpointing the particularity of their possessions. In the middle decades of the seventeenth century, the early years of lost property notices in newsbooks, there is evidence that some advertisements contained illustrations.

---

[117] Dorothy Kilner, *The Life and Perambulations of a Mouse, Vol. I* (London, 1790), 27.

However, the costs involved in producing and including such woodcuts were prohibitively expensive and short-lived.[118] Rather, over the long eighteenth century, it was the textual praxis of description that provided the primary means of making visible your things and laying claim to them should they be lost or stolen.

The centrality of descriptions in lost property and runaway notices remind us that in this period possession was not simply a physical act. To keep hold was not only to grasp at the thing, to lay a hand on it. Rather, possession was also dependent on knowledge, the ability to know and articulate its salient features. That different types of possessions were made visible through different characteristics – the number, the type, the material, the clothing – shows the diverse languages of possession at stake in this period. While description continued to be an important means of marking ownership, these languages of possession remained crucial.

The ability to produce a description and employ the correct language of possession relied on knowledge of the lost notices system but also of the possession. The construction of such knowledge further compounded the different languages of possession at stake. To know and recall the number of a bank note or a watchmaker's name relied on different practices and means of recollection to those employed when trying to recall what a servant was wearing on a particular day. These diverse practices also demonstrate the contrasting relationships of possession underway in this period, a diversity that becomes more complex still when we turn to the next chapter and the question of value.

---

[118] Jason McElligott, 'Advertising and Selling in Cromwellian Newsbooks' in Shanti Graheli (ed.), Buying and Selling: *The Business of Books in Early Modern Europe* (Leiden, 2019), 474.

6   Valuing Possessions

> Lost about eight Days ago, a young Spaniel dog, answers to the name of Rover; when lost he had a collar about his neck, having on it the name of Lord Byron, living in Great Marlborough Street; his colour is white, with liver colour ears, and a liver colour spot on his tail. Whoever brings him to Lawford's coffee house in Great Marlborough Street, shall have half a Guinea Reward, and no questions ask'd. Note, no greater reward will be offer'd for him, for he is no use to anybody, having never been broke.
> – *Daily Advertiser* (London), 11 December 1742

When Rover went missing in December 1742, his owner the twenty-year-old William Byron, 5th Baron Byron (1722–1798), followed the actions of many others and placed a notice in the *Daily Advertiser*. The notice described the distinguishing features of the dog. We learn that Rover was a young spaniel, with a white coat, liver-coloured ears and a liver spot on his tail. We are also told that he 'has never been broke'. We might surmise from this that he has not yet been taught the commands needed to hunt out game on the estate around Newstead Abbey.[1] Or perhaps that Rover was wont to ignore Byron when he stood there on Great Marlborough Street calling his name. The notice also makes the reader aware that when lost, Rover was wearing a collar, a sign to others that someone owned him and would notice his going missing. That the advertisement was placed eight days after he had gone was not necessarily a mark of any reticence to get him back. Byron being a lieutenant in the Navy, who only came to London when not at sea, it is possible that he had only a weak bond with Rover.[2] However, it is more probable that the young William Byron or a member of his household had made their own enquiries and when these proved fruitless, they resorted to placing a notice in the newspaper. The reward offered for the return of Rover was small, just half a guinea, but matched the amounts usually offered for lost spaniels in this period. The notice

---

[1] Ralph Beilby, *A General History of Quadrupeds* (2nd edn, London, 1791), 329–30.
[2] John Beckett and Sheila Aley, *Byron and Newstead: The Aristocrat and the Abbey* (Newark, DE and London, 2001), 40–41.

boldly claimed no greater reward would be proposed. It reached out but drew a line, 'for he is no use to anybody'.

Choosing to write a notice and paying for it to be advertised marked the lost item as valuable, but in the notices losers went further. Most of the lost notices included the offer of a reward. The central purpose of this chapter is to examine in greater detail what was at stake in the rewards offered for lost 'things'. To do so is to interrogate questions of value and why losers were so keen to reclaim. Historian Simon Middleton argues that while runaway notices in early American newspapers have received much attention, the rewards they included have not. He notes that the 'assumption has been that as a conventional feature of "runaway" advertisements, rewards provide little or no analytic purchase beyond measuring value and providing a medium of exchange, the reward is largely epiphenomenal to the transaction'.[3] Rather than regarding rewards as epiphenomenal, Middleton focuses on them to show the processes of commodification that shaped understandings of labour and people's lives in early America. This chapter follows Middleton's lead in recognising rewards as significant elements within lost notices. It argues, however, that their significance lies not only in their power to commodify. Rather than merely 'measuring value', the rewards raise important questions about the nature of value in eighteenth-century society. Here we begin to grapple more fully with the question of why eighteenth-century urban denizens worked so hard to reclaim their lost things. Possessions such as watches, financial instruments, dogs and people held economic value but by understanding rewards within the context of the notices themselves and within the political, social and cultural dynamics in which they operated, we see the wider range of values at work in 'things'.

Understanding Value

The question of value was deeply entangled with conceptions of property. In the 1762 copyright case, *Tonson v. Collins*, William Blackstone argued that 'Whatever...hath a *Value* is the Subject of Property'.[4] Although Blackstone produced this clear conception of the relationship between value and property in 1762, when he came to publish his *Commentaries on the Laws of England* in the later part of the decade, things were not so alluringly simple. As we learned in Chapter 1, the law was ambiguous as to what could and could not be considered property in this period and it certainly did not protect whatever 'hath a *Value*'. For instance, despite being valuable, the law was ambiguous as to whether dogs were personal property. The problem was that eighteenth-

---

[3] Simon Middleton, 'Runaways, Rewards, and the Social History of Money', *Early American Studies: An Interdisciplinary Journal*, 15:3 (2017), 622.

[4] As cited in Paul Langford, *Public Life and the Propertied Englishman 1689–1798* (Oxford, 1990), 3. Citation from the case of *Tonson v. Collins* (1762).

century British society saw value in almost everything. Even horse droppings and dust were regularly collected from the streets and sold. Different forms of detritus could achieve a ready market value.[5] At the same time, what value was, how it was produced and where it was located was distinctly open to interpretation in this period. In the late seventeenth century, the early modern 'reconceptualisation of value' intensified in the face of financial revolution. William Killigrew's proposal to parliament in 1663 to issue paper money and then its intensified use in the late seventeenth century to help realise war expenses meant a shift away from specie and towards paper.[6] Such changes have been characterised as a 'crisis in the notion of value'. Shifting the physical signifiers of value broached questions as to where worth was located, who produced it and how it might be distinguished.[7] Should value be in the thing, the silvery coin, or the name, or the text or the piece of paper announcing £1 to the bearer? It was difficult to know. This chapter sees lost notices as part of this uncertain world of value formation. It sees the rewards offered in lost and runaway notices as being reflective of the values at stake in property and simultaneously contributing to their formation.

Rewards largely worked in consort with the description of the possession, and other elements of the advertisement, to negotiate return. While some rewards mirrored the market values for those goods, others did not. Instead, they provide a means of considering the different values at stake and where those values might lie. Historian Rebecca L. Sprang argues that 'Value is a product of humans' interactions with objects and with each other.'[8] Yet losing things, this chapter argues, distinctly reorientates such interactions. Recent work by Aaron Hyman and Dana Leibsohn consolidates the importance of considering how loss is important to understanding value.[9] Hyman and Leibsohn examined the case of the *Santo Cristo de Burgos*, which left Manila in 1693 but was wrecked somewhere off the Oregon coastline. Although the wreck was never found, the sea slowly offered up parts of its cargo. Such items were then picked up by residents on the Oregon coast, particularly people known today as members of Nehalem-Tillamook and Clatsop communities.[10] Included in these coastal offerings were fragments of porcelain. Although such items were usually valued for their aesthetic qualities, the Clatsop and Nehalem-Tillamook peoples reworked these fragments into lethal arrowheads. The porcelain became detached from 'the frames of

---

[5] Jerry White, *London in the Eighteenth Century: A Great and Monstrous Thing* (London 2012), 199.
[6] Christine Desan, *Making Money: Coin, Currency and the Coming of Capitalism* (Oxford, 2014), 297–98.
[7] James Thompson, *Models of Value: Eighteenth-Century Political Economy and the Novel* (Durham, NC, and London, 1996), 2.
[8] Rebecca L. Sprang, *Stuff and Money in the Time of the French Revolution* (Cambridge, MA, 2017), 14.
[9] Aaron M. Hyman and Dana Leibsohn, 'Lost and Found at Sea, or a Shipwreck's Art History', *West 86th*, 28:1 (2021), 43–74.
[10] Hyman and Leibsohn, 'Lost and Found at Sea, or a Shipwreck's Art History', 55.

value that had animated their movement west from Manila' and was appreciated instead for its hardness and density.[11] Here, a reframing of value was instituted by a new set of possessors, who focused on porcelain's material qualities.

Hyman and Leibsohn's intervention encourages us to follow the thing and thus shift our analysis away from losers and towards new possessors to show how their interactions with the item produced new forms of value. Their work reminds us of the need to consider who creates value and how. Marxist theory asserts that an item's value is derived from the labour that is expended to produce it. Our view of the arrowheads might be different for example, if we focused more fully on the labour and skill expended by the Clatsop and Nehalem-Tillamook peoples in refashioning the porcelain pieces into arrowheads. In contrast, Georg Simmel argued that value emerges through exchange and is shaped by an individual's desire: the amount they are willing to pay for a given item. In the case of the arrowheads, it would be interesting to know whether they were exchanged onwards by the Clatsop and Nehalem-Tillamook peoples and the extent to which such exchanges produced further (and perhaps different) forms of value. More recently, Arjun Appadurai has further built on Simmel's insights to argue that exchange is an important producer of value both in formal and informal markets.[12] David Graeber has argued that Appadurai makes the radical move of 'writing as if all exchanges are simply about *things* and have nothing to do with making, maintaining, or severing social relationships'.[13] Certainly, Appadurai's work, and that of Igor Kopytoff, importantly focus on the ways in which things can accumulate meaning and value through their 'lives'.[14] Appadurai and Kopytoff see such lives as marked by different moments of exchange and thus that their circulation is intrinsically important. By contrast, Annette Weiner's concept of 'inalienable possessions' looks to those things which people try to ensure do not circulate.[15] These possessions are 'imbued with the intrinsic and ineffable identities of their owners' and 'are not easy to give away'. Rather the 'loss of such an inalienable possession diminishes the self and by extension, the group to which the person belongs' and so people work to avoid such loss.[16] Here, value is produced over

---

[11] Ibid., 56.
[12] Arjun Appadurai, 'Introduction: Commodities and the Politics of Value', in Arjun Appadurai (ed.), *The Social Life of Things: Commodities in Cultural Perspective* (Cambridge, 1986), 15.
[13] David Graeber, *Towards an Anthropological Theory of Value: The False Coin of Our Own Desire* (New York, NY and Basingstoke, 2001), 32.
[14] Igor Kopytoff, 'The Cultural Biography of Things: Commoditization as Process', in Arjun Appadurai (ed.), *The Social Life of Things: Commodities in Cultural Perspective* (Cambridge, 1986), 64–94.
[15] Annette B. Weiner, *Inalienable Possessions: The Paradox of Keeping-While-Giving* (Berkeley and Los Angeles, CA 1992), 7.
[16] Weiner, *Inalienable Possessions*, 6.

time through the thing's presence within and connection to a particular group and thus through the accumulation of meaning created by these relationships.

This chapter considers loss and value but takes a different track to that advocated by Hyman and Leibsohn. Rather than following the thing, it seeks to stay with the loser and the loss to consider how absence prompted articulations (and perhaps reformulations) of value. When things were lost, they were not destroyed; rather 'lost' denoted a situation in which the owner no longer had ready access. As such, being lost impacted the relationship that Weiner sees as fundamental to value and the interactions Sprang has identified. Instead, being lost makes crucial the owner's relationship to the thing but drives interactions into the realm of imagination. Seeking the return of an item speaks to its inalienability: the owner deems it irreplaceable, as it is that particular item that must be returned.

The rewards offered in lost notices were clearly shaped by values decided in the marketplace, especially when they involved items such as watches, which had a ready resale or pawn value. However, by reading the notices in their operational context and against other sources, we begin to see that they are also revealing of non-market values. Items were valued for their function, their symbolic importance, and their relationships to the owner and others. Similarly, that different rewards were offered for different types of 'things' is revealing of the range of values 'things' held in eighteenth-century society and culture. These diverse values motivated people to seek the return of their possessions. Such differences also show how value played a role in distinguishing between 'things' and the different relationships of possession that shaped them. As discussed in Chapter 1, and shown throughout this book, asking what it meant to own 'things' in an age in which it was possible to conceive of owning a watch, a banknote, a dog, but also people, is to probe questions of property, on the one hand, and issues of moral flatness on the other. What the book has begun to track and will develop further in this chapter is that over the eighteenth century, clearer distinctions between different kinds of 'things' emerged more fully, shaping understandings of property. Such distinctions did not magically appear. As we have long known, their construction has a history, and values played an important role.

In the next section, the chapter explores the different values at stake in financial instruments, watches and dogs to examine their varied importance in eighteenth-century society and culture. The chapter underlines how experiences of loss illuminated, and in some cases produced, value for historical actors. In the final section, the chapter explores more closely the outcomes people hoped rewards would produce. It does so by focusing on the notices written for 'runaways' and finds it was only notices for enslaved people (as opposed to those for apprentices, servants, spouses and soldiers) that consistently sought return. By analysing the notices for enslaved people alongside those for other 'runaways' but also for other 'things' such as watches and financial instruments, we find more evidence of *how* Britons enacted the commodification of humans. As the next two sections of the chapter explore, value was crucial to understanding and demarcating property in the eighteenth century.

Seeing Value

We know that there was a diversity of values at stake in watches, financial instruments, dogs and people in this period. Lost property notices and the system in which they existed provide an opportunity to see such values in motion, to think through the point at which value happens in the relationship between people and their possessions. We also gain a glimpse of times and places in which value was produced and see how these two dimensions (time and place) intersected. Loss and the rewards offered for return forced people to articulate a measure of value. Although in the case of possessions such as watches, the rewards offered align with market values, for other things, such as dogs, no such alignment took place. Here we gain an understanding of how, for certain things, other values existed, which were not demarcated by the market. Loss is particularly useful in illuminating the presence of such regimes because it creates a moment in which there is essentially a market of one. In these instances, it was for the owner to decide how much they would be prepared to pay to claim the object back and so *their* calculations of value (as opposed to those apparent to other participants in a marketplace) become central.

People used the newspaper advertisement not only to recover watches, snuffboxes and jewellery but also bank notes, coins, drafts, bills of exchange and promissory notes. The world of eighteenth-century Britain was alive with a diverse range of financial instruments and these items marked the pages of newspapers. Financial instruments provide particularly interesting case studies for thinking through value in the eighteenth century. They acted as measures of value and facilitated its movement across the global economy. Yet, the rewards offered for the return of financial instruments were low. As with bank notes, in the case of bills, the payor of a bill would be under obligation to pay any holder, even if the bill had been stolen. If the owner of the bill who had lost it or from whom it had been stolen wished to be paid, they would need to indemnify the payor in case the original document should be presented for payment by a third party. To avoid the risk of paying out the full amount via an indemnity if the original were presented, losers placed advertisements and offered a fraction of the face value as 'reward' to get the original document back.[17] A lost notice seeking to reclaim a bill drawn for 50l., which was placed

---

[17] *Peacock v. Rhodes* (1781), 99 E.R. 402. Many thanks to Richard Senior for alerting me to this case.

in the *Daily Advertiser* on 11 December 1742, offered a reward of only 10 shillings.[18] Similarly, a notice placed in 1771 to recover a promissory note for 90l. included a reward of only half a guinea.[19] In the early nineteenth century, a similar issue played out. In 1810, an advertisement noted that a draft worth '£5125l.' had been lost and offered just five guineas as reward.[20] If owners wanted to pay out more than a nominal amount in reward, they often opted to offer around 10 per cent of the financial instrument's stated value. When the grocers William Brooks and William Lawrence placed an advertisement for a 'Lost or mislaid' bank note worth twenty pounds, they offered a reward of two guineas. Unfortunately, the note did not re-emerge, but the Bank of England reimbursed the business partners in January 1753.[21] Similarly, when John Jones advertised his lost twenty-pound note in the *Daily Advertiser* on 19 December 1792, he offered three guineas for its return.[22] On 30 October, Jones had also alerted the Bank of England to his loss. He thought he must have burned the note with some 'loose papers'. On 4 November 1793, the Bank 'acquainted' him with its return.[23] In all but one of these five cases, the owner of the item stated that they had already taken steps to reduce the financial instrument's onward value and ability to circulate.[24] In fact, it was common to note that payment had been stopped across the lost notices for financial instruments. The notice from 11 December 1742 described how 'The Acceptance and Payment of the said Bill is stopt, and no greater Reward will be given'.[25] Similarly, the advertisement from 1771 noted that 'The above is stopt Payment, therefore is of no Use but to the Owner, neither will it be advertised again, nor any greater Reward offered.'[26] In the same vein, the notice from 1810 announced that 'As the draft is crossed Boldern, and every step taken to prevent its payment, no greater reward will be offered.'[27] Alongside offering up such warnings as to the difficulties people would face

---

[18] 'Lost on Thursday Evening last, near Aldgate', *Daily Advertiser* (London), 11 December 1742.
[19] 'Lost a Promissory Note, for 90 l. payable to Thomas Polley', *Daily Advertiser* (London), 21 December 1771.
[20] 'DRAFT LOST of Messrs Turner and Serntton', *The Times* (London), 28 December 1810.
[21] 'Lost or mislaid the 5th of December, 1751', *Daily Advertiser* (London), 18 December 1752. Details from the Bank of England Lost Books tell us that the 'losers' in this case were grocers William Brooks and William Lawrence. Bank of England Archive, Cashier's Department Record of Bank Notes Issue: Lost Book, 28 September 1751–8 February 1759, C101/9, f. 15.
[22] 'Lost a 20l Bank Note, No. 7800', *Daily Advertiser* (London), 19 December 1792.
[23] Bank of England Archive, Cashier's Department Record of Bank Notes Issue: Lost Book, 23 December 1791–28 November 1793, C101/19, f. 134.
[24] Only one of these notices did not state that payment had been stopped in some way. See 'Lost or mislaid the 5th of December, 1751', *Daily Advertiser* (London), 18 December 1752.
[25] 'Lost on Thursday Evening last, near Aldgate', *Daily Advertiser* (London), 11 December 1742.
[26] 'Lost a Promissory Note, for 90 l. payable to Thomas Polley', *Daily Advertiser* (London), 21 December 1771.
[27] 'DRAFT LOST of Messrs Turner and Serntton', *The Times* (London), 28 December 1810.

in gaining payment using the instrument, the notices themselves sought to make public the ownership of the bill, note or draft.

Prior to the 1812 Stanhope Act, it was up to individuals and businesses as to whether they would or would not accept a bank note.[28] In this period, tradespeople were often cautious in accepting, for fear that the note might be forged or stolen. They often relied on local knowledge – that the individual knew someone in the area or gave an address in the locality – when calculating whether to trust someone.[29] Another option was to check with the bank. In 1745, when John Mason came to the shop of Hinckley Phipps, a Linnen Draper in Cheapside, and presented a £20 note to purchase cloth for £2 13s, Phipps was annoyed. He did not want to part with so much change 'for so little Money being laid out'. He asked his servant to 'run down with it [the £20 note] to the Bank' to 'see whether it was a good Note' and soon heard that 'the Payment of it was stopt at the Bank'.[30] The Bank of England was well able to provide such a service due to the books recording lost notes, and more particularly the 'alphabet of lost Bank Notes' it insisted the cashiers refer to.[31] Despite such cautions, people could and did forge endorsements and sold notes and bills onto others.[32] We also know that individuals successfully used stolen bank notes in retail spaces. When appearing as a witness at the case of John Brinklow, the goldsmith Thomas Reynolds told how on 31 March 1760 he had baulked at accepting a £200 note from a customer but had accepted one for £25. As the goldsmith was soon to find out, the note had been stolen from Thomas Elrington earlier that day.[33] Nevertheless, that the rewards offered for financial instruments was relatively low suggests that 'stopping' strategies worked to some extent and that the return of the piece of paper was perhaps not as paramount as publicly marking ownership.

The low rewards often offered for financial instruments hides how even these things – often regarded as abstractions rather than physical objects – could hold other kinds of significance for their owners. We see such meanings come to the fore in Henry Fielding's novel *Tom Jones*, for instance when Tom

---

[28] Hiroki Shin, *The Age of Paper: The Bank Note, Communal Currency and British Society, 1790s–1830s* (Cambridge, 2024), 190.

[29] Hannah Barker and Sarah Green, 'Taking Money from Strangers: Traders' Responses to Banknotes and the Risks of Forgery in Late Georgian London', *Journal of British Studies*, 60 (2021), 599–601.

[30] *Old Bailey Proceedings Online* (hereafter '*OBPO*') (www.oldbaileyonline.org, version 8.0, 15 June 2023), December 1745, trial of John Mason (t17451204-3). I have been unable to find the corresponding record in the Bank of England Lost Books.

[31] Wilfred M. Acres, *The Bank of England from Within, 1694–1900* (Oxford, 1931), 607.

[32] Donna T. Andrew and Randall McGowen, *The Perreaus & Mrs. Rudd: Forgery and Betrayal in Eighteenth-Century London* (Berkeley, CA, 2001), 18.

[33] *OBPO* (www.oldbaileyonline.org, version 8.0, 16 June 2023), July 1763, trial of John Brinklow Francis Parsons (t17630706-24).

Jones finds Sophia Western's lost pocketbook, which contains a bank bill and feels reconnected with her. When Jones's travelling companion Benjamin Partridge hands Jones 'a little gilt pocket-book', which he 'found about two miles off', Jones is enraptured. He opens it and '(guess, reader, what he felt,) saw in the first page the words Sophia Western, written by her own fair hand'.[34] As Jones kisses the book, 'a piece of paper fell from its leaves to the ground, which Partridge took up, and delivered to Jones who presently perceived it to be a bank-bill'.[35] Sophia's writing and her name are instantly recognisable to Jones, making the bill emotionally valuable. James Thompson argues that bills were recognisable because of the 'individualised nature of paper money in the eighteenth century, which not only held the name of the drawer and the bearer, but often a number of intermediary bearers who had endorsed the bill'.[36] Such objects contained their own history. As such, these financial instruments could exist not only as measures of value, but marked identities and relationships, plotting courses as meaningful things. The presence of bills and notes at different points throughout *Tom Jones* and their position as decisive markers that reconnected characters and forwarded the plot shows how multivalent financial instruments could be.[37]

In contrast to the nominal rewards offered for financial instruments, those offered for watches largely aligned with the market values regularly given for such objects. As we saw in Chapter 3, watches remained one of the most significant categories of lost things appearing in newspaper advertisements. The central presence of watches in these notices is explained by the fact that watches were valuable items. Losers would also have been more than aware that watches were regularly stolen. In their study of some 35,540 trial accounts between 1740 and 1800, Anne Helmreich, Tim Hitchcock and William J. Turkel found that 90 per cent were for theft.[38] Of these, the most frequently appearing stolen items were handkerchiefs, with watches running a close second.[39] These objects were stolen because they were carried on the person in urban spaces and thus were available to thieves but also because watches could be easily sold on or pawned.[40] When in *The Adventures of a Watch* (1788), the watch was stolen on London's streets, it was immediately taken to

---

[34] Henry Fielding, *Tom Jones: History of a Foundling* [1749] (Harmondsworth, 1973), 561.
[35] Fielding, *Tom Jones*, 562. [36] Thompson, *Models of Value*, 137.
[37] Another example of such reconnection is when Squire Allworthy recognises a bank bill he had previously given to Tom Jones. See Fielding, *Tom Jones*, 819.
[38] Anne Helmreich, Tim Hitchcock and William J. Turkel, 'Rethinking Inventories in the Digital Age: The Case of the Old Bailey', *Journal of Art Historiography*, 11 (2014), 1.
[39] Helmreich, Hitchcock and Turkel, 'Rethinking Inventories in the Digital Age', 14.
[40] Alongside pawnshops, a ready second-hand market operated in England at this time. See Beverly Lemire, 'The Theft of Clothes and Popular Consumerism in Early Modern England', *Journal of Social History*, 24 (1990), 255–276; Sara Pennell, '"All but the Kitchen Sink": Household Sales and the Circulation of Second-Hand Goods in Early Modern England', in Jon

a pawnbroker and deposited for twenty guineas.[41] The narrative in *The Adventures* was credible because it took place so frequently. When William Tobin allegedly stole a watch with Arthur O'Hara in 1738, they took it to the pawnbroker Mr Grubb the next day. Although Grubb was keen to remind the court that he had asked multiple questions of the pair, he still received it and lent them 40s on it.[42] As we saw in Chapter 4, pawnbrokers were keen to present themselves as people who did not receive stolen goods, but this perception certainly continued into the 1780s. When 'losers' advertised their 'lost' watches then, they would have been very aware that their watch might well have been stolen and if so, there would be little time before it would be sold on or pawned to another. Understanding this dynamic – the spectre of a broader marketplace – shaped the rewards they were prepared to offer. Losers needed to act quickly and offer serious rewards.

E. P. Thompson estimated that in the mid eighteenth century, watches cost between £3 and £5, which was equal to a skilled labourer's monthly wage.[43] Such estimates are borne out in other sources: between 1740 and 1800, £4 was the average value of stolen watches noted in Old Bailey indictments.[44] The value that a stolen (and thus a used watch) was assigned was likely to be different to the average cost of buying a watch in this period, yet the two values closely align. The average reward offered in lost notices for the return of a watch in this period was £3 17s,[45] in other words, almost £4. Those who lost their watches in London were regularly prepared to pay something near the average market value to encourage others to return it. If we look closer though, we see that the average reward for the return of a lost watch changed over time. There were no lost notices for watches published in the *Daily Courant* in December 1702 and 1730, but there were watches in the December 1710 and 1720 issues. These notices offered an average reward of £1 11s. and £6 5s. respectively. The 1720 bump can perhaps be explained by the presence of Jonathan Wild in this period and his ability to negotiate for higher rewards. Following this, the average reward for the return of a lost watch in December 1742 was £2 10s., while for December 1752 it was £2 4s., for December

---

Stobart and Ilja Van Damme (eds), *Modernity and the Second-Hand Trade: European Consumption Cultures and Practices, 1700–1900* (Basingstoke, 2010), 37–56; Jon Stobart, 'Clothes, Cabinets and Carriages: Second-Hand Dealing in Eighteenth-Century England', in B. Blondé, P. Stabel, J. Stobart, I. Van Damme (ed.), *Buyers and Sellers: Retail Circuits and Practices in Medieval and Early Modern Europe* (Turnhout, 2006), 224–244.

[41] Anon., *The Adventures of a Watch* (London, 1788), 169.
[42] *OBPO* (www.oldbaileyonline.org, version 8.0, 16 June 2023), May 1738, trial of Arthur O'Hara William Tobin (t17380518-31).
[43] E. P. Thompson, 'Time, Work-Discipline, and Industrial Capitalism', *Past & Present*, 38 (1967), 67.
[44] Helmreich, Hitchcock and Turkel, 'Rethinking Inventories in the Digital Age', 15.
[45] Based on notices for lost watches appearing in the *Daily Courant* in December 1702, 1710, 1720 and 1730, the *Daily Advertiser* in December 1742, 1752, 1760, 1771, 1782 and 1792 and *The Times* in December 1800, 1810, 1820 and 1830.

1760 it was £2 2s., for December 1771 it was £2 5s. and for December 1782 it was £2 15s. Given that £4 was the average value of stolen watches noted in Old Bailey indictments between 1740 and 1800, in this same period, those who lost their watches paid under that average to reclaim them. By the 1790s, however, people were regularly offering more. In 1792, we see the average reward start to significantly rise with £4 1s. being offered, £5 5s. was the average reward offered in December 1800, no notices in 1810 and then £9 4s. was the average reward for watches in December 1820 and £4 2s. in December 1830. While the average reward offered changed over time, we see that people were willing to offer substantial sums across the period. That they were willing to pay such sums is indicative of their understanding of how watches held their value on secondary markets and of the ease with which someone might sell the item on. Owners would also have wanted to see the return of these possessions because, if cared for and repaired, watches held value over time and thus operated as a store of value, which could be easily pawned when necessary.

Alongside economic value, watches held use value in the eighteenth century. In this period, time became further ingrained as a means of navigating each day. Contemporary scholars have dispelled E. P. Thompson's arguments that it was industrial capitalism, and more particularly the factory, that inculcated a shift from task-orientated to time-orientated working.[46] Instead, historians have shown how there were high levels of 'clock-time awareness' in sixteenth- and seventeenth-century, even in rural, England.[47] They have also underlined the centrality of urbanisation (rather than industrialisation) as a means of consolidating the importance of clock time to the early modern working day.[48] Watches provided a means of navigating clock time. As we saw in earlier chapters, however, watches were valued not only as timepieces but also for their symbolic weight as markers of respectability and status. Watches were able to bear such weight because they were highly visible items, carried on the person.[49]

Owners were also prepared to pay out substantial rewards due to the inalienability of these objects. Annette Weiner has shown how inalienable possessions are those which 'are imbued with the intrinsic and ineffable identities of their owners'. As such, these possessions are likely 'kept by their owners from one generation to the next'.[50] Some watches were certainly understood to have such qualities. In his diary entry from 1764, Gervase Leveland recounted a

---

[46] Thompson, 'Time, Work-Discipline, and Industrial Capitalism', 56–97.
[47] Mark Hailwood, 'Time and Work in Rural England, 1500–1700', *Past & Present*, 248:1 (2020), 118.
[48] Mark Harrison, 'The Ordering of the Urban Environment: Time, Work and the Occurrence of Crowds 1790–1835', *Past & Present*, 110:1 (1986), 136.
[49] John Styles, *The Dress of the People: Everyday Fashion in Eighteenth-Century England* (New Haven, CT and London, 2007), 103.
[50] Weiner, *Inalienable Possessions*, 6.

conversation he had had in a coach on the road towards Turnham Green near London. He recorded how a gentleman had 'entertain'd us with fears of travelling for fear of losing his Family Watch'.[51] The gentleman needed to undertake a journey to Chatham but was worried about the potential dangers of travelling overland and the presence of highway robbers. Rather than the polite gentleman highwayman of the early eighteenth century, Leveland's travelling companion felt the highway robber as a distinctly violent threat.[52] Leveland acquainted the gentleman with the threats nearer to hand on the road to Turnham Green. The gentleman retorted he was sorry he had 'no Pistols' with him because he 'should be sorry to lose this Family Watch'. He then 'pull'd out an old Silver Watch with a Tortoise shell case inlaid with silver', which everyone 'commended to the skies'.[53] Similarly, Sylas Neville noted in his diary how his gold watch 'first belonged to his uncle' and as his uncle's coat of arms was engraved on the outer case, he had purchased another case for urban travails, in case he lost it.[54] Here we see how watches could be understood as items of economic value, of use value, but also as 'family' pieces that should be protected (by violent means if necessary) to ensure that they were retained over time and could be passed down between family members.

In contrast, another regularly appearing item in the lost notices – dogs – could not be passed down between generations, but these too appear to increasingly be treated like inalienable possessions, for which 'losers' offered higher and higher rewards. Lost notices marking the disappearance of canines usually offered a reward to encourage the return of the dog to a particular place and person. The average reward offered in notices between 1702 and 1830 was 13s.[55] The specific amount offered for lost dogs appears to have varied by breed, or as eighteenth-century Britons would have it, by kind. The average reward offered for dogs with no kind listed was 10s. For those dogs listed as spaniels, pointers and terriers the average reward offered was 11s, whereas that for greyhounds it was 16s. It is difficult to assess how much such a reward aligned with the market value of the dog itself. We know that different kinds were understood to have particular abilities and characters in this period and thus were likely sold for different prices.[56] While a King Charles spaniel was

---

[51] British Library, Diary of Gervase Leveland, July 1764–October 1765, BL Add MSS 19211, 33.
[52] Robert Shoemaker, 'The Street Robber and Gentleman Highwayman: Changing Representations and Perceptions of Robbery in London, 1690–1800', *Cultural and Social History*, 3 (2006), 382.
[53] British Library, Diary of Gervase Leveland, July 1764–October 1765, BL Add MSS 19211, 34.
[54] Basil Cozens-Hardy (ed.), *The Diary of Sylas Neville 1767–1788* (London and New York, NY, 1950), 28.
[55] This figure is drawn from an analysis of the December issues of the *Daily Courant* (1702, 1710, 1720, 1730), *Daily Advertiser* (1742, 1752, 1760, 1771, 1782, 1792) and *The Times* (1800, 1810, 1820, 1830). In these issues, 298 advertisements for lost dogs appeared. The average is taken from those advertisements listing a reward for the return of the dog.
[56] Ingrid H. Tague, *Animal Companions: Pets and Social Change in Eighteenth-Century Britain* (Philadelphia, PA, 2015), 36.

deemed an 'idle but innocent companion', the majority of spaniels undertook hunting roles.[57] Water spaniels were good at 'discovering the haunts of wild-ducks and other water fowl' and were known for their attentiveness to the commands of their masters.[58] Springer and cocker spaniels were similarly acknowledged as 'unwearied' pursuers of game, who were 'expert in raising woodcocks and stripes from their haunts in woods and marshes'.[59] Pointers were also employed in searching out game such as partridges and pheasants 'either for the gun or the net'. It was recognised though that an English pointer would require 'the greatest care and attention in breaking and training to the sport'.[60] Training a pointer was clearly no easy feat and took investments of time, skill and patience. Terriers and greyhounds were used in hunting that involved the chase rather than the gun or net. Terriers accompanied packs of hounds. They were there waiting when the hunt wished to force animals 'out of their coverts'.[61] In contrast, greyhounds were 'the fleetest of all Dogs', and they could 'outrun every animal of the chase'. They used their eyes rather than scents and would launch after anything that moved.[62] Greyhounds also held additional layers of cultural and social worth as they had long existed as symbols of elite status.[63] Given the extraordinary regard greyhounds received in British culture, it is perhaps unsurprising that they were brought to the capital, were often stolen or (as the notices would have it) 'lost' and that owners offered on average 16s for their return. Finally, the 20s that was on average offered for Newfoundlands was much greater than that for other breeds. These dogs were valued for their size and were seen as strong animals that could pull heavy loads, such as wood. They were also understood as dogs that could save lives, particularly when people were struggling in water. In his *A General History of Quadrupeds*, Ralph Beilby noted that 'The extraordinary sagacity of these Dogs, and their attachment to their masters, render them highly valuable in particular situations.'[64]

By the 1840s, as dog stealing and dog ransom became ever more organised, the rewards paid out by some individuals rose exponentially. In this period, there was growing agitation to move things on from the 1770 Act for Preventing the Stealing of Dogs. Although the 1770 Act had been formed specifically in response to 'the Practice of stealing Dogs', in the early decades of the nineteenth century, Londoners perceived that a further acceleration of the problem had taken place.[65] In July 1844, a Select Committee on Dog Stealing (Metropolis) was held to gather evidence on the extent of the problem and to find potential legislative solutions. Although the Select Committee took place outside of the chronological parameters of this book, it is included here

---

[57] Beilby, *A General History of Quadrupeds*, 331.   [58] Ibid., 329–330.   [59] Ibid., 331.
[60] Ibid., 324.   [61] Ibid., 315.   [62] Ibid., 313.
[63] Edmund Russell, *Greyhound Nation: A Coevolutionary History of England, 1200–1900* (Cambridge, 2018), 26.
[64] Beilby, *A General History of Quadrupeds*, 327.   [65] 10 Geo. III. C.18.

as a *history* of dog stealing in the capital. The witnesses that appeared before the Committee were asked not only to reflect upon the current problem but also how it had changed over time: they were asked to do historical work. The witnesses recognised this themselves and responded to it. Mr Joseph Shackell, an Inspector in the Metropolitan Police, appeared as a witness before the Committee on the 17 July 1844. Shackell had previously worked as a Bow Street Officer and then served in the Metropolitan Police Whitehall (A) division. He became a gaoler at Bow Street in 1834 before becoming its Principal Officer between 1836 and 1839. Shackell joined the Detective Department of the Metropolitan Police in 1844.[66] In his evidence to the Select Committee, Shackell asserted that he had much experience of dog stealing and dog thieves. He said he had long worked as a Metropolitan police officer in the parish of St. Luke's. More particularly, he stated that for the last fifteen years he had been employed in tracing lost dogs that were suspected to have been stolen.[67] He positioned himself as an old hand at the game: someone able to recount a history of dog stealing.

The different witnesses who appeared before the Select Committee joined in bemoaning that the major problem with dog stealing was that owners paid large sums to get their dog back. The witnesses felt that these owners created a ready and lucrative business for dog stealers. When giving his evidence, William Bishop, a gun-maker in Bond Street, produced a statement that listed 151 individuals who had money extorted from them to secure the return of their dog. The list included such exulted figures as the Bishop of Ely, His Royal Highness Prince George of Cambridge and the Duke of Beaufort, as well as less illustrious individuals such as a Mr Briggs and a Mrs Fletcher. The sums that Bishop reported they had paid ranged from £1 1s to £50 and many were over £5. Evidence from the sporting magazine, *Bell's Life in London and Sporting Chronicle*, shows that William Bishop had long been a key proponent of the Dog Stealing Bill.[68] The evidence he presented on exorbitant rewards was derived from a set of individuals he had knowingly chosen to make a case for the importance of the Bill. The social status of many of those listed shows us that they were in no way representative of British society more broadly, but they were telling. The picture Bishop sought to construct was one in which the

---

[66] Rachael Griffin, 'Detective Policing and the State in Nineteenth-Century England: The Detective Department of the London Metropolitan Police, 1842–1878' (Unpublished PhD Thesis, University of Western Ontario, 2015), 88.
[67] *Report from the Select Committee on Dog Stealing (Metropolis); together with the Minutes of Evidence Taken Before Them* (London, 1844), 16.
[68] See 'The Petition Against Dog Stealers', *Bell's Life in London and Sporting Chronicle* (London), Sunday 7 May 1843; 'The Dog-Stealing Petition', *Bell's Life in London and Sporting Chronicle* (London), Sunday 21 May 1843; 'The Dog Protection Bill', *Bell's Life in London and Sporting Chronicle* (London), Sunday 16 July 1843.

rewards offered had got out of hand. The rewards listed to the Select Committee were certainly much greater than those which appeared in newspaper lost notices. They provide evidence that in the early nineteenth century a step change took place in the problem of dog stealing in London. These seemingly exorbitant figures are also suggestive of how dogs were valuable for a range of reasons, and not simply those dictated by the marketplace.

Our old hand Joseph Shackell had a theory as to the values that large rewards were suggestive of, and he chose to share it with members of the 1844 Select Committee. Shackell described how owners who had lost their dogs or had them stolen 'would rather almost give anything than lose the dog': they felt that they had little to no control of the situation. His theory of the values at stake in these rewards was two-fold. He asserted that 'sometimes it is a favourite dog, and sometimes it is valuable, and in such a case they give a large reward'.[69] While some dogs proved valuable for the relationship they held with their owner then, others were simply 'valuable', by which we might assume he meant that they held a market value. The distinction drawn by Shackell suggests that he considered some forms of value more legible than others. Shackell's theory of value was reminiscent of that purported by William Blackstone in his *Commentaries on the Laws of England*, published in the 1760s. In his *Book II: Of the Rights of Things*, Blackstone had asserted that dogs 'only kept for pleasure, curiosity, or whim' had no intrinsic value but rather their worth depended 'only on the caprice of the owner'.[70] He imagined that value came to be constructed differently in dogs kept for pleasure, as opposed to those kept for work, or rather those that had value outside the realm of their owner. Blackstone began to assert the question later picked up by Shackell, namely that values produced by individuals had less credibility than those created collectively through processes of exchange. Dogs were subjected to these different fields of value and are highly illuminating of 'alternative' values operating outside of the marketplace in this period.

The marketplace perhaps held credence as an arbiter of value because dogs could readily achieve high prices. In 1773, Frances Burney noted in her journal how Mr Rishton had paid '3 guineas' for a dog, although she could not 'distinguish' the dog's '*sect*. [kind]'. Although Burney was not always sure of the type of dog concerned, Mr Rishton's dogs (and their values) clearly piqued her interest. She also noted that he had paid '5 guineas' for a 'Brace [a pair] of spaniels'.[71] These prices appear low in comparison to other claims.

---

[69] *Report from the Select Committee on Dog Stealing*, 16.
[70] William Blackstone, *Commentaries on the Laws of England Book II Of the Rights of Things* ed. Simon Stern (Oxford, 2016), 393.
[71] Frances Burney, *The Early Journals and Letter of Fanny Burney*, Vol. 1, 1768–1773 ed. Lars Troide (Oxford, 1988), 279 and 295.

In 1844, Vincent George Dowling, the editor of *Bell's Life*, asserted that he had known 'an instance in which as much as 150l. has been given for a dog'.[72] Hunting dogs sold for particularly large sums of money in the eighteenth and early nineteenth century. In his *General History of Quadrupeds* (1791), Ralph Beilby noted that he had heard that 'Mr Noel's' pack of fox-hounds (a pack being up to forty dogs) 'was sold to Sir Wm Lowther, bart. For 1000 guineas' (perhaps 25 guineas per dog).[73] At the 1844 Select Committee William Bishop, noted that he had known huge sums to be paid for sporting dogs. He knew of a '100 guineas bid for a pointer' and retrievers to have gone for 'Twenty guineas', while a brace of setters had reached 'forty-five guineas'.[74] Although such sums were proffered by Beilby and Bishop as exceptions, they provide some sense of the extreme prices people would pay for dogs (or at least the stories that could be told about them with some credibility). They reached exorbitant prices not only because of the type of dog they were and the uses to which they were put, but also because of the training invested in them. In his *The Universal Sportsmen*, William Augustus Osbaldiston laid out in detail the different stages of training required to allow greyhounds, pointers, setting dogs (such as spaniels) and terriers to participate in hunting. These processes could take from four months to well over a year, particularly in the case of pointers.[75] Rather than looks or build, Osbaldiston stressed that it was 'his breeding, training up, and coming of a good kind' that were 'the chief things'.[76] It was widely recognised that well-trained hunting dogs regularly achieved high prices on the market. As we saw at the start of this chapter, William Byron certainly knew a dog which had 'never been broke' was 'no use to anybody'.

The lost notices also provide evidence of the importance of human intervention – in other words of breeding, care and training – in producing value. Alongside specifying where and when the dog had been lost, in notices owners were also required to describe their dogs, often in detail. As discussed in Chapter 5, in doing so they sought to make their dog recognisable to others in the hope that this would aid the reclamation process. Alongside making listing of breed, colour, name and collar, some notices used their description of the physical makeup of the dog to list unique, distinguishing features. In 1710, 'a large Black and White Mungril [sic] or Cur Dog' was advertised as 'lost or stray'd' and a ten-shilling reward was offered. The dog was described as 'not

---

[72] *Report from the Select Committee on Dog Stealing*, 48.
[73] Beilby, *A General History of Quadrupeds*, 319.
[74] *Report from the Select Committee on Dog Stealing*, 26.
[75] For more on training pointers, see William Augustus Osbaldiston, *The Universal Sportsman: or, Nobleman, Gentleman, and Farmer's Dictionary of Recreation and Amusement* (Dublin, 1795), 542–548.
[76] Osbaldiston, *The Universal Sportsman*, 610.

very handsome to look upon'.[77] In December 1720, an advertisement noted that the 'small brown Spaniel Dog' who was 'lost from the Black Horse' was 'short Leg'd, full hung, and fat, a little white just under the Breast, the Hair about his Rump a little worn off with the Mange'.[78] Similarly, a 'Fallow Colour Greyhound' lost on the 25 November 1742 was described as 'old' and 'lame in his hind Legs'.[79] Around the same time, a 'small black Spaniel Bitch' was lost, and she was recognisable because 'her Ears rather short, and her Tail long'.[80] These idiosyncratic details were designed to mark the unique nature of the dog and make it recognisable amid all the other dogs in London. However, such details were important for other reasons too. We might read the mange and breakages not simply as idiosyncrasies, but more as defects. In writing the notices, owners sought to lessen the value of their dogs to prevent extortion.

Another common ploy of devaluation, as we saw at the start of the chapter, was to stress how ill-behaved and useless the dog was. Far from obedient sporting dogs, the pages of newspapers reveal a world of untrained canines who were no good for anything. A pointer dog 'strayed' in 1782 and the advertisement seeking his return noted he 'never was broke'.[81] Another pointer advertised as 'lost' in 1792 included a reward for half a guinea but noted that 'No greater Reward will be given, the Dog being old'.[82] In 1800 a white and liver-coloured pointer who was 'remarkably shy' was described as 'not broke in' and so 'no greater Reward than a GUINEA will be offered.[83] We cannot know whether the pointer was indeed shy and what exactly this might have meant. Including such details did less to make these dogs visible and more to make them appear worthless. By playing down the obedience or abilities of their dog, owners sought to ensure that the dog would not be sold on to others and that they, the owner, would not be extorted for £50. They also show that the owners knew the value of a young, well-trained, healthy dog, particularly a well-trained, healthy hunting dog, and they knew that any thief would know that value too. What is interesting is that no one saw the irony of multiple requests for mange-ridden, badly trained animals. The glaring problem here is that while the writers of these notices tried to insist that the dog was of no value, in writing and publishing they showed that the dog was certainly of

---

[77] 'Lost or Stray'd on Saturday the 11th Instant', *Daily Courant* (London), 16 February 1710.
[78] 'A small brown Spaniel Dog', *Daily Courant* (London), 20 December 1720.
[79] 'Lost on Thursday Morning the 25th instant', *Daily Advertiser*, 2 December 1742.
[80] 'Lost on Thursday Night last, a small black Spaniel Bitch', *Daily Advertiser* (London), 6 December 1742.
[81] 'Strayed, or otherwise conveyed away, a Pointer Dog', *Daily Advertiser* (London), 19 December 1782.
[82] 'A Pointer. Lost on Wednesday Afternoon', *Daily Advertiser* (London), 7 December 1792.
[83] 'LOST, on Wednesday Evening, about 4 o'clock', *The Times* (London), 27 January 1800.

value to *them*. In other words, they eloquently articulated the value they placed on the relationship of possession.

In his theory of value, Shackell considered two categories of valuable dog. One category contained dogs that were valuable on the marketplace due to their sporting prowess, but the other was dogs who were valuable to owners because they were a particular favourite. Other witnesses to the Select Committee also picked up on the power of affective relationships with dogs and the value this might produce. The Commissioner of the Metropolitan Police Richard Mayne thought that an owner would be prepared to pay more to get a dog back than a buyer would be prepared to pay to purchase it, because the owner felt 'affection' for it.[84] Similarly, George White, a dealer in livestock, dogs and other animals, told the Select Committee that 'When ladies and gentlemen are very much attached to their animals, they sometimes submit to give enormous rewards rather than be without their dogs.'[85] Given the importance of such relationships and their emotional weight, we might assume that they were discussed in lost notices. However, it was very rare for notices to make any mention of the importance of the dog or the emotions at stake. One notice from 1760, however, did allude to the importance of the dog's position in the family by noting that 'Musk' was 'of no other Value than having belong'd to a Family above ten Years'.[86] We know that this was not the only family to value a dog which 'has lost most of his Teeth, sits up, and has a narrow white Streak down his Forehead'. When his dog Vixen died, Thomas Pelham – Member of Parliament for Sussex and later 2nd Earl of Chichester – used his diary to mark the moment.[87] His notes reveal the central position that Vixen played in his life and the deep loss he felt at her death. On Tuesday 25 February 1794, he recorded that Vixen had died in the stable at four o'clock. Following her death, he ordered that she should be 'buried in our courtyard opposite my Window'.[88] After recording this detail, his prose style changes and he begins to address himself to Vixen directly. He tells her how he 'would have dropt a tear when I heard of your death' and went on to tell her that he would never forget a particular incident when he was ill. He remembered how, during a bout of sickness, Vixen had paid a 'daily visit at my door' and not being admitted had then gone to his mother's room and hidden under her bed. Pelham understood such actions to mean that 'if banished from me you would live only with those who were most attached

---

[84] *Report from the Select Committee on Dog Stealing*, 5. [85] Ibid., 43.
[86] *Daily Advertiser* (London), 30 April 1760.
[87] In the eighteenth century, owners wrote increasingly personal elegies and epitaphs for deceased pets. See Ingrid H. Tague, 'Dead Pets: Satire and Sentiment in British Elegies and Epitaphs for Animals', *Eighteenth-Century Studies*, 41:3 (2008), 289–306.
[88] British Library, Diary of Thomas Pelham, 30 November 1793–6 March 1794, BL Add 3629-33631, f. 37.

to me'. He then finishes his address by exclaiming 'May my life be as harmless & innocent as yours!'[89] Pelham's use of the diary to record the communication he wished to make directly to his dog is revealing of the affective connection he felt the two shared. Moreover, Vixen was not simply a companion; rather Pelham used what he perceived as Vixen's life as an inspiration for his own. People assumed increasingly meaningful relationships with dogs in the eighteenth century.

In her study of the social and material conditions of pet-keeping, Ingrid Tague found that in the eighteenth century the term pet came into usage in Britain to describe domesticated animals kept for pleasure or companionship.[90] Following this shift, pet-keeping then took off in the nineteenth century, as animals came to be seen as central to the construction of homes and families.[91] Dogs were an important part of this wider shift to understanding certain animals as pets, and over the late eighteenth and early nineteenth century, they increasingly came to be understood as 'favourites'. Despite not being alone in holding their dog as a 'favourite', Musk's family were unusual in admitting to such importance here in a lost notice published in the *Daily Advertiser*. People just did not admit to the emotional value of dogs in lost notices. In fact, they did not admit to the emotional value of any lost things, apart from occasionally when a family member had seemingly run away.[92] Such a lack of emotion stands in contrast to the use of emotion in other spaces, including courtrooms, in this period. In courtrooms, emotion played an important role as something that when displayed appropriately could demonstrate credibility and also elicit sympathy.[93] That the owners of Musk made the unusual move of admitting to the importance of their relationship with the dog and his emotional value to the family perhaps points to their lack of awareness as to the workings of the notices system or the intricacies of dog thefts. What they seem to misunderstand is that their valuing of the dog was already assumed and acknowledged as being of the greatest importance within this situation. It was this that might be played upon above all else.

While owners might not have mentioned emotional connections in the text of their notice, it was visible in the rewards they offered and the lengths to which they went to get their dog back. George Hoabdell's evidence to the Select Committee indicates that the rewards offered by dog owners often did

---

[89] British Library, Diary of Thomas Pelham, 30 November 1793–6 March 1794, BL Add 3629-33631, f. 37.
[90] Tague, *Animal Companions*, 3.
[91] Philip Howell, *At Home and Astray: The Domestic Dog in Victorian Britain* (Charlottesville, VA and London, 2015), 85.
[92] See for example, a notice in the *Daily Advertiser* on 6 December 1760, beginning 'Left his Parents on Thursday the 4th instant'. His 'disconsolate Father, Mr. John Little', was desperate for his son to return.
[93] Amy Milka and David Lemmings, 'Narratives of Feeling and Majesty: Mediated Emotions in the Eighteenth-Century Criminal Courtroom', *The Journal of Legal History*, 38:2 (2017), 162.

not align with the price that the dog in question might fetch on the market. Hoabdell, a dealer in dogs, told the Committee that he knew that "8l., 10l., 12l., or 14l. are paid for dogs when they are restored, which in trade, if they were sold, would not fetch 8s. or 10s".[94] There was no simple correlation between market value and reward, rather there was something else at stake, and witnesses before the Select Committee such as Shackell, Mayne and White, surmised that that something was affection. That this form of value existed, and that people were prepared to offer large rewards based on it, was clearly problematic. In an age that placed increasing faith in the marketplace as arbiter of value, this alternative regime needed to be dealt with and the means of doing so was to curb dog stealing. By doing so, dog owners would no longer be asked the question of how much their dog was worth to them and how much they would pay to see it returned to them.

Loss prompted questions of worth and illuminated the multiple forms of value at stake in possessions. Alongside market values, possessions were esteemed for the functions they performed, their role within familial networks, their symbolic importance and the status they held. They were also prized for the place they had held over time, the histories they had acquired and the stories that could be told of them. Lost notices did not bear witness to the emotional worth of these things, but in the rewards offered and the details included, they certainly showed that people knew their possessions, had relationships with them and identified within them. We see all these forms of value in things, but also in the rewards offered for lost things, we find evidence of forms of value, that operated differently to that found in the marketplace. Rather than what people paid to get something, we see what they would pay to get it back. In paying attention to this dynamic, we also begin to see how people assigned and prioritised different clusters of value to different things. People did not value a watch in the same way they valued a dog or a bank note. Particularly in the early nineteenth century, people were prepared to pay ever-more exorbitant rewards to reclaim the dog and have it back in their loving care. Such divergences were both reflective of how financial instruments, watches and dogs were understood but also produced such distinctions. These delineations based on value become clearer still if we shift our focus away from the reward and towards what the reward was offered for. As the next section will show, rewards were (and were decidedly not) offered for different services, sometimes for return, but sometimes 'losers' simply wanted information or to make sure no one else kept hold of the 'thing'. In viewing the different ends rewards sought, we further see how value came to be used to construct and police difference in the eighteenth century.

---

[94] *Report from the Select Committee on Dog Stealing*, 22.

What to Reward

Late seventeenth- and early eighteenth-century British culture did not recognise a sharp distinction between human beings and things. Such blurring occurred not only through cultural and legal forms, but also economically. Different areas of British society held a 'tendency to create equivalences between people and prices'.[95] The sale of enslaved people is the most obvious and extreme example of this tendency. However, prices were placed on people inhabiting other categories including women, children, servants and apprentices, shaping the rhetoric through which they were understood. At the same time, the authority granted to household heads provided the right to enforce discipline through violence and forge an understanding which objectified dependent persons. Historian Deborah Valenze has asserted that these understandings continued until the late decades of the eighteenth century, when antislavery campaigns 'called for a correction in the tendency ['to create equivalences between people and prices'] in its most extreme form'.[96] Within this wider political and cultural context of equivalencies between prices and people, and between people and things, we might assume that the rewards offered in runaway notices would operate similarly to those offered for objects and animals. However, notices advertising people as having run away, absconded or eloped offered rewards infrequently and when they did, they did so for a range of purposes.[97] In contrast to notices for lost bank notes, watches and spaniels, securing return was not always the primary purpose of 'runaway' notices. In fact, it was only the primary concern in notices for enslaved people. In this section of the chapter, we see both the possibilities of equating prices and people, but also how such equations worked differently in different instances. As such, it reminds us of the need to look both at a diverse range of relationships of possession but also to analyse them alongside each other to see how differences and similarities intensified the logics of commodification in some instances, and particularly in relation to the treatment of enslaved people in Britain.

Rather than encouraging the return of the runaway, notices frequently voiced that their purpose was to warn others against 'harbouring',

---

[95] Deborah Valenze, *The Social Life of Money in the English Past* (Cambridge, 2006), 223.
[96] Valenze, *The Social Life of Money in the English Past*, 223–225.
[97] As stated earlier, the sample includes all lost and runaway notices appearing in the *Daily Courant* in December 1702, 1710, 1720 and 1730, as well as all those in the *Daily Advertiser* in December 1742, 1752, 1760, 1771, 1782 and 1792, and those in *The Times* in December 1800, 1810, 1820 and 1830. Within this sample there were thirty-two notices (excluding duplicates) for deserting soldiers and 50 notices (excluding duplicates) for runaway apprentices. These figures sit in contrast to those for people of other occupations or status, such as servants (5), enslaved people (4) and 'lunaticks' (5). Children have not been included here as they are 'left' by others and are thus not cases of return. Neither have spouses as these notices deal with credit relations rather than offering rewards for return or information.

'employing', or 'entertaining' the person concerned. Such warnings were particularly abundant in the case of apprentices. In a period when the power of guilds to regulate trades was declining, masters found other ways to ensure that those who had not completed their apprenticeship might not work.[98] The warnings included in advertisements for runaway apprentices also suggest that masters sought to claim their rights to the apprentice by warning others off. Masters made investments of time and money in housing and training; these could be offset later in the term when the apprentice could work as a skilled labourer. An apprentice running away mid-term threatened this fragile calculation. Even though return is not mentioned, to warn others off might have also induced the apprentice to return by reducing alternative work opportunities. However, it must be remembered that apprenticeships were 'costly, long, and unstable' in this period.[99] That masters would have been aware of the precarity of apprenticeships and the high rates of dissolution is made apparent by the fact they rarely offered rewards and if they did offer a reward, they were unlikely to name the amount at stake. Apprenticeships often ended early, and apprentices regularly ran away; this was an understood and accepted part of the system.[100]

The notices also provide evidence that masters did not want their apprentices to return at all and actively sought to keep them away. In 1742, the stickmaker William Waring noted that he would break 'a Twopenny Oak Stick' across their backs if Edward Page's friends brought him home. Waring claimed that such compensation 'was a greater Reward than he [his apprentice Page] is worth, but still to be had'.[101] Similarly, in 1752, the packthread spinner and rope maker John Downes made clear that whoever harboured, employed or took onboard ship his apprentice Richard Waklin would be 'prosecuted as the Law directs'. At the same time, if anyone brought Waklin home, they would receive 'a Handful of Shop Dust for their Trouble'.[102] The carver and gilder John Robinson was not keen to see his apprentice again either. If anyone harboured or entertained William Clements, they would be 'prosecuted as the Law directs' and if they brought him to Robinson, they would 'receive as a Reward, an old Whitling Pan without a Bottom'.[103] The eighteenth century was a period in which everything held value, where broken items could always be repaired or repurposed. Nevertheless, these notices and the warnings they contain are suggestive of a world in which masters

---

[98] Patrick Wallis, 'Apprenticeship in England', in Maarten Prak and Patrick Wallis (eds), *Apprenticeship in Early Modern Europe* (Cambridge, 2019), 249.
[99] Patrick Wallis, 'Labor, Law, and Training in Early Modern London: Apprenticeship and the City's Institutions', *Journal of British Studies*, 51 (2012), 792.
[100] Wallis, 'Labor, Law, and Training in Early Modern London', 793.
[101] 'Whereas Edward Page, Apprentice to Mr. William Waring', *Daily Advertiser* (London), 18 December 1742.
[102] 'Whereas Richard Waklin, Apprentice to John Downes', *Daily Advertiser* (London), 4 December 1752.
[103] 'Whereas William Clements, Apprentice to Mr. John Robinson', *Daily Advertiser* (London), 27 December 1752.

sought to stave off the return of runaway apprentices, and a world in which there was a good joke to be had at the very idea of such an outcome. Return might be deeply unwelcome because masters could use such instances as grounds for the dissolution of the apprenticeship and to reduce the likelihood of being forced to return their premium.[104]

As with apprentices, servants also often ran away. As we discussed in Chapter 2, running away was a technical term, used to describe 'leaving a hiring before its term, or without notice'.[105] Undramatic, it was a mundane reality that allowed servants to break their contract. Perhaps due to its regularity, servants only occasionally appeared in runaway notices. We might also contend with the fact that for servants deemed valuable, masters and mistresses tried other tactics to ensure they stayed. Alongside formal renumeration, mistresses gave valued servants additional gifts to try to retain them over time. Elizabeth Shackleton provided her servant Nanny Nutter with 'a Halifax ribbon, a gauze cap with a spider thread lace border, a black silk laced handkerchief, a pair of old dimity pockets, an old worked muslin apron, a red and white handkerchief, an old mob, a yard of scarlet ribbon, and a pair of single lawn ruffles'.[106] Despite such inducements, Nutter absconded from the household on at least four occasions and in 1775, finally she ran away for good. The lack of notices for servants perhaps demonstrates their belief in other methods of retention. It also suggests that sometimes employers were reticent to encourage return.

The notices that were placed for absconding servants often sought other endings rather than return. Of the five notices that appear in this sample, two advertise servants who have left with stolen goods in tow. In these cases, rewards were offered (five pounds in the case of John Mills, three guineas in the case of Joseph Lovatt) to people who could 'apprehend' them or provide information so they may be 'apprehended'.[107] Given that a servant's annual wage in London was around £3 to £6 in the eighteenth century, these sums are monumental.[108] They suggest the importance of reclaiming the stolen goods and possibly prosecuting the servant. Yet, the sample also includes instances in which it was crucial that the servant return. A Mr Nixon demanded that his unnamed servant 'return to his said Master forthwith, or give immediate Notice where he may be wrote to or spoke with, in order that Affairs may be settled without proceeding to Extremities'. Otherwise, he threatened, 'no Cost or

---

[104] Wallis, 'Labor, Law, and Training in Early Modern London', 812.
[105] Carolyn Steedman, *Labours Lost: Domestic Service and the Making of Modern England* (Cambridge, 2009), 44.
[106] Amanda Vickery, *The Gentleman's Daughter: Women's Lives in Georgian England* (New Haven, CT and London, 2003), 144.
[107] 'Whereas John Mills, late Servant to William Langford', *Daily Courant* (London), 15 December 1710; 'Whereas a Servant Joseph Lovatt on Cock-Hill', *Daily Advertiser* (London), 11 December 1760.
[108] Paula Humfrey, 'Introduction', in Paula Humfrey (ed.), *The Experience of Domestic Service for Women in Early Modern London* (Farnham, 2011), 22.

Pains will be spared to find him out by advertising his Name and length, and any other Methods'.[109] This advertisement from 1760 perhaps points to another aspect at stake. In the eighteenth century, servants did not possess their own labour and contract it out to others, rather they accepted contracts in which they fulfilled their master or mistress's capacity to labour: they exercised it on their behalf.[110] Such conceptions caused much worry in the eighteenth century as to servants and their role in the social order. To have a servant runaway raised questions of the master and mistress, of what had happened to their capacity to labour, of where it had gone. Perhaps the disappearance of his unnamed servant challenged Mr Nixon's sense of self. Or perhaps the servant had simply run off with that week's takings.

As with servants, in the case of deserting soldiers, advertisements were placed not to secure return, but rather to reassert the importance of Crown authority through something akin to due process. Desertion was the most common crime tried by General Courts Martial in the eighteenth century. It was frequently punished with death, particularly in cases of desertion from the battlefield or to the enemies of the crown.[111] Advertisements for deserting soldiers included rewards as standard and sought information and/or capture. Rewards tended to be around one guinea and this reward was offered in addition to the statutory twenty-shilling reward outlined each year by the Mutiny Act.[112] Some of these notices offer rewards simply for information as to the whereabouts of the deserter involved. Most were more demanding, however, and required that the deserter be apprehended and taken to a gaol. The wording of these notices and the expectation that a reward would be paid for 'apprehension' highlights not only the importance of Crown authority and its consolidation but also to understandings of desertion as a particular act. 'Apprehension' and 'capture' suggest that force will be used to 'secure' the deserter and seek proceedings for their crime.

Similarly, questions of capacity and resistance were central to notices advertising enslaved people. These notices register that these individuals had acted of their own volition. They had not 'strayed' or 'got away'. Rather they had 'eloped' and 'runaway': they had acted with intention. At the same time, the notices also demonstrate an understanding that unlike white servants and apprentices, these individuals will not return of their own volition; they will not make that choice. Instead, they would need to be 'brought' by others. As we saw in Chapter 4, terms such as 'apprehend', 'take' and particularly 'bring' nodded to the forcible capture of the individual concerned. When

---

[109] 'Whereas a Covenant Servant to Mr. Nixon, of Clement's Lane', *Daily Advertiser* (London), 6 December 1760.

[110] Steedman, *Labours Lost*, 14.

[111] Joseph Cozens, '"The Blackest Perjury": Desertion, Miliary Justice, and Popular Politics in England, 1803–1805', *Labour History Review*, 79:3 (2014), 256.

[112] Cozens, '"The Blackest Perjury"', 267.

'James' a 'black Servant, brought over from Jamaica a few months ago' 'eloped' from 'his Master', the advertisement placed to facilitate his return noted that whoever 'apprehends him, and brings him' would receive 'a Guinea Reward'. It also warned that 'whoever harbours him shall be prosecuted according to Law, as he is his Master's purchased Property'.[113] Similarly, when 'Jeffreys', who was described in the notice as 'A Negro Boy, about sixteen Years of Age, tall and well made', 'ran away', his master 'James Pereira' aggressively advertised his demands. The notice asserted that 'Whoever will give Notice of him, so that he may be taken, or will bring him to James Pereira, Esq; (whose Property he is) ... shall have Two Guineas Reward; and whoever harbours him after this Advertisement, shall answer it at their Peril'.[114] These notices and the language used distinctly contrast with those for white apprentices and servants. In fact, reading the notices for enslaved people within the context of those for other types of 'runaways' *and* against those for lost 'things' more broadly, we are struck by how the language of the notices confined enslaved people 'in a depiction of violence and commodification from the perspective of the slave owner and other white authorities'.[115] A conclusion further consolidated by the enslavers use of the term 'property' in each notice. Such close textual analysis builds on the work of scholars such as Simon Newman to provide further evidence that despite legal ambiguities, Britons were clear that enslaved people could be openly understood as property on British shores and that they actively sought to keep hold.

Engaging more fully with the *how* of forcible capture and the commodification of enslaved people in Britain also reminds us of the radical act enslaved people completed when they ran away. They challenged (even if only temporarily) the understanding that they were property by finding a way (despite likely coercion and control) to act of their own volition and demonstrate their personhood. Enslaved people did not 'stray', they *chose* to run, they sought freedom and significantly the notices recognised this. At the same time, staying away and evading the force masters threatened and enacted further disrupted the possibility of imagining enslaved people as property. In describing 'Jeffreys', the notice records how it is 'supposed' that he is 'lurking about Covent-Garden and St. James's'. Here we see a glimpse of the attempts to find, follow and capture Jeffreys and his ability to continually outwit pursuit. These notices hold a series of contradictions about 'James' and 'Jeffreys'. They are simultaneously property to be held and harboured, and, at the same time they are people making decisions and acting of their own volition. That such

---

[113] 'Eloped on Wednesday last in the Evening', *Daily Advertiser* (London), 8 December 1760.
[114] 'Ran away about ten Days ago', *Daily Advertiser* (London), 16 December 1760.
[115] Marisa J. Fuentes, *Dispossessed Lives: Enslaved Women, Violence, and the Archive* (Philadelphia, PA, 2016), 44.

seeming contradictions could exist within the same historical record are unsurprising if seen in the wider imperial context of enslavement. Marisa Fuentes' research on Barbados has shown us how enslaved people could be legally perceived as 'a commodity without will' and yet could be tried for crimes.[116] As Chapter 1 underlined, to be an enslaved or previously enslaved person in Britain was to inhabit an ambiguous legal category. Such ambiguity allowed contradictory conceptions to be held simultaneously by white enslavers. The evidence of freedom seeking that such notices provide also underscore, however, that Black men and women enacted their understanding of themselves, as people with will and intention. As Douglas Lorimer argued long ago, through their actions these men and women voiced their claims to personhood.[117] Here, then, we also glimpse what Daina Ramey Berry has conceptualised as 'soul values': that Black men and women held 'self-worth' that existed beyond 'the "flesh and blood values" ascribed to their bodies' when enslaved.[118] Actions were important markers of self-possession and self-perception.

We must also remember that it was the actions of 'James' and 'Jeffreys' that prompted the creation of the historical record, fleeting, incomplete and unsatisfactory as it might be.[119] We learn that 'James' played the violin and held possessions: 'a blue Coat and Waistcoat with white Buttons, and crimson Worsted Breeches'. Although items such as the breeches might have been livery, they were nevertheless important in conferring maturity and manhood.[120] Might 'James' have been 'James Price', described as 'an adult Black' of 'New North Street', who was baptised in the parish of Saint George the Martyr, Queen Square on 1 October 1764?[121] Or perhaps he is James Baker, 'a Black Man 40 yrs old', who was baptised in the parish of Saint Marylebone in 1785?[122] We are made aware that 'Jeffreys' had 'a green Cloth Livery, with yellow Lace, the Coat lapelled, a black Velvet Cap, and Buckskin Breeches'. He took these possessions with him, needing clothes but also perhaps knowing that they would offer him a starting point, as property that

---

[116] Fuentes, *Dispossessed Lives*, 109. Catherine Hall has explored a similar paradox at work in eighteenth-century Jamaica. Catherine Hall, *Lucky Valley: Edward Long and the History of Racial Capitalism* (Cambridge, 2024), 329.
[117] Douglas Lorimer, 'Black Slaves and English Liberty: A Re-examination of Racial Slavery', *Immigrants and Minorities*, 3:2 (1984), 121.
[118] Daina Ramey Berry, *The Price for their Pound of Flesh: The Value of the Enslaved, from Womb to Grave in the Building of a Nation* (Boston, MA, 2017), 6.
[119] Saidiya Hartman, 'Venus in Two Acts', *Small Axe*, 26 (2008), 2.
[120] Karen Harvey, 'Men of Parts: Masculine Embodiment and the Male Leg in Eighteenth-Century England', *Journal of British Studies*, 54 (2015), 806.
[121] London Metropolitan Archives, London Metropolitan Archives Data Collections, Baptism record for Saint George the Martyr, Queen Square, 1 October 1764, Z/PROJECT/BAL/M/P82/GE02/001/1138.
[122] London Metropolitan Archives, London Metropolitan Archives Data Collections, Baptism record for Saint Marylebone, 3 November 1785, Z/PROJECT/BAL/M/P89/MRY1/008/1724.

could be pawned and thus quickly produce money. It was not only freedom seekers who sold their clothes to sustain themselves. For example, the servant Thomas Hughes was dismissed by his employer Lady Morton. Soon after, he returned to the house in Chiswick and stole money and various items of clothing. He swiftly sold the clothes to a second-hand clothes dealer and bought a new hat and coat, perhaps hoping to disguise himself.[123] A black velvet cap and buckskin breeches would have certainly provided for 'Jeffreys' when he pawned or sold them to on to one of the many second-hand clothes dealers in the city. In contrast to the more common breeches made from leather and cotton, buckskin breeches were of higher value.[124] Unlike Hughes, however, the cap and breeches were the clothes on his back, items which could have been understood as his possessions.[125] In leaving with these items, he made another claim to personhood through being a property owner. As Joseph H. Carens has noted in terms of C.B. Macpherson's concept of possessive individualism, 'To be an individual is to be an owner – in the first instance, an owner of one's own person and capacities, but also of what one acquires through the use of one's capacities.'[126] Although enslaved people did not own their person or capacities, through freedom seeking, they sought to lay claim to them and taking their clothes with them proved an important part of such a determination. Nevertheless, our glimpses of these two men are just that, half spied, barely visible. We can only root for them at a vast historical distance, hoping they quickly sold their clothes, connected with people who helped them, forged a life and were never found.

Notices announcing enslaved people as having run away largely ended in the 1780s.[127] While notices in the 1770s and 1780s were more ambiguous as to whether enslaved people could be understood as property, they were no less clear on the stakes at play. When 'George' a 'handsome Slave Boy, Native of Bengal' sought freedom the notice asserted that 'Whoever will bring him to his Master Mr Ruspini...shall be handsomely rewarded; and whoever harbours him will be sued.'[128] George's presence here reminds us that the British enacted forms of enslavement outside of the Caribbean and Americas in the eighteenth century. The British also utilised forms of (often domestic)

---

[123] J. M. Beattie, *The First English Detectives: The Bow Street Runners and the Policing of London, 1750–1840* (Oxford, 2014), 62–3.

[124] John Styles, *The Dress of the People: Everyday Fashion in Eighteenth-Century England* (New Haven, CT and London, 2007), 39.

[125] Laura Edwards, *Only the Clothes on Her Back: Clothing and the Hidden History of Power in the Nineteenth-Century United States* (New York, 2022), 1–2.

[126] Joseph H. Carens, 'Possessive Individualism and Democratic Theory: Macpherson's Legacy', in Joseph H. Carens (ed.), *Democracy and Possessive Individualism: The Intellectual Legacy of C. B. Macpherson* (Albany, NY, 1993), 2.

[127] Simon P. Newman, 'Freedom-Seeking Slaves in England and Scotland, 1700–1780', *English Historical Review*, 134:570 (2019), 1167.

[128] 'A Black Boy. Ran Away from His Master', *Daily Advertiser* (London), 20 December 1771.

enslavement within the Indian subcontinent and brought enslaved people with them from South Asia.[129] What the notice makes clear is that a 'handsome' reward is on offer for anyone who forcibly returns George to his 'Master Mr Ruspini'. Similarly, when 'Samuel Allen, a black Boy, about 16 Years of Age' was 'Lost, or supposed to lose his Way', the notice demanded that 'Whoever will bring' him 'shall receive Half a Guinea Reward'. It also threatened that 'Whoever shall harbour the said Samuel will be prosecuted, he being an indentured Servant.'[130] Here the notice seeks Samuel's forcible capture and return, but it also notes it will sue for services lost if someone takes Samuel in and employs him (especially now they are aware through the notice that Samuel's labour is owned by another).[131] The notice speaks to an idea that Samuel will be taken in by others and kept. It undermines his capacity for agency and self-possession but might also be half suggestive of the potential communities of support we explored in Chapter 2.

In contrast to the rewards offered for servants who had stolen goods, the rewards here seem minor, just half a guinea, a guinea or two guineas. It is difficult to decipher the values at stake or the calculation that has been made. Although we know that Black people were bought and sold in eighteenth-century Britain, we do not know the prices paid. Extant advertisements announced that people were 'To be dispos'd of' and 'To be SOLD', but they did not name the price.[132] The open advertising of the sale of people in England came increasingly to be regarded as problematic in the 1760s but only disappeared in the 1780s.[133] We might read the omission of prices in sale notices as attempts to seize the negotiating advantage rather than any coyness at the act of selling a human. Eighteenth-century English people wished to buy Black men and women because free and enslaved Black men who worked, or were forced to work, in British households were read as status symbols. In the seventeenth century, the elite began to commission portraits which included Black servants. They did so as a means of constructing their mastery over their

---

[129] Margot Finn, 'Slaves out of Context: Domestic Slavery and the Anglo-Indian Family, c.1780–1830', *Transactions of the Royal Historical Society*, 19 (2009), 183.
[130] 'Lost, or Supposed to Lose His Way', *Daily Advertiser* (London), 21 December 1782.
[131] Philip S. James and D. J. L. Brown, *General Principles of the Law of Torts* (London, 1978), 333.
[132] See 'Runaway Slaves in Eighteenth-Century Britain: 'For Sale' Advertisements', a PDF available on the Runaway Slaves in Britain: Bondage, Freedom & Race in the Eighteenth Century website (www.runaways.gla.ac.uk/for_sale/Runaway%20Slaves%20in%2018th%20C%20Britain%20-%20For%20Sale.pdf, accessed 26 May 2023). The sample of notices begin in 1705 and 1779. They were predominantly printed in London newspapers, but also in Liverpool, Bristol and Edinburgh papers.
[133] For example, Granville Sharp wrote to Lord Cambden in November 1769 to voice his approbation of the Lord Cambden's advertising as for sale a nameless eleven-year-old Black girl. See York Minster Archive, Letterbook of Granville Sharp 1768-73, COLL 1869/1, 31–33.

household and the world.¹³⁴ To enslave people was to understand them as 'things', as possessions, but also simultaneously as people. The runaway notices, written by enslavers, speaks to this 'logic'. Here, as with animals and objects, and in contrast to those for some other types of 'runaway', rewards were offered for the return of the person. Seeing these runaway notices in the context of the broader lost notices system reveals how particular the process of enslavement was and the violence it did to Black people in Britain. The descriptions included in runaway notices marks enslaved people out as person, the logic of the reward marks them out as 'thing'.

Conclusion

Focusing on the rewards offered in lost notices, and what those rewards were offered for, illuminates our understanding of the values at stake in people, animals and objects in the eighteenth century. We are alerted to how British people valued these different 'things' for the exchange values they could achieve, the functions they performed, their meanings and symbolic power and, ultimately, for the relationships that people had with them. Lost notices are a particularly important means of getting to these relationships and meanings. Rather than value produced in the marketplace, we have seen in this chapter that value was produced in a variety of times and places. It could be created when the watch was passed down as an heirloom, when the bill of exchange gained another signature, when the dog finally learned to answer to its name. It was created in the home, in the coffeehouse and on the hunting field. In exploring these values, we learn why owners were prepared to invest time, effort and money in getting their possessions back. Put simply, these were valuable things.

The production of *different* values for different things is also telling. They contributed to the broader eighteenth-century project of constructing categorical differences. We see that the lost notices offered different rewards for different things, but we also see that the lost notices offered rewards to ensure different outcomes for different 'things'. In other words, the values at stake acted to create distinction between different 'things' but so did the purposes to which such values were put. Such distinctions are most apparent when we see notices for watches, financial instruments, dogs and people side-by-side, but also when we assess how rewards worked differently in notices for different kinds of runaways. For instance, while rewards were customarily offered for

---

¹³⁴ Peter Erickson, 'Invisibility Speaks: Servants and Portraits in Early Modern Visual Culture', *Journal for Early Modern Cultural Studies*, 9:1 (2009), 34; Catherine Molineux, *Faces of Perfect Ebony: Encountering Atlantic Slavery in Imperial Britain* (Cambridge, MA, and London, 2012), 21 and 39.

information about or the capture of deserted soldiers, they were rarely offered for apprentices. It was only for enslaved people that rewards were offered to those who returned enslaved people to their 'masters'. In tracking rewards as a measure of value, but also as markers of action, the logic of distinction comes through more clearly.

While this chapter has sought to focus on possessions and the values which accrued to them, the next chapter changes tack by returning more fully to the relationship of possession. It questions why eighteenth-century Britons worked so hard to ensure the return of their 'things' and what this reveals not about the value of possessions, but rather of keeping hold of them.

7 Selfhood and the Importance of Keeping Hold

The preceding chapters have built an argument about the nature of possession in eighteenth-century culture. Those chapters have primarily looked to moveable forms of property and how people related to possessions by examining the idea of care. Care was a key means by which people made sense of possessions. They (and others) enacted different forms of care, not just the maintenance we are familiar with, but, as we have seen, keeping property secure, noting details, seeking out reclamation if it was lost. These forms of caring took place because, as we saw in Chapter 6, possessions were valuable. To have well-maintained possessions that were clean and neat also allowed people to accrue social and cultural capital. These clean, neat, ordered 'things' were signs of a good character. This, the final chapter in the book, seeks to lean on these arguments a little harder. It wants to build on the idea that people sought to reclaim their lost possessions because they were economically, culturally and socially valuable, to argue that there was more at stake in these acts of reclamation. This chapter pauses and sets a different pace. It asserts that there was value in the relationship of possession itself, or rather that there was value in being able to sustain the relationship of possession over time. Such value was accrued not simply by maintaining the possession, but rather by *keeping hold* of the possession, which was, as we have seen, a difficult task in the eighteenth century when objects might be dropped, dogs might run away and servants frequently absconded. The chapter explores these issues by looking to an imagining of what might happen if you could not keep hold. It focuses on loss and by looking to a particular genre of writing – novels – it tracks the cultural and social scripts loss animated.

Novels are useful for thinking through possession and loss because in the eighteenth-century, novelists were increasingly concerned with questions of ownership, particularly in relation to their work. Over the century, copyright shifted from being held by publishers to instead by authors.[1] The Donaldson dispute, heard in the House of Lords in 1774, marked the important resolution

---

[1] Ronan Deazley, *On the Origin of the Right to Copy: Charting the Movement of Copyright Law in Eighteenth-Century Britain (1695–1775)* (Oxford and Portland, OR, 2004), xix.

of the shift.² It changed what intellectual ownership was understood to be, how publication took place and who benefited from it. We see the importance of literary property at work in the career of Frances Burney (1752–1840). Burney's brother Charles (1757–1817) negotiated the sale of the copyright to her first novel *Evelina* (1778) to the publisher Lowndes.³ Despite its huge success, Burney received just twenty guineas.⁴ Her father, also Charles (1726–1814), negotiated the copyright for her much anticipated second novel *Cecilia*. However, he placed greater importance on connections and literary achievement than Burney's financial independence. As a result, the copyright for *Cecilia* (1782) was sold for just £250.⁵ Burney herself seems to have gained little of that sum, however, as the money remained in her father's care.⁶ For her final two novels, *Camilla* (1796) and *The Wanderer* (1814), Burney took control.⁷ Her brother Charles acted as her agent and she insisted the books be published by subscription, with Burney keeping the copyright and employing the bookseller who offered the highest bid. The issue of who it was that took control, who it was that benefited, is important. Burney had married the penniless General Alexandre d'Arblay (1748–1818) on 28 July 1793.⁸ Cheryl Turner reminds us that 'novels by married women were legally the property of their husbands, as were any profits from publication'.⁹ Yet D'Arblay seems unconcerned with such ownership claims. The letters between Charles and Frances arranging sale and copyright do not mention D'Arblay and evidence suggests he was largely unaware of such negotiations. *Camilla* (1796) earned Burney approximately £2,000 and allowed her to build Camilla Cottage.¹⁰ Here, as we saw in Chapters 1 and 4, we are struck by complexities of gendered patterns of ownership and how women worked around them. Burney was not alone in her negotiations for ownership and the losses and gains they entailed. Other novelists experienced them too. In fact, issues of property and possession loomed large in the lives of novelists and perhaps unsurprisingly, these preoccupations were given life in their

---

[2] Kevin Hart, *Samuel Johnson and the Culture of Property* (Cambridge, 1999), 5.
[3] Frances Burney, *Evelina, or The History of a Young Lady's Entrance into the World* [1778] (New York and London, 1965).
[4] Margaret Anne Doody, *Frances Burney: The Life in the Works* [1988] (Cambridge, 2010), 70.
[5] Doody, *Frances Burney*, 143; Catherine Gallagher, *Nobody's Story: The Vanishing Acts of Women Writers in the Marketplace, 1670–1820* (Oxford, 1994), 250.
[6] Doody, *Frances Burney*, 159.
[7] Frances Burney, *Camilla* [1796] (Oxford, 2009); Frances Burney, *The Wanderer* [1814] (Oxford, 2001).
[8] Frances Burney's income allowed them to marry. Queen Charlotte awarded Burney a pension of one hundred pounds per annum, which continued after her marriage. See Doody, *Frances Burney*, 201.
[9] Cheryl Turner, *Living by the Pen: Women Writers in the Eighteenth Century* (London, 1994), 100.
[10] Gallagher, *Nobody's Story*, 254.

novels.[11] Novels and novelists were not only impacted by questions of gender, status, value and property, they also actively shaped the terms of the discussion.[12] Novels are important in offering another window onto understanding the significance of the relationship of possession in eighteenth-century Britain.

In contrast to the chapters which have proceeded it, this chapter is much narrower in its focus. It attends to the novels of Frances Burney, and particularly her second novel, *Cecilia* (1782). The novel follows the tribulations of Cecilia Beverley, an heiress who will only retain her fortune if the man she marries takes her name.[13] Themes of possession and property thread through the fabric of the novel. Catherine Gallagher has argued that 'Perhaps no book in the annals of the English novel succeeds as thoroughly as this one [*Cecilia*] in focusing our apprehensive attention on a character's property.'[14] Cecilia has two fortunes. The first is a £10,000 bequest from her father, which Cecilia regards as her own property, even though she is not of age.[15] Before she comes of age, she has largely given it away to support her manipulative guardian Mr Harrel. Eventually, her second fortune of £3,000 per annum from her uncle's estate is also lost to her when she marries Mortimer Delvile, leading to wider questions about her identity. The climax of the novel finds Cecilia unable to account for herself; here she turns from subject to object. She is taken in by a pawnbroker and is advertised, like so many other lost 'things'.

What we find in *Cecilia* and see reflected in other novels, too, is the notion that 'things' were central to the formation of personhood and the self in this period.[16] We will not be surprised by this finding. We know, have known for a while, that this was the case. What has received less attention is what happened to such formations when things were lost. Margreta de Grazia's work suggests the longer histories at stake in this question.[17] Through an examination of William Shakespeare's 1606 play *King Lear*, de Grazia shows how 'Subjects and objects are so tightly bound in the play's economy that a subject cannot survive the loss of his or her possessions.'[18] Like de Grazia's work, this chapter remains embedded in literary sources but explores how these dynamics

---

[11] James Thompson, *Models of Value: Eighteenth-Century Political Economy and the Novel* (Durham, NC, and London, 1996), 175.
[12] Margot C. Finn, *The Character of Credit: Personal Debt in English Culture, 1740–1914* (Cambridge, 2003), 26.
[13] Frances Burney, *Cecilia* [1782] (Oxford, 2008), 898.   [14] Gallagher, *Nobody's Story*, 238.
[15] Ibid., 239; Thompson, *Models of Value*, 161.
[16] See, for example, Daniel Defoe, *Moll Flanders* [1722] (Oxford, 1998); Daniel Defoe, *Colonel Jack* [1722] (London, 1967); Samuel Richardson, *Pamela* [1740] (Oxford, 2001); Fielding, *Tom Jones*; Mary Wollstonecraft, *Mary* and *The Wrongs of Woman* [1798] (Oxford, 2009).
[17] Margreta de Grazia, 'The Ideology of Superfluous Things: King Lear as Period Piece', in Margreta de Grazia, Maureen Quilligan and Peter Stallybrass (eds), *Subject and Object in Renaissance Culture* (Cambridge, 1996), 17–42.
[18] de Grazia, 'The Ideology of Superfluous Things', 24.

of self, possession and loss operated in the eighteenth century. It examines what the loss of possessions might have meant in this period, as a way of better understanding why people worked hard to get things back. It suggests that exploring this problem of loss and losing within an eighteenth-century context takes us beyond the fictional kings and nobility focused on research in the seventeenth century. As growing numbers of people came to own a wider range of 'things' in the eighteenth century, the question of loss and its impact on self, personhood and character became much more widely applicable.

Self-Possession

In the eighteenth century, a reputable household was one that was ordered and neat. So too, to be of good character was to be composed and consistent. In this period, ever-greater value came to be placed on the concept of self-possession: the ability to control feelings and reactions. Self-possession was 'composure, equanimity, self-control'.[19] However, such composure had to appear 'natural'. The idea of self-possession emerged in the later seventeenth century and was first used in 1665. In 1745, the minister and author John Mason (1706–1763) developed these ideas more substantially in his *Self-Knowledge: A Treatise, Shewing the Nature and Benefit of the Important Science, and the Way to Attain It*.[20] Mason's treatise on self-knowledge has been described as 'one of the most popular works of moral advice and self-help of its time'.[21] It had gone through twenty editions by 1836 and was translated into several languages.[22] Here Mason argued for the importance of retaining control of the self and saw the 'Government' of thoughts and passions as central to good character.[23] Mason's treatise suggests that far from 'natural', self-possession was considered and practised: people invested in attaining it.

Ideas of self-command and self-control became particularly important to conceptions of polite masculinity in this period and remained so in the nineteenth century.[24] Self-control, or rather self-discipline, was also central

---

[19] 'self-possession, n.'. *OED Online*. June 2021. Oxford University Press. www.oed.com/view/Entry/175395?redirectedFrom=self-possession (accessed 31 August 2021).
[20] John Mason, *Self-Knowledge. A Treatise, Shewing the Nature and Benefit of the Important Science, and the Way to Attain It* [1745] (London, 1755).
[21] Alan Ruston, 'Mason, John (1706–1763), Independent Minister and Author', *Oxford Dictionary of National Biography*. 23 Sep. 2004; Accessed 15 June 2022. www.oxforddnb.com/view/10.1093/ref:odnb/9780198614128.001.0001/odnb-9780198614128-e-18283.
[22] Ruston, 'Mason, John (1706–1763), Independent minister and author'.
[23] Mason, *Self-Knowledge*, 156. For more on the centrality of the 'passions' in the eighteenth century (as opposed to emotions) see Thomas Dixon, *From Passions to Emotions: The Category of a Secular Psychological Category* (Cambridge, 2003), 4.
[24] Karen Harvey, 'The History of Masculinity, circa 1650–1800', *Journal of British Studies*, 44 (2005), 301; Joanne Begiato, *Manliness in Britain, 1760–1900: Bodies, Emotion and Material Culture* (Manchester, 2020), 9.

to the conceptions of polite femininity in this period, yet it existed as a form of 'ambivalent practice'. As Soile Ylivuori argues, 'self-control was required to fulfil the ideals of polite femininity', but 'it needed to be concealed, since engaging in self-discipline shook the allegedly natural core of women's gendered identity'.[25] For polite men and women, self-control was vital primarily due to concerns over its limitations and fragility. In considering the parameters of self-control, Mason was careful to consider such fragility and the ever-present possibilities of losing control. He advocated that one must consider 'in what Company you are most apt to lose the Possession and Government of yourself'. Once you have identified which company provides the greatest temptation to indulge in excess, Mason asserted that you should 'Flee that Company, avoid those Occasions'.[26] In his treatise, Mason sought to identify self-possession in social terms. It was people and particular occasions that contained the possibility of encouraging excess or unpredictability, this was where self-possession might be lost. His advice to flee such people and such events also suggests at the importance of time. Good character demanded that self-possession be sustained over time, rather than displayed in a static moment or temporary performance.

Patricia Meyer Spacks has argued that eighteenth-century novels were also attentive to issues of control and composure over time. Characters had to be consistent and unchanging. Part of the need for such consistency was embedded within the newness of the form itself; for extended plot lines to work, fictional characters needed to be consistent and recognisable to readers throughout. Similarly, such coherence spoke to concerns over the ever-growing range of external pressures and thus the greatest virtue a character might achieve was to 'remain essentially the same'.[27] Although characters such as Moll Flanders, Pamela Andrews, Tom Jones and Evelina Anville might struggle to define their 'proper social positions', such social fluctuation operated in marked contrast to personal stability.[28] Characters remained largely the same even if their social position radically altered. Moreover, Spacks takes this idea further, to argue that particular emphasis was placed on the importance of women achieving constancy and coherence over time.[29] The desire for coherence and stability of character maps on to broader eighteenth-century histories of the self. Following Dror Wahrman's arguments, we see that in the 1780s and 1790s a

---

[25] Soile Ylivuori, *Women and Politeness in Eighteenth-Century England: Bodies, Identities, and Power* (London, 2019), 18.
[26] Mason, *Self-Knowledge*, 63.
[27] Patricia Meyer Spacks, *Imagining a Self: Autobiography and Novel in Eighteenth-Century England* (Cambridge, MA and London, 1976), 8.
[28] Defoe, *Moll Flanders*; Richardson, *Pamela*; Fielding, *Tom Jones*; Burney, *Evelina*.
[29] Patricia Meyer Spacks, *Desire and Truth: Functions of Plot in Eighteenth-Century English Novels* (Chicago, IL and London, 1994), 93, 97, and 105.

new understanding emerged in which categories of identity such as gender, race and class came to be seen as part of an 'innate, fixed, determined core'.[30] While in this period ideas of personal development and change were embedded, so too was an idea of the self as something that could be realised and understood because it was essentially innate and fixed.

The burgeoning consumer culture of the eighteenth century allowed Britons the means to make their understandings of character, and more particularly, self, materially manifest. Changing understandings of worth and increasingly accessible consumer goods meant that the display of objects on the person became central to defining and expressing identity, particularly in urban spaces.[31] As we have seen, people could also be possessions and were utilised in forms of display and expression. However, it was not simply the having 'things' and the displaying of 'things' that was important. As we saw in Chapter 1, what one owned, what one was allowed to own, acted as a means of marking legal personalities and personhood.[32] In trying to understand the calculations eighteenth-century Londoners made when they devoted effort to finding lost possessions, this chapter suggests that changing understandings of self-possession were crucial. While, as the previous chapter showed, objects or 'things' themselves were important. Concern at preventing loss was linked to a wider moral view, which saw loss as carelessness and carelessness as slothful and problematic.[33] Similarly, as the possession of 'things' came to connected to ideas of personhood and identity, loss was considered not only in terms of the thing gone, but also in terms of what such loss might reveal about the owner. Careless, incoherent, unstable: the loss of possessions had consequences for how the owner might be understood by others and themselves. Loss had the ability to damage more than character; it had the ability to challenge the self, leaving one disoriented and dislocated. In other words, the relationship of possession, its twists and turns, was itself important.

Loss of Property, Loss of Self

Frances Burney's 1782 novel *Cecilia* is preoccupied with themes of property, possession and loss and their relation to conceptions of self and identity. The main protagonist Cecilia Beverley is an heiress, who after moving to London

---

[30] Dror Wahrman, *The Making of the Modern Self: Identity and Culture in Eighteenth-Century England* (New Haven, CT and London, 2006), 275.

[31] Alexandra Shepard, *Accounting for Oneself: Worth, Status, and the Social Order in Early Modern England* (Oxford, 2015), 311.

[32] Susan Staves, 'Chattel Property Rules and the Construction of Englishness, 1660–1800', *Law and History Review*, 12:1 (1994), 123.

[33] Bernard Mandeville, *An Enquiry into the Causes of the Frequent Executions at Tyburn* [1725] (Los Angeles, CA, 1964), 5; Henry Fielding, *An Enquiry into the Causes of the late Increase of Robbers, &c. with some Proposals for Remedying this Growing Evil* (2nd edn, London, 1751), 114.

to live with one of her guardians Mr Harrel, navigates the attentions of multiple men. Her fortune is dependent on her husband taking her name, a clause understood as deeply problematic by the parents of her potential suitor, Mortimer Delvile. Further on in the novel, when Mortimer asks her to marry him in secret to evade the strictures of his parents, Cecilia understands such secrecy as a threat to her values and thus to herself. Despite her concerns, the wedding goes ahead, but it is interrupted and stopped by an unknown woman, who we later find out has been placed there by Cecilia's supposed friend Mr Monckton, who wishes to ensure that Cecilia remains single in order that he might marry her once his unsuspecting elderly wife has died.[34] Later in the novel, Cecilia and Mortimer try to marry once more, this time under the premise that Cecilia will give up her fortune rather than Mortimer giving up his family name.[35] The wedding takes place and gains the blessing of Mortimer's mother, but not his father.[36] As for other married women of the period, Cecilia becomes covered by the legal personality of Mortimer: she becomes feme-covert, as opposed to feme-sole. However, as we explored in Chapter 1, an important space existed between the law of feme-covert and its lived reality. In fact, Amy Erickson has argued that English attempts to circumvent feme-covert led to the 'widespread use of a variety of complex forms of property transfer: legal instruments which were often also financial instruments'.[37] Settlements, trusts, contracts and bonds were used to ensure that married women could retain their property, or at least have access to it if the marriage ended. Yet in the novel, Cecilia does not have the protection of legal instruments; once she marries, her fortune of £3,000 per annum is no longer hers. Burney seeks to underline the significance of this transition by having her take Mortimer's name, thus breaking the inheritance clause, and compounding the notion that as a wife, and particularly as this wife, she has doubly lost her right to ownership. As such, *Cecilia* is very much a novel about property.

Although Cecilia's fortune is based on the profits accrued from land, the novel persistently focuses on money and thus movable forms of property. Money and financial instruments were increasingly understood as significant forms of property in the eighteenth century. Land had long existed as the central form of property and the means to a political identity. While seventeenth-century England had been deeply concerned with the question of land and its significance as the basis of civic virtue, the eighteenth century saw a shifting focus to questions about mobile forms of property.[38]

---

[34] Burney, *Cecilia*, 835. [35] Ibid., 803. [36] Ibid., 819.
[37] Amy Louise Erickson, 'Coverture and Capitalism', *History Workshop Journal*, 59 (2005), 5.
[38] J. G. A. Pocock, 'The Mobility of Property and the Rise of Eighteenth-Century Sociology', in Thomas Flanagan and Anthony Parel (eds), *Theories of Property: Aristotle to the Present* (Waterloo, 1979), 147.

The creation of the Bank of England in 1694 provided new forms of public credit and debt and thus new forms of movable and seemingly 'intangible' varieties of property.[39] These new forms of public credit and debt led to an expansion in the range and volume of the financial instruments on offer: mortgages, debt-instruments and stock boomed. While most government Treasury Orders were held by just twenty-five goldsmith bankers in 1672, by 1750, 60,000 individuals held government bonds.[40] Just as with other forms of property, these financial products were intrinsically linked to ideas of personhood. Commentators worried as to the kind of subjects that might emerge from such movable property. Land ownership had allowed for autonomy through the supply of armies, but worryingly those with wealth based on commercial interest would only be able to contribute to conflicts through the employment of mercenaries.[41] As forms that seemed to reduce autonomy by creating economic and social dependencies, they appeared deeply threatening to broader governance. As the daughter of 'a private country gentleman' whose ancestors had been 'rich farmers in the county of Suffolk', Cecilia's fortune emerges from older forms of property. Nevertheless, the novel focuses on the profits accrued from such agricultural ventures. It questions the forms of personhood constructed by such finances and the fragilities they created, especially for women. As such, the novel underlines the liveliness of discussions on mobile property, personhood and loss in eighteenth-century British culture.

Rather than ending with the wedding and marriage, the novel explores what follows: what happens when Cecilia loses her fortune, her property, completely. *Cecilia* has been interpreted as a novel about ownership, debt and personhood. Margaret Doody's reassessment of Burney's work in the late 1980s saw *Cecilia* interpreted as a novel concerned with the nature of independence, particularly the possibilities and challenges of female independence.[42] Doody showed how male advancement through the exploitation of women existed as a central issue within the novel. Building on such themes,

---

[39] James Tully, 'The Possessive Individualism Thesis: A Reconsideration in the Light of Recent Scholarship', in Joseph H. Carens (ed.), *Democracy and Possessive Individualism: The Intellectual Legacy of C. B. Macpherson* (Albany, NY, 1993), 35. For more on the questions of property rights in land and capital in eighteenth-century Britain see, Julian Hoppit, 'Compulsion, Compensation and Property Rights in Britain, 1688–1833', *Past & Present*, 210 (2011), 93–128; Joshua Getzler, 'Theories of Property and Economic Development', *Journal of Interdisciplinary History*, 26 (1996), 639–69. See also the key texts, Douglass C. North and Robert Paul Thomas, *The Rise of the Western World: A New Economic History* (Cambridge, 1973); Douglass C. North, *Structure and Change in Economic History* (New York, NY, 1981); Gregory Clark, 'The Political Foundations of Modern Economic Growth: England, 1540–1800', *Journal of Interdisciplinary History*, 26 (1996), 563–88; S. R. Epstein, *Freedom and Growth: The Rise of States and Markets in Europe, 1300–1750* (London, 2000).

[40] Christine Desan, *Making Money: Coin, Currency and the Coming of Capitalism* (Oxford, 2014), 254.

[41] Pocock, 'The Mobility of Property', 148. [42] Doody, *Frances Burney*, 113.

Catherine Gallagher highlighted how the plot of the novel focused on the importance (and seeming impossibility) of keeping a name and fortune. In *Cecilia*, the protagonist's name and fortune were not things to be achieved (as had been the case in *Evelina*), but rather the thornier problem of things to be maintained.[43] In the novel, Cecilia equates owning with owing and, only by the novel's end, understands these as two different entities.[44] James Thompson's interpretation built on Doody and Gallagher's to further underline the importance of debt and ownership within *Cecilia*. For Thompson, the novel highlights how eighteenth-century culture encouraged women to move from public to private spaces, and exist within the protection of men.[45] *Cecilia* underlines how men and women thus owned in different ways: while inheritance existed as a resolution for men, it operated as dissolution for women.[46] More recently, Katherine Binhammer has argued that while *Cecilia* seems to follow a courtship plot, it is instead its financial plot which is most pressing. In *Cecilia*, Burney explores how 'marriage arrives as financial ruin, not happy ending'.[47] Building on these interpretations, this chapter argues that while *Cecilia* highlights ownership as different for men and women, it also suggests at the rather radical notion that the *loss* of property was profound and important for women. In fact, throughout the novel, Burney returns again and again to how the loss of property particularly impacted women. By placing the novel within the broader cultures of and responses to loss explored in this book, we begin to see how Burney renders the loss of property as the loss of self for Cecilia and potentially for people more generally.

Following the wedding, Cecilia goes alone to her house in Suffolk, while Mortimer travels to Delvile Castle and then to France, and more particularly Nice, to look after his sick mother.[48] Back in Suffolk, it soon becomes clear that their marriage is public knowledge, and Cecilia's fortune is claimed by the next inheritor in line, Mr Eggleston. Cecilia, desiring the advice and support of her husband, travels to London to seek help getting to France. While in town, however, she comes across Mortimer and much confusion follows as he seeks to challenge Mr Belfield. As a result of witnessing such conflict without a full explanation and in fear for Mortimer's life, Cecilia becomes highly distressed traversing London's streets. Cecilia moves about without the protections of her servant, encounters a mob and flees the safety of her carriage, making her way alone through the streets. Finally, she runs into a pawnbroker's shop: 'wholly bereft of sense and recollection, she could give no account who she was,

---

[43] Gallagher, *Nobody's Story*, 232. [44] Ibid., 248. [45] Thompson, *Models of Value*, 158.
[46] Ibid., 174.
[47] Katherine Binhammer, *Downward Mobility: The Form of Capital and the Sentimental Novel* (Baltimore, MD, 2020), 114.
[48] Burney, *Cecilia*, 833.

whence she came, or whither she wished to go'.⁴⁹ Significantly, this event takes place soon after her realisation that she has changed her name and no longer possesses her inheritance. When she is no longer the owner of her fortune or herself, Cecilia becomes unable to give an account of 'who she was': she temporarily loses her sense of 'self'. Contemporary readers understood this scene as important and impactful.⁵⁰ In it, however, Burney played upon an established trope. Margreta de Grazia's analysis of *King Lear* has underlined how in the seventeenth century the loss of property had the potential to prove destructive. Dispossessed by his father, Edgar loses his estate and name. While Lear's madness is real, Edgar feigns madness and takes on the disguise of a Bedlam beggar.⁵¹ In *Lear*, however, disintegration due to the loss of property affects only men. Here in the eighteenth century, Burney asks us to consider how the loss of property (particularly mobile property) and of legal personhood has implications for women too. As such, the example set by Cecilia (just as with that set by her creator Frances Burney) also encourages us to consider in greater detail the gendered implications of loss and losing possession.

Seeing Cecilia

In this moment in the novel, as Cecilia enters the pawnbroker's shop and is unable to give an account of herself, she is 'found' by a pawnbroker and his wife. Having the pawnbroker and his wife as 'finders' proves a useful device. While a 'culture of appraisal' was widespread in seventeenth-century England, valuation increasingly became a specialist skill in the eighteenth century.⁵² As we saw in Chapter 4, pawnbrokers were understood to be adept at making quick valuations of the 'goods' on offer. However, in this instance, the pawnbrokers struggle to place Cecilia. At first, they believe she is 'a woman of the town'. They are quick to make a link between this seemingly 'ownerless' woman and her sexuality. But 'the evident distraction of her air and manner' show them they are mistaken. Their second guess is that 'she was broke lose [sic] from Bedlam'.⁵³ When Cecilia speaks to correct them, they become surer she is 'mad'. Finally, it is her clothes that prove most telling. The pawnbroker's wife notes that '"She's a gentlewoman, sure enough...because she's got such good things on."'⁵⁴ Later we learn that Cecilia was wearing a riding habit. Published six years after Joshua Reynolds completed his portrait

---

⁴⁹ Ibid., 898.
⁵⁰ Lars E. Troide and Stewart J. Cooke, *The Early Journals and Letters of Fanny Burney: Volume V, 1782–1783* (Oxford, 2012), 135.
⁵¹ de Grazia, 'The Ideology of Superfluous Things', 26.
⁵² Shepard, *Accounting for Oneself*, 2.   ⁵³ Burney, *Cecilia*, 897.   ⁵⁴ Ibid., 898.

of the infamous Lady Worsley in her red riding habit, readers of *Cecilia* might have had this outfit in mind as they read Burney's novel in 1782.[55] It is this outfit they might have been considering as they thought through Cecilia's 'good things'. By connecting to Lady Worsley, Burney also suggests at the sexual unravelling underway for Cecilia. The emphasis placed on Cecilia's 'good things' allows us to see how people deciphered each other through looking at clothes. However, such deciphering also appears partial and blurry: clothes only seem to show social status.

In the sixteenth and seventeenth centuries, clothing and adornments were understood to 'make the man'. We can see this idea most clearly in the person of the monarch. It was in the act of investiture, the putting on of clothes and crowns, that made the monarch. Clothing and adornments gave the person a form and a social function.[56] The same was true for those lower down the social scale. In this period, masters often clothed their servants and apprentices. Members of households were required to wear livery to mark them as belonging. Again, the putting on of clothes gave people form and their social function: it placed them in relation to others.[57] In the long eighteenth century, however, the relationship between objects and identity became more complex. For instance, wigs were popular with men from the late seventeenth century to the 1760s. In this period, following the logic of investiture, wigs were understood to confer upon the wearer certain corporate identities related to profession and rank.[58] Rather than the person underneath, the wig signalled someone's social identity. Within such calculations, however, there was room for play due to the assumed 'transformative power of possessions'.[59] Social identities could be temporarily 'tried on' through adopting specific wigs.

A similar logic was at play in gender identities and clothing. In the early eighteenth century, new identities could be worn and played with. As Dror Wahrman has noted, masquerades were 'large-scale, commercial, non-exclusive public' entertainments that emerged in London in the 1720s and claimed, 'a cultural prominence not easily rivalled by other features of eighteenth-century life'.[60] Masquerades encouraged participants to arrive in costumes and masks that made them unrecognisable. In fact, involvement in these entertainments allowed for temporary transformations. A contributor to the *Lady's Magazine* explained that 'every one divests himself of his borrowed

---

[55] Joshua Reynolds' oil on canvas entitled 'Lady Worsley' was completed in 1776. It resides in the collection of the Earl and Countess of Harewood House in Yorkshire.
[56] Ann Rosalind Jones and Peter Stallybrass, *Renaissance Clothing and the Materials of Memory* (Cambridge, 2000), 2.
[57] Jones and Stallybrass, *Renaissance Clothing*, 5.
[58] Lynn Festa, 'Personal Effects: Wigs and Possessive Individualism in the Long Eighteenth Century', *Eighteenth-Century Life*, 29:2 (2005), 59.
[59] Festa, 'Personal Effects', 63.   [60] Wahrman, *The Making of the Modern Self*, 158.

feathers, and following his natural propensity, assumes the character which suits him best'.[61] Such playful transformation was understood as celebratory rather than threatening. Yet, as Wahrman argues, 'the 1780s and 1790s witnessed the breathtaking free fall of the masquerade from the lofty heights of its former significance'.[62] Such changes in the final quarter of the eighteenth century, align with the emergence of new understandings of the self and identity. While previously, the self had been regarded as something to be produced and fashioned over time, in the later eighteenth century the idea of the individual, a unique and bounded self, began to take hold. We see this shift occurring in different spheres. Michael Mascuch marked the final decade of the eighteenth century as the moment that saw the rise of a new form of autobiography that told stories of personal and social development, marking the individual as unique.[63] Similarly, Lynn Hunt has noted that the new discourse around human rights, which emerged in the late eighteenth century, depended on an understanding of autonomy, and more particularly of individual bodies, as bounded and unique.[64] New understandings of the self as unique, innate and bounded had implications for identities and display. Possessions remained important to identities but rather than *conferring* an identity they were understood as needing to *reflect* an innately held self. The self, the subject, was understood as separate, an autonomy in part proven by the possession of things.

By the late eighteenth century, clothes were no longer used to *make* a social identity, or to temporarily play with identity. Instead, clothes came to act as signifiers of innate and fixed identities. Another way in which we might explain this shift is by remembering that the rise of bustling urban centres created spaces in which people needed to read identities *from* clothing and adornment. The possessions they displayed on themselves provided a vital means of navigating these increasingly complex social worlds. As we saw in the introduction to this book, Alexandra Shepard has recently argued that a shift took place in the late seventeenth and early eighteenth century in terms of the roles that objects played in 'securing personal and social identities'. Rather than possessions in the household acting as the basis of a person's worth, the selective display of objects started to become increasingly important in urban environments.[65] In evermore populous urban spaces, people needed ways of understanding each other. What accompanied you as you walked London's streets came to take on particular significance in this period. In the later eighteenth century, clothes did not make the person, they did not confer social identity, rather clothes reflected who the person was, and displayed that to

---

[61] As cited in Ibid., 161. [62] Wahrman, *The Making of the Modern Self*, 162.
[63] Michael Mascuch, *Origins of the Individualist Self: Autobiography and Self-Identity in England, 1591–1791* (Cambridge, 1997), 18.
[64] Lynn Hunt, *Inventing Human Rights: A History* (New York, NY, 2007), 29.
[65] Shepard, *Accounting for Oneself*, 311.

others.[66] In keeping with the arguments of this book, we might push this a little further to consider how it was not just clothes that people used in this way, but also watches, snuffboxes, canes, spaniels, greyhounds and even servants.

In *Cecilia*, the pawnbroker's wife can 'read' Cecilia's clothes and know her social identity: that she is a 'gentlewoman'. However, what we also learn from *Cecilia* is that clothes alone do not offer a 'reading' of personhood, nor of self. Rather, here we see the importance of the assemblage.[67] To understand a person, rather than simply their social position, 'viewers' needed to consider how clothes were worn, but also the other 'things' worn by and carried with the person, the body they were worn upon and the gestures and speech of that body. While social identities could be read from clothing, more complex understandings could only be derived from the interplay between different possessions, actions, and speech. It was assemblages of 'things' that allowed for fuller understandings of others. Similarly, in *Cecilia* we see the pawnbroker and his wife try to decipher the 'breathless and panting' Cecilia who has 'sunk upon' the floor of their shop 'with a look disconsolate and helpless'.[68] The pawnbroker and his wife decide that she is not a 'woman of the town'. Her 'air and manner' suggest she is something else. They decide she is 'quite crazy' when they hear her speak '"No, no – I am not mad"'.[69] It is her 'good things' that allow them to conceive that she is a gentlewoman, but they do not end their examination there. Instead, they insist on 'searching her pockets' and are deeply disappointed to learn they are entirely empty. In insisting on such a search, the pawnbroker and his wife make clear that they have no respect for Cecilia's privacy.[70] Without other clues, they see her as a mad gentlewoman who has got loose from her friends. In this scene, Burney points to the importance of the assemblage in understanding others. Clothes, demeanour, speech, and other objects carried upon the person come together to help (or hinder) Cecilia in expressing herself, and the pawnbroker and his wife in misunderstanding her. We begin to see that in the later eighteenth century, the self was demarcated through social, material and bodily means.

The wider array of things carried by and on the person not only offered a means of denoting the complexities of the self, they also denoted personhood and identity. In the eighteenth century, property was central to claims of legal

---

[66] Rebecca Earle, '"Two Pairs of Pink Satin Shoes!!" Race, Clothing and Identity in the Americas (Seventeenth–Nineteenth Centuries)', *History Workshop Journal*, 52 (2001), 181.
[67] For more on the relationship between identities, self and assemblages see Kate Smith, 'In Her Hands: Materializing Distinction in Georgian Britain', *Cultural and Social History*, 11:4 (2014), 490.
[68] Burney, *Cecilia*, 897.   [69] Ibid., 897.
[70] For more on the importance of tie pockets as a site of female interiority and privacy in the eighteenth century see Ariane Fennetaux, 'Women's Pockets and the Construction of Privacy in the Long Eighteenth Century', *Eighteenth Century Fiction*, 20:3 (2008), 308 and 325.

personality and personhood. The political scientist C. B. Macpherson drew attention to how property had been central to understandings of the individual in political thought from Hobbes to Bentham. Macpherson's concept of 'possessive individualism' asserted that the individual or person could be understood as the owner of their own person or capacities. Macpherson thus followed a Lockean model in which property was seen to extend out from one's ownership of oneself to one's ownership of objects in the world.[71] As Joseph H. Carens has noted more recently, for Macpherson 'To be an individual is to be an owner – in the first instance, an owner of one's own person and capacities, but also of what one acquires through the use of one's capacities.'[72] While Macpherson's interpretation of seventeenth- and eighteenth-century political thought has been challenged from multiple different angles, the centrality of property to the construction of the individual and of personhood has proven an important provocation to intellectual, social and cultural historians of eighteenth-century Britain.[73] Susan Staves has argued that in the eighteenth century, personhood relied upon being 'constructed out of ownership rights'. It was made up of 'what a particular person' was 'privileged or forbidden to own'.[74] We see such privileges and restrictions at stake across a range of 'things'. For example, if we think back to Chapter 1 and its examination of the legal strictures concerned with the ownership of dogs, we will remember that in the age of the Game Laws only certain individuals could own certain types of dogs. The legal regulation of property policed personalities by controlling the ownership of things.[75] Here, it was not simply 'real property' that was at stake, but 'movable property' too. The ownership of things was central to claims of personhood. Yet such possession was not abstract, it needed to be enacted and seen by others. Here in *Cecilia*, we see how to be reduced to only possessing the clothes one stood in and, as we will see later not possessing control over who had access to those clothes, was deeply problematic in eighteenth-century culture. With her clothes, Cecilia can make some claim to her social identity, but without control and without the superfluous goods that might also accompany her, without speech, without her husband, without her servant, she fails to make full claims to personhood.

The disintegration at stake in this moment and the loss of personhood it pertains to is further rendered by the ways in which others gain access to Cecilia. She has seemingly lost the power to protect the boundaries of herself, an important marker for women, and it is perhaps for this reason that the

---

[71] See footnote 39 in Lynn Festa, 'Person, Animal, Thing: The 1796 Dog Tax and the Right of Superfluous Things', *Eighteenth-Century Life*, 33:2 (2009), 13.
[72] Joseph H. Carens, 'Possessive Individualism and Democratic Theory: Macpherson's Legacy', in Joseph H. Carens (ed.), *Democracy and Possessive Individualism: The Intellectual Legacy of C. B. Macpherson* (Albany, NY, 1993), 2.
[73] For overview of critiques of Macpherson's thesis see Carens, 'Possessive Individualism', 1–18.
[74] Staves, 'Chattel Property Rules', 123.   [75] Festa, 'Person, Animal, Thing', 5.

pawnbroker and his wife initially think she might be a 'woman of the town'. With ready access to her body, Burney further shows Cecilia's loss of power and position.[76] Again, we are also met with hints of sexual unravelling. Making her way through the mob before getting to the pawnbroker's shop, Cecilia is 'spoken to repeatedly' and 'was even caught once or twice by her riding habit'.[77] Here Burney summons up an experience that had close echoes in eighteenth-century London. In 1786, Sophie von la Roche recorded how on exiting Covent Garden theatre a 'cry went out that pickpockets were among the crowd'. Von la Roche understands the threat to property and self and responds by acting: 'I had drawn my things around me as closely as possible, and clasped my bags tightly, so that they should be safe like my clothes.'[78] In the novel, Burney uses the mob scene to gesture towards the possibility that Cecilia's riding habit has become torn or disarrayed when she entered the pawnbroker's shop: that she is undone.[79] The loosening or loss of clothes was often understood as a sign of degeneration or madness in this period.[80] Alongside this, the mob does not steal her money that is being held by Mr Simkins who she leaves in frustration after his lengthy negotiations with the carriage driver and his bill, but they do 'rifle' through her pockets.[81] As discussed in Chapter 2, tie pockets existed as an important 'technology', which allowed women to keep their personal possessions safe, ordered and hidden on urban streets. The catching of her riding habit and the rifling of her pockets are important in understanding how Burney hints at Cecilia's loss of self-possession.

In the seventeenth and eighteenth centuries, earlier understandings of the humoral body as open and fluid were superseded. As medicine came to focus on muscles and nerve fibres, the body came to be seen as solid and defined: as bounded.[82] In medical discourse, the skin emerged as a particularly important boundary or surface. Yet the body as a delineated, individual entity had to be

---

[76] For the question of access (through clothing) as a marker of prostitution, see John Cleland's 1748–49 novel *Fanny Hill*. John Cleland, *Fanny Hill or Memoirs of a Woman of Pleasure* (London, 1985), 53.
[77] Burney, *Cecilia*, 897.
[78] Sophie von la Roche, *Sophie in London 1786* trans. Clare Williams (London, 1933), 218.
[79] 'I am undone', a religious reference, was a regularly repeated phrase in early modern prose, drama and poetry, to denote moral and economic ruin. It was also utilised in the eighteenth century; for instance see Colley Cibber, *Love's Last Shift; or, The Fool in Fashion* (The Hague, 1711), 97; Henry Fielding, *Love in Several Masques* (Dublin, 1728), 77; Richardson, *Pamela*, 103.
[80] de Grazia, 'The Ideology of Superfluous Things', 25; Karen Harvey, 'Men of Parts: Masculine Embodiment and the Male Leg in Eighteenth-Century England', *Journal of British Studies*, 54 (2015), 806.
[81] Burney, *Cecilia*, 898.
[82] Christopher E. Forth and Ivan Crozier (eds), *Body Parts: Critical Explorations in Corporeality* (Lanham, 2005), 5; Mikhail Bakhtin, *Rabelais and His World* (Bloomington, IL, 1984); Dorinda Outram, *The Body and the French Revolution* (New Haven, CT and London, 1989); Barbara Stafford, *Body Criticism: Imaging the Unseen in Enlightenment Art and Medicine* (Cambridge, 1991); Claudia Benthien, *Skin: On the Cultural Border between Self and World* (New York, 2002).

created and maintained daily, through rituals and practices as mundane as the increasing use of individual napkins.[83] Similarly, as Mechthild Fend's work on portraiture has shown, depictions were important. In portraits, the skin was increasingly depicted as a significant contour and boundary in the later eighteenth century.[84] While the skin could be understood to act as the surface of the body, clothing was also important in creating another envelope, and boundary.[85] Hence, in this period, as the bounded nature of the body became more important, permeating such boundaries took on new significance. Disruption of the border was problematic in that it was suggestive of looseness and fallibility. When others catch Cecilia's riding habit and rifle through her pockets, her sense of boundedness is threatened. Such an assault also creates disintegration. Once the mob have got to Cecilia's pockets, they take 'whatever else they contained'.[86] The ownership of possessions, even of superfluous things – the 'whatever else' – was an important demarcation of personhood.[87] To have those things taken sent the assemblage of the self into further disarray.

While historians have explored the centrality of ownership to claims of legal personality and personhood and the importance of things to the formation of the self, we know much less about what happened to such claims when possessions and property were lost. Here, in the moment where Cecilia has lost her inheritance, but also her money and even all her pockets contained, she is unable to give an account of herself: she has lost possession of herself. By focusing on these moments of loss, and how they were written and imagined within eighteenth-century novels, we begin to see that in this period such losses were understood to impact an individual's identity and their sense of self. While Chapter 4 showed that men might have used the lost notices more frequently than women, here we see that keeping hold and reclaiming possession had important implications for women. We start to recognise that people invested time, effort, and money in reclaiming their lost things, because to have them remain lost was to risk the ability to have, and express, a sense of self.

---

[83] For more on the use of individual napkins, see Dan Cruickshank and Neil Burton, *Life in the Georgian City* (London, 1990), 37.
[84] Mechthild Fend, 'Bodily and Pictorial Surfaces: Skin in French Art and Medicine, 1790–1860', *Art History*, 28:3 (2005), 312.
[85] Daniel Miller, 'Introduction,' in Susanne Kuchler and Daniel Miller, *Clothing as Material Culture* (Oxford, 2005), 15; Alexandra Warwick and Dani Cavallaro, *Fashioning the Frame: Boundaries, Dress and the Body* (Oxford, 1998), xv.
[86] Burney, *Cecilia*, 898.
[87] For an example of Frances Burney understanding superfluous goods (such as gloves in this case) as 'property' see Frances Burney, *The Early Journals and Letters of Fanny Burney*, Vol. III, 1778–1779, ed. Lars E. Troide and Stewart J. Cooke (Oxford, 1994), 443.

Cecilia as 'Thing'

In this scene within *Cecilia*, not only is Cecilia unable to give an account of herself, her personality and complexities are largely overlooked. Instead, people simply 'read' her. The pawnbroker's wife pays little attention to what Cecilia says, instead she conflates her with her 'good things'. Rather than a subject, in this scene, Cecilia is transformed into an object.[88] To further compound this allusion, Burney utilises a common cultural reference point in eighteenth-century Britain: 'lost' things. Cecilia is understood as an object come loose from its owner.

Realising that she is a gentlewoman and thus valued and possibly sought, the pawnbroker and his wife decide to take her in. As their companion in the act notes, 'if you were to take care of her a little while, ten to one but you'll get a reward for it'.[89] Cecilia is understood as a piece of lost property, which if taken 'care' of and returned will prove valuable to the finders. The logic of reclamation and rewards is shown to be broadly understood, or perhaps that pawnbrokers were particularly well-versed in calculating the possibilities of such transactions. As Chapter 4 showed, pawnbrokers played important roles in the 'lost' property system as 'finders' often called upon them to exchange the item. In *Cecilia*, Cecilia runs into a pawnbroker's shop herself, seemingly handing herself in for exchange.

Two days after Cecilia's appearance, the pawnbroker's wife Mrs Wyers is at a loss as to what to do. 'Two whole days passed thus; no enquiries reached Mrs. Wyers, and she found in the news-papers no advertisement.'[90] As we saw in Chapter 4, pawnbrokers actively read the lost notices placed in newspapers. Pawnbrokers were used to dealing with objects and advertisements, but in the case of Cecilia, Mrs Wyers is depicted as being uncertain. Only on asking 'the advice of some of her friends' as to 'what was proper for her to do', did she decide to place an advertisement in the newspaper – the *Daily Advertiser* (as we saw in Chapter 2, the bastion of lost notices) – herself.[91] It read:

MADNESS Whereas a crazy young lady, tall, fair complexioned, with blue eyes and light hair, ran into the Three Blue Balls, in————street, on Thursday night, the 2d instant, and has been kept there since out of charity. She was dressed in a riding habit. Whoever she belongs to is desired to send after her immediately. She has been treated with the utmost care and tenderness. She talks much of some person by the name of Delvile.

N. B. She had no money about her.

May, 1780

---

[88] Doody, *Frances Burney*, 142. [89] Burney, *Cecilia*, 898. [90] Ibid., 900.
[91] Ibid., 901.

As Margaret Doody has previously argued, in this scene Cecilia is transformed into a lost possession that can be sought out and reclaimed.[92] The notice follows some of the conventions of lost object notices: it lists where the object has been 'found', when and describes what it is. The notice included by Burney appears to recast Cecilia as an object put on display with the other goods in the pawnbroker's shop. Inert, Cecilia is waiting to be claimed. She can no longer lay claim to 'I'; rather she is described by others, she is 'A'. The notice consolidates this idea of objecthood by underscoring the 'care' that has been taken and by calling out to 'Whoever she belongs to'. Burney perhaps links back to the idea of Cecilia as newly married, as recently entering the state of feme covert and becoming the property of her husband. She is waiting to be claimed by her owner.

Yet this interpretation fails to capture the full complexity of the notice's significance here in the text. The tentative nature of the pawnbroker's wife's actions is suspect. Cases in the Old Bailey provide evidence that pawnbrokers not only regularly read and noted 'lost' notices, but they also placed them. For instance, in 1748, when the pawnbroker Isaac Peynon was offered a silver pint mug by Mary Jackson in what he considered to be suspicious circumstances, he stopped it and 'the same night I had it, I advertised it'.[93] In contrast, Mrs Wyers' waiting, her asking the advice of her friends, perhaps suggests at a central difficulty: what is Cecilia? In this moment, which is pointedly located in London, Burney utilises the possibilities offered by the 'lost' notices to examine Cecilia's position and personhood in more nuanced terms. Mrs Wyers' uncertainty and the notice she writes underlines the ambiguities and dangers faced by men, and more particularly here women, when they lost their property.

As well as being recast as an object, the notice underlines Cecilia's loss of self-possession. Her lack of control is at stake of course in her waiting to be reclaimed, in her being an object unable to act. It is also there in her being labelled as 'MADNESS', 'a crazy young lady'.[94] Eighteenth-century readers would have been unsurprised that the pawnbroker and his wife listed Cecilia as 'crazy'. They would have known, as the apothecary-surgeon's apprentice Samuel England did, that sudden exposure to excessive emotions – such as surprise, passion or anger – might lead to an imbalance of the humours or the

---

[92] Doody, *Frances Burney*, 142.
[93] *Old Bailey Proceedings Online* (www.oldbaileyonline.org, version 8.0, 14 April 2022), October 1748, trial of Mary Jackson (t17481012-12).
[94] Frances Burney herself showed an interest in 'madness' and recorded her discussions about it in her journals. See Burney, *The Early Journals and Letters of Fanny Burney*, Vol. I, 1768–1773, 92; Burney, *The Early Journals and Letters of Fanny Burney*, Vol. II, 1774–1777, 89.

disorder of the blood and thus cause a psychological ailment.[95] Moreover, they themselves might have read Cecilia's responses as 'madness'. Her breathlessness and panting, her 'look disconsolate and helpless' and her sinking upon the floor, were all recognised symptoms of hysteria in the eighteenth century.[96] Readers would also have recognised the nature of the notice Burney included. Notices appeared in eighteenth-century newspapers advertising that certain people labelled 'mad' had got lost. Just ten years after the publication of the *Cecilia*, we see an example of the finder and loser advertising for a certain Mary Beltey who had gone missing. On Saturday 8 December 1792, 'Friends' of Mary Beltey placed the following notice in the *Daily Advertiser*:

On Thursday the 29th of November, Mary Beltey eloped from her Friends; she is a middle-sized Person, about 40 Years of Age, of a dark Complexion, much Pockmarked; had on an old Mode black Silk Bonnet, a black Silk Cloak, with Lace round ditto, a sprigged Cotton Gown, black quilted Petticoat, dirty white Stockings, and much deranged in her Senses, very unwilling to speak. Whoever can give any Account of her to Mr. Overton, at the Workhouse, at Mile-End, shall be satisfied for their Trouble.[97]

'Deranged' and largely mute, Beltey – like Cecilia – seems unable or unwilling to give an account of herself. Beltey's confused state is further underlined by her 'dirty white Stockings'. As we have seen, lack of cleanliness was evidence of mismanagement, a household in disorder.[98] In this instance, dirty clothes were perhaps particularly egregious because Mary Beltey seems to have 'eloped' from a workhouse. In the eighteenth century, workhouses grew as one strand of the poor relief strategies utilised by parishes and of the survival strategies used by the poor.[99] Workhouses prided themselves on their commitment to cleanliness and particularly, clean clothing.[100] In multiple ways, Beltey appears to have stepped out (or been forced out) of a system and a series of expected behaviours. She is deemed unable to account for herself and is thus being sought and negotiated over.

It seems that Beltey's 'Friends' must have missed the advertisement placed almost a week prior to their own, which seems to describe finding Beltey:

---

[95] Wendy D. Churchill, *Female Patients in Early Modern Britain: Gender, Diagnosis, and Treatment* (Farnham, and Burlington, VT, 2012), 162–3. See also R. A. Houston, 'Madness and Gender in the Long Eighteenth Century', *Social History*, 27:3 (2002), 320–22.
[96] Burney, *Cecilia*, 897; Churchill, *Female Patients in Early Modern Britain*, 160.
[97] 'On Thursday the 29th of November', *Daily Advertiser* (London), 8 December 1792.
[98] Amanda Vickery, *The Gentleman's Daughter: Women's Lives in Georgian England* (New Haven, CT and London, 1998), 149–51.
[99] Tim Hitchcock and Robert Shoemaker, *London Lives: Poverty, Crime and the Making of a Modern City 1690–1800* (Cambridge, 2015), 133; Tim Hitchcock, *Down and Out in Eighteenth-Century London* (London, 2004), 7.
[100] Hitchcock, *Down and Out in Eighteenth-Century London*, 101 and 139.

228   Learning from Loss

A Woman disordered in her Mind was found near the Gates of the Foundling-Hospital on Thursday Evening last; she has spoken only a few incoherent Words, but has not mentioned her Name or from whence she came; she appears to be about 50 Years of Age, and her Dress is as follows, a dark-coloured printed Cotton Gown, black Stuff Petticoat, white Cotton Stockings, black Buckles in her Shoes, blue and white Check Apron, a good black Silk Cloak and Bonnet, and a black Silk Handkerchief trimmed with Crape [sic.]; it is supposed that she has wandered from her Friends, who are desired to apply to the Secretary or Matron of the Foundling-Hospital for further Information concerning her.[101]

The description marks Beltey as an older woman and has much less to say about the state of her stockings, but it is clearly Beltey: the two descriptions match. The notice shows that Beltey had been 'found' in the very centre of 'finding', the Foundling Hospital. After lobbying by Captain Thomas Coram (1668–1751), the hospital was granted a charter in 1739 and set up in Hatton Gardens in 1741. The Foundling Hospital arrived at its more established location of Lamb Conduit Fields in 1745. The purpose of the hospital was to care for war orphans, the children of the poor and needy and the children of those from different ranks born illegitimately, while granting some anonymity to their parents.[102] From the beginning, the Hospital operated a token system, whereby parents or carers would leave a token, which could be described if they sought the child's return at a later stage.[103] Here again, as we explored in Chapter 5, we see the importance of description, of describing things, in eighteenth-century culture. Small numbers of claims for return were made and continued to be made across the nineteenth century.[104] It seems likely that Mary Beltey would have found a way to return to Mr Overton at the workhouse at Mile-End. In the eighteenth century, most of the foundlings were sent by parish authorities.[105] If the notice published on Saturday 8 December was spotted by the Foundling Hospital, they would have had the means to contact the nearby workhouse and connect with the parish. Beltey would have been returned.

With only 'a few incoherent Words', Mary Beltey was clearly vulnerable. Discussed by others in short notices placed in eighteenth-century newspapers, we are perhaps disproportionately availed of the idea that Beltey had little control over her own life. However, the notices do show that for better or

---

[101] 'A Woman Disordered in Her Mind', *Daily Advertiser* (London), 3 December 1792.
[102] Alysa Levene, *Childcare, Health and Mortality at the London Foundling Hospital 1741–1800 'Left to the Mercy of the World'* (Manchester, 2007), 6.
[103] Gillian Clark, 'The Foundling Hospital and Its Token System', *Family & Community History*, 18:1 (2015), 54.
[104] Levene, *Childcare, Health and Mortality*, 18; Clark, 'The Foundling Hospital and its Token System', 59–61; Jessica A. Scheetz-Nguyen, 'Calculus of Respectability: Defining the World of Foundling Hospital Women and Children in Victoria London', *Annales de Demongraphie Historique*, 114:2 (2007), 29.
[105] Levene, *Childcare, Health and Mortality*, 36.

worse, Beltey had 'eloped', had managed to remove herself from the workhouse at Mile End and was found around five miles away in Bloomsbury.[106] Similarly, although the notice (and the scene more broadly) in *Cecilia* underlines Cecilia's loss of self-possession, her move from subject to object status, also includes the hint of personhood, of agency. Rather than *found*, the advertisement notes how Cecilia 'ran into the Three Blue Balls'. Mr and Mrs Wyers assume that Cecilia has run away from Bedlam. That they see Cecilia as a runaway is significant and is not simply marked by their noting she 'ran into' the shop, it is also hinted at in some of the conventions adhered to within the notice. Following the conventions of the 'runaway' notices, the advertisement begins by listing what Cecilia looks like. As Gwenda Morgan and Peter Rushton have argued, 'runaway' notices made visible the bodies of poor men by often focusing upon their hair, complexion and mannerisms.[107] Here Cecilia is made visible through the noting of her height, complexion, eyes and hair. Such identifiers mirror those noted in the 'runaway' notices examined in Chapter 5. Significantly, the description is the first time Cecilia is described to the reader in detail; at this point, the *reader* would not necessarily recognise her at all.

The notice also apes the conventions of the runaway notices by having someone else write the notice. As we saw in Chapters 4 and 5, 'runaway' notices were written by owners, commanders, masters or mistresses seeking the return of servants, enslaved people, apprentices or soldiers. As Konstantin Dierks work has shown us, writing (especially letter writing) acted as an important means by which the white middle classes accrued and asserted power in this period.[108] Their writing placed *their* desires front and centre. In placing a notice, the loser wanted the return of their property, whether that be a person or simply their capacities, or to warn off others from assuming possession of it. The floors needed cleaning and so did the pewter.[109] These notices, however, also allow us to glimpse the *actions* of the apprentice Charles Adams, as well as Ann Rowley the wife of John, and an enslaved boy from Bengal named George.[110] As explored in Chapter 2, servants,

---

[106] The use of the term 'eloped' is perhaps significant. As discussed in Chapter 2, 'eloped' was often used in notices placed by husbands advertising that their wife had left. It signalled that their wife had left with another man and thus that the husband incurred no future obligations towards her.

[107] Gwenda Morgan and Peter Rushton, 'Visible Bodies: Power, Subordination and Identity in the Eighteenth-Century Atlantic World', *Journal of Social History*, 39:1 (2005), 42–47; Malcolm Gaskill, *Crime and Mentalities in Early Modern England* (Cambridge, 2000), 168.

[108] Konstantin Dierks, *In My Power: Letter Writing and Communication in Early America* (Philadelphia, PA, 2009), 5.

[109] Mary Collier, *The Woman's Labour* (London, 1989), 23.

[110] 'Whereas Charles Adams, a Boy of about Fifteen, with a full round Face, and black Hair, born in Wales, went from his Master at Queen-street Coffee-house, Westminster', *Daily Courant* (London), 27 December 1720; 'Whereas Ann the Wife of John Rowley, Carpenter of Green Bank, near Tooley-Street, has eloped from her said Husband', *Daily Advertiser* (London),

apprentices, wives and enslaved people walked out and sought freedom or relief from violence or exploitation, or simply better conditions: more pay, more tea, less scrubbing. They did not write these notices, their *voices* cannot be found here, but their actions and *their* claims to self-possession are recorded within these notices.

Chapter 6 demonstrated how 'runaway' notices recorded acts of self-possession; here we also see that they are revealing of a very different set of losses and understandings of possession. They complicate our ability to make simple assessments of what it meant to possess things in the eighteenth century, and to whom. While lost notices exist as attempts to reclaim self-possession by getting stuff back, 'runaway' notices mark challenges to self-possession. Property has gone awry, an instance perhaps particularly disturbing in the case of servants and idea of them as phantom limbs, but perhaps even more so in the case of enslaved people. The enslaved person, the piece of 'property', has upped and left, challenging the 'owner's' project of self-possession. As we saw in Chapter 6, these notices also underlined that people were not objects, could not be property; after all, they moved of their own volition rather than being lost by being misplaced or dropped by another. Here then, in 'runaway' notices, we see claims to self-possession on the part of servants, spouses, apprentices and enslaved people and how these challenged others' ability to sustain self-possession. Although the notice for Cecilia is written to rather than by 'Whoever she belongs to', that it (briefly) notes her running, as well as her capture, allows Burney to suggest at the possibility of self-determination for wives and women, while also noting the structures that often secured its end.

Conclusion

Just after the advertisement had been sent off to be published, Cecilia's friend Mr Albany arrives at the pawnbroker's shop. He had heard that 'an unknown mad lady' was there, and wanting to aid this unfortunate woman, pays a call. He is astonished to find that the lady is indeed Cecilia and quickly finds out her maid Mary and husband Delvile. The advertisement is only seen and recognised by Cecilia's friend Henrietta Belfield. Seeing that the lady '*talked much of a person by the name of Delvile*' and recognising 'the description' and 'the account of the dress', Miss Belfield knew it was Cecilia.[111] Here Burney gestures towards the importance of female friendships and the possibilities

---

6 December 1752; 'A Black Boy. Ran away from his Master Mr Puspini, a handsome Slave Boy, Native of Bengal', *Daily Advertiser* (London), 20 December 1771.

[111] Burney, *Cecilia*, 913.

they held.[112] Yet when Henrietta arrives at the shop, she hardly recognises Cecilia due to her being motionless, her change in circumstances and her inability to speak. '"Who is this?"' she cries. However, once reunited with her servant, husband and friends, Cecilia is slowly returned to herself. She awakens and is 'quiet and composed', she is told what has happened, she begins to speak again and she regains self-possession.[113]

Cecilia explores how the loss of moveable property – everything from great fortunes down to servants and the 'whatever else' found in a woman's pockets – was understood to impact a person's sense of self and their ability to keep control, to remain self-possessed. The episode imagined within the pages of this highly popular novel is revealing of the broader concerns at stake in eighteenth-century British society and is suggestive of why people might have been prepared to expend effort, time and money not on seeking justice, but rather in ensuring the return of their possessions. Such care echoed religious and moral imperatives to treasure that given by the grace of God. Yet the desire to reclaim lost possessions contradicted sermons that told people to bear loss with patience, as a sign of chastisement from God. The desire to reclaim that we see again, and again, and again, in eighteenth-century newspapers, speaks more clearly to people's understanding not simply of possessions but of what it meant to possess. The climax in *Cecilia* tells us that because of the close relationship between property, personhood and the self, in fact that property and possessions operated as the legal and material manifestations of personhood and the self, the loss of such property was demonstrative of something more. To lose your property was to threaten your sense of self, particularly the coherent, stable self, which became increasingly valued in eighteenth-century British culture. For women, such loss of the self was perhaps more acutely threatening because they were often understood as household managers, as the preservers of possessions and thus the upholders of property relations over time.[114] If women lost their things and lost their self-possession, they could be understood as being hysterical or mad. Losing your things might leave you speechless. In eighteenth-century Britain, it was not simply the self that was important, but rather self-possession, self-control. Similarly, in eighteenth-century Britain, it was not just the *having* things that was important, but the *keeping* hold of them. In an age when people pawned goods on a regular basis or were increasingly jostled by the bustle of the urban space, such an ambition was startling difficult for most.

---

[112] Amanda Herbert, *Female Alliances: Gender, Identity, and Friendship in Early Modern Britain* (New Haven, CT and London, 2014).
[113] Burney, *Cecilia*, 920.   [114] Houston, 'Madness and Gender', 313.

Conclusion
Legacies of Loss

As this book has shown, across the long eighteenth century Londoners developed multiple systems through which they could hear about their lost and stolen possessions. Alongside the warning carrier notices, advertisements placed in daily newspapers and the printing of handbills, there is also evidence that Londoners attempted to establish a 'Lost and Found Office'.[1] Advertisements placed in the *Morning Post* and *Public Advertiser* in August 1777, and an extant handbill from the same year proclaimed that the Office had opened on Chancery Lane, 'the next House to Holborn' (Figure 8.1). It was advertised as a place where 'Every unfortunate Loser, and every honest and generous Finder ("by doing as they would be done by") may, in London, and its Environs, immediately recover, or restore, every Kind of Property lost or found'. Here was a space untainted by the tinge of stolen goods where losers could connect with virtuous finders, facilitating the return of their property. Even things of a small value could be reclaimed through this system. The Office and its services answered the problem of 'delicacy', which prevented some people from publicly 'exposing' their loss. In advertising the new service, the Lost and Found Office was acutely aware of the importance of anonymity. It recognised the potential loss of reputation attached to being seen as someone who lost their things. At the same time, servants and porters no longer needed to feel 'Anxiety and Distress' when they lost 'their own, or their employers Property'.

Later, on the 6 November 1777, the Office placed an advertisement in *The Morning Post, and Daily Advertiser* listing those items which were 'not yet restored', such as a 'Ladies Laced Ruffle', a 'Silver Watch' and a 'Large Spotted Pointer Dog'.[2] The continued presence of the ruffle, watch and dog at the Office suggests that all was not as it should have been in Chancery Lane. The advert in *The Morning Post* and *Daily Advertiser* also included multiple

---

[1] Alongside the handbill included in the text, advertisements announcing the opening of the Office were placed in *The Public Advertiser* on 14 August 1777 and *The Morning Post* on 15 August 1777.

[2] *The Morning Post and Daily Advertiser* (London), 6 November 1777.

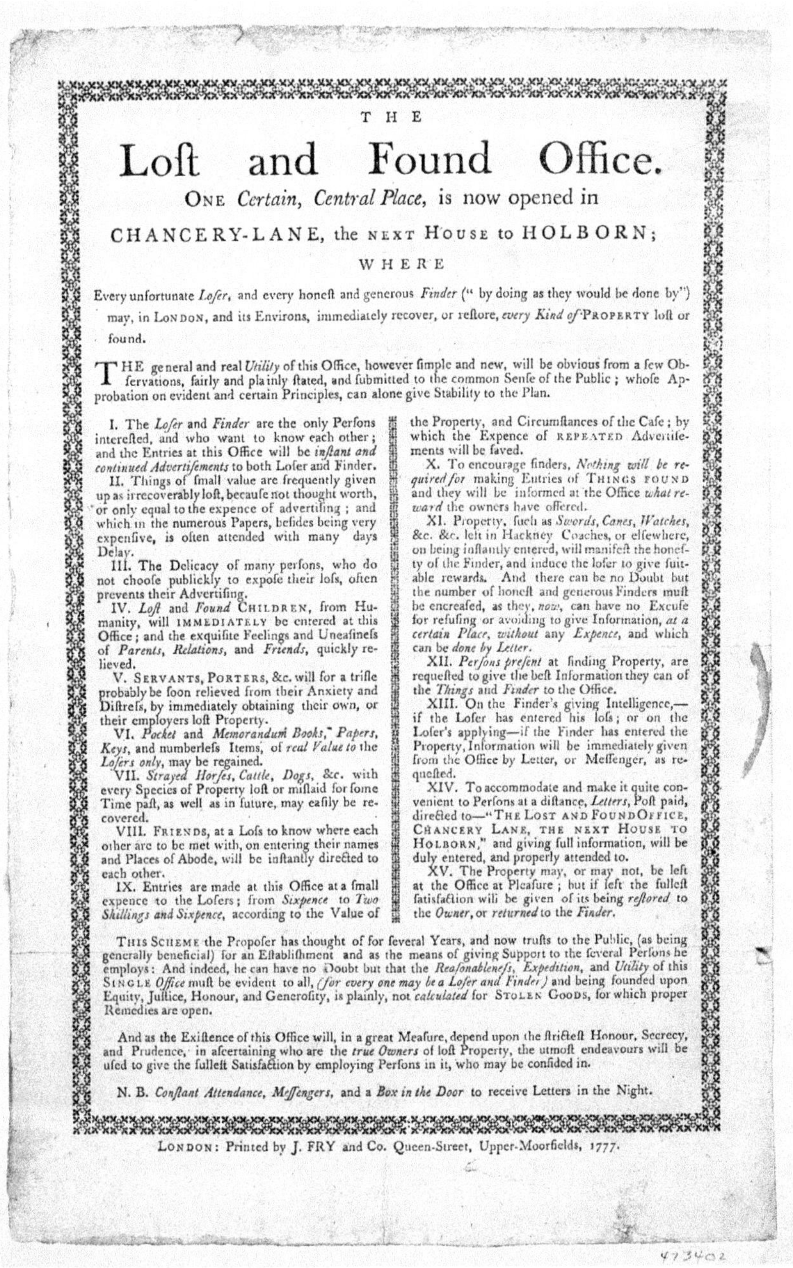

THE
Lost and Found Office.

ONE *Certain, Central Place*, is now opened in

CHANCERY-LANE, the NEXT HOUSE to HOLBORN;

WHERE

Every unfortunate *Loser*, and every honest and generous *Finder* ("by doing as they would be done by") may, in LONDON, and its Environs, immediately recover, or restore, *every Kind of* PROPERTY lost or found.

THE general and real *Utility* of this Office, however simple and new, will be obvious from a few Observations, fairly and plainly stated, and submitted to the common Sense of the Public; whose Approbation on evident and certain Principles, can alone give Stability to the Plan.

I. The *Loser* and *Finder* are the only Persons interested, and who want to know each other; and the Entries at this Office will be *instant and continued Advertisements* to both Loser and Finder.

II. Things of small value are frequently given up as irrecoverably lost, because not thought worth, or only equal to the expence of advertising; and which in the numerous Papers, besides being very expensive, is often attended with many days Delay.

III. The Delicacy of many persons, who do not choose publickly to expose their loss, often prevents their Advertising.

IV. *Lost* and *Found* CHILDREN, from Humanity, will IMMEDIATELY be entered at this Office; and the exquisite Feelings and Uneasiness of *Parents, Relations,* and *Friends,* quickly relieved.

V. SERVANTS, PORTERS, &c. will for a trifle probably be soon relieved from their Anxiety and Distress, by immediately obtaining their own, or their employers lost Property.

VI. *Pocket* and *Memorandum Books,* Papers, Keys, and numberless Items, of *real Value to the Losers only,* may be regained.

VII. *Strayed Horses, Cattle, Dogs,* &c. with every Species of Property lost or mislaid for some Time past, as well as in future, may easily be recovered.

VIII. FRIENDS, at a Loss to know where each other are to be met with, on entering their names and Places of Abode, will be instantly directed to each other.

IX. Entries are made at this Office at a small expence to the Losers; from *Sixpence* to *Two Shillings and Sixpence,* according to the Value of the Property, and Circumstances of the Case; by which the Expence of REPEATED Advertisements will be saved.

X. To encourage finders, *Nothing will be required for* making Entries of THINGS FOUND and they will be informed at the Office *what reward* the owners have offered.

XI. Property, such as *Swords, Canes, Watches,* &c. &c. left in Hackney Coaches, or elsewhere, on being instantly entered, will manifest the honesty of the Finder, and induce the loser to give suitable rewards. And there can be no Doubt but the number of honest and generous Finders must be encreased, as they, *now,* can have no Excuse for refusing or avoiding to give Information, *at a certain Place, without any Expence,* and which can be *done by Letter.*

XII. *Persons present* at finding Property, are requested to give the best Information they can of the *Things* and *Finder* to the Office.

XIII. On the Finder's giving Intelligence,— if the Loser has entered his loss; or on the Loser's applying—if the Finder has entered the Property, Information will be immediately given from the Office by Letter, or Messenger, as requested.

XIV. To accommodate and make it quite convenient to Persons at a distance, *Letters,* Post paid, directed to—"THE LOST AND FOUND OFFICE, CHANCERY LANE, THE NEXT HOUSE TO HOLBORN," and giving full information, will be duly entered, and properly attended to.

XV. The Property may, or may not, be left at the Office at Pleasure; but if left the fullest satisfaction will be given of its being *restored* to the *Owner,* or *returned* to the *Finder.*

THIS SCHEME the Proposer has thought of for several Years, and now trusts to the Public, (as being generally beneficial) for an Establishment and as the means of giving Support to the several Persons he employs: And indeed, he can have no Doubt but that the *Reasonableness, Expedition,* and *Utility* of this SINGLE *Office* must be evident to all, *(for every one may be a Loser and Finder,)* and being founded upon Equity, Justice, Honour, and Generosity, is plainly, not *calculated* for STOLEN GOODS, for which proper Remedies are open.

And as the Existence of this Office will, in a great Measure, depend upon the strictest Honour, Secrecy, and Prudence, in ascertaining who are the *true* Owners of lost Property, the utmost endeavours will be used to give the fullest Satisfaction by employing Persons in it, who may be confided in.

N. B. *Constant Attendance, Messengers,* and a *Box in the Door* to receive Letters in the Night.

LONDON: Printed by J. FRY and Co. Queen-Street, Upper-Moorfields, 1777.

Figure 8.1 'The Lost and Found Office', Handbill, 1777, 473402.
Image source: The Huntington Library, San Marino, California.

listings for lettings. That the Office diversified its listings to include lettings after less than three months in business also hints that it was experiencing problems. Evidence heard in a case at the Old Bailey in 1778 implies that Londoners quickly came to regard the Office as ineffective. The case, heard in January 1778, found George Glove not guilty of stealing a wooden box containing hair pins and clothes. John Vaughan, a servant of Mrs Barry, was asked to provide evidence in the case. He reported that he had forgotten to remove Mrs Barry's box from a coach and went to see the Hackney coachman the next day to get the box back. The coachman advised Vaughan to get bills printed, advertise in the daily papers and visit the 'lost and found office' on 'Chancery Lane'. Vaughan went to the Office, but the box was never heard of again.[3] After this ineffectual encounter, the Lost and Found Office itself seems to have disappeared, at least from the historical record.

The Office on Chancery Lane was not the first lost property office. Jonathan Wild named his office at the Old Bailey, 'The Lost Property Office'.[4] In Wild's case, the term 'lost' was something of a fantasy as he primarily dealt in stolen goods. The Lost and Found Office established on Chancery Lane in 1777 was by contrast an attempt to create a central site at which items found by disinterested individuals could be left, and to which 'Every unfortunate Loser' could apply. As such, the Office appears as a precursor to the modern lost property offices which emerged in the nineteenth century. The establishment of greater numbers of police offices from the 1790s onwards and then the beginnings of legislation, which demanded certain individuals, such as Hackney Coachmen, handed in items, meant there were places to receive found goods and people to find them from the early nineteenth century onwards. In 1777, however, this service, this ambition for institutionalisation did not flourish. The failure of the Office was perhaps the result of a lack of 'honest and generous' finders; it might also be explained by the efficacy of other means of reclaiming lost things. As we have seen, the Goldsmiths' Company's system of printed notices, which their beadles walked round to members of the luxury trades, and the handbills people printed, distributed and posted upon walls around the city meant urban dwellers had long accessed ways of chasing after their lost things. These earlier measures were consolidated in the eighteenth century by the activities of the Bank of England and of thief-takers but also by the rise of daily newspapers and the advertisements they contained. These innovative printed forms enlarged and expanded the possibilities of reclamation. In the

---

[3] *Old Bailey Proceedings Online* (www.oldbaileyonline.org, version 9.0) January 1778. Trial of GEORGE GLOVE (t17780115–1). Available at: www.oldbaileyonline.org/record/t17780115-1?text=%22george%20glove%22 (Accessed: 17 December 2023).
[4] Sean Silver, *The Mind is a Collection: Case Studies in Eighteenth-Century Thought* (Philadelphia, PA, 2015), 252.

period before modern lost property offices, these systems of return proved crucial.

Keeping Hold has explored these little-studied reclamation systems to show their vibrancy and importance in eighteenth-century culture, but also to examine Londoners' attitudes towards property and possession in this period. Its central finding is that people worked hard to reclaim property that went missing through forgetfulness or theft in eighteenth-century London. People cared for their possessions in the eighteenth century. To do so was part of constructing household order and signifying good character. They, or their servants, cleaned and maintained their things. When objects broke, people fixed them or sent them to specialists to be mended. Alongside these tasks, in the eighteenth century, taking care also meant knowing where the item was, securing it, making a note of its details and reclaiming it if it got lost. *Keeping Hold* has shown that people worked hard to keep track of and reclaim their lost things. They needed to work hard. The increased mobility and density of life meant things went missing and this was a period which retained the idea that everything had value. Scavengers, finders and dustmen scoured the streets collecting dust, excrement and scraps to sell on to others.[5] No *thing* would remain where you dropped it and in the bustle of the urban street it was difficult to know whether you had dropped it or whether a pickpocket's seamless motions had snatched it from you. Such realities meant that you could not simply return to the site where you thought it had been lost and you certainly could not rely on something calling itself the Lost and Found Office. Instead, you advertised, you described and you offered a reward. To lose something was not to chalk it up to experience but rather was a prompt to action. If you were a proper possessor, you found a way to get it back.

People pursued these means of reclamation because their possessions were valuable. As we have seen, the 'items' most frequently advertised in eighteenth-century newspapers were those of clear economic value. Watches and dogs were increasingly expensive things to obtain, while bills of exchange and bank notes were important to the circulation of wealth. Similarly, enslaved people were also economic assets that were highly valuable in this period. However, lost 'items' also held other forms of value. Watches were often unique 'family' items of sentimental value, passed down between generations. Although dogs did not exist as 'family' items in the way watches did, they clearly held emotional value in this period. No longer just owned for work or sport, dogs were increasingly understood as valuable for the companionship they offered. Not all advertisements sought the return of the 'thing' concerned. As we saw in Chapter 6, when employers, mistresses and masters wrote

---

[5] Jerry White, *London in the Eighteenth Century: A Great and Monstrous Thing* (London 2012), 199.

notices for servants and apprentices who had 'absconded' or 'eloped', they often sought to discourage return. In the case of spouses, the notices simply sought to mark the end of any financial responsibilities. The notice marked the end of any obligation to pay debts accrued by the spouse. In contrast, when enslavers wrote notices advertising that the person they enslaved had 'escaped', they were clear that they sought return and would reward those who used force to capture and return the person concerned. Freedom seekers escaped, but then had to evade captors to secure their future.

Keeping Hold has found that people sought to reclaim their property because it held economic, emotional and social value, but also because owners accrued value from maintaining possession. This book has argued that the relationship of possession was itself important. In the eighteenth century, the ability to maintain possession over time and to sustain a relationship of possession was an economic, social and cultural asset. Such calculations meant that when your possessions were lost, you also had a responsibility to reclaim them, to take care. To do so was to be a proper possessor, it was to be of good character and reputation, an ordered and upstanding individual. It is not necessarily all that surprising that people placed value on the ability to keep hold of things over time. If we look to real property, to land, we understand that there was a long history of placing great importance on keeping hold over time. In fact, the sharpening of the laws of primogeniture over the long eighteenth century were concerned with ensuring that land remained in the hands of certain families over generations. In this same period, we see similar ideas at work on a smaller scale too. But moveable property was distinct from real property. It held different forms of importance. Property – clothes, watches, jewellery, dogs, servants – was brought together in relationship to a particular person, especially in urban environments, to construct and display identity. Property acted as a material manifestation of the self and keeping hold of property provided a valuable means of showing your control and composure of that self. As explored in the final chapter of the book, if things were ill-maintained or were lost, such disorder reflected on the owner. Maintaining possession of your things was not just about retaining a good character, keeping your things in order also offered an important means of sustaining and showing self-possession.

Identifying the ambition of maintaining possession over time also raises questions about the difficulty of achieving it and the cultural and social work such an ambition might have done. We might understand maintaining possession as an exclusionary concept, which was difficult for most to achieve. As *Keeping Hold* has shown, in this period, it was hard to retain your things. In the eighteenth century, urban spaces were increasingly defined by their intensity. They were written and imagined as sites of hustle, bustle and hurrying. They existed in opposition to rural spaces that were conceived of in terms of calm and space. The hurry of cities, all those 'tides of passengers' upon the walkway of the pavement meant that it was more difficult to keep hold of your possessions.[6] The seemingly simple act of maintaining possession was dogged by an ever-widening range of threats from pickpockets to highwaymen, and from being jostled and dropping your gloves at the fair to having your dog run off in the park. Keeping hold required effort, it was something that needed to be enacted daily. Although, as we have seen, Londoners derived ways of reclaiming lost and stolen possessions, these systems required resources. As we saw in Chapter 4, while servants were expected to be aware of these systems and used them to reclaim their master's belongings, it was rarer for them to use it to reclaim their own property. While it was difficult to keep hold of your things then, it also required time, money and effort to reclaim them if they were lost. More broadly, in this period, most people regularly pawned their possessions. For them, the relationship of possession needed to be held lightly, and keeping hold of things over time must have been a trying proposition. It was not simply what you had that acted as a marker of status and character, but also your ability to keep hold of those things over time. The ability to care for possessions marked you out as a proper possessor and distinguished you from others.

Loss asked questions of how maintenance might be achieved and individuals used different tactics to sustain such relationships. Owners put their watches in fob pockets and secured them with a piece of string. If it was lost, they placed a notice in the newspaper and offered a high reward. Owners placed collars on their dogs and if their dog should be stolen or strayed, they placed a notice in a newspaper and tried to offer a low reward; if this failed, they offered as much as they could. As the century wore on, dog owners sought out dog sellers and dealers and asked for their advice and help when their dog went missing. By the early nineteenth century, they had little power in such circumstances and would offer high rewards to get their dog back. 'Owners' also placed collars on people to mark their enslavement and force them into staying. As we saw in Chapter 2, in early eighteenth-century London, an enslaved man named Richard navigated his way round the capital's streets while wearing a silver collar. If freedom seekers escaped, the 'owner' placed a notice in a newspaper and tried to ensure they were captured. As we saw in Chapter 4, William Beckford demanded someone 'bring him' the sixteen-year-old 'Charles'. Similarly, as we saw in Chapter 6, the enslaver of 'James' demanded someone bring him back and offered 'a Guinea Reward' for the service. Finding that keeping hold was an important ambition in eighteenth-century culture and society raises questions about its impacts, particularly in terms of

---

[6] John Gay, 'Trivia; or the Art of Walking the Streets of London', in John Gay, *Court Poems* (London, 1716), 19.

the different kinds of possession concerned. *Keeping Hold* has contributed to our understanding of human property through finding that enslaved people living in Britain were particularly vulnerable to the demands of keeping hold and the violence it inflicted. In contrast, masters and mistresses gave white servants a contract, wages and a gift of clothes. If they ran away, they often saw seeking return to be a futile move, but some did try to ensure no one else employed them. In the face of threats of loss, 'owners' sought to maintain possession through different means and reclaimed 'possessions' through different tactics. Such tactics show how these 'things' and the relationships of possession enacted towards them were differentiated. It allows us to see once again the violence of enslavement and how different values were placed on these 'things' and the relationship of possession at stake.

Keeping Hold has reoriented our view away from possessions and towards the relationship of possession itself. In doing so, it has shown the value and power that could be accrued not simply from having things in the eighteenth century, but rather from keeping hold of them. We see that maintaining possession was not a simple act and became more difficult as urbanisation intensified social contacts. In this analysis, we look past accumulation to instead see loss as a significant preoccupation in the eighteenth century. In their everyday lives, people sought to mitigate for the forms of loss they experienced. They developed new technologies to secure their possessions and formulated elaborate systems of reclamation to reconnect with lost things. While previously historians have largely understood possession as a self-evident relationship of little interest, here we have encountered its precarious nature and the impacts it had on understandings of character and of self. Keeping hold of your things, being seen to be able to take care of them, allowed you to accrue a marker of good character. But maintaining possession also did something more. It provided a material manifestation of your own self-possession: your self-control and poise. Keeping your things together was evidence of your ability to keep your self together. By contrast, the ripped dress, the open pocket, the cut ribbon, the lost glove denoted disorder.

The Importance of Finding

To look to these processes and practices of possession has been to tell a very eighteenth-century story. In this period, individuals engaged with print culture to reclaim their things. As such, individual actions created and sustained systems. While these people prized anonymity, their attempts at reclamation also relied on implicit assumptions about the possibilities of observation and connection among strangers in urban spaces. Often someone knew someone who knew something. Lost things came to be dealt with differently in the nineteenth century when an abstract bureaucracy emerged to manage them.[7] In the nineteenth century, things could be 'lost' in the way that we would recognise today. In other words, as 'modern' lost property offices emerged, it became possible to genuinely forget your purse or cane on a park bench, or in a Hackney coach, or as you wandered round the Great Exhibition, and get it back because someone had picked it up and deposited it at a designated site.

Increasingly, in the nineteenth century, people were encouraged to deposit objects that they found. As we learned in Chapter 4, in 1815, new legislation declared that 'every Driver in whose Coach or Chariot any Property whatever shall be left, by any Person or Persons hiring the same' needed to 'carry' and 'deposit' that property at the 'Hackney Coach Office'. Hackney coach drivers who failed to act would be fined 'a Penalty not exceeding Twenty Pounds'.[8] In 1831, new legislation placed a time limit of four days on such actions and in 1853 this was reduced to 24 hours.[9] From the 1790s onwards, police offices opened in different locations across London.[10] These offices provided sites which Londoners could take lost property to. By 1869, the Metropolitan Police established a centralised 'Lost Property Office' to which police offices could send lost items for processing. In the first year of operations, the Office received around 2,000 deposits. In 1925, the Office handled 163,579 deposits and it was decided that its offices were too small. In 1926, new purpose-built offices were constructed on Lambeth Road to handle the deluge of lost things.[11]

Similarly, people increasingly expected sites of public entertainment to have a lost property office. While at the Great Exhibition of 1851, attendants were expected to hand in to the police office any lost items they found; by 1862, the International Exhibition at South Kensington had its own lost property office.[12] An article in *The Era* declared that 'The Lost Property Office now contains a sufficient number and variety of articles to make up a very respectable display, and indeed there are very few of the thirty-six industrial classes of the Exhibition which could not be represented'.[13] The lost property office was almost as encyclopaedic (and as interesting) as the exhibition itself. That the office attracted such press attention suggests that lost property offices of this kind remained noteworthy rather than normalised by the mid nineteenth

---

[7] As such, London's lost property offices largely fit with James Vernon's rendering of the emergence of modern Britain. See James Vernon, *Distant Strangers: How Britain Became Modern* (Berkeley, CA, 2014), 16.
[8] 55 George III c.159.   [9] 1 & 2 William IV c.22; 16 & 17 Victoria c. 33.
[10] Clive Emsley, *Crime and Society in England, 1750–1900* [1987] (Edinburgh, 2010), 233.
[11] The National Archives, Metropolitan Police, 'Transfer of Lost Property and Public Carriage Offices to 109 Lambeth Road, 1919–1928', 1926, MEPO 2/5411, 90/BT/173.
[12] The National Archives, Metropolitan Police, 'Great Exhibition of the Works of Industry of all Nations 1851', MEPO 2/106.
[13] 'The Lost Property Office', *The Era* (London), Sunday, 28 September 1862.

century. Londoners were intrigued by the notion of the lost property office and all the forgetfulness and carelessness it suggested. Despite lost property offices becoming more ubiquitous, particularly with the onset of the railways, Londoners remained interested in what lost property offices were and what they contained into the late nineteenth and twentieth century.

By the 1920s, the possibility of losing things became understandable, not in terms of the social density of the urban space, but rather because of its speed. Writing a history of the Metropolitan Police's Lost Property Office in 1926, the author tried to explain why the number of deposits taken in by the Office had grown exponentially in the fifty-seven years between 1869 and 1926. Their explanation was the increased speed of transport. They considered that in 'the old days of the horse bus or the slow moving motor bus, it was possible for an article to be recovered if its loss was discovered on alighting'. The present day was a different story though. In the 1920s, 'the passenger no sooner alights than the vehicle has moved off too rapidly to be overtaken'. The author also had another explanation on hand: 'No doubt also there is a general tendency to carelessness on the part of the public.'[14] The importance of caring for possessions so crucial to eighteenth-century culture was largely thought to have dissipated by the early twentieth century. One of the other reasons deposits mounted in the Metropolitan Police's Lost Property Office was because owners often failed to seek out their lost possessions. A new culture of carelessness had seemingly arrived.

Occasionally a dog turned up at a lost property office, but by the end of the nineteenth century, their presence in these spaces was understood to be a category error. In this period, different kinds of lost things came to be dealt with quite differently. When a 'splendid Irish retriever' was 'found frolicking on the footbridge at Cannon Street', the station's lost property office decided to name him 'Whit' and make him a 'canine official with undefined duties'. When Whit finally died, his 'head was sent to a taxidermist' to be stuffed in order that it could then be hung up in the station-master's house.[15] As the journalist William FitzGerald sought to convey in his article on railway station lost property offices, the way he was treated marked Whit out as something special and unusual. In the second half of the nineteenth century, most lost dogs were delivered to the pound or a dogs' home, such as the one Mary Tealby (1801–1865) established in 1860.

In the 1850s, Tealby had established a 'canine asylum' at her home in Islington. As people started to deliver increasing numbers of dogs to her

---

[14] The National Archives, Metropolitan Police, MEPO 2/5411, 90/BT/173, 'Transfer of Lost Property and Public Carriage Offices to 109 Lambeth Road, 1919–1928', 1926, n.p.
[15] William G. FitzGerald, 'The Lost Property Office', *The Strand Magazine* (London), 10:81 (1895), 653.

doorstep, she decided to find larger premises and set up 'The Home for Lost and Starving Dogs'. The Home published its first prospectus on 2 October 1860 to reach a wider number of supporters and their funds.[16] The Home was significant in underlining how dogs were now associated with domestic settings. When not within a house, dogs were understood to either be lost (from their home) or starving (ownerless).[17] More particularly, the Home also demonstrated how dogs remained steeped in questions of value and property. The purpose of the Home was to return 'lost' dogs to their owners and to find new owners for dogs that were 'starving'. If new owners could not be found for the 'starving' dogs, they were killed, as the Home could ever only provide temporary refuge. As Philip Howell has argued, 'The mission of the Dogs' Home was after all to restore property, or else to turn strays into property.'[18] The importance of the Home increased after the Metropolitan Streets Act of 1867, which allowed the police to seize, detain and (after three days) destroy any apparently ownerless dog. A police order enacted on 6 June 1870 declared that all stray dogs would be sent to the Home. At this time, the Home was responsible for increasing numbers of dogs but also euthanised those that were not collected or sold on: those that were not 'valued'.[19]

Alongside these changes, the idea of the 'missing person' came into being in the mid nineteenth century. The earliest example of the term included in the *Oxford English Dictionary* dates from August 1850 and described people whose 'whereabouts are unknown'.[20] Following the Somerset ruling in 1772, newspaper notices placed to mark the escape of freedom seekers largely stopped, as did those announcing people for sale. As we saw in Chapter 1, any ambiguity as to the possibilities of owning and enslaving people in Britain ended in 1833 with parliamentary legislation on the abolition of slavery. While there were no longer notices for freedom seekers, notices for servants and apprentices also fell away. Notices placed for people who had runaway had largely ended by the 1830s, but it was still possible to advertise for people who had 'left home'. By the 1850s, the phenomenon of the missing person emerged more fully.

What we see in the establishment of these different institutions and practices – lost property offices, dogs' homes, missing person reports – is the assumption that in Britain objects, animals and people were different 'things' and needed to be treated in different ways. A dog could not go to a lost property office and a walking stick could not go to a dog's home. A missing

---

[16] Garry Jenkins, *A Home of Their Own: The Heart-Warming 150-Year History of Battersea Dogs and Cats Home* (London, 2010), 24–25.
[17] Philip Howell, *At Home and Astray: The Domestic Dog in Victorian Britain* (Charlottesville, VA and London, 2015), 75.
[18] Howell, *At Home and Astray*, 96.   [19] Ibid., 85–89.
[20] Robert Douglas-Fairhurst, *The Turning Point: A Year that Changed Dickens and the World* (London, 2021), 96.

person required a report to be written and information to be circulated. By the mid nineteenth century, the distinctions subtly at work in eighteenth-century notices had become more pronounced.

The establishment of these institutions was linked to the growing importance of the Metropolitan Police. London was increasingly filled with spaces that were regulated and policed and these institutions often served to further that end by putting things back in their place (or in a temporary refuge that marked them for what they were). The establishment of these institutions also marks the possibility of 'things' being genuinely lost and found. A person could go missing and be sought not because of their economic value as property nor because they had an occupation to fulfil but because they themselves were missed. A dog might stray and not be picked up and sold on by a thief but rather by a concerned citizen who would then take the poor wretch to the Home for Lost and Starving Dogs. A person might find a watch on the street and want to hand it in rather than taking it to the nearest pawnbroker. As such, these institutions also marked a changing relationship to possessions in urban spaces. New emphasis was placed not on the character of owners and their attempts to maintain possession but rather on urban denizens and their willingness to recognise and hand in 'lost' possessions: to act as good citizens. The late nineteenth century and early twentieth century had a very different story to tell about lost property, what it was and what it did in British society and culture. It is perhaps a story that looks more recognisable from our twenty-first century viewpoint. In contrast, in the eighteenth century, when everything was God given, when everything was valuable, it was important to take care of your things and pursue their reclamation should they get lost. In our moment of ecological crisis, where in the Global North unused things are thrown away with abandon and people struggle with 'clutter', we might look to this culture of care a little more closely to see what it offers. However, as we have seen in this book, we also need to reckon with how that same culture took 'care' of human possessions, seeking reclamation through forcible recapture. In the complex picture the past always offers, we must acknowledge that care could mean violence, as well as reconnection and repair.

Bibliography

Primary Sources

Archival Documents

Bank of England Archive, London
    C101, Cashier's Department Record of Bank Notes Issue: Lost Books.
Bedfordshire Record Office, Bedford
    L30/14/333, Wrest Park Manuscripts.
Bodleian Library, University of Oxford, Oxford
    John Johnson Collection of Ephemera.
    MS. Rawl. D. 1114, Diary of an anonymous man, 1 January 1710–31 August 1712.
British Library, London
    BL Add MSS 27951, Diary of an Anonymous Clergyman, August–October 1761 and August–September 1772.
    BL Add MSS 19211, Diary of Gervase Leveland, July 1764–October 1765.
    BL Add 33629–33631, Diary of Thomas Pelham, 30 November 1793–6 March 1794.
    BL Add MSS 32558, Diary of William Upcott of London, January 1803–1807, 1809, 1823.
Cadbury Research Library, University of Birmingham, Birmingham
    MS241, Journal of Annie Lambert, 1845–1846.
Gloucestershire Archives, Gloucester
    D3549/13/1, Lloyd-Baker family of Hardwick Court, Sharp Family, Granville Sharp (1735–1813), General Correspondence, c. 1772–c.1812.
The Goldsmiths' Company Library & Archive, London
    R13846, 'Copies of Warning Notices from a Private Collection'.
    Box O.J.V., Historic Warning Notices.
    Warning Carrier Book, 1744.
Guildhall Library, London
    CLC/B/215, Thwaites and Reed Collection.
    CLC/B/176, Parkinson and Frodsham Collection.

London Metropolitan Archive, London
　London Picture Archive.
　Baptism Records for Saint George the Martyr, Southwark.
　Baptism Records for Saint Marylebone, Westminster.
The National Archives, London
　PROB 11, Prerogative Court of Canterbury.
　MEPO 2/5411, Metropolitan Police: Office of the Commissioner, 1919–1928.
　MEPO 2/106, Metropolitan Police: Office of the Commissioner, 1851.
Tower Hamlets Local History Library, London
　P/GOF/1, Diary of Elijah Goff (Coal Merchants, St George in the East), 1788–1796.
York Minster Archives, York
　COLL 1896/1, 3, Letterbook of Granville Sharp, 1768–1773.

Museum Objects

Leeds Castle, Maidstone
　Dog Collar Collection.
Victoria and Albert Museum, London
　T.56-1940, Pocketbook, Embroidered Moroccan Leather, 1768.
　T.108-1953, Pocketbook, Red Morocco Leather, embroidered with Gilt Thread in Satin Stitch, Tétouan, Morocco 1776.
　T.51-1927, Pocketbook, Embroidered Velvet, Tunisia, 1774.
　T.143-1961, Pocketbook, Cream Silk, Lined with Pink Silk and Edged with Silver-Gilt Woven Lace, France, 1750s.
British Museum, London
　1912,1107.1, Gold Pair-Cased Cylinder Watch with Quarter-Repeat, George Graham, England, 1727.

Newspapers and Periodicals

Bell's Life in London and Sporting Chronicle
Boston News-Letter
Daily Advertiser
Daily Courant
The Era
General Advertiser
The Gentleman's Magazine
The India Gazette; or, Calcutta Public Advertiser
Lady's Magazine
London Evening Post
London Gazette
The London Packet and General Hue and Cry
The London Packet or New Lloyd's Evening Post
The Morning Post

Penny London Post or The Morning Advertiser
Post Boy
Public Advertiser
The Public Hue and Cry; or Sir John Fielding's General Preventive Plan
St. James's Evening Post
The Strand Magazine
The Times

Printed Primary Sources

Anon., *The Accomplished Lady's Delight in Cookery: Or, the Complete Servant's* [sic] *Maid's Guide* (Wolverhampton, 1780).
Anon., *The Adventures of a Silver Penny* (London, 1786).
Anon., *The Adventures of a Watch* (London, 1788).
Anon., *The Annual Register* (1771).
Anon., *The Bath and Bristol Guide: or, The Tradesman's and Traveller's Pocket Companion* (1765).
Anon., *The Biography of a Spaniel* (London, 1803).
Anon., *The Case of the Coffee-Men of London and Westminster* (London, 1728).
Anon., *Cato, or Interesting Adventures of a Dog of Sentiment* (London, 1816).
Anon., *The Compleat Modern Spy, for the Present Year* (London, 1781).
Anon., *The Countryman's Guide to London* (London, 1775).
Anon., *Domestic Management, Or the Art of Conducting a Family; With Instructions to Servants in General* (London, 1800).
Anon., *The Footman's Looking-Glass: Or, Proposals to the Livery Servants of London and Westminster, &c. For Bettering their Situations in Life, and Securing Their Credit in the World* (London, 1747).
Anon., *Hodson's Hackney Carriage Pocket Companion for 1839* (London, 1839).
Anon., *The Life and Glorious Actions of the Most Heroic and Magnanimous Jonathan Wilde* (1725).
Anon., *The London Companion, or an Account of the Fares of Hackney Coachmen, Chairmen and Watermen* (London, 1773).
Anon., *London Unmask'd: or the New Town Spy* (London, 1784?).
Anon., *Low-Life: Or One Half of the World Knows Not How the Other Half Live* (London, 1755).
Anon., *The Olio, Or, Museum of Entertainment* (1832).
Anon., *Onesimus; or, the Run-Away Servant Converted: A True Story* (London, 1795?).
Anon., *The Right of the City of London, and their Proceedings, Touching the Regulations of Hackney-Coaches, Standing in the Said City, and Liberties Thereof* (London, 1692/1693).
Anon., *The Servants Calling with Some Advice to the Apprentice* (London, 1725).
Anon., *The Sportsman's Dictionary; or, the Gentleman's Companion* (London, 1800).
Anon., *Tales of Chivalry; or, Perils by Flood and Field* (London, 1840).
Anon., *The Tradesman's and Travellers Pocket Companion: OR, THE Bath and Bristol Guide* (Bath, 1753).
Barker, Anne, *The Complete Servant Maid: Or Young Woman's Best Companion* (London, 1770).

Barrett, William, *The History and Antiquities of the City of Bristol* (Bristol, 1789).
Beilby, Ralph, *A General History of Quadrupeds*, 2nd edn (London, 1791).
Bishop, William, *Legal Protection of Dogs from the Increasing Evil of Dog-Stealers and Receivers* (London, 1844).
Blackstone, William, *Commentaries on the Laws of England: Book I Of the Rights of Persons* ed. Simon Stern (Oxford, 2016).
Blackstone, William, *Commentaries on the Laws of England: Book II Of the Rights of Things* ed. Simon Stern (Oxford, 2016).
Blackstone, William, *Commentaries on the Laws of England: Book IV Of Public Wrongs* ed. Simon Stern (Oxford, 2016).
Blackstone, William, *Commentaries on the Laws of England, Vol. 2* (London, 1774).
Blackstone, William, *Commentaries on the Law of England, Vol. 4* (London, 1774).
Bridges, Thomas, *The Adventures of a Bank-Note, Vol. I–IV* (London, 1771).
Burney, Frances, *The Early Journals and Letters of Fanny Burney, Vol. I 1768–1773* ed. Lars E. Troide (Oxford, 1988).
Burney, Frances, *The Early Journals and Letters of Fanny Burney, Vol. II 1774–1777* ed. Lars E. Troide (Oxford, 1988).
Burney, Frances, *The Early Journals and Letters of Fanny Burney, Vol. III 1778–1779* ed. Lars E. Troide and Stewart J. Cooke (Oxford, 1994).
Burney, Frances, *The Early Journals and Letters of Fanny Burney, Vol. IV The Streatham Years Part II 1780–1781* ed. Betty Rizzo (Oxford, 2003).
Burney, Frances, *The Early Journals and Letters of Fanny Burney, Vol. V 1782–1783* ed. Lars E. Troide and Stewart J. Cooke (Oxford, 2012).
Burney, Frances, *Evelina, or The History of a Young Lady's Entrance into the World* [1778] (New York and London, 1965).
Burney, Frances, *Cecilia* [1782] (Oxford, 2008).
Burney, Frances, *Camilla* [1796] (Oxford, 2009).
Burney, Frances, *The Wanderer* [1814] (Oxford, 2001).
Campbell, Robert, *The London Tradesman* (London, 1747).
Cibber, Colley, *Love's Last Shift; or, The Fool in Fashion* (The Hague, 1711).
Clapham, Samuel, *A Collection of the Several Points of Sessions' Law, Vol. 1* (London, 1818).
Clarkson, Thomas, *An Essay on the Slavery and Commerce of the Human Species* (London, 1786).
Clarkson, Thomas, *The Substance of the Evidence of Sundry Persons on the Slave-Trade, Collected in the Course of a Tour Made in the Autumn of the Year 1788* (London, 1789).
Cleland, John, *Fanny Hill or Memoirs of a Woman of Pleasure* (London, 1985).
Collier, Mary, *The Woman's Labour* (London, 1989).
Coventry, Francis, *The History of Pompey the Little*, ed. Nicholas Hudson [1751] (Buffalo, NY, 2008).
Cozens-Hardy, Basil (ed.), *The Diary of Sylas Neville 1767–1788* (London, 1950).
Crosby, B., *A Modern Sabbath, Or, A Sunday Ramble, and Sabbath-Day Journey* (London, 1794).
D. H., *The Life of Jonathan Wild, From His Birth to His Death* (Dublin, 1725).
Defoe, Daniel, *Moll Flanders* [1722] (Oxford, 1998).
Defoe, Daniel, *Colonel Jack* [1722] (London, 1967).
Defoe, Daniel, *The Life and Actions of Jonathan Wild, in Defoe on Sheppard and Wild* [1725], ed. Richard Holmes (London, 2004).

Equiano, Olaudah, *The Interesting Narrative and Other Writings* (London, 2003).
Fielding, Henry, *Love in Several Masques* (Dublin, 1728).
Fielding, Henry, *Tom Jones: History of a Foundling* [1749] (London, 1966).
Fielding, Henry, *An Enquiry into the Causes of the Late Increase of Robbers, &c. with Some Proposals for Remedying This Growing Evil*, 2nd edn (London, 1751).
Fielding, Sir John Jr and Richard King, *The New London Spy or a Modern Twenty-Four Hours Ramble through the Bills of Mortality* (London, 1771).
Fielding, Sir John, *Extracts from Such of the Penal Laws, As Particularly Relate to the Peace and Good Order of This Metropolis* (London, 1768).
Gay, John, *Court Poems* (London, 1716).
Godwin, William, *Caleb Williams* [1794] (Oxford, 2009).
Hale, Matthew, *The Analysis of the Law: Being a Scheme, or Abstract, Of the several Titles and Partitions of the Law of England Digested into Method*, 2nd edn (London, 1716).
Haywood, Eliza, *A Present for a Servant Maid* (London, 1743).
Hooke, Andrew, *Bristollia: or, Memoirs of the City of Bristol* (London, 1748).
Johnson, Mary, *Madam Johnson's Present: Or, the Best Instructions for Young Women, in Useful and Universal Knowledge*, 4th edn [1755] (London, 1766).
Johnson, Samuel, *A Dictionary of the English Language*, Vol. II (London, 1755).
Kenrick, William, *A New Dictionary of the English Language* (London, 1773).
Kilner, Dorothy, *The Life and Perambulations of a Mouse*, Vol. I (London, 1790).
Kilner, Dorothy, *The Adventures of a Hackney Coach*, 3rd edn (London, 1781).
King, Richard, *New Cheats of London Exposed* (London, 1780).
Locke, John, *Second Treatise of Government and A Letter Concerning Toleration* [1689] (Oxford, 2016).
Mandeville, Bernard, *An Enquiry into the Causes of the Frequent Executions at Tyburn* [1725] (Los Angeles, 1964).
Mason, John, *Self-Knowledge. A Treatise, Shewing the Nature and Benefit of the Important Science, and the Way to Attain It*, 3rd edn [1745] (London, 1755).
Osbaldiston, William Augustus, *The Universal Sportsman: or, Nobleman, Gentleman, and Farmer's Dictionary of Recreation and Amusement* (Dublin, 1795?).
Paget, Francis Edward, *Tales of the Village Children* (London, 1844).
Parker, George, *A View of Society and Manners in High and Low Life*, Vol. 2 (London, 1781).
Playford, John, *Vade Mecum, or The Necessary Companion* (London, 1680).
von Pückler-Muskau, Prince Hermann, *Letters of a Dead Man*, trans. Linda B. Parshall (Cambridge, 2016).
Richardson, Samuel, *Pamela* [1740] (Oxford, 2001).
Roach, I., *A Fortnight's Ramble through London, Or, A Complete Display of all the Cheats and Frauds Practised in the Great Metropolis* (London, 1795).
Roach, John, *Roach's London Pocket Pilot, Or Stranger's Guide through the Metropolis* (London, 1796).
von la Roche, Sophie, *Sophie in London 1786*, trans. Clare Williams (London, 1933).
Rosenberg, Jordy, *Confessions of the Fox* (London, 2018).
Sala, George Augustus, *Twice Round the Clock, Or the Hours of the Day and Night in London* [1858] (New York, 1971).
Scott, Helenus, *The Adventures of a Rupee* (London, 1782).
Selvon, Samuel, *The Lonely Londoners* [1956] (London, 2006).
Silverthorne, Elizabeth (ed.), *Deposition of Richard Wyatt, JP, 1767–1776* (Guildford, 1978).

Smeeton, George, *Doings in London; or Day and Night Scenes of the Frauds, Follies, Manners, and Depravities of the Metropolis* (London, 1828).
Smith, Capt. Alexander, *Memoirs of the Life and Times of the Famous Jonathan Wild* (London, 1726).
Smith, Patti, *M Train* (London and New York, 2016).
Stennett, Joseph, *The Works of the Late Reverend and Learned Mr. Joseph Stennett: In Five Volumes*, Vol. 3 (London, 1731–1732).
Strange, John, *A Collection of Select Cases Relating to Evidence. By a Late Barrister at Law* (London, 1754).
Talbot, Henry Fox, *The Pencil of Nature: The History of Photography* (London, 1844–1846).
Tillotson, John, *The Works of the Most Reverend Dr. John Tillotson, the Late Lord Archbishop of Canterbury* (London, 1735).
Trussler, John, *London Adviser and Guide* (London, 1786).
Ward, Edward, *The London-Spy Compleat. In eighteen parts* (London, 1703).
Wollstonecraft, Mary, *Mary and The Wrongs of Woman* [1798] (Oxford, 2009).
Wood, John, *Description of the Exchange* (Bath, 1745).
Woolf, Virginia, *Street Haunting: A London Adventure* [1927] (Nottingham, 2017).

Government Reports and Parliamentary Papers

Report from the Select Committee on Dog Stealing (Metropolis); Together with the Minutes of Evidence Taken Before Them (London, 1844).
House of Commons Transport Committee, *Seventh Report of Session 2010–2012: Taxis and Private Hire Vehicles: The Road to Reform* (London, 2011), Ev 66.

Digitized Sources

Seventeenth–Eighteenth Century Burney Collection Newspapers (www.galegroup.com)
Eighteenth-Century Collections Online (www.galegroup.com)
Oxford Dictionary of National Biography (www.oxforddnb.com)
Oxford English Dictionary Online (www.oed.com)
Proceedings of the Old Bailey Online, 1674–1913 (www.oldbaileyonline.org)
The Times Digital Archive (www.thetimes.co.uk/tto/archives/)

Secondary Sources

Books and Articles

Acres, Wilfred M., *The Bank of England from Within, 1694–1900*, vol. 2 (Oxford, 1931).
Almeroth-Williams, Thomas, *City of Beasts: How Animals Shaped Georgian London* (Manchester, 2019).
 'The Watchdogs of Georgian London: Non-Human Agency, Crime Prevention and Control of Urban Space', *The London Journal*, 43:3 (2018), 267–288.
Amussen, Susan Dwyer, *Caribbean Exchanges: Slavery and the Transformation of English Society, 1640–1700* (Chapel Hill, NC, 2007).

Bibliography

Andersson, Peter K., '"Bustling, Crowding, and Pushing": Pickpockets and the Nineteenth-Century Street Crowd', *Urban History*, 41:2 (2014), 291–310.

Andrew, Donna T. and Randall McGowen, *The Perreaus & Mrs. Rudd: Forgery and Betrayal in Eighteenth-Century London* (Berkeley, CA, 2001).

Appadurai, Arjun, 'Introduction: Commodities and the Politics of Value', in Arjun Appadurai (ed.), *The Social Life of Things: Commodities in Cultural Perspective* (Cambridge, 1986), 3–63.

   (ed.), *The Social Life of Things: Commodities in Cultural Perspective* (Cambridge, 1986).

Atkins, Peter (ed.), *Animal Cities: Beastly Urban Histories* (Farnham, 2012).

Aylmer, G. E., 'The Meaning and Definition of "Property" in Seventeenth-Century England', *Past & Present*, 86 (1980), 87–97.

Bachelard, Gaston, *The Poetics of Space: The Classic Look at How We Experience Intimates Places* (Boston, MA, 1994).

Bailey, Joanne, 'Favoured or Oppressed? Married Women, Property and "Coverture" in England, 1660–1800', *Continuity and Change*, 17:3 (2002), 351–372.

   Unquiet Lives: Marriage and Marriage Breakdown in England, 1660–1800 (Cambridge, 2003).

Bakhtin, Mikhail, *Rabelais and His World* (Bloomington, IL, 1984).

Barker, Hannah, *Newspapers, Politics and English Society 1695–1855* (Harlow, 2000).

Barker, Hannah and Sarah Green, 'Taking Money from Strangers: Traders' Responses to Banknotes and the Risks of Forgery in Late Georgian London', *Journal of British Studies*, 60 (2021), 585–608.

Barnard, John, D. F. McKenzie and Maureen Bell (eds.), *The Cambridge History of the Book in Britain, Volume 4: 1557–1695* (Cambridge, 2008).

Barrell, John, *The Spirit of Despotism: Invasions of Privacy in the 1790s* (Oxford, 2006).

Beattie, J. M., *Policing and Punishment in London, 1660–1750: Urban Crime and the Limits of Terror* (Oxford, 2001).

   Crime and Courts in England, 1660–1800 (Oxford, 2002).

   The First English Detectives: The Bow Street Runners and the Policing of London, 1750–1840 (Oxford, 2014).

   'Sir John Fielding and Public Justice: The Bow Street Magistrates' Court, 1754–1780', *Law and History Review*, 25:1 (2007), 61–100.

Beckert, Sven, *Empire of Cotton: A New History of Global Capitalism* (London, 2014).

Beckett, J. V., 'The Pattern of Landownership in England and Wales, 1660–1880', *The Economic History Review*, 37:1 (1984), 1–22.

Beckett, John and Sheila Aley, *Byron and Newstead: The Aristocrat and the Abbey* (Newark, DE and London, 2001).

Begiato, Joanne, *Manliness in Britain, 1760–1900: Bodies, Emotion and Material Culture* (Manchester, 2020).

Bender, John and Michael Marrinan (eds.), *Regimes of Description: In the Archive of the Eighteenth Century* (Stanford, CA, 2005).

Bender, John and Michael Marrinan, 'Introduction', in John Bender and Michael Marrinan (eds.), *Regimes of Description: In the Archive of the Eighteenth Century* (Stanford, CA, 2005), 1–10.

Benthien, Claudia, *Skin: On the Cultural Border between Self and World* (New York, NY, 2002).

Benton, Lauren, *Law and Colonial Cultures: Legal Regimes in World History, 1400–1900* (Cambridge, 2004).
Berg, Maxine, *Luxury and Pleasure in Eighteenth-Century Britain* (Oxford, 2005).
  'Cargoes: The Trade in Luxuries from Asia to Europe', in David Cannadine (ed.), *Empire, The Sea and Global History: Britain's Maritime World, c.1763–c.1840* (New York, NY and Hampshire, 2007), 60–82.
  'Women's Consumption and the Industrial Classes of Eighteenth-Century England', *Journal of Social History*, 30:2 (1996), 415–434.
Berg, Maxine and Helen Clifford, 'Selling Consumption in the Eighteenth Century: Advertising and the Trade Card in Britain and France', *Cultural and Social History*, 4:2 (2007), 145–170.
Berlant, Lauren, 'The Commons: Infrastructures for Troubling Times', *Environment and Planning D: Society and Space*, 34:3 (2016), 393–419.
Berry, Helen, 'Polite Consumption: Shopping in Eighteenth-Century England', *Transactions of the Royal Historical Society*, 12 (2002), 375–394.
Bille, Mikkel, Frida Hastrup and Tim Flohr Sørensen (eds.), *An Anthropology of Absence: Materialization of Transcendence and Loss* (New York, NY and London, 2010).
Bille, Mikkel, Frida Hastrup and Tim Flohr Sørensen, 'Introduction: An Anthropology of Absence', in Mikkel Bille, Frida Hastrup and Tim Flohr Sørensen (eds.), *An Anthropology of Absence: Materialization of Transcendence and Loss* (New York, NY and London, 2010), 3–22.
Binhammer, Katherine, *Downward Mobility: The Form of Capital and the Sentimental Novel* (Baltimore, MD, 2020).
Black, Jeremy, *The English Press in the Eighteenth Century* (Abingdon, 2010).
Blackwell, Mark (ed.), *The Secret Life of Things: Animals, Objects and It-Narratives in Eighteenth-Century England* (Lewisburg, PA, 2007).
Blondé, B., P. Stabel, J. Stobart and I. Van Damme (eds.), *Buyers and Sellers: Retail Circuits and Practices in Medieval and Early Modern Europe* (Turnhout, 2006).
Boulton, Jeremy, 'London 1540–1700', in Peter Clark, Martin J. Daunton and David Michael Palliser (eds.), *Cambridge Urban History of Britain, Vol. 2 1540–1840* (Cambridge, 2000), 315–346.
Braddick, Michael J. and Joanna Innes (eds.), *Suffering and Happiness in England 1550–1850: Narratives and Representations: A Collection to Honour Paul Slack* (Oxford, 2017).
Bray, Xavier, *Faithful and Fearless: Portraits of Dogs* (Lewes, 2021).
Brewer, Holly, 'Creating a Common Law of Slavery for England and Its New World Empire', *Law and History Review*, 39:3 (2021), 765–834.
Brewer, John and Roy Porter, *Consumption and the World of Goods* (London, 1993).
Brewer, John and Susan Staves (eds.), *Early Modern Conceptions of Property* (London and New York, NY, 1995).
Brewer, John and Susan Staves, 'Introduction', in John Brewer and Susan Staves (eds.), *Early Modern Conceptions of Property* (London and New York, NY, 1995), 1–20.
Briggs, Peter M., 'Satiric Strategy in Ned Ward's London Writings', *Eighteenth-Century Life*, 35:2 (2011), 76–101.
Brogan, Hugh, 'Clarkson, Thomas (1760–1846), slavery abolitionist', *Oxford Dictionary of National Biography*. 23 September 2004; Accessed

24 September 2021. www.oxforddnb.com/view/10.1093/ref:odnb/ 9780198614128.001.0001/odnb-9780198614128-e-5545.
Brown, Laura, *Homeless Dogs and Melancholy Apes: Humans and Other Animals in the Modern Literary Imagination* (Ithaca, NY, 2010).
Buggins, G. T. E. and A. J. Turner, 'The Context of Production, Identification and Dating of Clocks by A and J Thwaites', *Antiquarian Horology* 8:4 (1973), 372–381.
Burman, Barbara and Ariane Fennetaux, *The Pocket: A Hidden History of Women's Lives, 1660–1900* (New Haven, CT and London, 2019).
Burman, Barbara, 'Pocketing the Difference: Gender and Pockets in Nineteenth-Century Britain', *Gender & History*, 14:3 (2002), 447–469.
Bynum, Tara A., *Reading Pleasures: Everyday Black Lives in Early America* (Champaign, IL, 2023).
Cannadine, David (ed.), *Empire, The Sea and Global History: Britain's Maritime World, c.1763–c.1840* (New York, NY and Hampshire, 2007).
Carens, Joseph H. (ed.), *Democracy and Possessive Individualism: The Intellectual Legacy of C. B. Macpherson* (Albany, NY, 1993).
'Possessive Individualism and Democratic Theory: Macpherson's Legacy', in Joseph H. Carens (ed.), *Democracy and Possessive Individualism: The Intellectual Legacy of C. B. Macpherson* (Albany, NY, 1993), 1–18.
Carey, Daniel, *Locke, Shaftesbury, and Hutcheson: Contesting Diversity in the Enlightenment and Beyond* (Cambridge, 2009).
Christmas, William J., *The Lab'ring Muse: Work, Writing and the Social Order in English Plebian Poetry, 1730–1830* (Newark, NJ, 2001).
Churchill, David, *Crime Control and Everyday Life in the Victorian City: The Police and the Public* (Oxford, 2018).
Churchill, Wendy D., *Female Patients in Early Modern Britain: Gender, Diagnosis, and Treatment* (Farnham and Burlington, VT, 2012).
Clark, Peter, Martin J. Daunton and David Michael Palliser (eds.), *Cambridge Urban History of Britain, Vol. 2 1540–1840* (Cambridge, 2000).
Clark, Geoffrey, *Betting on Lives: The Culture of Life Insurance in England, 1695–1775* (Manchester, 1999).
Clark, Gillian, 'The Foundling Hospital and Its Token System', *Family & Community History*, 18:1 (2015), 53–68.
Clark, Gregory, 'The Political Foundations of Modern Economic Growth: England, 1540–1800', *Journal of Interdisciplinary History*, 26 (1996), 563–588.
Clayton, Mary and Robert Shoemaker, 'Blood Money and the Bloody Code: The Impact of Financial Rewards on Criminal Justice in Eighteenth-Century England', *Continuity and Change*, 37 (2022), 97–125.
Cowan, Brian, *The Social Life of Coffee: The Emergence of the British Coffeehouse* (New Haven, CT, 2005).
'Mr Spectator and the Coffeehouse Public Sphere', *Eighteenth-Century Studies*, 37:3 (2004), 345–366.
Coulton, Richard, '"The Darling of the Temple-Coffee-House Club": Science, Sociability and Satire in Early Eighteenth-Century London', *Journal for Eighteenth-Century Studies*, 35:1 (2012), 43–65.
Cox, Nancy, *The Complete Tradesman: A Study of Retailing, 1550–1820* (Aldershot and Vermont, NE, 2000).

Cozens, Joseph, '"The Blackest Perjury": Desertion, Military Justice, and Popular Politics in England, 1803–1805', *Labour History Review*, 79:3 (2014), 255–280.

Crane, Susan A., *Nothing Happened: A History* (Stanford, CA, 2020).

Cruickshank, Dan and Neil Burton, *Life in the Georgian City* (London, 1990).

Cutter, Martha J., '"As White as Most White Women": Racial Passing in Advertisements for Runaway Slaves and the Origins of a Multivalent Term', *American Studies*, 54:4 (2016), 73–97.

Daston, Lorraine J., 'The Domestication of Risk: Mathematical Probability and Insurance 1650–1830', in Lorenz Kruger, Lorraine Daston and Michael Heidelberg (eds.), *The Probabilistic Revolution* (Cambridge, MA and London, 1987), 237–260.

Deazley, Ronan, *On the Origin of the Right to Copy: Charting the Movement of Copyright Law in Eighteenth-Century Britain (1695–1775)* (Oxford and Portland, OR, 2004).

Dereli, Cynthia, 'In Search of a Poet: The Life and Work of Elizabeth Hands', *Women's Writing*, 8 (2001), 169–182.

Desan, Christine, *Making Money: Coin, Currency and the Coming of Capitalism* (Oxford, 2014).

Desmond, Ray, *Dictionary of British & Irish Botanists and Horticulturists* (London, 1994).

Devenney, James and Mel Kenny (eds.), *Consumer Credit, Debt and Investment in Europe* (Cambridge, 2012).

Dierks, Konstantin, *In My Power: Letter Writing and Communication in Early America* (Philadelphia, PA, 2009).

Dixon, Thomas, *From Passions to Emotions: The Category of a Secular Psychological Category* (Cambridge, 2003).

Donald, Moira and Linda Hurcombe (eds.), *Gender and Material Culture in Historical Perspective* (Basingstoke, 2000).

Donald, Moira, 'The Greatest Necessity of Every Rank of Men: Gender, Clocks and Watches', in Moira Donald and Linda Hurcombe (eds.), *Gender and Material Culture in Historical Perspective* (Basingstoke, 2000), 54–78.

Donington, Katie, *The Bonds of Family: Slavery, Commerce and Culture in the British Atlantic World* (Manchester, 2019).

Doody, Margaret Anne, *Frances Burney: The Life in the Works* (Cambridge, 2010).

Douglas-Fairhurst, Robert, *The Turning Point: A Year That Changed Dickens and the World* (London, 2021).

Downes, Stephanie, Sally Holloway and Sarah Randles, *Feeling Things: Objects and Emotions through History* (Oxford, 2018).

Earle, Peter, *The Making of the English Middle Class: Business, Society, and Family Life in London, 1660–1730* (Berkeley, CA, 1989).

A City Full of People: Men and Women of London, 1650–1750 (Methuen, MA, 1994).

Earle, Rebecca, '"Two Pairs of Pink Satin Shoes!!" Race, Clothing and Identity in the Americas (Seventeenth–Nineteenth Centuries)', *History Workshop Journal*, 52 (2001), 175–195.

Edwards, Laura, *Only the Clothes on Her Back: Clothing the Hidden History of Power in the Nineteenth-Century United States* (New York, NY, 2022).

Ellis, Markman, *The Coffee House: A Cultural History* (London, 2004).

'Suffering Things: Lapdogs, Slaves, and Counter-Sensibility', in Mark Blackwell (ed.), *The Secret Life of Things: Animals, Objects and It-Narratives in Eighteenth-Century England* (Lewisburg, PA, 2007), 92–113.
Emsley, Clive, *Crime and Society in England, 1750–1900* [1987] (Edinburgh, 2010).
Engerman, Stanley L., *Slavery, Emancipation and Freedom* (Baton Rouge, LA, 2007).
Epstein, S. R., *Freedom and Growth: The Rise of States and Markets in Europe, 1300–1750* (London, 2000).
Erickson, Amy Louise, *Women and Property in Early Modern England* (London, 1993).
'Coverture and Capitalism', *History Workshop Journal*, 59 (2005), 1–16.
Erickson, Peter, 'Invisibility Speaks: Servants and Portraits in Early Modern Visual Culture', *Journal for Early Modern Cultural Studies*, 9:1 (2009), 23–61.
Fend, Mechthild, 'Bodily and Pictorial Surfaces: Skin in French Art and Medicine, 1790–1860', *Art History*, 28:3 (2005), 311–339.
Fennetaux, Ariane, Amélie Junqua and Sophie Vasset (eds.), *The Afterlife of Used Things: Recycling in the Long Eighteenth Century* (New York, NY, 2014).
Fennetaux, Ariane, Amélie Junqua and Sophie Vasset, 'Introduction: The Many Lives of Recycling', in Ariane Fennetaux, Amélie Junqua and Sophie Vasset (eds.), *The Afterlife of Used Things: Recycling in the Long Eighteenth Century* (New York, NY, 2014), 1–10.
Fennetaux, Ariane, 'Women's Pockets and the Construction of Privacy in the Long Eighteenth Century', *Eighteenth Century Fiction*, 20:3 (2008), 307–334.
Fergus, Jan, 'Provincial Servants' Reading in the Late Eighteenth Century' in James Raven, Helen Small and Naomi Tadmor (eds.), *The Practice and Representation of Reading in England* (Cambridge, 1996), 202–225.
Festa, Lynn, *Sentimental Figures of Empire in Eighteenth-Century Britain and France* (Baltimore, MD, 2006).
Fiction Without Humanity: Person, Animal, Thing in Early Enlightenment Literature and Culture (Philadelphia, PA, 2019).
'Personal Effects: Wigs and Possessive Individualism in the Long Eighteenth Century', *Eighteenth-Century Life*, 29:2 (2005), 47–90.
'Person, Animal, Thing: The 1796 Dog Tax and the Right to Superfluous Things', *Eighteenth-Century Life*, 33:2 (2009), 1–44.
Finlay, Robert, *The Pilgrim Art: Cultures of Porcelain in World History* (Berkeley, CA and London, 2010).
Finn, Margot C., *The Character of Credit: Personal Debt in English Culture, 1740–1914* (Cambridge, 2003).
Finn, Margot, 'Women, Consumption and Coverture in England, c.1760–1860', *The Historical Journal*, 39:3 (1996), 703–722.
'Slaves Out of Context: Domestic Slavery and the Anglo-Indian Family, c. 1780–1830', *Transactions of the Royal Historical Society*, 19 (2009), 181–203.
Flanagan, Thomas and Anthony Parel (eds.), *Theories of Property: Aristotle to the Present* (Waterloo, ON, 1979).
Flather, Amanda, 'Gender, Space, and Place: The Experience of Service in the Early Modern Household, c.1580–1720', *Home Cultures*, 8:2 (2011), 171–188.
Floud, Roderick and Paul Johnson (eds.), *The Cambridge Economic History of Modern Britain, Volume 1, 1700–1860* (Cambridge, 2004).

Forth, Christopher E. and Ivan Crozier (eds.), *Body Parts: Critical Explorations in Corporeality* (Lanham, 2005).
Froide, Amy M., *Never Married: Singlewomen in Early Modern England* (New York, NY, 2005).
Fryer, Peter, *Staying Power: The History of Black People in Britain* (London, 1984).
Fuentes, Marisa J., *Dispossessed Lives: Enslaved Women, Violence, and the Archive* (Philadelphia, PA, 2016).
Gallagher, Catherine, *Nobody's Story: The Vanishing Acts of Women Writers in the Marketplace, 1670–1820* (Oxford, 1994).
Gaskill, Malcolm, *Crime and Mentalities in Early Modern England* (Cambridge, 2000).
Gattrell, Vic, *City of Laughter: Sex and Satire in Eighteenth-Century London* (London, 2006).
Gauci, Perry, *William Beckford: First Prime Minister of the London Empire* (New Haven, CT, 2013).
Gerzina, Greta Holbrook, *Black London: Life before Emancipation* (New Brunswick, 1995).
Getzler, Joshua, 'Theories of Property and Economic Development', *Journal of Interdisciplinary History*, 26 (1996), 639–669.
Gilbert, Pamela K., 'Introduction: Imagining Londons', in Pamela K. Gilbert (ed.), *Imagined Londons* (New York, NY, 2002).
(ed.), *Imagined Londons* (New York, NY, 2002).
Glaisyer, Natasha, '"The Most Universal Intelligencers": The Circulation of the *London Gazette* in the 1690s', *Media History*, 23:2 (2017), 256–280.
Gowing, Laura, *Common Bodies: Women, Touch and Power in Seventeenth-Century England* (New Haven, CT, 2003).
'Girls on Forms: Apprenticing Young Women in Seventeenth-Century London', *Journal of British Studies*, 55 (2016), 447–473.
Ingenious Trades: Women and Work in Seventeenth-Century London (Cambridge, 2022).
Graeber, David, *Towards an Anthropological Theory of Value: The False Coin of Our Own Desire* (New York, NY and Basingstoke, 2001).
Gray, Drew D., *Crime, Prosecution and Social Relations: The Summary Courts of the City of London in the Late Eighteenth Century* (London, 2009).
de Grazia, Margreta, 'The Ideology of Superfluous Things: King Lear as Period Piece', in Margreta de Grazia, Maureen Quilligan and Peter Stallybrass (eds.), *Subject and Object in Renaissance Culture* (Cambridge, 1996), 17–42.
de Grazia, Margreta, Maureen Quilligan and Peter Stallybrass (eds.), *Subject and Object in Renaissance Culture* (Cambridge, 1996).
Griffin, Carl, 'Becoming Private Property: Custom, Law, and the Geographies of "Ownership" in Eighteenth- and Nineteenth-Century England', *Environment and Planning A*, 42:3 (2010), 747–762.
Griffiths, Paul and Mark S.R. Jenner (eds.), *Londinopolis: Essays in the Cultural and Social History of Early Modern London* (Manchester and New York, NY, 2000).
Hailwood, Mark, *Alehouses and Good Fellowship in Early Modern England* (Martlesham, 2014).
'Time and Work in Rural England, 1500–1700', *Past & Present*, 248:1 (2020), 118.

Hamlett, Jane and Julie-Marie Strange, *Pet Revolution: Animals and the Making of Modern British Life* (London, 2023).

Hamling, Tara and Catherine Richardson (eds.), *Everyday Objects: Medieval and Early Modern Material Culture and Its Meaning* (Abingdon, 2010).

Hamon, Philippe and Patricia Baudoin, 'Rhetorical Status of the Descriptive,' *Yale French Studies*, 61 (1981), 1–26.

Hanley, Ryan, *Beyond Slavery and Abolition: Black British Writing c. 1770–1830* (Cambridge, 2019).

Harris, Michael, *London Newspapers in the Age of Walpole: A Study of the Origins of the Modern English Press* (London and Toronto, 1987).
   'London Newspapers', in Michael F. Suarez and Michael L. Turner (eds.), *The Cambridge History of the Book in Britain* (Cambridge, 2010), 413–433.

Harrison, Mark, 'The Ordering of the Urban Environment: Time, Work and the Occurrence of Crowds 1790–1835', *Past & Present*, 110:1 (1986), 134–168.

Hart, Kevin, *Samuel Johnson and the Culture of Property* (Cambridge, 1999).

Hartman, Saidiya, 'Venus in Two Acts', *Small Axe: A Journal of Criticism*, 12:2 (2008), 1–14.

Hartog, Hendrik, 'Pigs and Positivism', *Wisconsin Law Review*, 899 (1985), 1–26.

Harvey J. Kaye and Keith McClelland (eds.), *E. P. Thompson: Critical Perspectives* (Oxford, 1990).

Harvey, Karen, 'The History of Masculinity, circa 1650–1800', *Journal of British Studies*, 44 (2005), 296–311.
   'Men of Parts: Masculine Embodiment and the Male Leg in Eighteenth-Century England', *Journal of British Studies*, 54:4 (2015), 797–821.

Hay, Douglas and Francis Snyder (eds.), *Policing and Prosecution in Britain, 1750–1850* (Oxford, 1989).

Heller, Benjamin, 'The "Mene Peuple" and the Polite Spectator: The Individual in the Crowd at Eighteenth-Century London Fairs', *Past & Present*, 208 (2010), 131–157.

Helmreich, Anne, Tim Hitchcock and William J. Turkel, 'Rethinking Inventories in the Digital Age: The Case of the Old Bailey', *Journal of Art Historiography*, 11 (2014), 1–25.

Herbert, Amanda, *Female Alliances: Gender, Identity, and Friendship in Early Modern Britain* (New Haven, CT and London, 2014).

Hetherington, Kevin, 'Secondhandedness: Consumption, Disposal, and Absent Presence', *Environment and Planning D: Society and Space*, 22 (2004), 157–173.

Hitchcock, Tim and Robert Shoemaker, *London Lives: Poverty, Crime and the Making of a Modern City, 1690–1800* (Cambridge, 2015).

Hitchcock, Tim, *Down and Out in Eighteenth-Century London* (London, 2004).

Hitchcock, Tim and Heather Shore (eds.), *The Streets of London: From the Great Fire to the Great Stink* (London, 2003).
   'Confronting the Digital: Or How Academic History Writing Lost the Plot', *Cultural and Social History* 10:1 (2013), 9–23.

Holmes, Helen, *The Materiality of Nothing: Exploring Our Everyday Relationships with Objects Absent and Present* (Abingdon, 2023).

Hoppit, Julian, 'Compulsion, Compensation and Property Rights in Britain', *Past & Present*, 210 (2011), 93–128.

Horrell, Sara, Jane Humphries and Ken Sneath, 'Consumption Conundrums Unravelled', *Economic History Review*, 68:3 (2015), 830–857.
Houston, R. A., 'Madness and Gender in the Long Eighteenth Century', *Social History*, 27:3 (2002), 320–322.
Howell, Philip, *At Home and Astray: The Domestic Dog in Victorian Britain* (Charlottesville, VA and London, 2015).
  'Between the Muzzle and the Leash: Dog-Walking, Discipline and the Modern City', in Peter Atkins (ed.), *Animal Cities: Beastly Urban Histories* (Farnham, 2012), 221–241.
Howson, Gerald, *Thief-Taker General: The Rise and Fall of Jonathan Wild* (London, 1970).
Humfrey, Paula (ed.), *The Experience of Domestic Service for Women in Early Modern London* (Farnham, 2011).
Hunt, Lynn, *Inventing Human Rights: A History* (New York, NY, 2007).
Hunt, Margaret R., 'Wives and Marital "Rights" in the Court of Exchequer in the Early Eighteenth Century', in Paul Griffiths and Mark S. R. Jenner (eds.), *Londinopolis: Essays in the Cultural and Social History of Early Modern London* (Manchester, 2000), 107–129.
Hyman, Aaron M. and Dana Leibsohn, 'Lost and Found at Sea, or a Shipwreck's Art History', *West 86th*, 28:1 (2021), 43–74.
Jenkins, Garry, *A Home of Their Own: The Heart-Warming 150-Year History of Battersea Dogs and Cats Home* (London, 2010).
Jenner, Mark, 'Circulation and Disorder: London Streets and Hackney Coaches, c.1640–c.1740', in Tim Hitchcock and Heather Shore (eds.), *The Streets of London: From the Great Fire to the Great Stink* (London, 2003), 40–53.
Jones, Ann Rosalind and Peter Stallybrass, *Renaissance Clothing and the Materials of Memory* (Cambridge, 2000).
Jowett, Judy, 'The Warning Carriers: How Messengers of The Goldsmiths' Company Warned the Luxury Trades of Criminal Activities in Eighteenth-Century London', *Silver Studies*, 18 (2005), 1–144.
Kent, David A., 'Ubiquitous but Invisible: Female Domestic Servants in Mid-Eighteenth Century London', *History Workshop*, 28 (1989), 111–128.
  '"Gone for a Soldier": Family Breakdown and the Demography of Desertion in a London Parish, 1750–91', *Local Population Studies*, 45 (1990), 27–42.
Kesselring, Krista J. and Tim Stretton (eds.), *Married Women and the Law: Coverture in England and the Common Law World* (Montreal and Kingston, 2013).
Kesselring, Krista J. and Tim Stretton, 'Introduction: Coverture and Continuity' in Krista J. Kesselring and Tim Stretton (eds.), *Married Women and the Law: Coverture in England and the Common Law World* (Montreal and Kingston, 2013), 3–23.
King, Peter, *Crime, Justice and Discretion in England, 1740–1820* (Oxford, 2000).
  Crime and Law in England, 1750–1840: Remaking Justice from the Margins (Cambridge, 2009).
King, Steven and Alannah Tomkins (eds.), *The Poor in England 1700–1850: An Economy of Makeshifts* (Manchester, 2003).
Kingston, Christopher, 'Marine Insurance in Britain and America', *Journal of Economic History*, 67:2 (2007), 379–409.

Knepper, Paul, Jonathan Doak and Joanna Shapland (eds.), *Urban Crime Prevention and Restorative Justice: Effects of Social Technologies* (Abingdon, 2009).
Kopytoff, Igor, 'The Cultural Biography of Things: Commoditization as Process', in Arjun Appadurai (ed.), *The Social Life of Things: Commodities in Cultural Perspective* (Cambridge, 1986), 64–94.
Krausman Ben-Amos, Ilana, 'Failure to Become Freemen: Urban Apprentices in Early Modern England', *Social History*, 16:2 (1991), 155–172.
Kruger, Lorenz, Lorraine Daston and Michael Heidelberg (eds.), *The Probabilistic Revolution* (Cambridge, MA and London, 1987).
Kuchler, Susanne and Daniel Miller, *Clothing as Material Culture* (Oxford, 2005).
Kwint, Marcus, Christopher Breward and Jeremy Aynsley (eds.), *Material Memories: Design and Evocation* (Oxford, 1999).
Landry, Donna, *The Muses of Resistance: Labouring Class Women's Poetry in Britain, 1739–1796* (Cambridge, 1990).
Langford, Paul, *Public Life and the Propertied Englishman 1689–1798* (Oxford, 1990).
Latour, Bruno, *Reassembling the Social: An Introduction to Actor-Network-Theory* (Oxford, 2005).
Lamb, Jonathan, *The Things Things Say* (Princeton, NJ and Oxford, 2011).
Landau, Norma (ed.), *Law, Crime, and English Society, 1660–1830* (Cambridge, 2002).
Lane, Joan, *Apprenticeship in England, 1600–1914* (London, 1996).
Lemire, Beverly, *The Business of Everyday Life: Gender, Practice and Social Politics in England, c.1600–1900* (Manchester, 2005).
  'The Theft of Clothes and Popular Consumerism in Early Modern England', *Journal of Social History*, 24 (1990), 255–276.
Lemmings, David, 'Henry Fielding and English Crime and Justice Reportage, 1748–1752: Narratives of Panic, Authority and Emotion', *Huntington Library Quarterly*, 80:1 (2017), 71–97.
Levene, Alysa, *Childcare, Health and Mortality at the London Foundling Hospital 1741–1800 'Left to the Mercy of the World'* (Manchester, 2007).
Leonard, A. B., 'Underwriting British Trade to India and China, 1780–1835', *The Historical Journal*, 55:4 (2012), 983–1006.
  'Underwriting Marine Warfare: Insurance and Conflict in the Eighteenth Century', *International Journal of Maritime History*, 25:2 (2013), 173–185.
Leunig, Tim, Chris Minns and Patrick Wallis, 'Networks in the Premodern Economy: The Market for London Apprenticeships, 1600–1749', *The Journal of Economic History*, 71: 2 (2011), 413–443.
Liapi, Lena, *Roguery in Print: Crime and Culture in Early Modern London* (Martlesham, 2019).
Lieberman, David, 'Property, Commerce, and the Common Law: Attitudes to Legal Change in the Eighteenth Century', in John Brewer and Susan Staves (eds.), *Early Modern Conceptions of Property* (London and New York, NY, 1995), 144–160.
Lobban, Michael, 'Slavery, Insurance and the Law', *The Journal of Legal History*, 28:3 (2007), 319–328.
Lorimer, Douglas, 'Black Slaves and English Liberty: A Re-Examination of Racial Slavery', *Immigrants & Minorities*, 3 (1984), 121–150.
Lynch, Deidre, *The Economy of Character: Novels, Market Culture and the Business of Inner Meaning* (Chicago, IL, 1998).

McDonagh, Briony, *Elite Women and the Agricultural Landscape, 1700–1830* (Woodbridge, 2017).

MacKay, Lynn, 'Why They Stole: Women in the Old Bailey, 1779–1789', *Journal of Social History*, 32 (1999), 623–639.

Maclachlan, Ian, 'A Bloody Offal Nuisance: The Persistence of Private Slaughter-Houses in Nineteenth-Century London', *Urban History*, 34:2 (2007), 227–254.

Mascuch, Michael, *Origins of the Individualist Self: Autobiography and Self-Identity in England, 1591–1791* (Cambridge, 1997).

McConnell, Anita, 'From Craft Workshop to Big Business: The London Scientific Instrument Trade's Response to Increasing Demand, 1750–1820', *London Journal*, 19:1 (1994), 36–53.

McElligott, Jason, 'Advertising and Selling in Cromwellian Newsbooks' in Shanti Graheli (ed.), *Buying and Selling: The Business of Books in Early Modern Europe* (Leiden, 2019), 467–488.

McFall, Liz and Francis Dodsworth, 'Fabricating the Market: The Promotion of Life Assurance in the Long Nineteenth-Century', *Journal of Historical Sociology*, 22:1 (2009), 30–54.

Meldrum, Tim, *Domestic Service and Gender 1660–1750: Life and Work in the London Household* (Harlow, 2000).

Middleton, Simon, 'Runaways, Rewards, and the Social History of Money', *Early American Studies: An Interdisciplinary Journal*, 15:3 (2017), 617–647.

Milka, Amy and David Lemmings, 'Narratives of Feeling and Majesty: Mediated Emotions in the Eighteenth-Century Criminal Courtroom', *The Journal of Legal History*, 38:2 (2017), 155–178.

Miller, Daniel, 'Introduction,' in Susanne Kuchler and Daniel Miller, *Clothing as Material Culture* (Oxford, 2005), 1–20.

Mintz, Sidney, *Sweetness and Power: The Place of Sugar in Modern History* (New York, NY,1986).

Molineux, Catherine, *Faces of Perfect Ebony: Encountering Atlantic Slavery in Imperial Britain* (Cambridge, MA and London, 2012).

Morgan, Jennifer L., *Reckoning with Slavery: Gender, Kinship and Capitalism in the Early Black Atlantic* (Durham, NC and London, 2021).

Morgan, Gwenda and Peter Rushton, 'Visible Bodies: Power, Subordination and Identity in the Eighteenth-Century Atlantic World', *Journal of Social History*, 39:1 (2005), 39–64.

Munsche, P. M., *Gentlemen and Poachers: The English Games Laws, 1671–1831* (Cambridge, 1981).

Murdoch, Tessa, 'Second Generation Huguenot Craftsmen in London: from the "Warning Carriers" Walks', *Proceedings of the Huguenot Society of Great Britain and Ireland*, XXVI (1994–1997), 241–256.

Nacol, Emily C., *An Age of Risk: Politics and Economy in Early Modern Britain* (Princeton, NJ and Oxford, 2016).

Neeson, J. M., *Commoners: Common Rights, Enclosure and Social Change in England 1700–1820* (Cambridge, 1993).

Nelson, Carolyn and Matthew Secombe, 'The Creation of the Periodical Press, 1620–1695', in John Barnard, D. F. McKenzie and Maureen Bell (eds.), *The Cambridge History of the Book in Britain, Volume 4: 1557–1695* (Cambridge, 2008), 533–550.

Newman, Simon P., *Freedom Seekers: Escaping from Slavery in Restoration London* (London, 2022).
  'Rethinking Runaways in the British Atlantic World: Britain, the Caribbean, West Africa and North America', *Slavery & Abolition*, 38:1 (2017), 49–71.
  'Freedom-Seeking Slaves in England and Scotland, 1700–1780', *English Historical Review*, 134:570 (2019), 1136–1168.
North, Douglass C. and Robert Paul Thomas, *The Rise of the Western World: A New Economic History* (Cambridge, 1973).
North, Douglass C., *Structure and Change in Economic History* (New York, NY, 1981).
Nussbaum, Felicity, *The Limits of the Human: Fictions of Anomaly, Race and Gender in the Long Eighteenth Century* (Cambridge, 2003).
O'Byrne, Alison, 'The Art of Walking in London: Representing Urban Pedestrianism in the Early Nineteenth Century', *Romanticism*, 14:2 (2008), 94–107.
Paley, Ruth, 'Thief-Takers in London in the Age of the McDaniel Gang, c.1745–1754', in Douglas Hay and Francis Snyder (eds.), *Policing and Prosecution in Britain, 1750–1850* (Oxford, 1989), 301–340.
  'After *Somerset*: Mansfield, Slavery and the Law in England, 1772–1830', in Norma Landau (ed.), *Law, Crime, and English Society, 1660–1830* (Cambridge, 2002), 165–184.
Palk, Deidre, 'Private Crime in Public and Private Places: Pickpockets and Shoplifters in London, 1780–1823', in Tim Hitchcock and Heather Shore (eds.), *The Streets of London: From the Great Fire to the Great Stink* (London, 2003), 135–150.
Patterson, Orlando, *Slavery and Social Death: A Comparative Study* (Cambridge, MA, 1982).
Paul, Tawny, *The Poverty of Disaster: Debt and Insecurity in Eighteenth-Century Britain* (Cambridge, 2019).
Pearson, Robin, *Insuring the Industrial Revolution: Fire Insurance in Great Britain, 1700–1850* (Aldershot, 2004).
Pearson, Chris, *Dogopolis: How Dogs and Humans Made Modern New York, London, and Paris* (Chicago, IL, 2021).
Pennell, Sara, '"For a crack or flaw despis'd": Thinking about Ceramic Durability and the "Everyday" in Late Seventeenth- and Early Eighteenth-Century England,' in Tara Hamling and Catherine Richardson (eds.), *Everyday Objects: Medieval and Early Modern Material Culture and its Meaning* (Abingdon, 2010), 27–40.
  '"All but the Kitchen Sink": Household Sales and the Circulation of Second-Hand Goods in Early Modern England', in Jon Stobart and Ilja Van Damme (eds.), *Modernity and the Second-Hand Trade: European Consumption Cultures and Practices, 1700–1900* (Basingstoke, 2010), 37–56.
  'Invisible Mending: Ceramic Repair in Eighteenth-Century England', in Ariane Fennetaux, Amèlie Junqua and Sophie Vasset (eds.), *The Afterlife of Used Things: Recycling in the Long Eighteenth Century* (New York, NY, 2014), 107–121.
  'Happiness in Things? Plebian Experiences of Chattel "Property" in the Long Eighteenth Century', in Michael J. Braddick and Joanna Innes (eds.), *Suffering and Happiness in England 1550–1850: Narratives and Representations: A Collection to Honour Paul Slack* (Oxford, 2017), 208–226.

Pike, David L., *Metropolis on the Styx: The Underworlds of Modern Urban Culture, 1800–2001* (Ithaca, NY and London, 2007).
Pocock, J. G. A., 'The Mobility of Property and the Rise of Eighteenth-Century Sociology', in Thomas Flanagan and Anthony Parel (eds.), *Theories of Property: Aristotle to the Present* (Waterloo, ON, 1979), 141–166.
Poovey, Mary, *Genres of the Credit Economy: Mediating Value in Eighteenth- and Nineteenth-Century Britain* (Chicago, IL and London, 2008).
Prak, Maarten and Patrick Wallis (eds.), *Apprenticeship in Early Modern Europe* (Cambridge, 2019).
Prude, Jonathan, 'To Look upon the "Lower Sort": Runaway Ads and the Appearance of Unfree Laborers in America, 1750–1800', *The Journal of American History*, 78:1 (1991), 124–159.
Ogilvie, Brian W., *The Science of Describing: Natural History in Renaissance Europe* (Chicago, IL, 2006).
Oldham, James, *English Common Law in the Age of Mansfield* (Chapel Hill, NC, 2004).
Outram, Dorinda, *The Body and the French Revolution* (New Haven, CT and London, 1989).
Quinn, Stephen, 'Money, Finance and Capital Markets', in Roderick Floud and Paul Johnson (eds.), *The Cambridge Economic History of Modern Britain, Volume 1, 1700–1860* (Cambridge, 2004), 147–174.
Raven, James, Helen Small and Naomi Tadmor (eds.), *The Practice and Representation of Reading in England* (Cambridge, 1996).
Riello, Giorgio, *Cotton: The Fabric That Made the Modern World* (Cambridge, 2013).
Robbins, Bruce, *The Servant's Hand: English Fiction from Below* (Durham, NC and London, 1993).
Rushton, Pauline, 'Two Men's Leather Letter Cases: Mercantile Pride and Hierarchies of Display', in Chloe Wigston Smith and Beth Fowkes Tobin (eds.), *Small Things in the Eighteenth Century: The Political and Personal Value of the Miniature* (Cambridge, 2022), 172–186.
Russell, Edmund, *Greyhound Nation: A Coevolutionary History of England, 1200–1900* (Cambridge, 2018).
Ruston, Alan, 'Mason, John (1706–1763), Independent minister and author', *Oxford Dictionary of National Biography*. 23 September 2004; Accessed 15 June 2022. www.oxforddnb.com/view/10.1093/ref:odnb/9780198614128.001.0001/odnb-9780198614128-e-18283.
Rydén, Göran, 'Viewing and Walking: Swedish Visitors to Eighteenth-Century London', *Journal of Urban History*, 39:2 (2012), 255–274.
Scheetz-Nguyen, Jessica A., 'Calculus of Respectability: Defining the World of Foundling Hospital Women and Children in Victoria London', *Annales de démographie historique*, 114:2 (2007), 13–36.
Schwarz, Leonard, 'London 1700–1840', in Peter Clark, Martin J. Daunton and David Michael Palliser (eds.), *Cambridge Urban History of Britain, Vol. 2 1540–1840* (Cambridge, 2000), 641–671.
Scott, Susie, *The Social Life of Nothing: Silence, Invisibility and Emptiness in Tales of Lost Experience* (Abingdon, 2020).
Secord, William, *Dog Painting 1840–1940: A Social History of the Dog in Art* (London, 1992).

Sennefelt, Karin, 'A Discerning Eye: Visual Culture and Social Distinction in Early Modern Stockholm', *Cultural and Social History*, 12:2 (2015), 179–195.

Sewell, Jr, William H., 'How Classes Are Made: Critical Reflections on E. P. Thompson's Theory of Working-Class Formation', in Harvey J. Kaye and Keith McClelland (eds.), *E. P. Thompson: Critical Perspectives* (Oxford, 1990), 50–77.

Shepard, Alexandra, *Accounting for Oneself: Worth, Status, and the Social Order in Early Modern England* (Oxford, 2015).

Shoemaker, Robert, *Prosecution and Punishment: Petty Crime and the Law in London and Rural Middlesex, c. 1660–1725* (Cambridge, 1991).

The London Mob: Violence and Disorder in Eighteenth-Century England (London, 2007).

'The Street Robber and Gentleman Highwayman: Changing Representations and Perceptions of Robbery in London, 1690–1800', *Cultural and Social History*, 3 (2006), 381–405.

'The Old Bailey Proceedings and the Representation of Crime and Criminal Justice in Eighteenth-Century London', *Journal of British Studies*, 47:3 (2008), 559–580.

'Print Culture and the Creation of Public Knowledge about Crime in Eighteenth-Century London', in Paul Knepper, Jonathan Doak and Joanna Shapland (eds.), *Urban Crime Prevention and Restorative Justice: Effects of Social Technologies* (Abingdon, 2009), 1–22.

'Worrying about Crime: Experience, Moral Panics and Public Opinion in London, 1660–1800', *Past & Present*, 234 (2017), 71–100.

Shore, Heather, 'Crime, Criminal Networks and the Survival Strategies of the Poor in Early Eighteenth-Century London', in Steven King and Alannah Tomkins (eds.), *The Poor in England 1700–1850: An Economy of Makeshifts* (Manchester, 2003), 137–165.

Silver, Sean, *The Mind Is a Collection: Case Studies in Eighteenth-Century Thought* (Philadelphia, PA, 2015).

Singy, Patrick, 'Huber's Eyes: The Art of Scientific Observation before the Emergence of Positivism', *Representations*, 95 (2006), 54–75.

Smallwood, Stephanie E., *Saltwater Slavery: A Middle Passage from Africa to American Diaspora* (Cambridge, MA and London, 2008).

Smith, Bruce P., 'The Presumption of Guilt and the English Law of Theft, 1750–1850', *Law and History Review*, 23:1 (2005), 133–171.

Smith, Bruce, 'The Emergence of Public Prosecution in London, 1790–1850', *Yale Journal of Law & the Humanities*, 18:1 (2006), 29–62.

Smith, Chloe Wigston and Beth Fowkes Tobin (eds.), *Small Things in the Eighteenth Century: The Political and Personal Value of the Miniature* (Cambridge, 2022).

Smith, Kate, 'In Her Hands: Materializing Distinction in Georgian Britain', *Cultural and Social History*, 11:4 (2014), 489–506.

'Amidst Things: New Histories of Commodities, Capital and Consumption', *The Historical Journal*, 61:3 (2018), 841–861.

Spacks, Patricia Meyer, *Imagining a Self: Autobiography and Novel in Eighteenth-Century England* (Cambridge, MA and London, 1976).

Desire and Truth: Functions of Plot in Eighteenth-Century English Novels (Chicago, IL and London, 1994).

Privacy: Concealing the Eighteenth-Century Self (Chicago, IL and London, 2003).

Spencer, Jane, *Writing about Animals in the Age of Revolution* (Oxford, 2020).
Sprang, Rebecca L., *Stuff and Money in the Time of the French Revolution* (Cambridge, MA, 2017).
Stafford, Barbara, *Body Criticism: Imaging the Unseen in Enlightenment Art and Medicine* (Cambridge, 1991).
Stalnaker, Joanna, *The Unfinished Enlightenment: Description in the Age of the Encyclopaedia* (Ithaca, NY, 2010).
Staves, Susan, *Married Women's Separate Property in England, 1660–1833* (Cambridge, MA and London, 1990).
  'Chattel Property Rules and the Construction of Englishness, 1660–1800', *Law and History Review*, 12:1 (1994), 123–153.
Steedman, Carolyn, *Labours Lost: Domestic Service and the Making of Modern England* (Cambridge, 2009).
  An Everyday Life of the English Working Class: Work, Self and Sociability in the Early Nineteenth Century (Cambridge, 2013).
  History and the Law: A Love Story (Cambridge, 2020).
  'Servants and Their Relationship to the Unconscious', *Journal of British Studies*, 42 (2003), 316–350.
  'Intimacy in Research: Accounting for It', *History of the Human Sciences*, 21:4 (2008), 17–33.
Stewart, Susan, 'Prologue: From the Museum of Touch', in Marcus Kwint, Christopher Breward and Jeremy Aynsley (eds.), *Material Memories: Design and Evocation* (Oxford, 1999), 17–36.
Stobart, Jon, Andrew Hann and Victoria Morgan, *Spaces of Consumption: Leisure and Shopping in the English Town, c. 1680–1830* (London and New York, NY, 2007).
Stobart, Jon and Ilja Van Damme (eds.), *Modernity and the Second-Hand Trade: European Consumption Cultures and Practices, 1700–1900* (Basingstoke, 2010).
Stobart, Jon, 'Clothes, Cabinets and Carriages: Second-Hand Dealing in Eighteenth-Century England', in B. Blonde, P. Stabel, J. Stobart and I. Van Damme (eds.), *Buyers and Sellers: Retail Circuits and Practices in Medieval and Early Modern Europe* (Turnhout, 2006), 224–244.
Stoler, Ann Laura, *Along the Archival Grain. Epistemic Anxieties and Colonial Common-Sense* (Princeton, NJ, 2009).
Strasser, Susan, *Waste and Want: A Social History of Trash* (New York, NY, 1999).
Styles, John and Amanda Vickery (eds.), *Gender, Taste and Material Culture in Britain and North America 1700–1800* (London and New Haven, CT, 2006).
Styles, John, *The Dress of the People: Everyday Fashion in Eighteenth-Century England* (London and New Haven, CT, 2007).
  'Sir John Fielding and the Problem of Criminal Investigation in Eighteenth-Century England', *Transactions of the Royal Historical Society*, 33 (1983), 127–149.
  'Print and Policing: Crime Advertising in Eighteenth-Century Provincial England', in Douglas Hay and Francis Snyder (eds.), *Policing and Prosecution in Britain, 1750–1850* (Oxford, 1989), 55–112.
Swain, Warren and Karen Fairweather, 'The Legal Regulation of Pawnbroking in England, A Brief History', in James Devenney and Mel Kenny (eds.), *Consumer Credit, Debt and Investment in Europe* (Cambridge, 2012), 142–159.

Sweet, Rosemary, *The Writing of Urban Histories in Eighteenth-Century England* (Oxford, 1997).
Tague, Ingrid H., *Animal Companions: Pets and Social Change in Eighteenth-Century Britain* (Philadelphia, PA, 2015).
'Eighteenth-Century English Debates on a Dog Tax', *The Historical Journal*, 51 (2008), 901–920.
'Dead Pets: Satire and Sentiment in British Elegies and Epitaphs for Animals', *Eighteenth-Century Studies*, 41:3 (2008), 289–306.
Thompson, E. P., *The Making of the English Working Class* [1963] (London, 2013).
Customs in Common (London, 1993).
'Time, Work-Discipline, and Industrial Capitalism', *Past & Present*, 38 (1967), 67.
Thompson, James, *Models of Value: Eighteenth-Century Political Economy and the Novel* (Durham, NC, 1996).
Town, Edward and Angela McShane (eds.), *Marking Time: Objects, People, and Their Lives, 1500–1800* (New Haven, CT and London, 2020).
Tully, James, 'The Possessive Individualism Thesis: A Reconsideration in the Light of Recent Scholarship', in Joseph H. Carens (ed.), *Democracy and Possessive Individualism: The Intellectual Legacy of C. B. Macpherson* (Albany, NY, 1993), 19–44.
Turner, Cheryl, *Living by the Pen: Women Writers in the Eighteenth Century* (London, 1994).
Valenze, Deborah, *The Social Life of Money in the English Past* (Cambridge, 2006).
Vernon, James, *Distant Strangers: How Britain Became Modern* (Berkeley, CA, 2014).
Vickery, Amanda, *The Gentleman's Daughter: Women's Lives in Georgian England* (New Haven, CT and London, 1998).
Behind Closed Doors: At Home in Georgian England (New Haven, CT and London, 2009).
'"Neat and Not Too Showey": Words and Wallpaper in Regency England', in John Styles and Amanda Vickery (eds.), *Gender, Taste, and Material Culture in Britain and North America 1700–1800* (New Haven, CT and London, 2006), 201–219.
'His and Hers: Gender, Consumption and Household Accounting in Eighteenth-Century England', *Past & Present Supp.*, 1 (2006), 12–38.
Wahrman, Dror, *The Making of the Modern Self: Identity and Culture in Eighteenth-Century England* (New Haven, CT and London, 2006).
Waldstreicher, David, 'Reading the Runaways: Self-Fashioning, Print Culture, and Confidence in Slavery in the Eighteenth-Century Mid-Atlantic', *The William and Mary Quarterly*, 56:2 (1999), 243–272.
Wales, Tim, 'Thief-Takers and Their Clients in Later Stuart London', in Paul Griffiths and Mark S. R. Jenner (eds.), *Londinopolis: Essays in the Cultural and Social History of Early Modern London* (Manchester and New York, NY, 2000), 67–85.
Wall, Cynthia, *The Prose of Things: Transformations of Description in the Eighteenth Century* (Chicago, IL, 2006).
Wallis, Patrick, 'Labor, Law, and Training in Early Modern London: Apprenticeship and the City's Institutions', *Journal of British Studies*, 51 (2012), 791–819.
'Apprenticeship in England', in Maarten Prak and Patrick Wallis (eds.), *Apprenticeship in Early Modern Europe* (Cambridge, 2019), 275–276.

Walsh, Claire, 'Shop Design and the Display of Goods in Eighteenth-Century London', *Journal of Design History*, 8:3 (1995), 157–176.
Walsham, Alexandra, *Providence in Early Modern England* (Oxford, 2003).
Walvin, James, *Sugar: The World Corrupted, From Slavery to Obesity* (London, 2017).
Warwick, Alexandra and Dani Cavallaro, *Fashioning the Frame: Boundaries, Dress and the Body* (Oxford, 1998).
Weatherill, Lorna, *Consumer Behaviour and Material Culture in Britain 1660–1760* (London, 1996).
— 'The Meaning of Consumer Behaviour in Late Seventeenth- and Early Eighteenth-Century England', in John Brewer and Roy Porter (eds.), *Consumption and the World of Goods* (London, 1993), 206–227.
Weiner, Annette B., *Inalienable Possessions: The Paradox of Keeping-While-Giving* (Berkeley and Los Angeles, CA, 1992).
Werrett, Simon, *Thrifty Science: Making the Most of Materials in the History of Experiment* (Chicago, IL and London, 2019).
Wilson, Lee B., *Bonds of Empire: The English Origins of Slave Law in South Carolina and British Plantation America, 1660–1783* (Cambridge, 2021).
White, Jerry, *London in the Eighteenth Century: A Great and Monstrous Thing* (London, 2012).
Wiecek, William M., 'Somerset: Lord Mansfield and the Legitimacy of Slavery in the Anglo-American World', *The University of Chicago Law Review*, 42:1 (1974), 86–146.
Williams, Raymond, *Keywords: A Vocabulary of Culture and Society* (London, 2014).
Wittgenstein, Ludwig, *Philosophical Investigations*, 4th edn, trans. G. E. M. Anscombe, P. M. S. Hacker and Joachim Schulte (Oxford, 2009).
Worboys, Michael, Julie-Marie Strange and Neil Pemberton, *The Invention of the Modern Dog: Breed and Blood in Victorian Britain* (Baltimore, MD, 2018).
Wyett, Jodi L., 'The Lap of Luxury: Lapdogs, Literature, and Social Meaning in the "Long" Eighteenth Century', *Lit: Literature Interpretation Theory*, 10:4 (1999), 275–301.
Ylivuori, Soile, *Women and Politeness in Eighteenth-Century England: Bodies, Identities, and Power* (London, 2019).

Unpublished Theses

Griffin, Rachael, 'Detective Policing and the State in Nineteenth-Century England: The Detective Department of the London Metropolitan Police, 1842–1878' (Unpublished PhD Thesis, University of Western Ontario, 2015).
Smoak, Katherine, 'Circulating Counterfeits: Making Money and Its Meanings in the Eighteenth-Century British Atlantic World' (Unpublished PhD Thesis, John Hopkins University, 2018).

Index

abolition movement, 37, 39–41, 46, *See also* slavery and enslaved people
Adams, Charles, 167, 229
Addison, Joseph, 19
Adventures of a Bank-Note, The (Bridges), 56, 66
Adventures of a Hackney Coach, The (Kilner), 137
Adventures of a Rupee, The (Scott), 57, 66
Adventures of a Silver Penny, The, 57
Adventures of a Watch, The, 54–55, 66, 187–188
Allen, Samuel, 206
anchors, lost, 21, 99
Annis, John, 74–75
Appadurai, Arjun, 182
apprentices
    clothing for, 219
    legal protection for, 131–132
    manuals for, 70–71
    mobility of, 71
    proximity to employers, 175–177
    runaway apprentices, 72–73, 130, 133–134, 166–167
    value of and rewards for, 199–201

Bank of England, 55–56, 94–95, 156–158, 170, 185–186, 215–216, 234
Bank Restriction Period, 55–56, 170
Barrett, William, 59
Beckford, William, 134–135, 237
Beggar's Opera, The (Gay), 113
Beilby, Ralph, 164, 191, 194
Beltey, Mary, 227–229
Bender, John, 154
Berry, Daina Ramey, 204
bill stickers, 118
Bille, Mikkel, 13–14
bills of exchange, 8, 55, 103, 125, 158, 169, 184, 207, 235
Binhammer, Katherine, 217

Bishop, William, 192–194
Black, James, 167
Blackstone, William, 30
    on animals, 49–52, 193
    on chattels, 7–8, 33–35
    on coverture, 42
    on finding unclaimed things, 67
    on freedom of enslaved persons in England, 34–35, 37
    on labour and servants, 46
    on nature of property, 31
    on value, 24, 180
Boddice, Rob, 14
Boston News-Letter, 97
Bourk, Alexander, 136–137
Boyce, Robert, 56
Bready, William, 94
Bridges, Thomas, 56
Bristol, 59
Brooks, William, 185
Brown, Ann, 67–68
Brown, Christopher L., 11
Brown, Thomas, 141–142
Burney, Charles (Frances's brother), 210
Burney, Charles (Frances's father), 210
Burney, Frances
    Camilla, 210
    Cecilia, 118–119, 210–211, 214–219, 221–227, 229–231
    Evelina, 210, 213, 217
    marriage to Alexandre d'Arblay, 210
    on dog prices, 193
    on purchased shoes, 1, 14, 16
    The Wanderer, 210
Butts v. Penny, 36–37
Byers, George, 117
Byron, William, 179–180, 194

Caleb Williams (Godwin), 69
calotypes, 151
Camilla (Burney), 210

capitalism
  industrial, 189
  racial, 2
care and caring. *See also* knowledge of
    possessions
  enslaved people and, 75–76, 83, 85, 135
  found notices and, 126
  Hackney coachmen and, 140
  in *Cecilia* (Burney), 225–226, 231
  Mandeville on, 113–114, 128
  reclamation and, 90, 235–236
  relationship of possession and, 3–7, 25, 80, 169, 209, 237–238
  security technologies and, 19, 169
  urban environments and, 61, 65, 68, 78
  violence and, 83, 85, 242
Carens, Joseph H., 205, 222
Cartwright, Thomas, 133
Cato, or Interesting Adventures of a Dog of Sentiment, 6, 77–78, 82, 145
Cavendish, William (5th Duke of Devonshire), 48
Cecilia (Burney), 118–119, 210–211, 214–219, 221–227, 229–231
character
  care of possessions and, 6–7, 128, 169, 209
  consistency of, 213–214
  dependence on labour and knowledge of others, 174
  household order and, 4–5, 235
  lost notices and, 131, 133
  of servants, 70
  relationship of possession and, 6–7, 24–25, 114, 237
  returning lost items and, 126, 133, 242
  runaway notices and, 74
  self-possession and, 212–214, 236, 238
chattels. *See under* possessions
city guidebooks, 59–61, 78, 85, 127, 147
  Doings in London (Smeeton), 62–63
  London Adviser and Guide (Trusler), 66–67, 81, 139, 170, 172
  New Cheats of London (King), 65, 80–81
  The Countryman's Guide to London, 63, 65
  The London Spy (Ward), 62–65, 78
  The New London Spy (Fielding and King), 63, 65
  The Stranger's Guide through London and Westminster, 62
Clarkson, Thomas, 40–41
Clatsop community, 181–182
Clay, Charles, 162
Clements, William, 200
coachmen. *See* Hackney coachmen
coffeehouses, 19, 136–137, 207

Colderhead, Alexander, 172–173
Cole, Aquila, 132–133
Cope, Charles, 132–133, 147
Coram, Thomas, 228
corn, 7, 34
Coventry, Francis, 29–31, 49–50, 58, 144–145
coverture, 42–45, 53–54
crime literature, 64–66
crime prevention. *See* policing and crime prevention
Crosby, Robert, 67–68, 123

d'Arblay, Alexandre, 210
Dacus, Lucy, 14
Daguerre, Louis-Jacques-Mandé, 151
daguerreotypes, 151
Daily Advertiser, 21, 97, 109
  coachmen mentioned in notices, 138
  found item notices, 108, 126
  in *Cecilia* (Burney), 118–119, 225
  lost dog notices, 83, 147, 179, 197
  lost financial instrument notices, 157, 185
  lost notice layout and positioning, 101–102
  lost notice trends and statistics, 97–100, 103–104, 114–116
  lost notices versus runaway notices, 107
  lost watch notices, 90, 124, 132, 137, 161–162
  pawnbroker practices and, 143
  runaway notices, 109, 114–116, 133–134, 167
  stolen notice trends and statistics, 103–105
  stopt notices, 107
Daily Courant, 20, 96–97, 111, 113
  coachmen mentioned in notices, 138
  found item notices, 108
  lost notice layout and positioning, 101
  lost notice trends and statistics, 99–100
  lost notices versus runaway notices, 107
  lost watch notices, 188
  runaway notices, 107, 109
  stolen notice trends and statistics, 104–105
  stopt notices, 107
Davis, Robert, 117, 170–171
de Grazia, Margreta, 211, 218
debt, 10, 16
  in *Cecilia* (Burney), 216–217
  marriage and, 43–44, 74, 236
debt and credit, public, 216
debtor prisons, 114
Defoe, Daniel, 112–113, 119, 154, 213
Desan, Christine, 55, 160
description, 151–156, *See also* knowledge of possessions
  of dogs, 163–166
  of financial instruments, 156–161

Index 267

of people, 166–169
of watches, 161–163
desertion, military, 202
Dictionary of the English Language, A (Johnson), 12
Dierks, Konstantin, 229
dogs, 47–54
  as pets, 51, 57, 164, 197
  as property, 47–54
  descriptions of, 163–166
  dog collars, 53, 77, 82–83, 86, 129, 179, 237
  dog stealing, 50–54, 77–78, 145–147, 165, 191–193
  Dog Stealing Act of 1770, 50–52, 77, 145, 191
  Dog Stealing Act of 1845, 53
  fictional stories of, 6, 29–31, 49–50, 77–78, 82, 144–145
  Home for Lost and Starving Dogs, 240–241
  knowledge and memory of, 174–175
  lost notices for, 82–83, 145–146, 163–166
  Select Committee on Dog Stealing (Metropolis), 52–54, 146–147, 191–198
  value of and rewards for, 190–198
domestic management, 4–5, 235
Doody, Margaret, 216–217, 226
Dowling, Vincent George, 54, 146, 194
Downes, John, 200

Earle, Peter, 71
Ellicott, John, 161, 172
Elrington, Thomas, 186
Enquiry into the Causes of the late Increase of Robbers, An (Fielding), 119, 141
enslaved people. *See* freedom seekers, *See* slavery and enslaved people
Equiano, Olaudah, 74–75
Erickson, Amy, 215
Evans, Jane, 83–84
Evelina (Burney), 210, 213, 217
Evelyn, John, 91
Exchequer bills, 8, 125, 169
experience, conceptual understandings of, 14–15
Extracts from such of the Penal Laws (Fielding), 75

Fend, Mechthild, 224
Festa, Lynn, 9–10
Fewtrell, James, 167
Fielding, Charles, 79–80
Fielding, Henry, 106, 119–120, 213
  An Enquiry into the Causes of the late Increase of Robbers, 119, 141
  Tom Jones, 186–187
Fielding, John, 75, 119–121, 143, 162, 174

Fielding, John, junior, 63
financial instruments
  as property, 55–57
  descriptions of, 156–161
  identity and, 187
  knowledge and memory of, 169–171
  value of and rewards for, 184–187
Finn, Margot, 6, 10
FitzGerald, William, 240
Flanders, Moll (Defoe), 213
Fleming, Abraham, 164
Footman's Looking Glass, The, 70
Forbes v. Cochrane, 41
forged bank notes, 56, 170, 186
found and stopt notices, 106–107, 126–127, 143
Foundling Hospital, 228
freedom seekers, 22–23, 75–76, 134–135, 166, 204–205, 214, 236–237, 241
Fryer, Peter, 75
Fuentes, Marisa J., 22

Gaffney, Patrick, 93–94
Gahagen, Constantine, 140–141, 174
Gallagher, Catherine, 211, 217
Galway v. Vadee, 37
Game Act of 1671, 48
Game Laws, 222
Gay, John, 113
Geertz, Clifford, 15
gender
  identity and, 213–214, 219–220
  loss and, 218, 226, 231
  lost notices system and, 128–129, 224
  marriage and property rights, 42–45
  ownership and, 3, 210–211
General History of Quadrupeds, A (Beilby), 164, 191, 194
Glaisyer, Natasha, 96, 118
Glove, George, 234
Godwin, William, 69
Goff, Elijah, 172, 174
Goldsmiths' Company, 90–95, 99, 114, 124, 234
Graeber, David, 182
Great Exhibition of 1851, 239
Great Fire of London, 16, 63
guidebooks. *See* city guidebooks
guilds, 200

Hackney Carriage Act of 1831, 140
Hackney Coach Office, 140, 239
Hackney coachmen, 23, 117, 137–140, 144, 147, 234
Hally, Thomas, 162
Hamilton, Frances, 40

268   Index

handbills, 19, 91, 94–96, 101, 116–117, 124, 232, 234
Hardwick, John, 53
Harper, Samuel, 173
Harris, Michael, 19, 115
Hastrup, Frida, 13–14
Haywood, Eliza, 70
Heaven, Samuel, 174
Helmreich, Anne, 187
Hetherington, Kevin, 13
History of Pompey the Little, The (Coventry), 29–31, 49–50, 58, 144–145
Hitchcock, Tim, 187
Hitchin, Charles, 110–111
Hoabdell, George, 146, 197–198
Hodson, Joseph, 170
Holmes, Helen, 13–14
Holt, John, 36–37
Hooke, Andrew, 59
household order, 4–5, 235
Howe, Charlotte, 38–39, 41
Howe, Tyringham, 38–39
Howell, Philip, 241
Hubbard, Clifford, 164
Hudson, John, 170–171
Hughes, Thomas, 171, 205
humanity, 9–10, 103
Humfrey, Paula, 71
Hunt, Lynn, 220
Hyman, Aaron, 181–183

identity
  Cecilia (Burney) and, 214, 222
  clothing and social identity, 219–222
  financial instruments and, 187
  inalienable possessions and, 182, 189
  land ownership and, 215
  loss and, 214–218, 224
  newspapers and, 119
  self-possession and, 212–214
  urban environments and, 6, 70, 236
  wigs and social identity, 219
immoveable property, 33
India Gazette, 98
industrialisation, 189
insurance industry, 16
Interesting Narrative of the Life of Olaudah Equiano, The (Equiano), 74–75
International Exhibition of 1862, 239–240

Jacob, Lazrous, 137
jewellers, 91, 144
jewels and jewellery, 21, 64, 99, 184, 236
  as chattel, 7, 34
  diamond rings, 126–127
  gold rings, 128
Johnson, Samuel, 12, 25, 67, 141

Jones, Grace, 39
Jones, John, 185
Jones, Thomas, 156–157
Jowett, Judy, 92

Kenrick, William, 12
Kesselring, Krista J., 42
keys, 99
keys, lost, 21
Killigrew, William, 181
Kilner, Dorothy
  The Adventures of a Hackney Coach, 137
  The Life and Perambulations of a Mouse, 5–6
King Lear (Shakespeare), 211, 218
King, Richard, 63, 65, 80–81
Knight v. Wedderburn, 36, 38, 41
knowledge of possessions, 23, 169
  dogs, 174–175
  familiarity and, 171
  financial instruments, 169–171
  memory aids, 153, 155–156, 177
  proximity and, 175
  servants and apprentices, 173–177
  watches, 171–174
knowledge, collective, 174
knowledge, household, 174
knowledge, local, 186
Kopytoff, Igor, 182

Lady's Magazine, 219
Lambert, Annie, 173
land ownership, 3, 216
Lawrence, William, 185
Lee, Leonard, 94
Leibsohn, Dana, 181–183
Leveland, Gervase, 138, 189–190
Licensing Act of 1695, 19, 96
Life of Wild, The (Defoe), 112–113
Lloyd, Edward, 171
Lloyd, Samuel, 156
Locke, John, 31–32, 35, 40, 46, 222
London, 59–61, *See also* city guidebooks
  crime and, 17–18
  migration and, 17, 60–61
  population statistics, 17, 60
  print culture and, 61–68
  runaway dogs in print culture, 76–78
  runaways in print culture, 69–76
London Gazette
  influence of, 96, 118
  lost notices, 98–100
Lord Mayor's Court, 72–73, 132
Lorimer, Douglas, 204
loss, 12–17, 58, 232–238, *See also* warning carrier notice system, lost notices
  ambiguities of loss, 66

Index

anthropology on, 13–14
Burney on, 1, 14, 16, 25
identity and, 214–218
in novels and plays, 209–212, 214–218, 222–224, 226, 229, 231
Johnson on, 12
of possessions, 17–23
of self-possession, 217, 223, 226, 229, 231
preventing loss, 78–85, 142, 237–238
relationship of possession and, 214
sociology on, 13
urban environments and, 17–19, 35, 59–61, 66, 68–69, 76
value and, 181–184, 198
Lost and Found Office, 232–235
lost notices, 21–22, 90–91, 96–100, 109, 112–113
description in, 156–169
intended readers, 133–147
items mentioned frequently in, 8
pawnbrokers and, 226
placers of, 128–133
popularity of, 20
system of, 20, 172–173
trends and statistics, 97–100, 104, 116
Lost Property Office, 239–240
luxury trades, 91–92, 124, 234

Macpherson, C. B., 205, 222
Mandeville, Bernard, 113–114, 119, 128
Mansfield, Lord (William Murray), 38–39, 42, 56, 58, 135
Marrinan, Michael, 154
Mascuch, Michael, 220
Mason, John, 186, 212–213
Mayne, Richard, 52–53, 146, 196, 198
McDaniel, Stephen, 114
Middlesex Justice Act of 1792, 120
Middleton, Simon, 180
Miller v. Race, 56
Molineux, Catherine, 36
Monro, John, 121–123
Morgan, Gwenda, 229
moveable property, 4, 7, 25, 29, 33, 215–216, 222, 231, 236
Mutiny Acts, 202

necessaries, 43–44
Nehalem-Tillamook community, 181–182
Neville, Sylas, 81, 190
Newman, Simon P., 22–23, 84, 203
newspapers, 19–23, *See also London Gazette*, runaway notices, found and stopt notices, lost notices, *Times, The, Daily Courant, Daily Advertiser*
growth of, 114–119

history of lost notices, 96–103
Nutter, Nancy, 16, 176, 201

O'Hara, Arthur, 188
Ogilvie, Brian, 153–154
Onesimus, 69–70
Osbaldiston, William Augustus, 194

Page, Philip, 174
Paget, Francis Edward, 81
Paley, Ruth, 41, 114
Pamela (Richardson), 213
paraphernalia, 43
Paul, Tawny, 10, 16
pawnbrokers, 94, 117, 122, 147, 174, 187–188
in *Cecilia* (Burney), 211, 217–218, 221–223, 225–226, 230
legal cases, 67–68, 140–144
stopt notices and, 106
Pelham, Thomas, 196–197
Pencil of Nature, The (Talbot), 151–153
Peynon, Isaac, 226
Pharez, Richard, 143–144
Phillips, Avis, 166–167
Phipps, Hinckley, 186
photographs, 151–153, 155, 177
pickpocketing, 64–66, 68, 78, 122, 223, 235, 237
Piggott, Thomas, 89–91, 106, 124, 161–162, 174
Pike, David, 61
pin money, 43
pocketbooks, 67, 79–80, 82, 159–161, 170, 187
pockets
fob pockets, 80
men's pockets, 79–81
tie pockets, 79
Polak, Marcus, 128
policing and crime prevention, 119–121
Bow Street runners, 120–121
Metropolitan Police, 52, 146, 192, 239–240, 242
possessions, 7–12, *See also* property, value and rewards, description, relationship of possessions, care and caring, lost notices
Burney on, 1
care of, 4–7
chattel law, 7–8, 33–35, 57
chattels personal (chattels moveable), 7–8, 29, 33–34, 57
dogs as, 47–54
financial instruments as, 55–57
legal and philosophical conceptions of, 31–35, 53–54, 57–58
loss of, 17–23
marriage and, 43, 45

possessions (cont.)
  people as, 40, 47, 69
  reclamation of, 19–23
  security technologies of, 78–85
  servants and, 45
  urban environments and, 17–19, 63–68, 76, 85–86, 90
  value and, 24–25
  watches as, 54–55
Potter, Christopher, 173
Present for a Servant Maid, A (Haywood), 70
Prince, Mary, 39
probate inventories, 2, 4, 12, 142
promissory notes, 55, 156, 160, 170, 184
property. *See also* possessions
  dogs as, 47–54
  financial instruments as, 55–57
  immoveable property, 33
  labouring servants and, 45–47
  legal and philosophical conceptions of, 31–35, 57–58
  legal types of, 33
  people as, 36–42
  watches as, 54–55
  wives and, 42–45
Public Advertiser, 20, 120, 142–143, 232
Pyne, William, 117–118

Quare, Daniel, 162

racial capitalism, 2
Rainsford, Richard, 36
Ranson, Thomas, 56
relationship of possession, 2–3, 8, 11–17, 24–25, 211
  as active process, 125
  Burney on, 1
  care and, 3–7, 25, 80, 169, 209
  character and, 6–7, 114, 238
  dogs and, 49
  newspapers and, 100, 103
  urban environments and, 78
  value of, 24–25, 196, 209, 214, 236–237
Robin John, Ancona Robin, 41
Robin John, Ephraim, 41
Robinson, Frederick, 16–17
Robinson, John, 200
Robinson, Thomas, 16–17
runaway apprentices, 72–73, 130, 133–134, 166–167
runaway dogs, 76–78
runaway notices, 20–22, 24, 84, 100, 107–109, 133–135
  costs of, 96–97
  for enslaved persons, 183–184
  frequency of, 115–116
  intended readers of, 133–135, 153
  placers of, 128–130
  positioning of, 101, 103
runaway servants, 78
  reasons for leaving, 71–72
  servant manuals and, 70–71
  stories of, 69–70
runaway spouses, 73–74
runaways
  descriptions of, 166–169, 177–178
  in print culture, 69–76
  value of and rewards for, 180–207
Rushton, Peter, 229

Savage, Lawrence, 141
Schröder, Samuel, 62
Scott, Susie, 13
Second Treatise of Government (Locke), 31–32
self-knowledge, 212
self-possession, 25, 204, 206, 212–214, 223, 226, 229–231, 236, 238
self-worth, 3, 204
servants, 45–47
  clothing for, 219
  knowledge and, 173–177
  legal protection for, 131–132
  manuals for, 70–71
  mobility of, 71
  proximity to employers, 175–177
  value of and rewards for, 201–202
  wages of, 201
Servants Calling with Some Advice to the Apprentice,The, 70
Settlement Act of 1662, 39, 132
Sewell, William H., Jr., 14–15
Shackell, Joseph, 146, 192–193, 196, 198
Shackleton, Elizabeth, 16, 176, 201
Shakespeare, William, 211, 218
Shanley v. Harvey, 37
Sharp, Granville, 38, 75, 85, 134–135
Shepard, Alexandra, 6, 220
Shin, Hiroki, 95, 157, 170
Shipley, Francis, 142
shoplifting, 112
Simmel, Georg, 182
slave trade, 36
Slavery Abolition Act, 41, 241
slavery and enslaved people. *See also* abolition movement
  Blackstone on, 33–35, 37
  care and, 75–76, 83, 85, 135
  collars and chains used on enslaved people, 83–85, 237

in print culture, 69–76
property and, 36–42, 53
value of and rewards for, 181–208, 235–236
Smeeton, George, 62–63
Smith, Anne, 83–84
Smith, Mark, 14
snuffboxes, 21, 79, 93, 97, 99, 184, 221
Sørensen, Tim Flohr, 13–14
Somerset v. Stewart, 36–38, 41, 75, 135, 241
Spacks, Patricia Meyer, 213
Spencer, Jane, 10
Sprang, Rebecca L., 24, 181, 183
St Paul's Cathedral, 62, 85
Stalnaker, Joanna, 154
Stanhope Act, 55–56, 186
Staves, Susan, 7, 222
Steedman, Carolyn, 15, 39, 46
Stewart, Charles, 37, *See also Somerset v. Stewart*
stolen notices, 103–105, 143
Stretton, Tim, 42

Tague, Ingrid, 175, 197
Talbot, Charles, 37
Talbot, William Henry Fox, 151–153, 155, 177
Tales of the Village Children (Paget), 81
taverns, 19, 75, 89, 93, 136
Tealby, Mary, 240–241
thief-takers, 20, 91, 109–111, 114, 118, 127, 234
Thompson, E. P., 14, 188–189
Thompson, James, 56, 187, 217
Times, The, 20, 97, 104, 115
  coachmen mentioned in notices, 139
  found item notices, 108
  lost financial instrument notices, 158
  lost notice layout and positioning, 101
  lost notice trends and statistics, 97–100
  runaway notices, 109, 115–116
  stolen notice trends and statistics, 104–105
  stopt notices, 107
Tise, Thomas, 133, 167
Tobin, William, 188
Tom Jones (Fielding), 186–187, 213
Tompion, Thomas, 162
Tonson v. Collins, 180
Townsend, Henry Hare, 80
trade routes, global, 2
Trussler, John, 66–67, 81, 139, 170, 172
Turkel, William J., 187
Turner, William, 137

Upcott, William, 71
urbanization, 6, 61, 189, 238

Valenze, Deborah, 10–11, 199
value and rewards, 179–184
  apprentices and, 199–201
  deserting soldiers and, 202
  dogs and, 190–198
  enslaved people and, 202–208
  financial instruments and, 184–187
  runaways and, 181–207
  servants and, 201–202
  watches and, 187–190
value and valuing, 24–25
Vaughan, John, 234
Vines, Samuel, 123
von la Roche, Sophie, 81, 101, 126, 223
von Pückler-Muskau, Hermann, 17, 67, 159

Wahrman, Dror, 213, 219–220
Waklin, Richard, 200
Wall, Cynthia, 154
Wanderer, The (Burney), 210
Ward, Edward, 62–65, 78
Ward, John, 162
Waring, William, 200
warning carrier notice system, 90–96, 99, 136, 144, 232
watch theft, 54–55, 89–90
watches
  as property, 54–55
  descriptions of, 161–163
  knowledge and memory of, 171–174
  lost watch notices, 90, 124, 132, 137, 161–162, 188
  value of and rewards for, 187–190
Wayte, Margaret, 122–123
Weeden, James, 174
Weiner, Annette, 182–183, 189
Wellstead, Richard, 167
White, George, 196, 198
Wilberforce, William, 40
Wild, Jonathan, 111–114, 146, 158, 188, 234
wills, 12, 154–155
Wingfield, George, 121–123
Wittgenstein, Ludwig, 171–172
Wood, John, 59, 67
working class, 14
Wright, George Thomas, 167–168

Yates, Edward, 174
Ylivuori, Soile, 213
Yorke, Philip, 37

For EU product safety concerns, contact us at Calle de José Abascal, 56–1°, 28003 Madrid, Spain or eugpsr@cambridge.org.

www.ingramcontent.com/pod-product-compliance
Ingram Content Group UK Ltd.
Pitfield, Milton Keynes, MK11 3LW, UK
UKHW022139240226
468380UK00018B/383